Specific Learning Difficulties (Dyslexia)

Challenges and Responses

Specific Learning Difficulties (Dyslexia)

Challenges and Responses

A national inquiry coordinated and written
by Peter D. Pumfrey and Rea Reason
together with a working group of educational
psychologists

London and New York

First published 1991
by NFER-Nelson Publishing

Reprinted 1991

Reprinted 1992 (twice), 1993, 1994 and 1995
by Routledge
11 New Fetter Lane, London EC4P 4EE

Simultaneously published in the USA and Canada
by Routledge
29 West 35th Street, New York, NY 10001

Printed and bound in Great Britain by
Mackays of Chatham PLC, Chatham, Kent

NFER-Nelson would like to acknowledge Zachary Gordon Burgess,
who wrote the letter appearing opposite page 1 of this book and used in
the cover design. Our thanks also to his aunt, Mrs Helen Gordon.

We are also grateful to Frank Pert, who compiled the author and subject indexes.

British Library Cataloguing in Publication Data
A catalogue record for this book is available from the British Library

ISBN 0-415-06470-8

Contents

List of Tables and Figures
Preface
Acknowledgements
Abbreviations

List of Tables

List of Figures

Preface

In 1988 the Committee of the Division of Educational and Child Psychology of the British Psychological Society decided to take further its report published in 1984 entitled *Specific Learning Difficulties: The 'Specific Reading Difficulties' versus 'Dyslexia' Controversy Resolved?* The Association of Educational Psychologists accepted an invitation to be involved in the work.

The inquiry was to be national and called *Specific Learning Difficulties (Dyslexia): Challenges, Responses and Recommendations.* Peter D. Pumfrey and Rea Reason were invited to organize and coordinate the work and to write the final report. A group of qualified and experienced educational psychologists, from eight local education authorities, joined the team which thus comprised the following members:

Betty Allan
Robin Bartlett
John Coleman
Mary Dean
Ann Forrester
Margaret Gregory
Robin Hedderly
Peter Pumfrey
Rea Reason
David Webster (AEP representative)
John Wilkins

The inquiry had two main aims: firstly, to provide a wide-ranging account of current theory and research with regard to specific learning difficulties and, secondly, to investigate relevant educational policies and practices.

Information was collected from the beginning of January 1989. The actions listed below show the scope of the work that was carried out and also indicate the structure of the book.

- The historical context was reviewed and key theoretical and practical issues are presented in Section A.
- A comprehensive review of pertinent theory and research was undertaken from three complementary viewpoints: psychological, psychoeducational and psychomedical. This work is described in Sections B, C and D.
- Relevant educational policies and practices were surveyed. Results are reported in Section E, which covers the following aspects:
  (i)   Policies of local education authorities.
  (ii) Practices of educational psychologists.
  (iii) Policies of examination boards on dispensations for pupils deemed to have specific learning difficulties.

(iv) Views were also sought from a wide range of voluntary bodies; professional psychological organizations in other countries; the general public; other psychologists within the British Psychological Society; and the Department of Education and Science.

Most chapters conclude with a set of recommendations agreed by all members of the working group. The recommendations are not intended to be detailed or revolutionary; their main purpose is to represent a consensus of opinion. The recommendations, however, provide a 'checklist' against which one can appraise the theoretical stances and approaches of individuals and the policies and practices of schools and local education authorities.

Abbreviations

AEP	Association of Educational Psychologists
AMMA	Assistant Masters and Mistresses Association
BDA	British Dyslexia Association
BMA	British Medical Association
BPsS	British Psychological Society
DCP	Division of Clinical Psychology of the British Psychological Society
DD	Defining Dyslexia
DECP	Division of Educational and Child Psychology of the British Psychological Society
DES	Department of Education and Science
DI	Dyslexia Institute
DUB	Dyslexia Unit, Bangor
EP	Educational Psychologist
GEST	Grants for Educational Support and Training
GRIST	Grant Related In-Service Training
HMI	Her Majesty's Inspectorate
IEP	Individual Education Programme
INSET	In-Service Education of Teachers
IT	Information Technology
LEA	Local Education Authority
LEATGS	Local Education Authority Training Grant Scheme
LMS	Local Management of Schools
NARE	National Association of Remedial Education
NASUWT	National Association of Schoolmasters, Union of Women Teachers
NC	National Curriculum
NCC	National Curriculum Council
NUT	National Union of Teachers
RSA	Royal Society of Arts
SDECP	Scottish Division of Educational and Child Psychology of the British Psychological Society
SEAC	School Examinations and Assessment Council
SEMERC	Special Education Microelectronics in Education Resources Centres
SEN	Special Educational Needs
SpLD	Specific Learning Difficulties
UKRA	United Kingdom Reading Association

Acknowledgements

Knowledge will forever govern ignorance; and a people who mean to be their own governors must arm themselves with the power which knowledge gives. (James Madison, 4 August 1822)

The Division of Educational and Child Psychology (DECP) of the British Psychological Society has a long-standing tradition of undertaking studies in fields of applied psychology that are of professional and public concern. Such areas are typically controversial and complex. The topic of specific learning difficulties (specific developmental dyslexia) is one of these.

This book is a result of an institutional initiative, collaborative endeavours involving statutory and voluntary groups, integrated with individual responses and applications to a variety of challenging invitations and tasks. respectively. The working group that completed this task under the direction ci Peter D. Pumfrey and Rea Reason is indebted to many sources for the support and encouragement that they received in completing their work.

The committee and the membership of the Division of Educational and Child Psychology provided both financial and professional support. The enthusiastic collaboration of the committee and membership of the Association of Educational Psychologists, particularly in the two surveys of policy and practice that were carried out as one aspect of this inquiry, added immensely to the interest and importance of the work. The cooperation of the Department of Education and Science and the examination boards, together with offical responses from a range of key voluntary organizations, further enriched the study. The many individuals who contacted the inquiry provided important clinical insights into the emotional, intellectual, motivational, administrative, legal and financial issues involved. Without these contributions, our work would have been the poorer.

Students and staff at the Centre for Educational Guidance and Special Needs of the University of Manchester School of Education provided a stimulating and supportive professional context within which the project was based.

The issues identified, evidence presented and recommendations made do not represent the views of the Division of Educational and Child Psychology. What is presented are the views of the working group alone.

The challenges of conceptualizing, identifying and minimizing the adverse effects on individuals with specific learning difficulties (specific developmental dyslexia) are great. This book testifies to what has been achieved, to what is currently being done and indicates what has yet to be accomplished. We remain optimistic.

Now to put into effect all the suggestions which I have given is the province of prayer, perhaps, or exhortation. And even to follow zealously the majority of them demands good fortune and much careful attention, but to accomplish this lies within the capability of man.
(Plutarch, 46–120, The Education of Children, Vol. 1 of Plutarch's *Moralia*)

Such faults that remain in the present book are the sole responsibility of the co-ordinators.

PETER D. PUMFREY
REA REASON

December 1990

March 8th

Dear Mr Pumfrey.
I am ten. I did not injoy life until
I got hellp because the techer say
(thinking thay no evrything) "you
are lase and norty...
    Now I am haveinghellp
I can rit letters and storys and
eneyfing I wont to. But speling is
stil a lital bit difacelt.
    I fink evre scool have a speshal
techer tat thchis chrivin to try and
get rid of ther Broblern. When the
techer told me to rit I wood sit
thon and antil it got difelcett
and sumthing alluay corl my
alenchon and I wood mes a round
and get told off ond I did not
lisk life then.
    I have riton a book and I have
folocopeed it for you. I am going
to rit a Book and it is about two
mice that go to the city and met
ampeooth   Love
            From
            Zachary

SECTION A: CHALLENGES

This section comprises outlines of the historical and contemporary contexts within which the natures of, and relationships between, specific learning difficulties and specific development dyslexia have been, and are, conducted. Key theoretical issues are identified. Their implications for more effectively conceptualizing, identifying, predicting and alleviating the varied patterns of learning difficulties are considered. The ambiguous nature of the legal rights of pupils in England and Wales deemed to have special educational needs in general, and the subset of those experiencing specific learning difficulties in particular, is discussed. Related administrative and financial implications are examined in the light of the Education Act 1981 and the Education Reform Act 1988.

Chapter 1

Background to the Current Scene

Introduction

The unexpected intrigues. Explanations are sought. The fittest survive. This is why specific learning difficulties (dyslexia) is a controversial topic. We are intrigued; we seek explanations; we discuss and investigate their merits; we disagree. The process continues. 'If a man begin with certainties, he shall end in doubts; but if he will be content to begin with doubts, he shall end in certainties.' This was Bacon's maxim in 'The Advancement of Learning'. It stands the test of time.

Children are both similar and different. As a group, they can be characterized by a wide range of 'within-child' attributes: physical, emotional, social, intellectual and motivational. Contexts in which the child is brought up present additional external dimensions. Both sets interact. The uniqueness of the individual at a given time can be viewed as a pattern of points in *n*-dimensional space. The processes that occur during development are often identified using such variables.

All children are capable of learning. Some learn more rapidly than others. Children who learn rapidly are, in common parlance, considered to be 'bright', 'quick', 'able'. An absolute term is used when a relative one would be more valid. 'Intelligent' is another frequently used term. All of these labels simplify complexities. In this sense, no one has ever seen 'intelligence' (in contrast to its alternative meaning of 'information'). We observe behaviours that we classify as being intelligent. From a range of these we infer the construct of 'intelligence'. In Western society it is a highly regarded attribute.

Typically, the more intelligent the child, the more rapidly will he or she learn skills dependent on symbolic thinking. These include those of literacy and numeracy. When a child considered to be intelligent has great difficulties in acquiring such cognitive skills as reading, it flies in the face of common experience. Are such pupils best described as having specific learning difficulties or would it be more accurate to call them dyslexic? Whatever term is used, the unexpected has occurred. Why? Can anything be done? If so, what?

We are witnessing a new technological revolution. It makes the effects of earlier ones pall into insignificance in their effects on our species and our planet. Information technology (IT) impinges increasingly on all in our society, primarily as consumers, secondly as users and thirdly (a very small minority) as developers. IT makes available an ever-increasing amount and variety of information in different forms for myriad purposes. It increases dramatically the control that potentially we can exercise over our environments and, reciprocally, the control that can be exercised over individuals and groups. What implications do such developments have for the education of children and for the work of educational practitioners?

Achievements, at one time considered as remote as horizons, have been attained in IT. Computer synthesized speech is available. Using an optical scanner, a blind person can 'read' text via either the auditory or tactile senses. Speech can be electronically converted into text. Correct spelling and syntax can virtually be assured. Electronic translation of languages is possible. Computations can be carried out more rapidly and accurately by computers than by human beings. Computer-assisted learning and interactive video are but two other examples of growth areas. Artificial intelligence is more than a concept. Computerized testing and 'expert systems' are others of importance to those whose work involves assessing children. It behoves all inhabitants of this impending brave new world to be sensitive to the ultimate danger of overdependence on systems understood by few.

In passing, it is interesting to note that the notions of 'linear' and 'branching' programmed learning advocated many years ago by Skinner and Crowder now have an adequate technology to support the development and application of their complementary learning theories. Children's learning can be enhanced by IT applications. The microcomputer is to the educational practitioner what the telescope and the microscope were to the astronomer and the biologist, with at least one important difference: the possibilities for developing theory and practice that it opens up are even greater (Seymour, 1986; GB.DES, 1988a; US Office of Education (USOE), 1988).

The importance of IT in the education of all children in the UK is, in part, attested to by the work carried out at 14 Regional Information Centres (RICs) established under the DES Microelectronic Education Programme. The interests of children with special educational needs were catered for by four Special Education Centres (SEMERCs) sited in Newcastle, Manchester, Redbridge and Bristol and linked to the 14 RICs. Changes in the funding of the Microelectronics Education Programme have led to a consortia of local education authorities (LEAs) taking responsibility for the former SEMERCs. Undoubtedly IT will contribute significantly to helping children become literate and numerate. In time, is it likely to make such skills redundant?

In such a climate it is sometimes claimed that helping children to become, for example, literate is preparing them for life in the previous century. Typically, such comments are made by individuals who are highly accomplished in all aspects of communication. Edmund Leach, former Provost of King's College, Cambridge, has written on such lines. In the USA the late Marshall Macluhan presented similar arguments on the basis of the revolution in IT in which we are all participants. Such arguments are based on a failure to appreciate the complexities and importance of literacy as determinants of children's cognitive, social and emotional development. In his essay *Of Studies*, Bacon was almost certainly nearer the truth when he wrote 'Reading maketh a full man; conference a ready man and writing an exact man'. In Somerset Maugham's short story *The Verger*, illiteracy led to success and affluence. In life, it was Maugham's ability to read and write that resulted in his influence and prosperity.

Literacy and numeracy are amplifiers of human abilities. They are both applications of the symbolic thinking that is characteristic of the species. They matter because they facilitate communication and the control that we have over our environments. In Western industrial societies, not to be literate is to be seriously and progressively disadvantaged, both materially and in terms of access to cultural enrichment. For the literate individual to tell the illiterate that the skills are unimportant is as objectionable in its thoughtlessness as Marie Antoinette's advice to the starving French peasantry. (For somewhat suspect historical and cultural reasons, to be innumerate is more readily admitted and acceptable in our society.) When, for example, it is thought that children's reading standards have declined, considerable public concern is manifest.

Understanding the processes that lead to literacy is still in its infancy. Controversies abound. These concern the nature of the processes, why some children have difficulties and what can be done to alleviate these. The conceptual complexity of this field, the problems of devising and carrying out both basic and applied research that will resolve controversial issues, the ambiguities in the terminology used by those engaged in this work, all testify to our limited knowledge. These considerations highlight the importance of the field as a continuing challenge to the educational psychologists' and teachers' professional skills. At the centre of the issue is the nature and extent of inter-individual and intra-individual differences in cognitive processes, and the modifiability of these.

It is important to acknowledge professional limitations. It is equally necessary to make clear that valuable contributions have been, and are being, made by individuals from many disciplines. Later chapters on psychological, psychoeducational and psychomedical contributions underline this point. The early psychologists in the late 19th century pioneered psychologically based methods of helping children and parents. The first officially appointed local authority educational psychologist in the UK was C. Burt with the London County Council in 1913. Despite their relatively recent arrival on the scene, educational psychologists as a group have taken a particular interest in literacy and numeracy, with specific attention to the former. The work of Burt (1921) and Schonell (1942–55) represents the early stages of a continuing involvement (GB.DES, 1968; Sampson, 1975, 1976, 1980). As the number of practising educational and child psychologists has increased, so has their contribution to many aspects of applied psychology. The understanding, assessment and improvement of children's literacy skills has been a major focus. This interest derives from the key role of literacy in general, and reading in particular, in the educative process. It also owes much to educational and child psychologists' experience as qualified teachers and from the professional challenges involved in conceptualizing and facilitating children's ability to read, write and spell (see Moseley and Nichol, 1986; Reason and Boote, 1986; Webster and McConnell, 1987; Thomson, 1988a; Tyler and Elliott, 1988; Pumfrey and Elliott, 1990).

Teachers and psychologists have also contributed to the resolution of controversies in this field. The Tizard Report, *Children with Specific Reading Difficulties*, was published 19 years ago (GB.DES, 1972). Its nine major recommendations had important policy implications for LEAs concerning the organization of identification procedures, teaching strategies and the establishment of record systems. Record systems were required to allow the evaluation of the short-term and long-term progress of children '...suffering from reading backwardness of all kinds'. The committee also noted that the term 'dyslexia' had been used so loosely as to make it valueless. They acknowledged the possibility that a minority of children with severe reading difficulties, often accompanied by spelling, writing and number problems, met *some* of the criteria of 'specific developmental dyslexia'. Despite this, the committee cast doubts on the validity of a syndrome of 'developmental dyslexia' with a specific underlying cause and specific symptoms. They concluded that it would be better to adopt the more usefully descriptive term 'specific reading difficulties' to indicate the problems of the *relatively small* proportion of pupils '...whose reading (and perhaps writing, spelling and number) abilities are significantly below the standards which their abilities in other spheres would lead one to accept' (ibid., p. 3).

Tansley and Panckhurst (1981) subsequently published a major and wide-ranging review of research entitled *Children with Specific Learning Difficulties*. Its prime concern was 'with children who exhibit severe difficulties in reading', although associated problems in areas such as spelling, writing, arithmetic and speech are included and given brief consideration. In the introduction to that book, the Department of Education and Science recommends the review to those working in the field of specific learning difficulties.

The Minister of State for Education and Science in a House of Lords debate (*Hansard*, 14.1.1981) and the Parliamentary Under Secretary of State for the Department of Education and Science, in a Special Standing Committee (10.3.1981), made it clear that children handicapped by dyslexia were included in the definition of special educational needs given in the Education Act 1981.

Quoting from the Minister of State:

> I am hopeful that the removal of categories of handicap and the new arrangements for the assessment of special educational needs will end the arguments which have taken place over what is dyslexia. Whatever the cause or nature of the condition commonly called dyslexia, its manifestation is that the child has difficulty in reading, writing and spelling. The degree of difficulty should be revealed by assessment, and local education authorities will have to make appropriate arrangements for meeting the individual educational needs of children, whatever the cause...

Eight days later in the House of Lords, the Minister of State said:

> It is only right in our consideration of this Bill that we do not overlook the special educational needs of children with learning difficulties in reading, writing, spelling or mathematics. We understand the pain and distress of a child who is neither lazy nor backward but who is unable to learn to read or

write at the same pace as his peers, and that this is a proper cause for concern.

At the fifth sitting of the Special Standing Committee on the Education Bill 1981 held on 10 March, the Under Secretary of State had referred to dyslexia as a condition '...which is difficult to define' and that 'certain educationalists presume that it does not exist'. He continued:

There is much sterile argument over what is or is not dyslexia, when it has become clear to all that the child concerned has a learning difficulty. There is no argument about whether he has a learning difficulty; the argument is over the definition of what has brought about that learning difficulty. Our definition [Clause 1 of the Bill which states that 'For the purposes of this Act a child has "special education needs" if he has a learning difficulty which called for special educational provision to be made for him"' and Subsection (a) 'A child has a "learning difficulty" if he has a significantly greater difficulty in learning than the majority of children of his age'] therefore deliberately focuses on learning difficulty as the key factor in deciding whether a child has special educational needs.

Later the Under Secretary said

...the baffling condition popularly known as dyslexia, a category which is difficult to pin down but which exists as a learning difficulty. Of that there is no doubt. That group will be covered by paragraph (a) of the definition.

Publication of the Education Act 1981 and of Circular 8/81 was followed by Circular 1/83 in which advice was given on assessments and statements of special educational needs (GB.DES, 1981a, 1983). It was within this context that educational and child psychologists were required to make assessments concerning specific learning difficulties (dyslexia). Many educational and child psychologists had, and still have, serious reservations concerning the validity of the concept of 'dyslexia'. They were also aware that one consequence of the debates surrounding the Education Act 1981 had been to increase markedly public awareness of the concept and use of the label. Many psychologists were willing to use the term descriptively but without necessarily accepting the neurological and aetiological implications associated with specific developmental dyslexia by some professionals. Disinterested observers might wonder how this disassociation could be achieved. Other educational and child psychologists remained unwilling to use a concept that they considered invalid on the evidence available. The situation is one in which friction between believers and sceptics, between parents and psychologists, between psychologists and psychologists, can easily arise.

It has been asserted that many parents find it emotionally difficult to accept that their child could be a poor reader, especially if the parents themselves are highly literate. In part, this reaction may be because of the general relationship between intelligence and literacy skills. In many cases a label indicating a medical condition as being the cause was, for certain parents and their children, seen as helpful. Some critics referred to dyslexia as a syndrome shown by the children of middle class parents. How justified is this assertion?

Background to the 'specific learning difficulties' versus 'dyslexia' controversy

The existence and labelling of a condition requires that it should satisfy one or more of the following criteria. It should have distinct (a) aetiology, (b) identifying characteristics, (c) prognosis or (d) response to interventions. How do the terms 'specific learning difficulties' and 'dyslexia' measure up against such criteria?

Quite clearly the first term refers to a variety of conditions. It is an 'umbrella' concept crucially dependent on how one defines the term 'specific'. The second one initially appears unitary in character. If this is the case, then we may have a simple class inclusion relationship. However, there is considerable evidence suggesting that what is referred to as 'dyslexia' could more readily be considered as a variety of 'dyslexias'. Evidence and arguments for and against this assertion have been summarized by Bryant (1985), Rack and Snowling (1985) and Snowling (1987). The nature of both concepts and their relationships remains controversial. The in-fighting between proponents of the two terms has become unnecessarily intemperate at times. The late Professor Meredith of the University of Leeds scathingly referred to dyslexia as 'The unidentified flying object of psychology'. Observers might well ask: Why is there a controversy concerning the merits of the terms 'specific learning difficulties' and 'dyslexia' to describe certain children who experience difficulty in learning to read? Is the controversy an unnecessary academic and professional luxury? Are various authors correct in asserting that the name given to the condition is immaterial? Or does the existence of such a dispute stimulate the investigations on which advances in the ability to conceptualize, predict and control reading development depend? Is it sufficient to claim that 'We do not have a medical condition called dyslexia. We have an educational problem about how to teach more effectively?' (Whittaker, 1981). Is dyslexia the prerogative of conceptual flat-earthers? Is it valid to assert that '…devotion to an outmoded concept in the field of learning seems to inspire those who work so hard to keep the dyslexia issue alive?' (Whittaker, 1982). In a detailed six-page submission to the current inquiry the same educational psychologist concludes:

> Let us deal with learning difficulties and specific learning difficulties as they arise and abandon the attempt to define a concept, half-medical, half-educational, half-magic (the reported healing aspect of shouting 'I am dyslexic, I am dyslexic'). What this hybrid of a concept represents can as easily be defined in clear behavioural terms and plain English. (Whittaker, 1989a)

A subsequent public criticism of psychologists who remain unconvinced by evidence for her case appeared in a trenchant letter to *The Psychologist* (Whittaker, 1989b). At the First International Conference of the British Dyslexia Association (1989), Feuerstein, of *Instrumental Enrichment* fame, suggested that the concept of dyslexia was used as an 'alibi' for ineffectiveness at times by some professionals. The tenacity with which certain professionals and parents hold or reject the belief that dyslexia is a specific condition or handicap and the reasons why their views will be exceedingly difficult to alter have been commented on by many workers over the years (such as Campion, 1982). Agreements accrue slowly.

The psychological approach to learning and development with its emphasis on learning processes and products, the psychoeducational focusing on pedagogy and the medical model with its disorder/disease-treatment orientation almost inevitably lead to contrasting interpretations of certain (not all) literacy difficulties. The observers' inevitably restricted conceptual frameworks resulting from their professional training predispose them to different levels of analysis and towards particular interpretations. Such studies should be complementary (Quin and Macauslan, 1986).

Meetings between representatives of the Schools Council, CSE (Certificate of Secondary Education) and GCE (General Certificate of Education) Boards and the British Medical Association held in 1979 and 1980 were unable to formulate a working definition of the term dyslexia. In the *BMA News Review*, the British Medical Association advised their members that dyslexia was not basically a medical problem. As a learning disability, its certification was the province of the educational psychologist (British Medical Association, 1980). Neurologists disagree. The World Federation of Neurology produced definitions in 1968 of both 'dyslexia' and 'specific development dyslexia' (Critchley, 1970). Dyslexia is defined as '...a disorder in children who, despite conventional classroom experience, fail to attain the language skills of reading, writing and spelling commensurate with their intellectual abilities'. Specific developmental dyslexia is defined as '...a disorder manifested by difficulty in learning to read despite conventional instruction, adequate intelligence, and socio-cultural opportunity. It is dependent upon fundamental cognitive disabilities which are frequently of constitutional origin' (ibid., p. 26). The basis for the existence of a specific type of developmental dyslexia includes persistence into adulthood, distinctive and specific errors in reading and spelling, familial incidence of the condition and a greater frequency in males. When later presenting an overview of the field, Critchley emphasizes that the condition is '...cognitive in essence and usually genetically determined'. He also emphasizes the importance of early identification and the possibility of remedial help leading to considerable improvements. He regrets the confusion between specific developmental dyslexia and acquired dyslexia. The latter is a consequence of some damage to the central nervous system (CNS), for example, by injury or infection. In the case of specific developmental dyslexia he claimed that minor neurological abnormalities are to be found on examination. 'I have always insisted that the diagnosis of specific developmental dyslexia is a medical responsibility. This view is not popular among certain educational psychologists, but its truth can scarcely be denied' (Critchley, 1981, p. 2). Recent advanced work in neurology supports Critchley's comments concerning the neurological integrity of children identified as having specific developmental dyslexia. These findings may, if anything, strengthen the case for neurologists' involvement in assessment and diagnosis.

The importance of neuropsychological findings concerning brain function in general, and specific developmental dyslexia in particular, is difficult to deny. The pioneer work on aphasias (a general term for disturbances of language due to brain lesions) carried out during the 19th century by Broca and Wernicke led to the identification of areas of the brain implicated in the expressive and receptive aphasias, respectively. More recently, an autopsy carried out on a dyslexic child who died from a vascular malformation in the cerebellum '...revealed an atypical cortical gyral pattern with microgyria and pachygyria, as well as absence of the typical pattern of six well-differentiated layers of cortex' (Drake, 1968, referred to in Pirozzolo, 1979, p. ix). Masland cites both the preceding case and one reported by Galaburda. Each case was deemed to be 'a developmental dyslexic'. Each also suffered from epilepsy (Masland, 1981). By 1989 it was reported that Galaburda had now carried out autopsies on a total of nine dyslexics, seven boys and two girls (Masland, 1990). In the boys, anomalous developments in the auditory areas of the brain were identified. In contrast, the girls showed scars suggestive of injury in late pregnancy or early infancy. From the aetiological viewpoint, such findings matter. They could also have important implications for interventions: but the numbers are extremely small and considerable caution in interpreting the findings is essential. The examination of living brains processing information is of more immediate relevance to the work of educational practitioners. This has been achieved by other techniques such as brain stimulation, electroencephalographic studies and the use of radioactively labelled sugar. These techniques help to identify patterns of brain activity and to relate these to a variety of stimuli and responses. For example, activities such as word reading, analysis of meaning, listening and speaking have been related to patterns of brain activity identified by the amount of energy being used in different parts of the brain. It has been unequivocally demonstrated that it is work to think. Where this work is done can be neurologically investigated (Masland, 1990). Increasingly sophisticated, non-intrusive investigative techniques such as transcranial Doppler sonography, magnetic resonance imaging and computerized tomography are available for research into the working of the living brain (Weinberger, 1989). This issue is considered more fully in Chapter 9).

An adequate understanding of aetiology, prognosis and the effects of interventions on children's reading difficulties is unlikely to derive from the efforts of any one group of specialists. Educational psychologists who have suggested that the aetiologies of specific reading difficulties (dyslexia) are relatively unimportant, compared with the identification and alleviation of such difficulties, reveal a questionable certitude. If, as has been suggested, the brain of a 'dyslexic' person is 'miswired', it is not a point to be dismissed lightly (Geschwind, 1980).

Knowledge of the nature of the development of literacy skills of normal children and of children having specific learning difficulties (dyslexia) is paradoxically extensive and limited. There is a proliferation of empirical findings, but a dearth of agreement on many important issues. In psychology, the limitations are in large measure a consequence of an inadequate taxonomy. Even if we limit ourselves to the receptive language skills of silent reading, we have a proliferation of ambiguous terminology. The case for improving this situation, and ways of doing it, are important issues for educational psychologists (Elliott, 1990a).

The Ninth World Congress on Reading was held in Dublin in July 1982. Constance McCullough, a world authority on the identification and alleviation of children's reading difficulties, described her own experience of suddenly losing the ability to read. Her reflections on this event and on her subsequent long, drawn out process of recovery underlined the need for, and importance of, interprofessional cooperation in conceptualizing, identifying and minimizing all severe reading difficulties. Hers was a case of acquired dyslexia. It was on the basis of analogical reasoning applied to children who had not suffered an insult to their brain, but who showed symptoms markedly like those of cases of acquired dyslexia, that led to the postulation of a syndrome-specific developmental dyslexia. Although argument by analogy has serious weaknesses and can lead to category errors, in this instance it has generated a great deal of research, a lot of heat and a little light. The First International Conference of the British Dyslexia Association was held in 1989. Those fortunate enough to attend were impressed at the way in which people working in a range of disciplines were studying different aspects of specific learning difficulties (dyslexia). Whilst it is only one position, and a controversial one at that, the British Dyslexia Association accepts the two terms as virtually synonymous: they are not necessarily correct.

The historical context

As noted above, the medical profession has had a long involvement in the diagnosis and treatment of aphasias. Identification of a specific aphasic loss of the ability to read, 'word blindness', is usually credited to a German physician, Kussmaul, in 1877 (Critchley, 1970). A further ten years passed before the word 'dyslexia' was used to describe the acquired condition (Berlin, 1887). In December 1895 a Glasgow eye-surgeon called Hinshelwood wrote to the *Lancet* on the topic of word blindness and visual memory in adult aphasics. This note stimulated a general practitioner, living in Seaford on the south coast of England and acting as attending physician to a preparatory school, to describe in the *British Medical Journal* the case of a 14-year-old boy who could not master the art of reading and who had great difficulties in spelling and writing. In his article entitled 'A case of congenital word blindness', the boy 'Percy F.' was described as one of the brightest in the class. He had exceptional talents in, for example, mathematics and was capable of carrying out binomial expansions with ease. In the opinions of the boy's teachers, if all the teaching had been oral, the boy would have been at the top of the class in his work. As it was, he was struggling at the bottom of the class. To account for the disability, Morgan suggested that the brain region suspected of being structurally damaged by disease in acquired dyslexia (the left angular gyrus) was underdeveloped in this adolescent. He noted that the condition 'is unique, so far as I know, in that it follows no injury of illness, but is evidently congenital, and due most probably to defective development of ... the left angular gyrus'. Thus maturational lag in the development of particular areas of the brain subserving processes involved in dealing with textual materials was conceived by analogy (Pringle-Morgan, 1896).

Several weeks prior to the publication of Pringle-Morgan's paper, James Kerr, Medical Officer of Health in the city of Bradford, Yorkshire, described in his annual report the existence in local schools of some pupils who appeared to show what he described as 'congenital word-blindness'. Kerr was awarded the Howard Medal by the Royal Statistical Society in the same year for an essay based on his work in Bradford. It included the observation that reading and writing difficulties occurred in children having no other apparent cognitive disabilities. Pringle-Morgan and Kerr made their discoveries independently. Both are generally acknowledged to be the 'discoverers' of developmental dyslexia, though the former is more frequently mentioned in the literature. Thus the medical involvement and interest in certain cases of reading, writing and spelling difficulties in children has a lengthy history.

It was not long before the term 'congenital word blindness' was recognized as a clinical condition by investigators in several countries. The literature contains many case studies, right up to the present day. Over the years these case studies have become increasingly elaborate as investigative techniques have developed. It is interesting and informative to read these accounts in order to note the developing sophistication being brought to the description, the techniques of investigation and the interpretation of the data. But the core concerns remain very similar: an unexpected discrepancy between aspects of the child's severe difficulties in dealing with textual materials contrasted with evidence of considerable intellectual abilities in other fields (Hinshelwood, 1900, 1902, 1904, 1907; Rutherford, 1909; Hallgren, 1950; Miles, 1961; Bakker and Satz, 1970; Naidoo, 1972; Levy, 1982; Seymour, 1986; Hulme, 1989; Richards, 1989). An account entitled *Dyslexia: A Hundred Years On*, written by two well-known authorities, provides further historical details plus contemporary considerations of key theoretical and applied issues (Miles and Miles, 1990).

A number of autobiographical accounts describe in detail the pressures exerted on children and adults who, for no readily apparent reason, experienced tremendous difficulty in achieving literacy. The strategies and subterfuges adopted to cope with these stresses are vividly revealed (Herman, 1959; Newby, 1969; Phemister, 1973; Hampshire, 1981; Harvey, 1983; Lysley, 1989). The letter written to the current inquiry by Zachary underlines the problems and the anguish involved (reproduced at the front of this book).

In the 1920s, an American psychiatrist named Orton noted that an unusually high proportion of children with 'specific reading disability' had pronounced reversal and orientation difficulties in reading and writing. Some showed complete mirror reversal of words. The children also tended to be left-handed, or to have no established lateral preference at an age when this was usually firmly established. Conflicting laterality of eye and hand was frequently noted. Orton hypothesized that, for *some* children, reading difficulties were the symptom of a failure of one of the cerebral hemispheres to become the dominant control centre for speech, language and motor functions (Orton, 1925, 1937). His theorizing concerning 'engrams' or patterns in the right and left hemispheres was never substantiated and the hypothesized aetiological relationship between laterality and reading difficulties were also questioned (Spache, 1976). Despite this, developmental delays were increasingly hypothesized as responsible for many of the neurological difficulties underlying the symptoms. Orton stimulated important work on the teaching of children with severe and prolonged reading difficulties. His methods developed from the assumption that 'dyslexia' was a problem of linguistic development. Careful observation, an individual profile of the child's abilities, the noting of 'instructional errors' (currently called 'miscues' in oral reading), attention to the child's emotional reaction and an individually tailored and responsive intervention programme characterized this approach. On the basis of work with about 1000 dyslexic children, Orton offered flexible guidelines for interventions that have found many supporters. The Orton Society was founded in 1949 in the USA. It is currently influential in coordinating and disseminating research into developmental deficits of language development. Additionally, this society is concerned with the provision of facilities and the development of intervention programmes (Richardson, 1989).

Orton's observations concerning the particular problems that dyslexics had with printed symbols, especially reversible letters and words, such as b/d, p/q, no/on, was/saw, stimulated interest in the notion that dyslexia was a consequence of visual and perceptual difficulties. This led to studies of visual information processing by such children. One group of workers presented children with various visual stimuli, mainly letters, each divided into two parts. First, one half of the stimulus was presented. After a specified time it was removed and the other half of the stimulus was shown. The children were required to report when an integrated single stimulus was perceived. The findings showed that visual information remained in iconic memory for some 50 per cent longer in dyslexic than in non-dyslexic children. It took the former children longer to proceed to the next stage of visual information processing. This led to the conclusion that in activities such as reading, where successive bits of visual information had to be integrated over time, the reading progress of dyslexic children would be slower than that of their non-dyslexic peers (Stanley, 1975). More recently, it has been proposed that dyslexic children experience difficulties when visual stimuli have to be named. Children were shown pairs of letters that were either physically identical (such as AA) or different (AB or Aa). The task was to decide whether the items within a pair were the same or different. For all subjects, AA was more rapidly and accurately dealt with than Aa or Bb. The second task is seen as requiring retrieval of letter representations from memory whereas the first depended on judgements made on a physical basis (Ellis, 1981). A comparison was made of mental-age matched skilled and disabled readers' performances in tracing, and then drawing from memory, meaningless angular shapes using (i) unnamed and then (ii) arbitrarily assigned verbal labels. In relation to their ability to reproduce shapes from memory under the first condition, the groups did not differ. When verbal labels were added, the disabled readers performed less adequately. This is interpreted as demonstrating their difficulties in integrating visual and verbal codes (Swanson, 1984).

As would be expected bearing in mind the complexities of specific learning difficulties (dyslexia), evidence and arguments concerning the importance of visual and verbal coding deficits in dyslexia are extensive (Snowling, 1985, 1987). A number of carefully carried out studies indicate the importance of verbal memory and phoneme segmentation (Pumfrey and Elliott, 1990).

The first Wordblind Institute was established by Norrie in Denmark in 1936. In 1963 the Invalid Children's Aid Association established the Word Blind Centre for Dyslexic Children in London. It closed in 1972 because of lack of funds. However, between 1965 and 1972 eight voluntary local dyslexia associations were started. The British Dyslexia Association was formed in 1972. Since 1977 this organization has had formal links with the DES. Local branches can now be found in most parts of the country. The BDA organized its first international conference in 1989. The event was extremely well attended and successful. At the conference, a special interest group for professionals involved in the field was established. A number of educational and child psychologists are members. Its second international conference was held at Oxford in April 1991. That event was also very successful with many high quality contributions from eminent workers (Snowling and Thomson, 1991).

Much earlier, the North Surrey Dyslexic Society sponsored the Dyslexia Institute at Staines, which published the now defunct *Dyslexia Review*. A new training unit called the City of London Dyslexia Institute opened at Coram's Fields, Guildford Street, London WC1 in 1982. Other voluntary associations involved in this field include the Cambridge Specific Learning Disabilities Group, The Gifted Children's information Centre, the Helen Arkell Dyslexia Centre, Invalid Children's Aid Nationwide and the National Bureau for Handicapped Students. The addresses of these and other bodies are readily available (Brett, 1990). The Foundation for the Education of the Underachieving and Dyslexic is one of the more recent arrivals on the British educational scene. It opened a residential school in 1982. This is one of the seven independent schools working in this particular field that have been inspected and are currently recognized by the DES.

An even more recently established group called 'Defining Dyslexia' has its head-quarters in Ruislip. It is active in encouraging the training of teachers in the identification and alleviation of specific learning difficulties (dyslexia).

An increasing number of private sector schools are offering specialist help for children who may be categorized as having 'specific reading difficulties', 'specific learning difficulties', or 'dyslexia' (School Fees Insurance Agency, 1989). A survey by the Dyslexia Institute of over 1200 independent schools in the UK and the Irish Republic received an 80 per cent response rate. A press report stated that nearly 80 per cent of such schools '...will take dyslexics' (*Times Educational Supplement*, 1982). Since the implementation of the Education Act 1981 in April 1983, the topics of specific learning difficulties and dyslexia have received considerable public discussion. Private school provision in this field appears to have expanded since then, and new courses of training for teachers have been established.

Elsewhere the Specific Learning Difficulties Association has evolved from the dyslexic associations in Australia and New Zealand. In the USA the term 'specific learning disabilities' is enshrined in legislation. Conceptually it is very similar to the notion of 'specific learning difficulties' used in this country. As here, it subsumes dyslexia. The Americans are far more explicit in their operational definitions of the condition(s) and of eligibility for funds under Federal and State provisions than is the practice in the UK (Elliott, 1990a).

Research into children identified as *underachieving* in literacy has been a long-standing professional interest at universities. That tradition continues (Colt-heart, 1987a; Pumfrey and Elliott, 1990). The pioneer British work based on the Remedial Education Centre established by Schonell and Wall at the University of Birmingham is an important example. The centre worked in cooperation with the Department of Paediatrics and Child Health, Birmingham schools and other adjacent LEAs. The ethos was multidisciplinary but the impetus for the establishment and development of the centre came from psychologists involved in education. The contributions of Kelmer-Pringle and Phillips as later directors of the centre extended its influence throughout Britain and overseas (Sampson, 1980).

Hospitals also showed an early and continuing interest in the diagnosis and treatment of specific learning difficulties (dyslexia). St Bartholomew's, London, was involved from the early 1950s. The Royal Berkshire Hospital, Reading, has carried out research into children with reading difficulties. Although the project was based in the Orthoptic Department, the study was multidisciplinary. The work of the Learning Disabilities Clinic at St Thomas's Hospital, London, is also widely known (Quin and Macauslan, 1986).

The preceding examples of private sector, university and hospital initiatives are intended only to be indicative. The range and variety of initiatives aiming to optimize children's literacy development in general, and reading in particular, are considerable and likely to increase. The success of the Education Reform Act 1988 and the increase in attainments anticipated through the National Curriculum require improved literacy.

Public and professional interest in this field is also marked. An earlier extensive computer review of the literature on 'dyslexia' carried out at the Department of Communication Studies of Sheffield City Polytechnic makes the point (Wheeler, 1979). From Wheeler's next base at the National Institute for Higher Education, Dublin, a search of the 1979 to 1982 literature has also been completed; publications proliferate (Evans, 1982). Subsequent computer searches carried out at the John Rylands University Library, Manchester, in connection with the 1989 inquiry covered several extensive data bases. These included the *American Educational Resources Information Centres*, the British Education Index and *Medline*. From the period January 1980 to March 1989, over 1000 references to pertinent publications were located.

The severe and prolonged difficulties in learning to read, spell and write experienced by some otherwise intellectually competent children pose a profound challenge to members of the many helping professions involved. Individuals who have experienced problems in learning to read have been active in establishing organizations independent of the state educational system to help children with similar problems. Such pressure groups have successfully influenced aspects of the educational policies and practices of the government, of some schools and of the examination boards.

Despite the use of the adjective 'specific', much of the research on specific reading difficulties (dyslexia) has involved a somewhat non-specific group of children failing to read at an expected level. Difficulties in agreeing, or even making explicit, the theoretical basis for expectations concerning reading attainments and other literacy skills, impede progress in describing, identifying, predicting progress and developing effective interventions. Coupled with problems in theoretically conceptualizing and operationally defining the cognitive characteristics of children having specific learning difficulties (dyslexia), this leads to incidence estimates that vary from 0.3 per cent to over 30 per cent (Cornwall, Hedderly and Pumfrey, 1984). It is possible to find research in which, for example, dyslexia is operationally defined as six months behind grade level in reading.

Definition largely determines incidence. Imprecise definitions linked to legal/administrative procedures lead to varying incidences. If one accepts the assumptions that dyslexia is a subset of specific learning difficulties, rather than synonymous with it (as some assert), the incidence of the former should be smaller than the incidence of the latter. The procedures of 'statementing' children with special educational needs under the provisions of the Education Act 1981 does not necessarily identify all children with specific learning difficulties and/or dyslexia, but must include a considerable proportion of them. Using the formal procedure of statementing as one criteria of incidence, LEA services show identification rates that vary between 0.04 per cent and 4.2 per cent (Select Committee on Education, Science and the Arts, 1987). Such a hundredfold variation raises many questions concerning what is being identified and the policies and practices of LEAs that lead to such huge differences.

A plethora of ambiguous terms purports to clarify the situation; labels such as slow reader, backward reader, retarded reader, a child with specific reading/ spelling/writing difficulties, a child with specific retardation in reading, dyslexia, developmental dyslexia, strephosymbolia and a host of others exist. These exacerbate the problems of comparison between studies. Typically, terms with Greek roots come from one group of professionals. Less etymologically obscure but equally vague terms come from other professionals. The flippant but pointed comment 'Do not adjust your minds: there is a fault in reality' could well be expected, were the issues involved not so serious.

Despite their inevitable limitations, current American attempts to address the central taxonomic issues hold more promise than the nebulous superordinate concept of 'special educational needs' under which specific learning difficulties and dyslexia are subsumed in the UK (Elliott, 1990a; Pumfrey and Mittler,

Table 1.1: Some pertinent definitions

Special educational needs. 'A child has special educational needs if he has a "learning difficulty" which calls for special educational provision to be made for him' (Section 1, Education Act 1981).

Special educational provision. That provision 'which is additional to, or otherwise different from, the educational provision made generally in LEA schools for children of his age' (Section 1, Education Act 1981).

Learning difficulty. 'A child has a learning difficulty if he has significantly greater difficulty in learning than the majority of children of that age, or he has a disability which either prevents or hinders him from making use of the educational facilities of a kind generally provided in schools, within the area of the local authority concerned, for children of his age' (Section 1, Education Act 1981).

Dyslexia. 'A disorder in children who, despite conventional classroom experience, fail to attain the language skills of reading, writing and spelling commensurate with their intellectual abilities' (World Federation of Neurology, 1968).

*Dyslexia.** 'We define dyslexia as a specific difficulty in learning, constitutional in origin, in one or more of reading, spelling and written language which may be accompanied by difficulty in number work. It is particularly related to mastering and using written language (alphabetical, numerical and musical notation) although often affecting oral language to some degree' (British Dyslexia Association, 1989).

Specific developmental dyslexia. 'A disorder manifested by difficulty in learning to read despite conventional instruction, adequate intelligence, and socio-cultural opportunity. It depends on fundamental cognitive disabilities which are frequently of constitutional origin' (World Federation of Neurology, 1968).

Specific reading retardation. '… an attainment on either reading accuracy or reading comprehension which was 28 months or more below the level predicted on the basis of each child's age and short *WISC* I.Q.' (Rutter, Tizard and Whitmore, 1970, p. 36).

Specific learning difficulties. 'Children with specific learning difficulties are those who in the absence of sensory defect or overt organic damage, have an intractable learning problem in one or more of reading, writing, spelling and mathematics, and who do not respond to normal teaching. For these children, early identification, sensitive encouragement and specific remedial arrangements are necessary' (Tansley and Panckhurst, 1981, p. 259).

*Specific learning difficulties.** These 'are defined as organising or learning deficiencies which restrict the student's competencies in information processing, in motor skills and working memory, so causing limitations in some or all of the skills of speech, reading, spelling, writing, essay writing, numeracy and behaviour' (Dyslexia Institute, 1989).

Specific reading difficulties. A descriptive term used to indicate the problems of the relatively small proportion of pupils 'whose reading (and perhaps writing, spelling and number) abilities are significantly below the standards which their abilities in other spheres would lead one to expect' (GB. DES, 1972, p. 3).

Learning disability. 'A disorder in one or more of the basic psychological processes involved in understanding or using language, spoken or written, which may manifest itself in an imperfect ability to listen, think, speak, read, write, spell or do mathematical calculations' (United States Education for All Handicapped Children Act, PL 94–142, 1975). (NB: The definition specifically excludes visual, hearing or motor handicaps, mental retardation, and the effect of environmental, cultural, or economic disadvantage.)

---

* The most recent definitions of the terms 'dyslexia' and 'specific learning difficulties' given above represent an expansion of the concepts. The more that each expands, the greater the likelihood that one will become redundant.

1989). The variety of labels used in the research literature, as represented by those listed in Table 1.1, makes the point (see p. 14).

Adams, cited by Stauffer, Abrams and Pikulski (1978), reviewed definitions of the term 'dyslexia' in psychological and medical dictionaries and of its use by psychologists, educators, neurologists and psychiatrists. He identified 32 differing definitions leading him to the conclusion that the meaning of the term '...is obscure and it has divided the efforts of professional men when collaboration would have been the better course' (Adams, 1969, p. 616). It is a concern that is reiterated regularly.

Cruickshank, reported in Cornwall, Hedderly and Pumfrey (1984), noted that:

> If a child diagnosed as dyslexic in Philadelphia moved to Bucks County, ten miles north, he would be called a child with language disorder. In Montgomery County, Maryland, a few miles south, he would be called a child with special or specific language problems. In Michigan, he would be called a child with a perceptual disturbance. In California he would be called either a child with educational handicaps or a neurologically handicapped child. In Florida and New York State, he would be called a brain injured child. In Colorado, the child would be classified as having minimal brain dysfunction. (p. 13)

The debate concerning the definition of specific learning difficulties in this country is paralleled in the USA, and elsewhere, in relation to the definition of the psychoeducational and legal concept of 'learning disabilities'.

In an informed and challenging analysis, one authority has pointed to a consensus emerging in this field in relation to the conceptual definition of the condition (Hammill, 1990). Such a consensus is seen as the essential first step towards an operational definition.

Hammill examined 28 textbooks on learning disabilities published between 1982 and 1989. These were considered representative of books used as introductory or methods texts in teacher training courses. Beginning with Kirk's (1962) initiative in defining the term, Hammill presents 11 definitions.

He then identifies nine conceptual elements against which the definitions can be compared. These elements are as follows.

- Underachievement determination.
- Central nervous system dysfunction aetiology.
- Process involvement.
- Present through lifespan.
- Specification of spoken language problems as potential learning disabilities.
- Specification of academic problems as potential learning disabilities.
- Specification of conceptual problems as potential learning disabilities.
- Specification of other conditions as potential learning disabilities.
- Allowance for the multihandicapping nature of learning disabilities.

Hammill considers that the definitions in Table 1.2 fall into two distinct clusters. The first of these includes nos 2, 4, 5 and 8 from the table. A composite derived from these four is deemed '... painfully obscure and obviously unacceptable. It is easy to see why most professionals have moved in the definitional direction indicated by cluster 2' (Hammill, 1990, p. 81). A composite definition drawing on

Table 1.2: American definitions of learning disabilities

---

(1) Kirk (1962, p. 263)
'A learning disability refers to a retardation, disorder, or delayed development in one or more of the processes of speech, language, reading, writing, arithmetic, or other school subjects resulting from a psychological handicap caused by a possible cerebral dysfunction and/or emotional or behavioural disturbances. It is not the result of mental retardation, sensory deprivation, or cultural and instructional factors.'

(2) Bateman (1965, p. 220)
'Children who have learning disorders are those who manifest an educationally significant discrepancy between their estimated intellectual potential and actual level of performance related to basic disorders in the learning process, which may or may not be accompanied by demonstrable central nervous dysfunction, and which are not secondary to generalised mental retardation, educational or cultural deprivation, severe emotional disturbance or sensory loss.'

(3) National Advisory Committee on Handicapped Children (1968, p. 34)
'Children with special (specific) learning disabilities exhibit a disorder in one or more of the basic psychological processes involved in understanding or in using spoken and written language. These may be manifested in disorders of listening, thinking, talking, reading, writing, spelling or arithmetic. They include conditions which have been referred to as perceptual handicaps, brain injury, minimal brain dysfunction, dyslexia, developmental aphasia etc. They do not include learning problems that are due primarily to visual, hearing or motor handicaps, to mental retardation, emotional disturbance, or to environmental disadvantage.'

(4) Kass and Myklebust (1969, pp. 378–9)
'Learning disability refers to one or more significant deficits in essential learning processes requiring special education techniques for remediation.
  * Children with learning disability generally demonstrate a discrepancy between expected and actual achievement in one or more areas such as spoken, read, or written language, mathematics, and spatial orientation.
  * The learning disability referred to is not primarily the result of sensory, motor, intellectual, or emotional handicap, or lack of opportunity to learn.
  * Significant deficits are defined in terms of accepted diagnostic procedures in education and psychology.
  * Essential learning processes are those currently referred to in behavioural science as involving perception, integration, and expression, either verbal or non-verbal.
  * Special education techniques for remediation refers to educational planning based on the diagnostic procedures and results.'

(5) Wepman et al. (1975, p. 306)
'Specific learning disability, as defined here, refers to those children of any age who demonstrate a substantial deficiency in a particular aspect of academic achievement because of perceptual or perceptual–motor handicaps, irrespective of etiology or other contributing factors. The term perceptual as used here relates to those mental (neurological) processes through which the child acquires ... basic alphabets of sound and forms.'

(6) United States Office of Education (1976, p. 52405)
'A specific learning disability may be found if a child has a severe discrepancy between achievement and intellectual ability in one or more of several areas: oral expression, written expression, listening comprehension or reading comprehension, basic reading skills, mathematics calculation, mathematics reasoning, or spelling. A "severe discrepancy" is defined to exist when achievement in one or more of the areas falls at or below 50% of the child's expected achievement level, when age and previous educational experiences are taken into consideration.'

Table 1.2 cont.

---

(7) United States Office of Education (1977, p. 65083)
'The term "specific learning disability" means a disorder in one or more of the basic psychological processes involved in understanding or in using language, spoken or written, which may manifest itself in an imperfect ability to listen, speak, read, write, spell, or to do mathematical calculations. The term includes such conditions as perceptual handicaps, brain injury, minimal brain dysfunction, dyslexia, and developmental aphasia. The term does not include children who have learning disabilities which are primarily the result of visual, hearing or motor handicaps, or mental retardation, or emotional disturbance, or of environmental, cultural, or economic disadvantage.'

(8) Council for Exceptional Children, Division for Children with Learning Disabilities (Siegel and Gold, 1982, p. 14)
'A child with learning disabilities is one with adequate mental ability, sensory processes, and emotional stability who has specific deficits in perceptual, integrative, or expressive processes which impair learning efficiency. This includes children who have central nervous system dysfunction which is expressed primarily in impaired efficiency.'

(9) Association for Children with Learning Disabilities (1986, p. 15)
'Specific Learning Difficulties is a chronic condition of presumed neurological origin which selectively interferes with the development, integration, and/or demonstration of verbal and/or non-verbal abilities. Specific Learning Disabilities exist as a distinct handicapping condition and varies in its manifestations and in degree of severity. Throughout life, the condition can affect self-esteem, education, vocation, socialisation, and/or daily living activities.'

(10) Interagency Committee on Learning Disabilities (1987, p. 222)
'Learning disabilities is a generic term that refers to a heterogeneous group of disorders manifested by significant difficulties in the acquisition and use of listening, speaking, reading, writing, reasoning, or mathematical abilities, or of social skills. These disorders are intrinsic to the individual and presumed to be due to central nervous system dysfunction. Even though a learning disability may occur concomitantly with other handicapping conditions (e.g. sensory impairment, mental retardation, social and emotional disturbance) with socioenvironmental influences (e.g. cultural differences, insufficient or inappropriate instruction, psychogenic factors) and especially attention deficit disorder, all of which may cause learning problems, a learning disability is not the direct result of those conditions or influences.'

(11) National Joint Committee on Learning Disabilities (1988, p. 1)
'*Learning disabilities* is a general term that refers to a heterogeneous group of disorders manifested by significant difficulties in the acquisition and use of listening, speaking, reading, writing, reasoning, or mathematical abilities. These disorders are intrinsic to the individual, presumed to be due to central nervous system dysfunctions, and may occur across the life span. Problems in self-regulatory behaviours, social perception, and social interaction may exist with learning disabilities but do not themselves constitute a learning disability. Although learning disabilities may occur concomitantly with other handicapping conditions (for example, sensory impairment, mental retardation, serious emotional disturbances) or with extrinsic influences (such as cultural differences, insufficient or inappropriate instruction), they are not the result of those conditions or influences.'

---

the other seven definitions comprising cluster 2 is considered to be '...nearly identical to those of Kirk, NACHC [National Advisory Committee on Handicapped Children], the 1987 USOE [United States Office of Education] and the NJCLD [National Joint Committee on Learning Disabilities]. By comparing the composite '... with the four definitions, one can note agreement on eight of the nine elements. This represents 89% agreement on critical definitional characteristics' (ibid., p. 81).

Hammill concludes from his analysis that, surprisingly, considerable agreement exists between definitions proposed by various groups. Of the definitions currently available, he considers that given by the NJCLD to be probably the best current descriptive statement concerning the nature of learning disabilities.

Whilst not all readers will agree with either Hammill's assumptions, criteria or judgements, his presentation will undoubtedly stimulate discussion of the conceptual basis of learning disabilities.

Stringent criticisms of work in the field of learning disabilities (LD) have been presented by Kavale and Forness (1985). Are these authors (who are not alone) correct in arguing that learning disabilities represents a 'pseudoscience' and is 'a victim of its own history'? Do the same comments apply to the concepts of specific learning difficulties (dyslexia) currently in use in the UK? Have Kavale and Forness demonstrated unequivocally that:

> ...the important (and legitimate) study of LD can be called a science in no significant sense, and the continued application of this misleading metaphor can only vitiate and distort research efforts. We are *not* saying that LD should not be empirical, that LD should not essay a tough-minded analysis of events, or that LD should not apply statistical (and mathematical) methods. We *are* saying that in studying LD, particularly in terms of notions like learning, language, cognition, perception, attention, motivation, information processing and so on, concepts such as 'law', 'theory', 'model', 'measurement', 'control' and the like do not behave sufficiently like their counterparts in the established sciences to justify their extensions to LD science.

Coupled with their criticism of unreflective empiricism, this leads to the assertion that work in the LD field shows '...not the qualities of a discipline based on science but, rather, one based on deceit' (ibid., p. 141). They see the central problem of work in the LD field as having to account for the nature of LD phenomena in general at the conceptual and philosophical level. For them, there has been an unhelpful imbalance between the empirical and the conceptual aspects of work in this field.

Conceptualizations of what is meant by learning disabilities in the USA, and what is meant by specific learning difficulties (dyslexia) in the UK are essential concomitants of improved operational definitions and decision-making concerning identification and alleviation that is public and valid.

In the past, a similar catalogue could have been made out for various parts of the UK. The range and variety of diagnostic terminology was used neither because of the perversity of those involved nor because of an unwillingness to communicate and cooperate. In large measure, the terminological confusions were (and remain) attributable to the complexities of the issues, the involvement of different professions, the contrasting levels and natures of explanatory theories available, the different interventions advocated and the evidence adduced as to the efficacy of the latter. In addition, the legal and administrative procedures concerning the identification and alleviation of both specific learning difficulties and dyslexia further confound the issue. The claim that categories of handicap had been abolished under the provisions of the Education Act 1981 was misleading. Superordinate categories were established. Either a child did or did not have special educational needs. If these existed, the child was or was not 'statemented'.

This confusion concerning the use of the terms specific learning difficulties and dyslexia has led some psychologists and teachers to assert that aetiological considerations are largely irrelevant. They believe, as do parents, that attention should be focused on identifying effective interventions. The assertion is suspect, albeit understandable. Aetiologies are important and cannot lightly be ignored. Increasingly, neurological, psychological and educational evidence points to groups of pupils having specific learning difficulties (dyslexia) with contrasting aetiologies and presenting performance characteristics (Singleton, 1987; Tyler and Elliott, 1988; van der Leij, 1989; Masland, 1990). Other workers disagree. They consider that all backward readers form part of a continuum, that inter-individual differences are quantitative and not qualitative, and that the concept of dyslexia does not exist as a clinical entity (Bryant, 1985).

The search for valid means of identifying pupils with specific learning difficulties (dyslexia) is characterized by the problems identified above. Had the search been successful, incidence rates would have much more in common than is currently the case. Despite this difficulty, the search for effective interventions continues. This path has its own considerable difficulties (Wilsher, 1990).

Elliott (1990a) has described how in America the application of Public Law 94–142, *Education for All Handicapped Children Act* seeks to impose a degree of order in this terminological jungle (United States Office of Education, 1975). In the UK the use of specific categories of handicap was largely abandoned as a consequence of the provisions of the Education Act 1981. In the USA, categories were retained. Specific learning disability is one of these. It has been operationally defined, albeit not identically, in all states. Interestingly, this particular category of handicap has grown markedly over recent years and is now the largest in the American educational system. The relationship with funding arrangements is seen by some as contributory to a situation currently causing considerable concern (Kavale and Forness, 1985; Elliott, 1990a).

A major problem with categories in the field of specific learning difficulties (dyslexia) in the UK is that the boundaries between children deemed to exhibit the condition tend to be arbitrary. If these boundaries were clearer than they are in terms of pupil characteristics, decision-making concerning resource allocation would not be any easier. It would, however, be more explicit and defensible than the current situation. As has been argued elsewhere, the learning of virtually *all* children can be enhanced and their attainments improved. Educational and child psychologists and teachers have a very considerable, albeit imperfect, understanding of the developmental, cognitive, socio-emotional and motivational factors involved. Pedagogic expertise, materials and methods are extensive. They are also expensive. Awareness of the costs involved in making provisions for pupils with special educational needs is currently being highlighted by the development of Local Management of Schools (LMS) (GB.DES, 1988c). The application of this professional knowledge and expertise to help pupils with specific learning difficulties (dyslexia) requires additional resources. That means money. Usually this comes from the public purse. There are many competing claims for such limited funds as are available. It is for society, via the votes of its citizens, to determine priorities and the resources allocated to them. In this area there is one certainty: demand for public funds from pressure groups will always exceed provision. In their capacity as disinterested professionals, it is for educational and child psychologists to view the entire field of individual differences between pupils and contribute to local and national discussions on resource allocation and priorities. Children with specific learning difficulties (dyslexia) are but one group for whom a case can be made. Inevitably and justifiably, pressure groups headed by charitable and professional organizations will also be involved. Controversy over funding will continue in parallel with the unresolved theoretical issues specified earlier. Even if these could be resolved, and it may be that they cannot by their very nature, the funding issue would remain contentious (Pumfrey and Mittler, 1989). This issue is addressed in more detail in Chapters 6 and 8.

In the earlier DECP report, replies were received from 62 principal educational psychologists employed by LEAs. Of these, 66 per cent answered positively to the question 'Do you subscribe to the view that a specific category of need exists that can be isolated from general reading retardation?' When asked to comment on the terminological issues involved, two related concerns emerged. Firstly, there was an awareness of the ambiguities and other deficiencies in the then current terminology used. The second concern was with the idiosyncratic patterns of abilities and needs of each individual child. That concern with individual differences remains central to the work of psychologists and teachers.

Since 1983, the concepts of specific learning difficulties and dyslexia have increasingly permeated the vocabulary of the populace. In relation to dyslexia, this is particularly the case. It has been observed that whereas in the past the term dyslexia was used with an unjustified infrequency, nowadays it is used with an unjustified frequency. The accuracy of such a statement is unknown, but it conveys a feeling of concern felt by some professionals. The power of fashion in education and psychology cannot be ignored.

Over many years educational and child psychologists, whilst accepting the existence of 'acquired dyslexias', have tended to be suspicious of the term 'specific developmental dyslexia'. The current abbreviation of this in popular usage to 'dyslexia' tends to be accepted as a shorthand that allows communication between parents and professionals. The aetiological, prognostic and resource implications of the term remain a communicative quagmire, frequently unrecognized until misunderstandings have developed. The increasing acknowledgement that there could be a variety of specific developmental dyslexias and that these could be included under the term specific learning difficulties provided an administrative avenue that to some psychologists looks like a conceptual cul-de-sac.

The previous DECP report anticipated that the precision with which children's learning difficulties in general and specific learning difficulties (dyslexia) in particular could be specified was likely to increase. Developments in this field have been greatly promoted by the increasing availability of microcomputer applications in testing, learning and teaching. A hitherto unavailable degree of control in psychological experimentation has opened up rapidly (Seymour, 1986). To the educational and child psychologist and teacher trying to understand, predict and enhance children's learning, the advent of the microcomputer has been analogous to the benefits to biologists in their specialism following the development of the microscope. And that is almost certainly an understatement.

Recent reports and reflections

A 'Cook's tour' of important reports and other publications is listed in Table 1.3. It plots key documents indicating how an earlier discussion concerning dyslexia, specific reading difficulties and some of their variants has developed to date. The Chronically Sick and Disabled Persons Act 1970 required that every LEA provide information to the Secretary of State on '...special educational facilities for children who suffer from acute dyslexia'. Authorities were also required to provide '...special educational treatment ... for children suffering from acute dyslexia'. The use of the term 'acute dyslexia' was confusing. In the medical sense,

Table 1.3: Legislation and reports

Date	Title
1970	Chronically Sick and Disabled Persons Act.
1972	Children with Specific Reading Difficulties (GB.DES, 1972) (Chairman: Professor J. Tizard).
1975	A Language for Life (GB.DES, 1975b) (Chairman: Sir A. Bullock).
1978	Special Educational Needs (GB.DES, 1978) (Chairperson: Mrs H. M. Warnock).
1981	DES sponsored review by the NFER: Children with Specific Learning Difficulties (Tansley and Panckhurst, 1981).
1981	Circular 8/81: Education Act 1981 (GB.DES, 1981a).
1983	Education (Special Educational Needs) Regulations 1983.
1983	Circular 1/83: Assessments and Statements of Special Educational Needs within the Education, Health and Social Services (GB.DES, 1983).
1987	Special Educational Needs: Implementation of the Education Act 1981 (House of Commons Education, Science and Arts Committee, 1987) (Chairman: Sir William van Straubenzee).
1987	Report of the Task Group on Assessment and Testing (GB.DES/WO, 1987a) (Chairman: Professor P. J. Black).
1988	Education Reform Act.
1988	Report of the Committee of Inquiry into the Teaching of English Language (GB.DES, 1988b) (Chairman: Professor J. Kingman).
1988	English for ages 5 to 11: Proposals of the Secretaries of State (GB.DES/WO, 1988). (Chairman: Professor B. Cox).
1988	Circular 7/88: Local Management of Schools (GB.DES, 1988c).
1989	Circular 5/89: School Curriculum and Assessment (GB.DES. 1989c).
1989	English in the National Curriculum (GB.DES, 1989a).
1989	Circular 8/89: Education Reform Act 1988 – Temporary Exceptions to the National Curriculum (GB.DES, 1989e).
1989	Circular 22/89: Assessments and Statements of Special Educational Needs: Procedures within the Education, Health and Social Services (GB.DES, 1989f).
1990	Education (Special Educational Needs) (Amendment) Regulations (1990) No. 1524 (Statutory instrument, 1990).
1990	Circular 9/90: The Education (National Curriculum) (Assessment arrangements for English, Mathematics and Science) Order 1990 (GB.DES, 1990a).

acute means 'coming sharply to a crisis'. The severe reading difficulties referred
to in the Act were not of that nature. If the term 'acute' is interpreted as meaning
'severe', the degree of severity was not defined. The Secretary of State referred
the issue to the Advisory Committee on Handicapped Children for their views. A
subcommittee was set up with Professor J. Tizard as Chairman. Its report
(referred to at the beginning of this chapter), *Children with Specific Reading
Difficulties* (GB.DES, 1972), considered the utility of the terms 'dyslexia', 'acute
dyslexia', 'developmental dyslexia' and 'specific developmental dyslexia'. It
was accepted that some children did experience severe and often long-lasting difficulties in learning to read and '...fulfil some of the criteria of specific developmental dyslexia'. However, the evidence for a syndrome of 'developmental
dyslexia' was discounted. The report recommended the adoption of the term
'specific reading difficulties' as the most appropriate one to use in describing the
difficulties of the small group of children whose reading (and perhaps writing,
spelling and number) is 'significantly below the standards which their abilities in
other spheres would lead one to expect' (GB.DES, 1972).

Intra-individual discrepancies in cognitive functions were referred to, but the
precise pattern of abilities characterizing children deemed to have specific reading difficulties remained obscure. Reference to a discrepancy between assessments of general ability and of reading or other language attainments begs more
questions than it answers. The psychological and psychometric limitations of
such procedures have been a focus of psychological concern for many years.
This is not to say that such procedures are valueless; merely that considerable
caution is required when using such data. Profile interpretation is complex, even
when well-constructed normative tests are used. When criterion-referenced tests
of unknown reliabilities and validities are used (an increasingly common practice), it is likely that even more error variance pervades the picture. As knowledge of patterns of intra-individual differences in cognitive abilities was limited,
the failure of the committee to specify an identification procedure capable of
commanding acceptance by all professional groups was symptomatic of the prevailing state of knowledge in this area.

In 1972 an NFER report, *The Trend of Reading Standards*, indicated a decline
in attainments at particular age levels (Start and Wells, 1972). Shortly after the
publication of this report, the Secretary of State for Education set up a committee
of inquiry under the chairmanship of Sir Alan Bullock. Its brief was to consider
in the school context all aspects of the teaching of English including reading,
writing, spelling and speech.

In their report, the committee recognized that the term 'dyslexic' was used to
describe a small group of children whose difficulties in learning to read are not
attributable to 'limited ability or ... emotional or extraneous factors' (GB.DES,
1975b, p. 268). The term 'dyslexic' is criticized because of the lack of an agreed
operational definition or indication of means of alleviating the difficulty. 'A
more helpful term to describe the situation of these children is specific reading
retardation' (ibid., p. 268). This had been defined as 'a syndrome characterized
by severe reading difficulties which are not accountable for in terms of low intelligence and which are not explicable merely in terms of the lower end of a normal distribution of reading skills' (Rutter and Yule, 1973). These authors stressed
that 'specific reading retardation', in their terminology, has no implications concerning aetiology and does not imply any unitary causal factors. The appeal at
that time of their chosen terminology was due, in part, to the extensive epidemiological studies and the clear identification procedures adopted by these workers.

These identification procedures represented an explicit operational means of identifying children with specific reading retardation. The arbitrary nature of the dividing line between children deemed to be in this category and those excluded was, and remains, a matter of controversy. Subsequent work has indicated that a ceiling effect in the tests used by Rutter and Yule contributed to the 'hump' in the distribution of underachievement they had identified and interpreted. Work with a sample of ten-year-old pupils derived from the Child Health and Education Study failed to replicate their findings. The researcher identified no 'hump' and stated that specific reading retardation was the extreme of the continuum of underachievement (Rodgers, 1983). The findings from the two studies are not entirely incompatible.

The appropriateness of the term specific reading retardation has been criticized as insufficiently broad to encompass developmental dyslexia. Critchley has argued that the etymology of the word dyslexia

> ...expresses admirably a difficulty – not in reading – but in the use of words, how they are identified, what they signify, how they are handled in combination, how they are pronounced and how they are spelt ... The natural history of a dyslexic schoolboy is usually one of steady improvement in his ability to read, but the other troubles or epiphenomena are then highlighted. The term specific reading retardation is, therefore, not appropriate as it indicates an isolated symptom, whereas developmental dyslexia is a complex syndrome. (Critchley, 1981, p. 2)

All of the major voluntary organizations concerned with dyslexia subscribe to this position.

The next major report pertinent to the issue was that of the Committee of Enquiry into the Education of Handicapped Children and Young People (the Warnock Report; GB.DES, 1978). The term 'acute dyslexia' appears in the report (para. 2.83), which despite this manages to concur with the conclusions of the earlier Tizard Report (ibid., para. 11.47). The Warnock Report states that, as yet

> Although there are no agreed criteria for distinguishing those children with severe and long-term difficulties in reading, writing and spelling from others who may require remedial teaching in these areas, there are nevertheless children whose disabilities are marked but whose general ability is at least average and for whom distinctive arrangements are necessary. (para. 11.48)

In reorientating the conceptual framework within which special educational provision is made from one based on discrete categories of handicap to the specification of a continuum of special educational needs, the Warnock Report led to professional rethinking, legislation (the Education Act 1981) and its related circulars and regulations, and to an important survey of the field (Tansley and Panckhurst, 1981).

It must be recognized that the concept of *needs* in general and *special educational needs* in particular is not as straightforward a notion in theory and in practice as might first appear. When basic physiological requirements for survival have been met, higher order needs emerge, as indicated in Maslow's need hierarchy. To specify such higher order needs for the entire population is one means of asserting a moral imperative; to do so for *particular* groups, rather than for the entire population, can be to claim a priority for those groups. It is a semi-covert way of asserting what ought to be done without necessarily making explicit the assumptions, values and empirical evidence on which the assertion is based and from which the justification of prioritizing particular needs derives. It can be asserted that all children need to be literate in a Western industrialized, democratic society. Such a claim can be questioned on various grounds. The assertion certainly requires qualification if it is to be of value in advancing public knowledge of the individual and institutional economic and emotional costs/benefits involved. Claims that, for example, any child having specific learning difficulties (dyslexia) should receive special consideration and resources requires justification. The American Right to Read programme was initiated in September 1969. Its goal was that no one should leave school without the skill and the desire to read to the full limits of their capability. The programme was the focus of a tremendous national effort. The legislation on which it was based was rescinded in 1979 and replaced by Title II of Public Law 95–561, Basic Skills Improvement. Eliminating reading difficulties may well be impossible; reducing them is not. The literacy difficulties of children with specific learning difficulties (dyslexia) present tremendous personal and professional challenges.

In the UK, the Warnock Report advocated that the term 'children with learning difficulties' be used in future to describe both pupils at that time categorized as educationally subnormal plus those who were typically the concern of various remedial services. This new label would therefore include the range of other competing and overlapping labels previously used to describe differing groups of children with serious and prolonged difficulties in learning to read. It was also suggested that children with 'specific reading difficulties' might be described as 'having specific learning difficulties' (GB.DES, 1978, para. 3.26).

A subsequent survey of the research literature on children with specific learning difficulties had, as a prime concern, children manifesting severe reading difficulties, though problems with spelling, writing, arithmetic and speech were also considered (Tansley and Panckhurst, 1981). After reviewing a wide range of evidence and opinion, a definition of specific learning difficulties is proposed in the final chapter. It states:

> Children with specific learning difficulties are those who in the absence of sensory defect or overt organic damage, have an intractable learning problem in one or more of reading, writing, spelling and mathematics, and who do not respond to normal teaching. For these children, early identification, sensitive encouragement, special teaching and specific remedial arrangements are necessary. (ibid., p. 259)

This definition has the clarity of oxtail soup. It can be argued that its use reflects the uncertainties of, and disagreements between, various groups of professionals. Others consider that its advantages outweigh its opacity. As detailed earlier in this chapter, the term 'learning difficulty' is contained in the Education Act 1981 and in subsequent circulars and regulations. The term also is disastrously ill-defined. Despite this, it is included in the latest revision of an earlier circular specifying procedures within the Departments of Education, Health and Social Services to be adopted in making assessment and statements of special educational needs (GB.DES, 1989f). The DES considers that the term includes children with specific learning difficulties and also covers children identified as being dyslexic. The imprecise and circular nature of the legal definition represents an administrative nightmare for parents and professionals seeking to establish the legal responsibilities of LEAs concerning such children. Actions have to be brought before the courts in order to clarify the law. Case law then establishes precedents concerning provision. Coupled with official statements to the effect that up to 1 in 5 pupils will probably, at some time during their school career, experience such needs, public expectations have been significantly increased. Resources have not. Educational and child psychologists are increasingly being called as witnesses in cases where an LEA and a parent acting on behalf of a child brings an LEA to court for allegedly not making suitable provision for a child claimed to have specific learning difficulties (dyslexia). If expensive and drawn out legalities are to be reduced, clearer guidelines for decision-making by education, health and social services are required. Are they possible?

Tansley and Panckhurst disagreed with the plea in the Warnock Report for distinctive arrangements being made to identify and help children whose reading difficulties were severe and chronic but whose general abilities were at least average. The term 'specific learning difficulties' as used by Tansley becomes included in the generic term 'learning difficulties' as used in the Warnock Report and the Education Act, 1981. They claimed that the available evidence did not justify the exclusive categorization advocated by the Warnock Report and by the British Dyslexia Association.

Speaking at the fifth sitting of the special standing committee on the Education Bill 1981 held on 10 March in the House of Commons, the Under Secretary of State for Education commented on the issue: '...the baffling condition popularly known as dyslexia, a category which it is difficult to pin down but which exists as a learning difficulty. Of that there is no doubt. That group will be covered...'.

The Education Act 1981 (Circular 8/81 and Circular 22/89; GB.DES, 1981a, 1989f) are seen by the British Dyslexia Association as making it a duty for LEAs to provide resources to identify and alleviate specific learning difficulties as defined in the Warnock Report. 'The British Dyslexia Association regard the Education Act 1981 as a gesture of good faith on the part of the Government in accepting responsibility for the provision of appropriate remedial education for this group of children which does not fall into one of the hitherto specified categories', according to a letter from the chairman of the BDA in the *Times Educational Supplement* of 27 November 1981. The position remains valid for the BDA in 1991.

The Education Act 1981 made important changes to the law on the provision of education to all children with special educational needs. LEAs were charged with responsibilities to make an assessment of those children in their area with special educational needs who require, or may require, special educational provision. Children under the age of five years are also covered by the provisions. Such identification and assessment procedures might, or might not, lead to the preparation of a formal statement on the child under the Act. The general rule is that LEAs are expected to afford the protection of a statement to all children who have 'severe or complex learning difficulties' which require the provision of extra resources in ordinary schools, and in all cases where the child is expected to spend most of the day in special facilities of various types. Currently this group of children comprises about 2 per cent of the total school population in England. In that population up to 20 per cent of pupils may at some time be expected to have special educational needs, according to the Warnock Report.

Section 7 (2) further requires LEAs to arrange that the special educational provision specified in a statement is made for the child, unless the parent has made
suitable alternative arrangements. LEAs are also required to keep their arrangements for special educational provision under review. The concept of learning
difficulties is central. Section 1 (2) of the Act states that a child has a 'learning
difficulty' if:

- he has a significantly greater difficulty in learning than the majority of his
  age;
- he has a disability which either prevents or hinders him from making use
  of educational facilities of a kind generally provided in schools, within the
  area of the local authority concerned, for children of his age...

Explanations of the provisions of the Education Act 1981 involve circulars
(guidelines) outlining the intentions stated in the Act and the means whereby
these intentions can be translated into practice. Circulars are accompanied by
statutory instruments (regulations) in which particular issues are dealt with in
detail. Circular 1/83 on *Assessments and Statements of Special Educational
Needs* led to extended discussions (GB.DES, 1983).

In order to clarify the effects of the Education Reform Act 1988 in this area,
Circular 1/83 has now been revised as Circular 22/89 (GB.DES, 1989f). It re-
states the points from Section 1 of the Education Act 1981 defining special educational needs in relation to learning difficulties and disabilities and also defines
the meaning of special educational provision. The revised circular addresses
developments that have taken place since 1981. The implications of the Education Reform Act 1988 are considered, in particular those related to the requirements of the National Curriculum and the effects of the Local Management of
Schools on the financing of special needs provision for children with special
educational needs but without statements. LEAs will have discretion over
whether or not they delegate provision for statemented pupils in ordinary schools
and special units organized as a part of ordinary schools. This saga is likely to
run for some considerable time before the many contentious issues concerning
identification, provision, National Curriculum modifications and disapplications,
and financing are recognized and dealt with. LEA and school policies and practices will be under a greater degree of scrutiny than previously. Accountability
rules. One important administrative change is that the maximum time taken for
the completion of the statement should not exceed six months, other than in
exceptional circumstances.

It is possible that the implementation of the Education Reform Act 1988 and
LMS will lead to a revision of the extent to which LEAs will give pupils with
special educational needs legal entitlement to extra help. Circular 1/83 implied
that all children with severe and complex learning difficulties might expect to
have a statement setting out the additional provision that they required. The latest
advice in the revised circular modifies guidance on the operation of the Education Act 1981 dealing with children with special needs. An Appeal Court
ruling confirmed that a local authority, having taken advice, could decide not to
make a statement even though special educational needs had been identified. Circular 22/89 implies that LEAs are only obliged to make a statement of provision
for children in special schools.

Pupils cannot be exempted from any part of the National Curriculum without
detailed justification. This will involve assessment and the preparation of a statement. The number of junior school pupils for whom statements of special educa-

tional needs have been requested is already rising and likely to rise further. The option of exempting statemented pupils from parts of the National Curriculum exists. There is a danger that, if a child's learning difficulties require formal curricular modifications or exclusions, integration into the subject-oriented secondary school curriculum could be made more difficult. Temporary exemptions are also possible (GB.DES, 1989g).

Statements have to be very precise concerning the modifications or disapplications of the National Curriculum that are prescribed for an individual pupil. The LEA must also consider the provision it proposes to substitute for anything excluded in order to ensure that the child has access to a broad and balanced curriculum. The requirements are specified in the Education (Special Educational Needs) (Amendment) Regulations 1990 (Statutory Instrument 1990, no. 1524).

Pupils with learning difficulties attending mainstream schools with the protection of a statement have the specified additional resources funded by the LEA. The arrival of LMS suggests that schools will be keen to ensure that this situation continues. The point that pupils cannot permanently be exempted from parts of the National Curriculum without an assessment and statement is also pertinent. This will make it harder for LEAs to defend the segregation of pupils with special educational needs in general, including those deemed to have specific learning difficulties (dyslexia) in particular. Circular 22/89 advises that a statement must not be limited to those needs that the LEA can meet. A full description of a child's needs must be provided irrespective of whether or not the authority has the resources to meet these (GB.DES, 1989f).

The new Circular (22/89; GB.DES, 1989f) has caused concern. How will it impinge on provision for children with specific learning difficulties (dyslexia)? A barrister who is also a director of the Dyslexia Institute has been quoted as saying that 'The new emphasis gives the impression that local authorities can pick and choose which children they statement according to how they feel – which they can't' (Hackett, 1989). The scene is set for further legal actions. Whether this will generate greater resources for children who experience specific learning difficulties (dyslexia) is a moot point. Inevitably educational and child psychologists will be involved in such cases. Their professional competence and judgement will be subject to examination in a forum and mode for which few members of the profession are adequately trained.

In October 1983 a mother of two dyslexic children was convicted by magistrates for deliberately keeping the children away from an Essex school. It was reported that the LEA agreed that both children needed special tuition and offered four hours of remedial tuition weekly for each child at their primary school. One of the children had received private tuition at the Dyslexia Institute at Chelmsford. The mother considered that her children's educational needs could only be met at an independent boarding school for dyslexic children in Kent. Because her children were increasingly unhappy at the local state school, the mother withdrew them and was subsequently prosecuted. In this instance the magistrates deferred sentence until they obtained a ruling from the Secretary of State for Education concerning the education that the LEA should provide for the children. In the north-west of England in 1988, another parent argued a similar case. The consequence of a statement was that the child was placed in an independent school claiming to provide the required expertise. The case was to be reviewed each year, as is required by the statementing procedure. The instance is not an isolated one. LEAs are designed to carry out legal duties. Where these duties concerning pupils with specific learning difficulties (dyslexia) are unclear, conflicts between parents and the LEA will inevitably arise. After attempts at reconciliation between the parties fail, the legal system can be invoked.

Letters to the current DECP inquiry represent the tip of an iceberg of parental concern. They underline the great variations between LEAs in their policies and provision concerning pupils considered to have specific learning difficulties (dyslexia). In view of the lack of professional agreement on the identification of such special educational needs referred to earlier, no early resolution is in sight. The frustration, anxiety and anger created fuels the demand by parents for legal action. Rightly or wrongly, many parents see this as the only way of obtaining the additional help that their child requires. The battle for resources from a limited public pool will continue (Chasty and Friel, 1991).

Interest, both popular and scientific, in the field of specific learning difficulties (dyslexia) is increasing. The number of voluntary organizations active in this area is one index. In 1989 the British Dyslexia Association held its first international conference (Hales et al., 1990). The second was held in 1991. Interest in both, as indicated by the numbers attending and the papers presented, was considerable. At the first of these conferences, a special interest group of psychologists involved in this field was formed. They have a central role in resource allocation to pupils with special educational needs, including those deemed to have specific learning difficulties (dyslexia). Sadly, few psychologists joined.

As part of the current enquiry, the DES was asked for the number of appeals received under Section 5(6) of the Education Act 1981. In a letter dated 15 September 1989, we were informed that 'The Secretary of State has received a total of 144 appeals under Section 5(6) of the 1981 Act. Twenty-four appeals were received in the period January to December, 1988. In a subsequent letter dated 16 November 1990, it was stated that in 1989 alone 'The Secretary of State received a total of 99 appeals under the Education Act 1981. Of this total 50 were under Section 5(6) and 49 under Section 8(6) of the 1981 Act'.

The DES does not have separate figures for the number of appeals on behalf of children with specific learning difficulties. It would be interesting to know whether the apparent trend to increasing use of litigation and appeal procedures indicated in the above figures is continuing. It would be of particular interest to know whether pupils with specific learning difficulties are increasingly involved in such actions. Voluntary associations have suggested that this is the case. Is it a trend that is likely to continue?

It should be noted that, despite problems of identification, dyslexia is a registerable disability for the purposes of employment, YTS and employment training.

Dyslexic clients who wish to register as disabled should contact the Disablement Resettlement Officer at a Jobcentre and present evidence of dyslexia. This can be a letter from a general practitioner or an educational psychologist's report indicating that the client has dyslexia or specific learning difficulties.

In making an award to a student entering higher education the DES may include an additional grant known as a 'Cost of Disability Allowance'. In 1990, this could be an additional £760.00 per annum. This would enable a student having specific learning difficulties (dyslexia) to pay for the additional equipment and services necessary for effective study. For example, this could include a wordprocessor, spellcheck typewriter, taped books, microcassette tape recorder, pocket electronic dictionary or a reader (Dayan and Augur, 1990).

Prior to further or higher education, the examination boards are empowered to make special arrangements for candidates with specific learning difficulties (dyslexia). This matter is dealt with in detail in Chapter 16.

According to the 19th century philosopher Spencer, the evolution of human opinion is characterized by three phases: 'the unanimity of the ignorant, the disagreement of the enquiring and the unanimity of the wise'. A major problem is the ease with which phase three is confused with phase one.

The 'disagreement of the enquiring' characterizes the 'specific learning difficulties' versus 'dyslexia' controversy. If different groups of professionals show a critical tolerance of alternative possibilities during this phase, movement towards wisdom might be more rapid. Hypothesis, antithesis and synthesis represent important means of advancing knowledge. Though subject to the vagaries of fashion, the underlying strength of the scientific method is one that must be capitalized upon by those seeking to understand the nature of, and relationships between, specific learning difficulties and dyslexia.

In the present state of knowledge, the terminological jungle, which has been briefly explored, is likely to flourish. New labels are being continually developed. 'Pure reading disability' was one recent variant. A proliferation of conceptually and empirically ill-defined labels typically leads to breakdowns in communication between parties discussing the same phenomena. There are ways of changing this situation.

Another philosopher's thoughts, if accepted, can assist in this process. Bentham (1748–1832) stated 'He who thinks and thinks for himself will always have a claim to our thanks; *it is no matter if it be right or wrong so as it be explicit*. If it be right, it will serve as a guide to direct; if wrong, as a beacon to warn'. Both consequences are valuable.

By being explicit and tolerant in this vital field of professional activity, we can ensure that controversy is a constructive activity.

Summary: background to the inquiry and the current scene

- The literacy of our country's children is a crucial educational objective. It is an amplifier of human abilities. Delivery of the National Curriculum requires that children learn to read, spell and write and that standards and progress in literacy be optimized.
- In our present state of knowledge there are many inter- and intra-professional differences concerning the conceptualization, aetiologies, identification procedures and treatment of children with reading and related learning difficulties.
- Developments since the Tizard Report in 1972, culminating in the Education Act 1981, the Education Reform Act 1988, and Circular 22/89, indicate the need for a reappraisal of earlier formations. Both scientific and administrative/legal considerations have important implications for pupils with specific learning difficulties (dyslexia), their parents and professionals.
- 'Coming events cast their shadows before.' The historical background to the specific learning difficulties (dyslexia) controversy is outlined. The contemporary DES administrative resolution assumes dyslexia to be a subset of specific learning difficulties. This assumption is itself controversial. It has contributed to inconsistencies between LEAs concerning the incidence of specific learning difficulties (dyslexia). Huge variations in the use of the state-

menting procedure for such individual pupils under the provisions of the Education Act 1981, its circulars and regulations, highlight a continuing challenge.

- A survey of recent official reports outlines how the controversy has evolved. The use of the term 'specific learning difficulties' provides an administrative 'umbrella'. It is far from conceptually or operationally 'leakproof'.
- Limitations in the psychological concepts of both specific learning difficulties and dyslexia include their apparent *lack* of specificity.
- The Education Act 1981 has encouraged voluntary groups, such as the British Dyslexia Association, and several others to press for resources to help those children whose interests they represent.
- The relative merits of the claims of different groups of children with broadly similar special educational needs on already scarce professional resources for assessment and teaching will continue to be controversial. The financial and resource implications under the Education Reform Act 1988 of Local Management of Schools will heighten tensions between groups representing competing interests.
- Communication and cooperation between professionals of differing orientations and disciplines is essential in furthering the dialectic on which advances in professional competence depends. No single professional discipline, no one pressure group, has a freehold on expertise in this exceedingly complex field.

Recommendations

1.1. Each LEA produce an updated policy document on pupils with specific learning difficulties and that teachers and educational psychologists facilitate such developments.

1.2. Contributions from psychology, education and medicine be integrated in developing an understanding of the natures, incidences and alleviation of specific learning difficulties.

1.3. All professionals encourage cooperation between statutory and voluntary organization concerned with any pupil currently identified as experiencing specific learning difficulties.

1.4. Teachers and educational psychologists accept that parents and some professional workers will continue to use the term 'dyslexia' in various ways.

1.5. Efforts be made by educationalists to reach provisional agreement on the presenting characteristics of pupils experiencing specific learning difficulties, using theoretically based empirical definitions.

1.6. In cooperation with schools, psychological services build up epidemiological data on the nature, extent and responses to interventions of children experiencing specific learning difficulties.

Chapter 2

Specific Learning Difficulties (Dyslexia): Issues

Introduction

The purpose of this chapter is to identify a number of controversial theoretical, pedagogic and administrative issues concerning specific learning difficulties and dyslexia. An appreciation of these underlines the point that there exist valid reasons for disagreements between equally well informed individuals. The issues are as follows.

- Specific learning difficulties and the National Curriculum.
- Differing professional viewpoints.
- Specific learning difficulties and specific developmental dyslexia: concerns over definitions.
- Diagnosis: a suspect concept in psychology and education?
- Potential versus performance.
- 'Top-down' versus 'Bottom-up' versus 'interactive' theories.
- Qualitative versus quantitative differences between pupils.
- Subtypes.
- Evaluation/measurement.
- Early identification.
- Specific learning difficulties (dyslexia) in adulthood.
- Administrative/legal issues.

Different professions have important common concerns when working with children experiencing specific learning difficulties.

The existence of a syndrome or syndromes such as specific learning difficulties (dyslexia) requires that one or more of the following characteristics should distinctly differentiate the pupils affected from their peers.

- Aetiology.
- Presenting characteristics.
- Identification.
- Prognoses.
- Effective interventions.

Considerable amounts of empirical data exists concerning each of the above areas in relation to specific learning difficulties (dyslexia). It is frequently the interpretation of these data that is central to the controversy concerning the nature, or even the existence, of such conditions. Problems of interpretation arise mainly because of the lack of theoretical agreement concerning the development of language abilities in general and of patterns of difficulty known as specific learning difficulties (dyslexia) in particular. A second concern is that the ability to identify the condition or conditions does not imply that there are agreed effective interventions. Some of these difficulties can be reduced if communication between various interested parties is improved.

Since the first DECP survey was carried out, communication between educational psychologists employed by statutory bodies (such as LEAs, health authorities and social service departments) and the voluntary bodies working for pupils with specific learning difficulties (dyslexia) has increased and improved. Communications between experts from various disciplines have similarly developed. In acknowledgement of the importance of the differing but complementary contributions of such groups, Chapters 3 to 11 present ideas and findings drawn from the psychological, psychoeducational and psychomedical literatures.

Issues

Specific learning difficulties and the National Curriculum

(NB: Observations concerning the historical context of the Education Act 1981 and the Education Reform Act 1988 are also included in Chapter 1.)

If, for whatever reasons, a pupil has specific, serious and prolonged difficulties in any one or more of the skills of listening, talking, reading, spelling, writing or mathematics, what balance does the National Curriculum provide between educational opportunities and obstacles?

Under the provisions of the Education Reform Act 1988, a National Curriculum applicable to all pupils 5 to 16 years of age in all maintained schools is now a legal requirement (GB.DES, 1988e, Ch. 40). Whilst the means exist legally to modify or disapply the requirements of the National Curriculum for pupils under specified circumstances, the procedures appear to be designed to discourage such steps. Although it will be many years before the full provisions of the Education Reform Act are in operation, fundamental changes in the ways in which teachers and schools organize and assess the work carried out are already under way. The advent of the financial delegation of budgets to schools leads the way to every educational activity being costed. Will such developments alter the priority and resources allocated to children with specific learning difficulties (dyslexia), either by the school within its delegated budget or by the LEA in relation to centrally retained services? It must be remembered that the requirements of the Education Act 1981 remain operative, in addition to those of the Education Reform Act 1988.

In every maintained school, the curriculum must include religious education for all pupils. Additionally, 'core' and 'foundation' subjects must be included. English, mathematics and science are designated core subjects. In Wales, Welsh is a core subject in Welsh-speaking schools. The core subjects are viewed as incorporating essential concepts, knowledge and skills that are required if other learning is to take place effectively. The foundation subjects are history, geography, design and technology, music, art and physical education. During the secondary school period, a modern foreign language is to be included.

In each area of the curriculum, attainment targets will be specified for up to ten levels of attainment covering the age range from 5 to 16 years. These attainment targets are defined in the Act as '...the knowledge, skills and understanding which pupils of different abilities and maturities are expected to have by the end of each key stage' (GB.DES, 1988e, para. 2). The same Act defines 'programmes of study'. These comprise '...the matters, skills and processes which are required to be taught to pupils of different abilities and maturities during each key stage' in each subject area (ibid., para. 2). A national system of assessment will monitor what children '...should normally be expected to know, understand and be able to do at the ages of 7, 11, 14 and 16. This will enable the progress of each child to be measured against national standards' (GB.DES, 1989a, para. 6.4). The normative focus is important and cannot be ignored. Those familiar with the vast range of inter-individual differences in attainments between pupils at any age will know of the inherent problems of motivation when relative attainments are emphasized. For pupils with specific learning difficulties this issue is particularly crucial.

The assessment system is intended to provide reliable and valid formative, summative and evaluative information that can be used in measuring individual pupils' attainments and progress (GB.DES/WO, 1987a, b). Currently (1991) Standard Assessment Tasks (SATs) in the core subjects have been developed by the National Foundation for Educational Research to provide a means of carrying out such assessments. Increasing weight is being given to the role of continuous assessment by teachers at Key Stage 1. Whether the combined assessments will be of benefit to pupils and teachers remains an open question.

The National Curriculum Council has produced general guidance for those dealing with children with special needs. This includes modification and disapplication procedures, revising statements of special educational needs and temporary exceptions from the National Curriculum (National Curriculum Council, 1989a, b). The implications of the Education Reform Act 1988 and its effects on pupils experiencing specific learning difficulties will have to be carefully monitored (Pumfrey, 1990a, b).

The rhetoric associated with the Act emphasizes entitlement and access to the National Curriculum for all pupils. Public and professional sensitivity to pupils' attainments in, for example, reading, is one continuing related concern. Claims that the mean reading test scores of seven- to eight-year-old pupils in nine LEAs had fallen over the period 1985–90 created considerable alarm (Turner, 1990). This prompted action by the DES at most atypical speed. HMI carried out a survey of the teaching and learning of reading in primary schools (GB.DES, 1991a). The National Foundation for Educational Research was asked to carry out a related survey of LEA evidence on standards of reading of seven-year-old children (GB.DES, 1991b). Both reports counsel caution for a number of technical reasons concerning sampling and test validities. The standards and progress of pupils with specific learning difficulties (dyslexia) were not addressed.

The reality of inter- and intra-individual differences in pupils' physical, emotional, social, intellectual and motivational characteristics will continue differentially to affect children's absolute and relative standards and progress in the subjects listed, and in many others.

Children with specific learning difficulties (dyslexia) will find the concepts of curricular entitlement and access of little utility unless the professional expertise and time required to enable them to increase their literacy attainments are made available. Oversimplified, if one cannot read, how can the current legislation be made to help rather than to hinder?

Differing professional viewpoints

It is clear from the points made so far in Chapters 1 and 2 that theoretical ideas concerning the nature of specific learning difficulties and of dyslexia are controversial. Different professional groups view the phenomena from different standpoints and bring particular knowledge and expertise to bear. Within each of these professional groups there are many subgroups. There are also important theoretical disagreements between the members of each group. These differences are reflected in their work with children. These professional differences can have important effects on pupils and also on parents' perceptions of the services of psychologists as indicated by the following.

> It was six men of Hindustan
> To learning much inclined
> Who went to see the elephant
> (Though all of them were blind),
> That each by observation
> Might satisfy his mind.
>
> The first approached the elephant
> And happening to fall
> Against its broad and sturdy side
> At once began to bawl
> 'God bless me! but the elephant
> Is very like a wall!'
>
> The *second*, feeling of the tusk,
> Cried, 'Ho! what have we here
> So very round and smooth and sharp?
> To me 'tis mighty clear
> This wonder of an elephant
> Is very like a spear!'...
>
> And so these men of Hindustan
> Disputed loud and long,
> Each in his own opinion
> Exceeding stiff and strong,
> Though *each* was *partly* in the right,
> They *all* were in the wrong. (J. G. Saxe)

Disagreements concerning the characteristics of tangible objects can occur when the data bases of observers differ. Even when these data bases are potentially the same, the conceptual constraints of the different professions can lead to different interpretations. When we consider the nature and extent of children's specific learning difficulties, a tolerance of other professions' contributions to an ongoing debate is imperative in the interests of the clients whom the professions exist to serve. In varying degrees, we all have conceptual 'blind spots'.

There are contrasting professional emphases on, for example, neurological, cognitive, affective and motivational (contextual) dimensions of specific learning difficulties (dyslexia) (Coltheart, 1987a, b; Gentile and McMillan, 1987; Gjessing and Karlsen, 1989; Miles and Miles, 1990; Pavlidis, 1990a, b).

Specific learning difficulties and specific developmental dyslexia: concerns over definition

Are the terms 'specific learning difficulties' and 'dyslexia' synonyms? Do they represent a class inclusion relationship? Are both of these relationships inadequate? The term 'dyslexia' includes acquired and developmental forms. In children the developmental form has the more cumbersome name 'specific developmental dyslexia'. For various reasons, including the apparent ease of communication, some voluntary organizations have shortened this term to 'dyslexia' in their literature. As noted earlier, the notion of specific developmental dyslexia was established on the basis of analogical reasoning. Although the surface symptoms of acquired dyslexia and specific developmental dyslexia have much in common, it does not follow that their causes, prognoses or intervention/ treatment are necessarily similar. In the current discussion the word dyslexia is used as a contraction of the longer term specific developmental dyslexia. This is in recognition of the common usage by parents. Here it is used in a descriptive sense only, whereby it indicates a set of presenting symptoms.

At school, the majority of children move from illiteracy and innumeracy to competence in language and number. They move at different rates. Verbal and numerical languages are facets of language in general. Language itself is only one aspect of communication. Communication comprises only one aspect of the symbolic thinking that is characteristic of the species. Specific learning difficulties can be defined at different levels. The most general of these is related to different aspects of symbolic thinking.

Current definitions of dyslexia have been extended from an early concern with receptive and expressive language abilities to include alphabetic, numerical and musical notation systems by the British Dyslexia Association. The Dyslexia Institute construes children's specific learning difficulties in terms of information processing (see Table 1.1). If it is also accepted that there are different types of dyslexia, the convergence of concepts of specific learning difficulties and specific developmental dyslexia is apparent. The use of the term dyslexia in the *singular* can give a misleading impression. However, not all workers accept that there are qualitative differences between children who experience specific learning difficulties and those who do not. The balance of the evidence collected during the present inquiry suggests that these are important qualitative differences between pupils and that these have pedagogic implications for interventions.

Returning to the initial questions, some workers consider the terms specific learning difficulties and dyslexia to be synonymous. Others accept the class inclusion relationship while some see more complex relationships between the concepts (see Chapter 14 for the views of educational psychologists).

Diagnosis: a suspect concept in psychology and education?

The medical model of human functioning based on the concepts of diagnosis and treatment has received considerable criticism in the psychological literature. Currently, the work of the educational psychologist is frequently construed as identifying inter- and intra-individual differences in children's characteristics (cognitive, affective, conative and contextual) and planning ways of facilitating more effective learning. Educational psychologists are aware of the dangers of the slippery slope from individual differences to deviations, difficulties, disabilities, deficits and defects. Despite this, the concepts of diagnosis/treatment and identification/intervention are not mutually exclusive.

Diagnosis is the process of identifying disorders from their symptoms. Technically diagnosis means only the identification and labelling of a disorder. In the Penguin *Dictionary of Psychology* this definition has been extended to the 'determination of the nature of an abnormality, disorder or disease' (Drever, 1964). However, in education diagnosis typically includes the planning of interventions. These are based on an evaluation of the child's characteristics and circumstances, a consideration of possible causes and the likely effects of pedagogic programmes aimed to improve the child's learning.

Psychologically and educationally, by diagnosing learning difficulties, the nature of the processes involved in pupils' performances are explored. This involves carefully considering the functional relationships between the cognitive processes underpinning literacy, and their links with performances. These are first steps. For the teacher, identification is a process whereby hypotheses concerning the nature of a difficulty can be investigated with a view to constructive interventions. The pupil's relative strengths and weaknesses can be identified, thus assisting in planning a programme that will capitalize on strengths and help to improve skills found to be weak. The educational context is essential.

Educational psychologists and teachers struggle with many dilemmas. For example, they are expected to respect the individuality, the uniqueness of the child. At the same time they are also expected to ensure that pupils conform to certain patterns of behaviour (within limits). For example, children are expected to learn to read, spell and write at school. Often those children falling at the lower end of hypothesized normal distributions of surface characteristics (such as reading attainments) or inferred attributes (such as general or specific intellectual abilities) are diagnosed as 'having reading difficulties'. A subset of these pupils may be considered as having specific learning difficulties or dyslexia.

To some extent the difficulties in symbolic thinking in general, and reading in particular, that such children experience are generated by society's desire for a conformity that may well be at variance with the nature of human beings. This should not be taken as indicating a belief that the improvement of, for example, reading skills and the identification and alleviation of specific learning difficulties cannot be achieved. The complexities of the reading process mean that it is possible for a range of ineffective reading strategies and negative attitudes to be learned by the child. These can be modified, given the necessary resources. The issue is partly financial and partly political (Pumfrey and Mittler, 1989; Pumfrey, 1991).

In some cases, a child's reading and writing difficulties may arise from a physical abnormality, disorder or disease. For example, vision or hearing may be intermittently impaired. An impairment of neurological functions can adversely affect a child's speed of information processing. This, in turn, may reduce the child's ability to extract or to convey meaning using symbolic materials. The diagnosis of such conditions can lead to effective treatment resulting in improved functioning. However, in the majority of cases of such learning difficulties, highly specific causes cannot be identified.

The identification of specific learning difficulties is not an esoteric exercise carried out solely by highly trained specialist support teachers or educational psychologists. It is carried out at many levels. The class teacher is constantly engaged in informal diagnoses of children's general learning difficulties and in making modifications to the experiences that children encounter. A relatively small proportion of such pupils will have specific learning difficulties. Interventions are planned to facilitate the child's progress, irrespective of the levels of his or her relative skills. If this informal approach is unsuccessful, the teacher may initiate a more detailed examination of the child's difficulties, still within the classroom. If the difficulties continue, referral will probably be made to someone with more specialized knowledge or expertise such as a specialist support teacher, an educational or child psychologist, or a member of a medical team. If the pupil's problem continues to give concern, the formal procedure of preparing a statement of special educational needs under the provisions of the Education Act 1981 can be initiated. Parents have a right to request such an assessment. This type of assessment always involves a multidisciplinary team, which includes the parents. In many ways the expertise brought to bear is similar to that which was used when child guidance work was started in Britain. The context of assessment has always been seen as important although emphases have changed with time.

At all levels the diagnosis of learning difficulties in general, and specific learning difficulties in particular, can be viewed as a process of hypothesis generation and testing. Identification is followed by an intervention. The result leads to a further modification of the hypothesis and, if necessary, of the intervention. Put more prosaically, from a 'bottom-up', theoretical viewpoint, 'Tommy cannot synthesize short phonically regular words; why not? Perhaps it is because ..., so I will arrange for him to ... and see if it helps. If it doesn't, I'll have to think again'. All teachers need to be aware of the principles of educational diagnosis. The majority have not been adequately trained in this field (Pumfrey, 1990b). By virtue of their training, educational psychologists have a contribution to make in this area.

Potential versus performance

The comment 'could do better' has echoed down the history of education. It continues today, particularly in the field of specific learning difficulties and dyslexia. Made either on a pupil's school report, or verbally by a teacher to a parent or a pupil concerning the pupil's performance, it signals concern. Increasingly it is being said by the parents of pupils, including those parents who consider that their child has specific learning difficulties or dyslexia.

Most children become literate and numerate at school, albeit at different rates. Bright children typically do so more rapidly than less bright ones. What is one to make of the child who shows clear evidence of being bright, but makes very slow or negligible progress in these important basic skills? Do such pupils represent a 'special case' as suggested in the official reports discussed earlier? If identified, would such children repay the investment of time and expertise by making rapid progress? To use a term that was employed in one influential 1960s publication, do such pupils represent the most 'salvageable' by virtue of their apparent brightness? (Collins, 1961). It depends largely on the causes of a pupil's lack of progress. If these are attributable to environmental deficiencies, such as a lack of opportunity, encouragement, support, materials or sound teaching, such children are likely to make rapid progress if given extra help. If the causes are attributable to within-pupil characteristics, they are likely to make no greater progress than other pupils experiencing difficulties in learning.

In a class including the three boys described in Table 2.1, is it possible to claim that one should be accorded a higher priority than the others in terms of

extra help? Irrespective of whether your answer is 'yes' or 'no', it becomes
necessary to justify the decision. This involves a consideration of the costs involved in terms of teacher expertise, time and money.

Table 2.1: Illustration of pupils of differing abilities at different ages (years)

	John	Jack	James
Chronological age (CA)	10	10	10
Reading age (RA)	6	6	6
Mental age (MA)	12	10	8
CA – RA	4	4	4
MA – RA	6	4	2

The concept of 'underachievement' is based on the assumption that there is an
unexpected discrepancy between the standard of work that the pupil is producing
and what, for various reasons, the child is considered capable of producing.
There are many reasons for such discrepancies. These can be attributed to
'within-child' attributes, to environmental conditions or to interactions between
these two major groups of possible influences on achievement.

'Underachievement' is related to the concept of 'potential'. The latter has
many meanings. In the field under consideration, underachievement refers to un-
exerted, unrealized or undeveloped intellectual capabilities (Harris and Hodges,
1981). The concept of potential relates to inferred intellectual capabilities. It is
also controversial. One reason for this is that it raises questions about the contributions of heredity and the environment, and interactions between these, on
the realization of potential in children's learning abilities. A common shorthand
for 'potential' used by both parents and professionals is the psychological concept of 'intelligence'. Some children are more intelligent than others. Different
theories exist concerning the structure, development and modifiability of human
intelligence. In Western culture, intelligence is a valued attribute.

At its most general level, intelligence is an abstract notion. It can *never* be
directly observed: but behaviours that are classified as intelligent, or otherwise,
are regularly seen and labelled. From the observation of such behaviours, the
concept of intelligence is inferred. The circularity in the process is apparent.
Vernon labelled the inferred psychological construct 'Intelligence A'; observed
intelligent behaviours in their multitudinous forms he designated as 'Intelligence
B'; and that sample of 'Intelligence B' measured by intelligence tests was called
'Intelligence C' (Vernon, 1979).

The concept of intelligence is valuable if it helps to describe, predict and control (to the benefit of individuals and groups) different aspects of development,
including literacy and numeracy. In many cases, it can help in such endeavours.
When discussing intelligence, it is usually helpful to indicate whether one is
using the term at level A, B or C. Children differ markedly in virtually every
attribute that one can identify. Some children are seen as more intelligent than
others. Intelligence tests provide various means of measuring different aspects of
this concept. The *Wechsler Intelligence Scales for Children (Revised) (WISC-R)*
is one of many available measures of aspects of 'Intelligence C' (Weschler,
1974). In practice this particular test provides different but related measures of
intelligence based on a profile of subtest scores. This profile can be used in the

diagnosis of reading/learning disability (Searls, 1985). Recently the validity and utility of the concepts of intelligence have been questioned in some quarters. Alternative terms such as 'ability' or 'abilities' are used instead in describing batteries of tests used to assess children. The *British Ability Scales* (Elliott, 1983) is one example. Its American development, published in 1990, is called the *Differential Ability Scales* (Elliott, 1990b).

One body of opinion believes that any pupil whose relative attainment is significantly lower than his or her ability (usually as measured by an intelligence test) is an underachiever: the intelligence test is seen as a measure of potential. Others argue that since half the population have relative attainments that are higher than their intelligence scores suggest, the idea of intelligence test scores as an index of potential achievement is logically flawed. Many hold that the difference between attainments and the average performance of the age-group is a better basis for determining the need for educational help. Yet others believe that 'both the alternatives are too simple as principles for determining whether or not a child is underachieving' (Williams, 1988, p. 2). There are many ways of theoretically and operationally defining underachievement and of identifying groups of children who can then be said to have specific learning difficulties or – in the USA – specific learning disabilities (Elliott, 1990a). There is no consensus as to which tests of intelligence and attainments should be used in identifying children with specific learning difficulties or dyslexia. It is interesting to note that in the USA 57 per cent of the states include achievement discrepancy criteria in the guidelines on procedures for identifying children with specific learning disabilities. The argument that discrepancy definitions of reading disability involving intelligence test scores represent a 'dead end' has been recently and cogently made (Stanovich, 1991).

It is worth reiterating that professionals have sufficient expertise to help virtually *any* pupil to improve their literacy and numeracy skills. The improvements that can be achieved are, in part, dependent on the expertise and time that can be allocated. However, the experts cannot make all pupils equal in their attainments; nor can they necessarily make the attainments of pupils with specific learning difficulties (dyslexia) match their measured mental ages. Children experiencing such difficulties can be identified. The priority that the nation gives to such individuals is a political question. The demand on the public purse of this particular (legally recognized) group of pupils is just one of many. The Education Act 1981 raised parental expectations concerning provision for up to 20 per cent of the school population deemed likely to have special educational needs at some time during their school career. Unfortunately, no additional resources have been made available (Pumfrey and Mittler, 1989).

Whether we give additional help to either James or John or Jack, or to some combination of the three, is an issue that is one of values and priorities. It is also one of resources. The financial implications of the Local Management of Schools will increasingly highlight the cost of providing additional resources for any pupil experiencing specific learning difficulties (dyslexia). The parents of all three boys have no doubts that their particular child needs, and merits, additional help.

'Top-down' versus 'bottom-up' versus 'interactive' theories and their pedagogic implications

There are contrasting views concerning the nature of language abilities and their development. They each have implications for pedagogy in general, and for the teaching and learning of reading in particular. For example, the 'top-down' approach is typically advocated by those who have been influenced by the work of psycholinguists. The theory that good readers can use a direct route from text to meaning that minimizes the role of the decoding process has been one of the strongest arguments for 'top-down' models. Proponents of the 'top-down' theory consider that, in learning complex skills, the most effective and common procedure is to engage in complex activities. Using an analogy, we learn to swim by swimming and not by doing bench exercises on dry land. Similarly, we best learn to talk by talking and to read by reading. The subskills into which reading, for example, can be analysed are learned as a by-product of encounters with texts that convey psychologically significant messages. When applied to the teaching and learning of reading, the approach stresses the importance of meaning, the acceptance of 'miscues' in oral reading as providing the teacher with a window on the individual pupil's reading processes, the 'language experience' approach to literacy, and the use of 'real books'.

Other workers consider that the learning of subskills can help in the mastery of more complex skills. 'Master the simple before tackling the complex' is the cry: conquer conservation of number before trying integral calculus; calculate a mean before carrying out a factor analysis; learn simple pieces of music before attempting a piano concerto by Brahms. The strategy is an extremely ancient and pervasive one. Language is a complex skill; so is reading. When applied to the teaching and learning of reading, the 'bottom-up' approach leads to practices such as task analysis, precision teaching, programmed learning and graded reading schemes.

Held rigidly, both the 'bottom-up' and the 'top-down' models have serious shortcomings. Some children have great difficulties in understanding the sound–symbol system based on the alphabetic notation. They can become frustrated by their inability to decode text into sound. Others can become so attentive to the decoding process that they give insufficient attention to the meaning of the message. The 'top-down' orientation also has its limitations. In the extreme, it could lead to children failing to give sufficient attention to the detailed information contained in a text. Their own predictions, guesses and elaborations may create idiosyncratic interpretations that may fail to give the reader access to the author's thoughts and feelings. This may be of less immediate importance in reading a novel than in reading a set of instructions, a recipe or other textual materials in which detail can be vital.

Statutory and voluntary organizations concerned with helping children with specific learning difficulties (dyslexia) recognize the importance of identifying the strengths and weaknesses of the individual pupil. The individual programme that is designed for a child is intended to capitalize on the pupil's strengths and to alleviate weaknesses. Currently, an individualized multisensory approach in which phonics play a large part is favoured by the majority of the specialist organizations. Such approaches have a distinctly 'bottom-up' flavour. The extremely popular 'Alpha to Omega' approach is but one example of many similar systems (Hornsby and Sher, 1975); there are many other systems (Naidoo, 1988). Yet others adopt a contrasting approach based on 'icons'. This is more akin to a 'top-down' orientation (Brown, 1990). The identification of which approach suits which children at which particular stages in their learning presents a continuing challenge. The uniqueness of the child demands that the teacher understands the importance of differential diagnosis, and its limitations, in the current state of knowledge.

If either of the above two models had been adequate to ensure children's literacy, it is highly likely that the other would have disappeared without trace. There is evidence that a number of children educated under either system continue to experience serious and prolonged specific learning difficulties. This includes failing to learn to read, spell or write.

A combination of the 'top-down' and 'bottom-up' approaches has much to commend it (see Chapter 3). The narrowness that can be associated with either position in isolation is avoided. Options are opened up. The teacher's repertoire includes a larger range of strategies for responding to specific learning difficulties than would be the case if he or she declared sole allegiance to one extreme or the other (May, 1986; Reason, 1990b). Unsurprisingly, a small-scale survey carried out by one of the authors suggested that most teachers adopt an eclectic position, apparently reflecting pragmatism in the classroom (Pumfrey, 1990b).

What happens when the teacher is faced with a pupil who fails to make progress no matter which approach is tried? There are some such pupils. No method is a panacea capable of alleviating the literacy difficulties of all pupils suffering from specific learning difficulties (dyslexia). Fortunately, there are constructive strategies, many methods and a wide range of materials and media available. The pupil with even the most severe difficulties can be helped (Pumfrey, 1991). The cost/benefit ratio of providing that help presents a moral question to us both as individuals and as a society.

Qualitative versus quantitative differences between pupils

Some workers consider that the differences between children who learn to read easily and those who do not are quantitative (Bryant and Bradley, 1985; Bryant and Impey, 1986). If this is the case, it follows that all children need help in developing the same skills. Some children will require more help than others, including those seen as having severe and prolonged specific learning difficulties. The concept of specific learning difficulties (dyslexia) and the possible existence of qualitatively different patterns of attributes and interventions can be viewed as an irrelevance. If common crucial skills underpinning a failure in reading (and spelling) can be identified and effective interventions developed, all children can be helped. Currently the importance of phonemic awareness is receiving considerable attention (Bryant, 1990; Bradley, 1990; Cataldo and Ellis, 1990; Snowling, 1990) (see Chapter 5 for further details).

Other workers point to important differences between normal readers and those children who experience severe and prolonged difficulties in becoming literate. They consider that some of these differences can be qualitative in nature (Snowling, 1985; Coltheart, 1987b; Tyler and Elliot, 1988; Gjessing and Karlsen, 1989; Tyler, 1990). The controversy is important, leading directly to a closely related methodological concern.

Subtypes

If there are qualitative differences between pupils' abilities, it is possible that they will need different teaching and use different learning techniques. In the field of sensory difficulties, partially hearing pupils can be considered as having qualitatively different information processing attributes to partially sighted pupils. The methods used to teach the two groups have considerable differences. There is an ongoing search for methods that are effective for pupils with qualitatively different characteristics. In the literature, it is frequently referred to as the search for aptitude × instruction interactions (AIIs), and it is continuing (Freebody and Tirre, 1985; Carbo, Dunn and Dunn, 1986).

The two positions are not necessarily mutually exclusive, provided that we distinguish between 'trait' and 'type' and consider the relationship between these methodological concepts. A trait can be defined as a one-dimensional attribute that has a range within which all pupils can be ranked. Individual differences can be expressed quantitatively, and the variability between individuals can be extensive; for example, in 'phonological awareness'. In contrast, a classification of pupils by type puts pupils into a limited number of theoretically related categories of attribute patterns. The patterns are defined as a variety of associated qualitative dimensions, such as 'auditory dyslexia' and 'visual dyslexia'.

It is clear that, in principle, qualitative attributes can be quantified. A distinction between 'monothetic' and 'polythetic' typologies is helpful at this point. A typology is monothetic if it assumes that a unique set of attributes, traits or characteristics is both necessary and sufficient to determine membership of a given cell in the typology. In contrast, a polythetic typology groups together those pupils having the largest number of attributes, traits or dimensions in common. No single trait is necessary, nor is it sufficient for membership. The monothetic assumption maximizes similarities between pupils within each cell in the classification. Because empirical testing is far from completely valid, it would be highly improbable that every individual would fall neatly within one category. The polythetic alternative is a compromise solution.

Such considerations contribute towards the increasingly frequent use of the phrase 'a variable syndrome' to describe specific learning difficulties (dyslexia). The imprecision of the term is itself a continuing challenge to both theoreticians and practitioners (Miles and Miles, 1990).

Evaluation/measurement

Earlier this century, Thorndike wrote 'Whatever exists exists in some quantity and can, in principle, be measured.' More critically, the quantification of information is one important means of advancing knowledge in this (or any) field. It would be helpful if estimates of the incidence of specific learning difficulties (dyslexia) showed greater consistency. Estimates varying from less than 1 per cent to over 30 per cent have been reported in the literature (Cornwall, Hedderly and Pumfrey, 1984). The point is highlighted in the following critical quotations from British Dyslexia Association publications. They have been used by the National Association for Remedial Education, a group with a long-standing involvement in the identification and alleviation of severe and prolonged learning difficulties, to question the reality of the concept of dyslexia. 'Dyslexia is a disorder of learning to read, write and spell – it is conservatively estimated to affect 4% of the population at all levels of intelligence' (BDA Press Release, 1985). Two years later, this had become 'as many as 10% of the whole population' (British Dyslexia Association Appeal Brochure, 1987) (Bushell and Cripps, 1988). What are we to believe?

Valid and reliable means of measuring and describing pupils' attributes, such as their abilities, attainments and attitudes, are essential if we are to conceptualize, predict and enhance professionals' control over the development of children's literacy abilities. Measurement enables teachers and research workers to operationalize aspects of the cognitive, emotional and motivational literacy-related attributes of individuals and groups. Professional accountability requires that modes of assessment are valid, public and replicable.

The different but complementary types of information elicited by the wide variety of tests and assessment techniques available can be used for a considerable range of purposes. The uses and limitations of observational, criterion-referenced, informal and normative assessment techniques are increasingly being appreciated. Teachers are showing an enhanced awareness of the different types of validities and reliabilities, and their interrelationships, in relation to educational diagnostic decision-making (Sumner, 1987). The knowledge of how various types of assessment instruments can be constructed is also increasing. The effective utilization of the information provided by an assessment technique requires an appreciation of such issues. Such technical understanding has been the preserve mostly of specialists, such as psychologists and remedial or support teachers, who have taken courses of advanced training. The field is continuously developing (Pumfrey, 1985, 1990b, c; Assessment of Performance Unit, 1988).

The key role to be played by teachers in evaluating the attainments and progress of individual pupils under the requirements of the National Curriculum highlights the point. In the field of English, the five profile components of speaking and listening, reading, writing, spelling and handwriting each have associated Programmes of Study and Attainment Targets. Standard Assessment Tasks have been developed to facilitate the assessment of pupils (GB.DES/WO, 1989). A massive amount of in-service training in the assessment of English in the National Curriculum is currently in hand.

The identification of pupils' special educational needs is also required by law. According to the Department of Education and Science, this includes pupils with specific learning difficulties and dyslexia. At present there are no commonly agreed operational definitions of specific learning difficulties (dyslexia). In such circumstances, argument will proliferate. An increased use of tests and assessment techniques is likely because these provide evidence that is explicit and, in one sense, objective. This is a small but important step in clarifying the nature and incidence of specific learning difficulties (dyslexia). Arguments concerning the interpretations of such data will continue until theoretical issues are resolved. There is nothing as practical as a valid theory.

Early identification

It is often argued that the early identification of literacy difficulties can lead to more effective interventions, rather than ignoring the difficulties until they become unambiguously clear. Without the use of any formal tests, after a period of teaching the class teacher in an infant school can identify those pupils who do or do not experience difficulties in becoming literate. The question that arises is 'Why wait for a child to fail, if failure can be anticipated?' If future difficulties can be anticipated, might they not be prevented or reduced? For example, it is possible to administer a battery of tests and assessment techniques to children *before* they learn to read. The children can then be followed up. By correlating the children's scores on the initial battery (predictor scores) with their later reading attainments (criterion scores), pre-reading predictors of later success or failure in learning to read can be identified. However, correlation does not imply causality; for example, it has been established that knowledge of letter names is one of the best predictors of later reading attainments (Hammill and McNutt, 1981). It does not follow that the teaching of letter names to children who are starting to learn to read will significantly affect their later success or failure in reading. Other more powerful determinants are probably at work.

In addition, on the basis of such correlations between pupils' scores on predictor tests and later criterion tests of reading attainment, attempts have been made to nominate children at the pre-reading stage as being 'at risk' or 'not at risk' of experiencing reading difficulties at a later stage in their education. The great danger here is that children will be wrongly classified. Some children who will not subsequently fail will be classified as 'at risk'. Others who will subsequently fail may earlier be classified as 'not at risk' (Potton, 1983; Pearson and Lindsay, 1986). The educational efficacy of such predictive screening procedures is suspect, but they can have considerable concurrent educational utility. Despite this cautionary comment, the research strategy remains important if the complexities of the development of reading and other literacy attainments are to be better understood.

A number of research workers and LEAs have developed systems for the early identification of reading difficulties. They have also developed materials intended to alleviate difficulties that are identified. An extensive selection of materials and methods has been produced to help the teacher in integrating the testing and teaching of reading (and other skills). These are listed in Chapter 7. They differ in their theoretical bases and the amount of empirical validation presented. Each has its own strengths and weaknesses.

It is important to recognize that children differ markedly in virtually every literacy-related attribute. A clearer appreciation of both inter- and intra-individual differences at particular stages in the development of literacy skills will help to identify those areas where early interventions can help to reduce difficulties later on. Such knowledge will not prove to be a panacea. Even if every seven-year-old pupil was able to read leading articles in *The Times* with accuracy and understanding, some would do so more accurately, more rapidly and with greater comprehension than others. At such an improbably high level of reading attainment would those who were slower, less accurate and showing less understanding be labelled as having reading difficulties? Within this group would we then search for pupils with specific learning difficulties (dyslexia)?

There is a danger in not being able to recognize the nature and extent of individual differences in literacy-related skills, which presents a continuing professional challenge. It is an essential adjunct to accepting the importance of individual differences. The danger of inappropriately labelling the normal as 'at risk' must be avoided, unless a convincing case is presented.

Specific learning difficulties (dyslexia) in adulthood

It can be argued that specific learning difficulties (dyslexia) vary according to aetiologies, prognoses, responses to interventions and the passage of time. Evidence from neurological, neuropsychological and genetic research typically supports the existence of heterogeneity in such respects; twin studies demonstrate the hereditability of certain disabilities. Research findings also suggest that specific learning difficulties are characteristically long-standing. Pupils identified as dyslexic continue in adulthood to experience specific learning difficulties that adversely affect their performances in various aspects of numeracy and literacy (Pavlidis, 1990a, b). Put simply, specific learning difficulties are rarely completely alleviated. Fortunately, a variety of techniques can be taught to help individuals to minimize the restrictions imposed by the condition on the accessibility of information in, for example, reading and other aspects of text processing.

Despite the opportunities afforded by upward of ten years of full-time education between the ages of 5 and 16 years, many school-leavers and adults in the UK have difficulties in the basic skills of literacy and numeracy. According to the evidence from the longitudinal National Child Development Study (NCDS) about the incidence of self-admitted difficulties in literacy and numeracy of 23-year-old adults, about 13 per cent considered that they had difficulties with reading, writing or basic mathematics. 'If 23 year olds are no better or no worse than other young people and adults (and there is no really reliable evidence either way) then almost six million people would appear to have significant problems with fundamental basic skills in the UK' (Adult Literacy and Basic Skills Unit (ALBSU, 1988). It is also estimated that this includes 400,000 adults and young people 'who cannot read at all' (ibid., p. 3). Additionally, it is reported by ALBSU that evidence from a MORI Poll commissioned by Granada Television's *World in Action* programme early in 1987 supported the findings of the NCDS survey. A survey carried out in 1987 by the Manpower Services Commission among long-term unemployed adults indicated that a minimum of 20 per cent had substantial problems in literacy and/or numeracy. There is inevitably a considerable margin of error in such figures. While one may have reservations about the validity of the generalizations explicit in such estimates, there is little doubt that a serious problem exists. The ALBSU exists to meet such educational needs when an individual is ready to acknowledge the existence of a difficulty and is motivated to deal with it. The considerable demand for the services of ALBSU indicates the existence of a serious problem of adult illiteracy and innumeracy. Among ALBSU's clients will be a number, although a small minority, who would have demonstrated specific as opposed to general learning difficulties at school.

A relatively small number of pupils diagnosed at an earlier stage as having specific learning difficulties (dyslexia) have gone on to higher education. If their problems have been in reading, writing and spelling, they are likely to require considerable support from the institution if they are to complete their courses successfully. This will include concessions in respect of examination arrangements (see Chapter 16). Without such support the consequences can be tragic. The recent case of the dyslexic student who passed GCSE and A-level examinations but who committed suicide after subsequently failing his first-year examinations in higher education, despite being at the institution with a well-developed student support service, provides a salutary warning.

In Denmark, according to Kristin Illeborg of the Dyslexia Institute in Copenhagen, those with severe difficulties in reading can be helped by the use of a small yellow card. It was invented some years ago by Bodil Holsting. The text on it says 'Jeg er ordblind' (I am wordblind). Also on the front is the inter-European dyslexia logo. On the back of the card the owner can record their name, address, telephone number and social security number. The card can be used, for example, in public offices or other places where help may be required in filling in forms. The use of the card is reported as having been widely accepted. It saves users from the embarrassment of explaining their difficulties to strangers. It also enables people to be helpful. In Denmark the card is distributed by the National Association for the Cause of Severely Disabled Readers (Landsforeningen for Ordblindesagen).

Is the idea one that would be of value in other countries?

Administrative/legal issues

Continuing administrative problems in the identification, alleviation and prevention of specific learning difficulties perturb many professionals, parents and
pupils. The purpose of this section is to outline the contemporary legislative context in England and Wales and to identify particular concerns that arise in relation to special educational needs in general and specific learning difficulties
(dyslexia) in particular.

Education is a political issue. The expenditure on education in England and
Wales during 1988–89 was £18.41 billion. During 1989–90 it was estimated to
increase to £19.57 billion. The cost per year per pupil in a state primary school
is approximately £1100. Some LEAs spend far more than this per pupil and
others are more economical. The smaller the pupil–teacher ratio in the LEA,
the higher the annual cost of education per pupil. Even in the ordinary school,
small group or individual tuition is expensive. The annual cost per pupil of
various forms of special education provided by the state and the private sector
are far more expensive than the normal state day school. A year at a residential
school can cost over £12,000 per pupil. In this context, politicians are probably
pleased that the acknowledged social and educational advantages of integration,
education in the community and a 'whole-school' approach to meeting *all*
special educational needs might also be linked to financial savings. However,
LEAs still have responsibilities to assess and meet the needs of pupils with
specific learning difficulties (dyslexia) under the provisions of the Education
Act 1981. The pressures on LEA finances have considerable implications for
their policy and practice in meeting their legal obligations. The pool of resources
is limited (see Chapters 6 and 8 for further discussion of these issues).

The 1981 Education Act, its implementation in 1983 and the subsequent
numerous related circulars and regulations have highlighted many issues concerning policy and practice in the field of special educational needs in general
and of specific learning difficulties (dyslexia) in particular. The Department of
Education and Science and the Department of Health have been monitoring
various aspects of the 1981 Education Act. Commissioned evaluative research
has been carried out by the National Foundation for Educational Research, the
University of London Institute of Education, the University of Manchester and
Huddersfield Polytechnic. In addition, the Select Committee on Education,
Science and Arts carried out its own investigations. Its report was published in
June 1987 (Select Committee on Education, Science and Arts, 1987). The
government's response was published on 4 December 1987, in the form of a
memorandum deposited in the House of Commons library. It includes the state-
ment that:

> There is a strong case for more guidance about identifying the wider range
> of special educational needs and about when a statement of such needs
> might be required. We recommend that national guidance on such [special
> education] provision should be given ... we are in no doubt that aspects of
> the present system are not working satisfactorily. The weight of evidence
> shows on balance that it is the way these statutory procedures operate which
> is unsatisfactory, not their scope and purpose. The Committee recommends
> that the Department should examine closely ways in which procedures for
> assessment and making statements ... could be improved. (Secretary of
> State for Education, 1987)

In August, 1988, the Education Reform Act was passed. The National Curriculum and its associated Attainment Targets and Programmes of Study are now being introduced into state schools. Local Financial Management of Schools is also being introduced (GB.DES, 1988c). This further highlights financial and staffing issues. All these changes have important resource implications for pupils deemed to have specific learning difficulties (Hart and Hellyer, 1989).

Arrangements for carrying out assessments and making, or not making, statements of individual pupil's SENs under the Education Act 1981 were originally detailed in Circular 1/83 (GB.DES, 1983). The DES revised that circular to take into account changes that have taken place since 1983. To this end, a draft Circular was widely distributed on 21 December 1988 (GB.DES, 1988d). In it the concept of '...the child's *true learning potential*' is used (ibid., para. 88) (original emphasis). Despite having their attention drawn to this particular point, the term was retained when the final version appeared in Circular 22/89 (GB.DES, 1989f).

Its very use in the document raises important issues concerning the relationships between a pupil's 'potential' and attainments, as noted earlier. Why should significant discrepancies between these two factors cause concern? How can each be assessed? How valid is the identification of such discrepancies in identifying children with SpLDs? Can such information help in deciding which individuals should receive additional educational resources, such as extra small group and/or individual work? How much will this cost? From where will the money come? Is the additional investment worthwhile? The issues are weighty ones to which there are no simple answers that command consensus.

The revised circular reaffirms a system of assessment and statementing that is broadly based and involves the family. Some observers see the circular as describing the ideal. This should not be confused with what happens in practice. The fact is that the earlier Circular 1/83 and the subsequent associated regulations have *not* noticeably harmonized practices of LEAs concerning the assessment of children with specific learning difficulties (dyslexia). There is marked heterogeneity in LEAs' policies and practices. For example, the proportion of pupils statemented in LEAs ranges from 0.04 per cent to 4.2 per cent, a 100-fold difference. Overall the figure stands at 1.7 per cent of the total population of statutory school age. This is but one cause of concern (Select Committee on Education, Science and Arts, 1987). Only an extremely small number of statemented pupils are classified as having SpLD (dyslexia).

Other critics consider Circular 22/89 little more than a public relations exercise in which acceptable sentiments are expressed and which describes detailed administrative procedures. The time for completion of the statementing procedure for a pupil has been set at six months. These procedures are themselves complex, time-consuming and extremely costly. The revised Circular 22/89 still signally fails to address equally important issues concerning the assessment techniques and the operational definition of the criteria that are the essential tools of an accountable decision-making process. In this respect, the circular takes flexibility to the point of flabbiness. Recognizing that a circular is only advisory and that clarifications of issues typically appear in subsequent regulations, the track history of Circular 1/83 does not augur well for the future of Circular 22/89. Little appears to have been learned in the intervening six years. Whilst reference is made to the need for assessments and statements to take account of the National Curriculum both initially and at each subsequent review, the circular gives no indication as to how this might be done. This may be either because *there is no consensus* as to what is appropriate, or that the expense of what is required could be politically unacceptable. 'Keep things vague' could be the unwritten, possibly unavoidable, administrative dictum governing proposals in the circular to either or both contingencies. In a democracy, when professionals cannot agree, politicians, administrators and the legal professions make arrangements for the resolution of differences via the courts in the final analysis.

As with the present arrangements, plenty of room for disagreements exists within the revised circular concerning whether or not a child has specific learning difficulties (dyslexia) and whether or not special provision should be made. The scenario is one in which parents are increasingly likely to have recourse to the courts. Independent chartered educational psychologists are likely to be asked for second opinions concerning the merits of particular cases. Our adversarial judicial system will then continue its due process. Case law and precedent will determine the legal definition of specific learning difficulties (dyslexia), the rights and responsibilities of parents, pupils and LEAs (Chasty and Friel, 1991).

Within the National Curriculum, assessments of pupils' attainments and progress are to be reported at the end of each school year when the majority of a cohort reaches the age of 7, 11, 14 or 16 years. Each of the subject working groups defines programmes of study and specified attainment targets. Ten levels are used to cover the full range of progress that children of different abilities should achieve between the ages of 5 and 16 years. Levels 1 to 5 represent the range of attainment levels which should be reached by children from the ages of 5 to 11. Thus the average seven-year-old is expected to reach attainment level 2 whilst a typical 11-year-old is expected to reach attainment level 4. This is *not* a refined grading system (GB.DES/WO, 1987a, b; GB.DES, 1989c).

English is one of the three core subjects of the National Curriculum. In discussing SENs, the importance of children being enabled '…to perform in English to their full *potential*' has been stressed in the Cox Report (GB.DES/WO, 1988, para. 13.15) (original emphasis). After widespread consultation, the revised recommendations, published in March 1989, reduced the original six attainment targets to five. These targets specify what pupils should know, understand and be able to do between the ages of 5 and 11 years. In summary, these are as follows (GB.DES/WO, 1989):

- Profile component 1:   Speaking and Listening (Attainment Target 1)
- Profile component 2:   Reading (Attainment Target 2)
- Profile component 3:   Writing (Attainment Targets 3, 4 and 5: Writing, Spelling and Handwriting)

Can this be 'A Curriculum for All'? (National Curriculum Council, 1989a, b). Without the development of adequate listening, speaking, reading, writing and spelling skills, the National Curriculum cannot be delivered (Pumfrey, 1990a). 'A Level 1 performance should always be a signal for further investigation. This might, for example, reveal that a child who appeared to be a slow learner, or inattentive, was in fact showing symptoms of specific learning difficulties (dyslexia)…' (GB.DES/WO, 1988, para. 13.6).

How will such investigations be carried out, and by whom? It appears likely that the statementing procedures referred to earlier will be increasingly used. Under Section 1 of the 1981 Education Act, a child is deemed to

...have special educational needs if they have a learning difficulty which calls for special educational provision to be made for them. *Learning difficulty* is defined in terms of children who have a significantly greater difficulty in learning than the majority of children of their age; and/or have a disability which either prevents or hinders them from making use of educational facilities of a kind generally provided in schools in their LEA area for children of their age...

Special educational provision means educational provision that is additional to, or otherwise different from, that made generally for children of the same age in schools maintained by the LEA concerned. Such provision is expensive. Public resources are limited. Letters received in the current inquiry bear eloquent testimony to the anger and frustration felt by many parents of pupils identified as having specific learning difficulties (dyslexia). They are but one of many such groups fighting for resources.

Provisions within the Education Act 1988 allow exceptions, exclusions, disapplications and modifications of the National Curriculum for children with SENs. Fortunately, these can only be made in individual cases for children with statements. The full participation of parents and professionals is required, and decisions are subject to appeal. Blanket exemptions for groups of pupils or types of school are allowed subject to detailed statutory consultation.

The parents of children with specific learning difficulties (dyslexia) frequently experience considerable problems in obtaining from LEAs the special educational provision that they consider their children need. One of the consequences of LMS is that all educational activities will be costed. The legal obligations on LEAs and schools to provide resources for the assessment and alleviation of specific learning difficulties (dyslexia) are likely to lead to considerably more legal actions by pressure groups backing disaffected parents. This may eventually lead to greater professional agreement concerning the operational definition of specific learning difficulties (dyslexia), and the public funding available (Elliott, 1990a).

Summary

The 12 issues that have been identified testify to the controversies that characterize this field. Entirely legitimate theoretical differences exist concerning the nature of specific learning difficulties and dyslexia, and their interrelationship. These theoretical differences have important implications for practices intended to anticipate, minimize the likelihood or to alleviate learners' difficulties. In part, because of the almost inevitable professional 'tunnel vision' of individuals trained in any particular field with its expertise and concerns, members of the teaching, psychological and medical professions often fail to appreciate the value of interdisciplinary efforts in conceptualizing, predicting and alleviating specific learning difficulties.

No single profession and no single professional has a freehold on expertise in these three concerns. The accounts of theory, research and applications from the psychological, educational and medical perspectives presented in Sections B, C and D (Chapters 3 to 11) make the point. The line 'Though each was partly in the right, they all were in the wrong' (see p. 34) contains an important truth that all groups interested in this field would do well to remember, considering the current state of knowledge. Fortunately, there is increasing communication between different groups of professionals. Expertise and understanding are far from perfect, but undoubtedly exist within all the groups specified. Individuals with specific learning difficulties can be helped.

The availability of this expertise is limited. It is also expensive. Demand for publicly funded professional services exceeds the financial and personnel resources available to LEAs. The Education Act 1981, the Education Reform Act 1988 and their associated circulars and regulations seek to target expertise where it is most needed. In law, there are clearly specified LEA responsibilities for identifying children with special educational needs in general and with specific learning difficulties in particular. The latter is only one of a set of competing claims on resources from children with other learning difficulties. The keys to the legal identification of pupils falling within these categories lie in quantitative and/or qualitative inter- and intra-individual differences. The specification and operational definition of attributes characterizing specific learning difficulties are highly controversial issues.

Until there is agreement, albeit provisional, concerning the theoretical basis and operational definition of these attributes, disagreements between whether an LEA is, or is not, fulfilling its legal obligations to children with specific learning difficulties are sometimes resolved by the judgement of the courts. In the meantime, further collaborative research is required if the scientific and legal controversies identified are to be resolved.

Despite such uncertainties, LEAs have legal responsibilities to identify and assess pupils with specific learning difficulties and, where considered necessary, to provide additional resources from the public purse. That purse is not bottomless. The values of our society determine its depth and the priority accorded to the many claims on it.

Recommendations

2.1. Professionals and parents be aware of the scientific, pedagogic, administrative and financial implications of the issues outlined in this chapter.

2.2. All of the many interested parties contribute towards a wider public appreciation of the complexities and costs involved.

2.3. Longitudinal cohort research by multidisciplinary teams be further developed into the nature, incidence, prognosis, presenting characteristics and responses to intervention of specific learning difficulties.

SECTION B: PSYCHOLOGICAL RESPONSES

This section emphasizes the wide range of psychological theory and research relevant to those concerned with the identification and alleviation of specific learning difficulties. The first chapter starts deliberately with a broad perspective of literacy and literacy learning. The second evaluates approaches that acknowledge the anguish and embarrassment of persistent failure in reading and writing. Finally, the third chapter reviews the extensive body of cognitive research focusing on difficulties with print recognition and reproduction.

Chapter 3

A Broader Perspective

Introduction

The purpose of this chapter is to put the 'specific' into the context of the 'general'. Whilst research into specific learning difficulties has largely focused on the written word and its elements (see Chapter 5), other aspects of literacy learning might have been taken for granted. It needs to be emphasized, therefore, that print recognition is embedded in a broader perspective that forms the basis for the development of particular skills. This viewpoint does not deny that some children have marked and debilitating specific difficulties with print. It stresses the importance of a wider focus on psychological theory and research relevant to those concerned with the identification and alleviation of such difficulties.

Current theory about literacy regards reading and writing as processes reflecting social, political and cultural influences. The emphasis is on meaning in its broadest sense (Ferreiro and Teberovsky, 1983; Wallace, 1986; Branston, 1988). The shift away from perceptual aspects has been illustrated by Reid (1983), who compared the indexes of two books from the forties and fifties with three from the sixties and seventies. While the earlier books referred to visual perception, discrimination, eye movements, association, word shape and Gestalt theory, the later publications devoted their attention to language, speech, syntax, sentence patterns, prediction, context and concepts of print. Underpinning that change was a greater understanding of the nature of language and language acquisition. The development of literacy in children was viewed in relation to the development of the oral language which preceded it.

That emphasis has also been evident in the present inquiry into specific learning difficulties (dyslexia). The previous version, reported in 1984, listed particular methods of assessment and intervention which also involved underlying perceptual subskills (Frostig, Lefever and Whittlesey, 1964; Frostig and Horne, 1964; Kirk, McCarthy and Kirk, 1968). Few British educational psychologists made use of these techniques and then only rarely. Respondents to the current inquiry regarded specific learning difficulties as relating to print recognition and reproduction conceptualized in a way which took account of the wider psychological and educational context (see Chapter 14).

Chapters 6 and 7 describe the instructional implications of different views of literacy, including that which sees the learner using prior knowledge about language and 'life' to make sense of the text. This chapter is limited to some of the psychological theory underpinning that learning and refers only briefly to educational methodology.

The scope of psychology

Having considered a range of publications about dyslexia, such as those reviewed in Chapter 5, Hynds (1987) comes to the conclusion that a preoccupation with graphophonic elements has resulted in an ignorance of developmental language research and the interaction of semantic, syntactic and bibliographical cues in making sense of print. All these 'cues' can be regarded as referring to the general expectations of meaning in life which enable the reader to predict the content, language and functions of the text.

Meek (1982) too has had the impression that psychological models are solely concerned with breaking reading up into stages and teaching each stage in turn. As much of psychological research has been compartmentalized into particular areas, it is not surprising to find psychological theory represented in these narrow ways in educational contexts. Take, for example, cognitive research into word recognition. Work has mainly centred on the single word and the elements within it not because researchers have been unaware of the wider linguistic aspects but because the number of variables to be examined and controlled has already been more than sufficient. Furthermore, a primary interest has been to model human information processing. The study of reading, including impairments or deficits, has been undertaken to test these models and, in many cases, educational implications have rarely been mentioned.

It should be recognized that research into cognitive processes is not synonymous with research into the teaching of reading and writing. Consequently, the stages defined by authors such as Frith (1985) or Seymour and McGregor (1984), described in more detail in Chapter 5, do not necessarily imply a sequence of teaching goals as has been assumed by Sterne (1990). The search for causal relationships with predictive validity may emphasize particular aspects, such as phonological awareness (Bryant and Bradley, 1985), but has not been intended as a prescription of overall approaches to learning. There is no 'holy grail' that, when discovered, will obviate the need for assessment and intervention on a broad front for either individuals or groups.

The separation of psychological research into different branches or sub-areas presents problems to applied practitioners. It would be suspect, for example, to consider cognitive aspects in isolation from emotional and social influences. Even academic psychology is moving towards holistic approaches represented by framework theories in cognitive science. These frameworks seek to synthesize agreements between theories and to make naturalistic observations in order to derive useful working approximations (Reason, 1990a). Their purpose is to draw out and combine that which is of practical relevance rather than set up studies to support or refute particular theoretical stances. Similarly, the context of education requires comprehensive knowledge of all aspects so that informed choices can be made for particular children and situations.

Linking assessment with intervention, Wedell (1970) was one of the first to devise procedural flow diagrams which placed emphasis on 'hypothesis testing' through systematic questions related to interventions. Although such problem-solving heuristics provide useful rules of thumb, their linear nature might lead to over-ready applications of familiar solutions. It seems that the principal objection of proponents of 'psycholinguistic' orientations to literacy (such as Goodman, 1967; Meek, 1982; Smith, 1985) is the precipitate narrowing of strategies to print-related practice alone. Their overall orientation is expressed well by Branston (1988): 'The litmus test for any and all activities in the reading classroom is whether they are experienced by the child as directly meaningful, intrinsically rewarding and therefore worthwhile'.

Practitioners tend to combine that which they see as useful into workable plans of action. In daily work their 'hypotheses' become generalizations drawn from every aspect of psychology and education. The broader their knowledge base the less they run the risk of over-focusing on limited aspects. Eclecticism has its merits.

Systematic observation and measurement of the interactive relationships between semantic, syntactic and grapho-phonic elements is difficult and time-consuming. It is much easier to administer a few standardized tests of relatively isolated elements. If one adds to that the range of interrelated social and emotional factors which contribute to a child's development in a complex and incremental way, then teasing out particular measures can seem irrelevant. Consequently, proponents of 'psycholinguistic' approaches base their views on general psychological theory and research into early language development. There is *no specific body of empirical evidence* comparable to that which exists for word recognition as described in Chapter 5. The long pedigree of psychological theory underpinning psycholinguistic viewpoints is described briefly below. Its bearing on pupils regarded as having specific learning difficulties is considered.

Schema theories

Bartlett's (1932) enduring phrase, 'effort after meaning', encapsulated his views. He introduced the notion of 'schema' to explain the systematic errors that were made when recalling pictorial or textual material. The errors occurred because the new material was being related to established knowledge structures 'schemata'. A 'schema' was defined by Bartlett as 'an active organisation of past reactions, or of past experiences' which then lead to '...the tendency to interpret present material in accordance with the general character of earlier experience'.

Kelly's (1955) personal construct theory also merits mention in this context. The actions of individuals are regarded as consistent with the meanings they impose on their experiences. Those meanings are determined by individual perceptions in the light of their own unique histories (Bannister and Fransella, 1971; Beail, 1985; Phillips, 1989). Indeed, Ravenette (1979) has described these processes in relation to the emotional underpinnings of specific learning difficulties (see Chapter 4).

In reading and writing, learners bring along their expectations and 'schema' developed about the nature of language and communication. They make predictions about content, interest and language structures and, furthermore, their predictions and expectations extend to knowledge about words and the letter strings of which those words are made up.

Recent work exploring 'schema' effects in reading has been reviewed, for example, by Garner (1988). While much of the research has been concerned with adult readers, results have shown that younger and poorer readers have little awareness that they must attempt to make sense of a text. They tend to focus on reading as a decoding process, rather than as a meaning-getting process (Baker and Brown, 1984). Furthermore, they are less likely to notice that they are not understanding the text (Garner and Reis, 1981). At first sight, research reviewed by Stanovich (1980) contradicts these findings. Poor readers have been observed to use context more than good readers to 'guess' words they cannot read. Stanovich concludes that those who are weak at word recognition need to rely more on context to compensate for their deficient use of graphic information. Even here, however, poor readers have turned to the context to facilitate decoding; their focus and interest has not necessarily been on the meaning-getting process. Whilst pupils with specific learning difficulties may behave in this manner, it should be noted that some may show particular strengths in understanding the meaning of the text when presented orally.

The reader's purpose is to make sense of the purposes and thoughts conveyed by the author. As described by Rumelhart (1980), if a reader arrives at the 'schema' intended by the author, then the text has been comprehended. If the reader can find no 'schema' to accept the textual information, the text is not understood. And if the reader finds 'schema' other than those intended by the author, the text is misrepresented or creatively interpreted.

This analysis points to factors associated with the text itself. It is not surprising to find learners regarding reading only as a decoding process if texts have been contrived to develop the deciphering of print through carefully controlled vocabularies, or reading schemes. The current emphasis on 'real books', written by authors for children because they have something to communicate has, in principle, rejected the use of reading schemes. Meanwhile some publishers have attempted to make the content of these schemes more meaningful while, of necessity, retaining the restricted vocabularies required by structured repetitive approaches recommended by those concerned with word recognition skills. Root (1986) and Donaldson (1988) argue convincingly that the use of reading schemes does not necessarily deprive children of access to stories, poems and information books. What matters is that schemes are used flexibly and imaginatively together with a wider range of children's literature and that teachers themselves have an interest in and knowledge of that literature.

To summarize, the current view of 'schema' is of higher order, generic cognitive structures which underlie all aspects of human knowledge and skill (Reason, 1990a). Although their processing lies beyond the direct reach of awareness, their products – words, images, feelings and actions – are central to involvement in literacy. These are the products children bring to the reading task which determine whether they become readers with a lifelong interest in books and other written information or whether they see reading as a job to be done through deciphering the text.

The social and cultural context of learning

Learning, thought and knowledge are not only functions of the way the individual learns or thinks, but are in essence social and interactive (Bruner, 1986). The development of common shared knowledge, between the pupils themselves and between teachers and pupils, has been investigated by those concerned with social interaction in the classroom (Driver, 1983; Willes, 1983; Bennett *et al.*, 1984; Edwards and Mercer, 1987; Bruner and Haste, 1990).

Bruner comes to the conclusion that most learning in most settings is a communal activity, 'a sharing of the culture'. He uses the notion of culture to describe the educational contexts in which teachers and pupils negotiate meanings and the teacher acts in a way that supports a participatory and future-oriented process of education. This general learning environment should also be available to those who have specific difficulties with print, an aspect returned to in Chapter 8 concerning ways of facilitating access to the curriculum.

Cultural 'scripts' for social situations influence the way texts are comprehended. Wallace (1986) provides a range of illustrations to show how universal events, such as births and marriages, are understood according to the particular traditions they draw on. An extract from the Link-Up Reading Scheme (Auntie Pat in Hospital) makes the point with regard to young children who may not know that flower buying is part of the 'script' for visiting people in hospital. Without that knowledge, children find it difficult to use reading experience to learn about the nature of print. The problems of pupils with specific learning difficulties might thus be exacerbated through inappropriate choices of content. In a pluralistic society teaching needs to emphasize the validity of black experience, perspectives and culture. The variety of content should ensure that specific learning difficulties are not defined in terms of socio-cultural background.

If reading is regarded as 'visually guided thinking' (Neisser, 1967), then the content provides the starting point for word recognition. That content needs to be relevant and interesting. When pupils read and write together with their teachers, parents or friends, and they spend much time talking about the content that they enjoy, these shared activities can be described as 'the social and interactive learning of visually guided thinking' (Reason, 1990b). It is particularly important to ensure that this ethos is not lost when pupils experience specific learning difficulties.

Early language and literacy development

Bartlett's (1932) 'effort after meaning' becomes a unifying theme for research into early development of language and thought that has its roots in the work of Vygotsky (1962, 1978). The research undertaken by Wells and his co-workers has been particularly influential in demonstrating that language acquisition requires a shared purpose of making sense of the situation (Wells, 1985a). Transcripts of interactions between mothers and children illustrate the way parents respond to their children's utterances by guessing at the message the child is trying to convey and then giving continuity and reciprocity to the interaction. There is no planned sequence of instruction but a sharing of meaning in the context of 'real life'. Parallels have then been extended to reading: a sharing of meaning in the context of 'real books'.

Resulting from that interaction, most children have a great deal of knowledge about print prior to school, not only with book reading but in relation to the signs and symbols that surround them in their environment (Torrey, 1979; Goodman, 1983; Hall, 1987). Where there are specific learning difficulties, children may not be able to take full advantage of these early interactions. Difficulties might indeed be compounded when there is little opportunity for incidental learning about signs and symbols and also specific learning difficulties with print. This demonstrates the interdependence of environmental factors and within-child variables.

Wells (1985b) has highlighted the effects of certain pre-school language experiences at home that assist the child in dealing with the symbolic, relatively context-independent, nature of language characteristic of written stories and information. Of the activities recorded, listening to a story read or told was significantly associated both with knowledge of literacy and reading comprehension at the age of seven. Wells noted that the stories gave the child the opportunity to discover the power of language to create and explore alternative possible worlds. The transcripts showed, however, that it was not only the reading of the stories, as such, but the talk and discussion which related the content to children's own experiences. Children were encouraged to reflect upon and ask questions about the events that occurred, their causes, consequences and significance. Of prime importance was the parents' own enjoyment of reading. For some parents, it was a task they performed with difficulty and, not surprisingly, those parents who reported that they did not enjoy reading to their children also reported that their children did not enjoy being read to.

Further evidence has been provided by Torrance and Olson (1985), relating children's competence in early language with their later progress in literacy. The strongest correlate of reading ability was the variety of cognitive verbs used by the children; better readers used more abstract verbs such as 'think', 'know', 'decide' and 'wonder'. These verbs were part of a system of concepts for decontextualizing language and thought. It was not clear, however, whether the good reader's competence with these verbs was a by-product of being exposed to the literate language of written text or a prerequisite for it.

The plight of parents not knowing how to help has been highlighted previously by the Plowden Report (GB.DES, 1967). Results of earlier work were not strongly associated with achievements in reading (Newson and Newson, 1977; Moon and Wells, 1979). Furthermore, if little progress was being made, tensions between parent and child could become marked (Glynn and McNaughton, 1985). In contrast, more recent studies involving parents in reading together with their children have produced positive results (Hewison and Tizard, 1980; Hannon and Jackson, 1987). The theoretical basis for these later initiatives has come largely from the notions of language learning described in this chapter (for example Wells, 1985b). Parents and children have been assisted in focusing on the enjoyment derived from the content of the text (Branston and Provis, 1986). As will be described in Chapter 4, these aspects have had an important bearing on the emotional factors associated with specific learning difficulties.

Although children learning to read already possess or acquire a wide range of knowledge and skills, there are considerable individual differences (Clark, 1976). Success in reading is likely to come from understanding concepts about print and the idea that the spoken word can be represented by writing (Francis, 1982). It would appear, however, that word awareness develops slowly and, while the ability to segment speech into words may not be essential for reading to begin, it is likely to facilitate progress (Ehri, 1979).

Even after months of schooling some children may be unsure about these concepts (Clay, 1979a, b). On entry to school two-thirds of the children studied by Clay understood the idea that print rather than the picture alone told the story. Two per cent of children were still confused about this at age six years. Some also took a long time to discover that it is necessary to move in a left to right direction to read in English. These directional variables were highly correlated with reading attainment and could be linked to writing, an important way of helping children to acquire the necessary concepts (Chomsky, 1979).

The studies by Clay suggest that cues from language are supplemented by learning in other areas, such as letter knowledge, word knowledge and letter–sound associations. Clay's observations that children making slow progress do not hear the sound sequences in words agrees with the research by Bryant and Bradley (1985) who found that the achievement of nursery children on rhyming and alliteration tasks was related to their progress in reading and spelling four years later. They argue that skills in phonemic analysis help children to learn to read, and training in sound categorization can improve reading progress. They recommend activities in the nursery or reception class that encourage the use of alliteration as well as rhyme, songs and poetry, a recommendation which fits in well with research concerned with specific learning difficulties (see Chapter 5).

Bryant and Impey (1986) then go on to challenge the work of those who have drawn parallels between adults who, due to injury, have lost some aspect of their ability to read (acquired dyslexia) and children who experience marked difficulties in learning to read (developmental dyslexia). Their view is that these typologies of defect are not relevant to children who they regard as being delayed, particularly in developing phonology. Coltheart (1987b) responds forcibly to Bryant and Impey. According to Coltheart, some children acquire visual or phonological word recognition skills abnormally slowly, thus there is a defect. This debate does not currently have any clear implications for practitioners in terms of educational methodology. All one can say is that the term 'delay' sounds more optimistic than the term 'defect'. Those struggling with what will seem to them a lifelong disability might find little grounds for such optimism.

Implications for intervention

Educationally relevant psychological debate centres on the extent to which phonological awareness and word recognition should be taught directly. Smith (1978), for example, writes that learning to read does not require the memorization of phonic rules or lists of words; such subskills are taken care of in the course of reading with assistance as long as children have the opportunity to generate and test their own hypotheses about reading. The prerequisites for learning to read and write are then an adequate understanding of the purposes of language, and plenty of opportunity both to use that language and to predict the way it is represented in a visual form as written text. This provides a starting point for considering the additional help required by those regarded as having specific learning difficulties.

Observations indicate that children making slow progress in literacy read much less than those making good progress (Clay, 1979a, b). In the first year at school the high progress group read an estimated 20,000 words while those making the least progress read an estimated 5000 words. This discrepancy was thought to be an underestimate as the low progress group was also known to be reading and writing at home to a lesser extent. Other studies have noted differences in the amount of time spent 'on task' during reading (Cambrell, Wilson and Gantt, 1981) and writing (Fonseca, 1990).

These observations demonstrate the cumulative effects of early difficulties. Some children increasingly avoid reading and writing, becoming unmotivated and unwilling to take the risks of guessing at meaning described by Smith (1978). The resultant lack of opportunity to develop underlying competencies can then contribute to specific learning difficulties (Stanovich, 1986). If certain cognitive abilities develop as a consequence of the growing reading skills of the child, it may not only be the underlying functions which dictate the course of reading development but the language experiences associated with the processes of learning to read.

It follows that children with difficulties require more enjoyable opportunities for supported reading and writing using methods based on shared activities (Branston and Provis, 1986; Davis and Stubbs, 1988). These methods regard print recognition as a product derived from a focus on content; there is no struggle with deciphering individual words. Arguably, the reduction of stress associated with a fear of failure along with the sense of warmth, intimacy and shared interest between those involved may be responsible for the positive outcomes reported.

The promotion of the whole language and reading experience from the very start has been labelled the 'top-down' approach. It contrasts with the controlled presentation of practice tasks concerned with letter sounds and word recognition – the 'bottom-up' approach – that assumes that complex skills need to be built up from their elements.

The theoretical basis for the 'bottom-up' approach originates, in part, from research concerned with the difficulties some children have with print recognition. Emphasis now shifts to the cognitive complexities underlying acquisition of literacy, and reading is no longer regarded as a natural extension of primary linguistic activity. Instead, discussion centres on the fundamental differences between the skills involved in dealing with print and in dealing with speech. As outlined by Bertelson (1986), learning to read is regarded as an explicit manipulation of the units for which the written symbols stand.

Instructional methodology concerned with word recognition tends to involve structured cumulative programmes of instruction in the form of the objectives approach (Solity and Bull, 1987), direct instruction (Carnine and Silbert, 1979) and the 'multisensory' practice of phonics (Hornsby and Shear, 1975; Hickey, 1977). Structured reading schemes based on a limited vocabulary can also be regarded as belonging to this category. The main assumptions are that the reading and writing curriculum can be drawn up as a hierarchy of target skills to be mastered and that sufficient practice of a specified task increases the probability of success.

While this agrees quite well with the focus of those cognitive psychologists concerned with the single word and its elements, it differs from holistic 'top-down' approaches. The different emphases of the 'top-down' and 'bottom-up' orientations to instruction are summarized in Table 3.1. 'Top-down' starts from shared interest, gentle assistance and plenty of opportunity. Most children learn to recognize printed words by attending first to higher order knowledge about language and life in general. In contrast, the 'bottom-up' way of teaching assumes that word recognition skills are learnt through structured cumulative methods of instruction; thus complex skills are built up from their elements, the letter strings within words. It should be emphasized that neither approach denies the importance of print recognition and reproduction.

Table 3.1: A summary of 'top-down' and 'bottom-up' approaches to literacy learning

Top-down	Bottom-up
Instruction progresses from the general to the specific; children begin with stories and poems and word recognition skills follow	Instruction progresses from letters and words to sentences and stories, from specifics to the general
'Effort after meaning' is the source of literacy	Emphasis is on grapho-phonic symbols and word recognition
Learning requires shared interest, gentle assistance and plenty of opportunity	Learning requires structured cumulative methods of instruction
Poor readers may not use higher order knowledge about language to predict and guide lower level word recognition skills	Poor readers cannot attend to content while they are laboriously deciphering print

Jansen (1985) has objected to an either/or way of representing the two approaches. He writes:

> What is right at one level of teaching reading may be insufficient at another level of teaching reading and wrong at yet another. ...[it] is not a question of teaching either this way or that way, but in most cases of teaching both this way and that way. (p. 172)

Can the two paradigms be combined to form one coherent approach if one of them starts from content, and word recognition follows, and the other from word recognition, and content follows? The practice of 'both', that is supported reading and writing *and* instruction in letter and word recognition, would seem obvious to most practitioners. Indeed, a small-scale study of the work of 188 class teachers showed that their practice represented an interactive eclecticism incorporating both the grapho-phonic and the psycholinguistic orientations (Pumfrey, 1990b). But the issue still remains – which of the rationales dominates in informing the overall ethos for instruction?

A partial answer can be derived from a framework drawn by Reason (1990b) which incorporates specific learning difficulties. It takes the form of an up-turned triangle reproduced in Figure 3.1. The first and largest segment of the triangle refers to the context of learning. Mentioned in that segment are phrases taken from the writings of Bartlett and Bruner, already described. Bartlett's 'effort after

Figure 3.1: Ingredients of literacy (from Reason, 1990b)

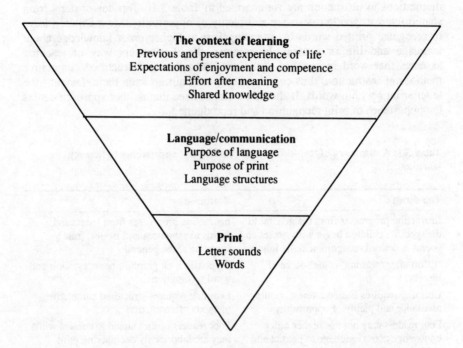

The context of learning
Previous and present experience of 'life'
Expectations of enjoyment and competence
Effort after meaning
Shared knowledge

Language/communication
Purpose of language
Purpose of print
Language structures

Print
Letter sounds
Words

meaning', based on previous and present experiences of life, determines whether the purposes and thoughts of the author can make sense to the reader. Bruner's emphasis on the sharing of knowledge and culture points to the interactive nature of learning. Personal expectations of competence and enjoyment become determined by many social and emotional factors considered in Chapter 4.

The second segment of the triangle is concerned with all these general aspects in relation to language learning and its purpose of communication. It links with 'top-down' views which promote the whole language and reading experience from the very start; thus, children learn to speak and read by being involved in these activities and, assisted by parents, teachers and friends, gradually joining in that which makes sense to them.

The nature of print now becomes a small, but essential, third segment of the triangle. It is dependent on the major areas of learning in the larger segments. The additional features of print, concerned with grapho-phonic elements, can become the cause of considerable, even apparently intractable, difficulties for some children.

Specific learning difficulties (dyslexia) can be conceptualized within this framework. Definitions tend to focus on the apex of the inverted triangle (that is on deficient recognition and reproduction of print) and assume that the experiences associated with other, broader aspects of the triangle have taken place. If instruction has concentrated on the 'bottom-up' approach, however, the learner may have missed out on the wider experience prerequisite for developing and testing hypothesis about the nature of print (Smith, 1978). Isolated practice of word recognition then ignores the language cues based on content and can make the task of learning something difficult so much harder.

It is argued that intervention for pupils with specific learning difficulties should not ignore opportunity for meaningful assisted reading and writing. The amount of productive and enjoyable time spent on activities to do with the appreciation of the content of nursery rhymes, poetry and literature, combined with plenty of supported reading and writing, would meet both the emotional and the broader cognitive needs of the pupil.

Although not addressing specific learning difficulties in particular, that ethos is reflected in a resource pack concerned with the English National Curriculum at Key Stage 1, developed by a working party of teachers in Manchester (Manchester City Council Education Department, 1989). They consider instruction under three headings: shared, guided and independent. The shared learning concentrates on content and supported enjoyment of that content; guided learning takes particular instructional points arising from the shared content, such as letter sounds; independent learning assumes that the pupil can enjoy the content without assistance.

The National Curriculum in English at Key Stage 1 (GB.DES, 1989a) gives pupils much opportunity to show what they can do in terms of the two large segments at the top of Figure 3.1. If assistance is provided with print recognition and reproduction, pupils with specific learning difficulties are able to demonstrate what they can achieve rather than having to concentrate only on their difficulties. This obviously does not deny the need for additional help with the print aspects of literacy.

Figure 3.1 represents an overall educational ethos that favours the 'top-down' rationale. Are there instances, however, where the third small segment, concerned with print, becomes so dominant that the other aspects pale into significance? In other words, in what circumstances might the framework represented by the triangle become turned on its head so that grapho-phonic elements occupy the largest segment?

Subjective perceptions are important. Those struggling with decoding are not likely to refer to a lack of meaningful learning experiences but to trouble with print. As argued by Sterne (1990), loving books is not necessarily a guarantee for learning to read and write.

Emotional aspects play a central role. As described in Chapter 4, learners with decoding difficulties place greater strain on the limited capacity of working memory, further reduced by anxiety associated with a sense of failure with print.

The considerable body of work concerned with phonology and word recognition, reviewed in Chapter 5, gives priority to print. Broader considerations play a secondary role. Even the 'interactive–compensatory' hypothesis has word recognition as its focus (Stanovich, 1980). Stanovich suggests that learners compensate for deficiency in one source of information about words by relying more on information from other sources. Consequently, they rely more on context because they process words less efficiently. It is the utilization of context and higher order language skills as compensatory strategies that underlies some of the current instruction for pupils with specific difficulties (see Reason and Boote, 1986).

Vellutino (1987) argues for a balanced programme which makes generous use of both the holistic/meaning and the analytic/phonetic approach to the instruction of children with specific learning difficulties in literacy. The focus of his research has been on word recognition and the guided learning suggested by Cotterell (1985) would fit his recommendations. Those starting from the meaning-getting process will, however, introduce word-building as part of a broader programme illustrated by the work of Holdaway (1980). Differences then persist with regard to the overall educational ethos in which the instruction takes place.

Implications for identification

In a broader perspective, the process of identification starts by examining instructional conditions. In assessing the needs of the individual, previous opportunities to learn become the focus. The severity of literacy difficulties can then be considered a function of the extent and quality of the teaching that has already taken place. That history takes account of individual learning and language experience, the school's policies and practices and the learner's own approaches and views. It draws on both past and present information about the way the individual responds to instruction.

Summary

The separation of psychology into different branches or sub-areas presents problems for applied practitioners who need to combine what they see as useful into workable plans of action. The wider their knowledge base the less they run the risk of over-focusing on limited aspects.

Literacy learning, as an extension of oral language, does not draw on a specific body of empirical evidence comparable to that which exists for print recognition. But there is a long pedigree of general psychological theory and research underpinning these approaches. That work has been described under the headings of 'schema theories', 'the social and cultural context of learning' and 'early language and literacy development'.

It has been argued that supported reading and writing provide an opportunity to develop underlying competencies. Furthermore, the cumulative effects of early difficulties can result in a lack of that opportunity. Specific learning difficulties are described within a framework that takes account of the context of learning, including personal expectations of enjoyment and competence, the purpose of language and the nature of print recognition. It is also recognized that some children have very serious difficulties. Implications for identification and intervention, emphasized in this chapter, consider the overall ethos of instruction, previous learning experiences and the views of the learner.

Recommendations

3.1. Specific learning difficulties be considered within an overall educational context that takes account of previous opportunities to learn.
3.2. Practitioners ensure that their knowledge base remains sufficiently broad to avoid over-ready focus on limited aspects of literacy acquisition.
3.3. Practitioners inform themselves of research about language and literacy development in general, the social and interactive nature of learning, and the perceptions of the learners themselves.
3.4. The validity of black experience, perspectives and culture reflected in the literature of a pluralistic society be recognized.

3.5. Specific learning difficulties must not become defined in terms of socio-cultural background.

3.6. Research into the effects of different approaches to supporting pupils with specific learning difficulties be undertaken.

Chapter 4

Emotional and Social Factors

The views of the learner

> Then he reddened furiously, felt his bowels sink with shame, scratched out what he had written, made an agonised effort to think of something in the real composition style, failed, became sullen with rage and humiliation, put the pen down and would have been torn to pieces rather than attempt to write another word. (Lawrence, 1915, p. 17)

This well-known quote from *The Rainbow* illustrates that sense of frustration and anger which can be engendered by learning difficulties. Failing readers have to cope not only with their own self-doubts but also with the knowledge that their poor progress, far from being a secret shame, often becomes a public failure (Gaines, 1989).

There is little systematic documentation of the views and feelings expressed by the children themselves. Publications include personal accounts by adult dyslexics (such as Arkell, n.d.) and parents' descriptions of the plight of their children (Melck, 1986). The stream of correspondence to voluntary associations reinforces this point. Indeed, letters received from parents in response to the present inquiry comment on their children's perceptions. The following two quotes provide a flavour of the responses:

> His concentration is poor but he is a real individual and likes to stand out from the crowd – possibly to compensate for his other shortcomings of which he is intensely aware.

> It is not only the person involved who has difficulties but all who come into contact with them share the frustration and concern.

The views of one teenager are described in some detail in Chapter 8 and a letter received from Zachary has been reproduced in full at the front of this book. Zachary's letter illustrates his essentially positive attitude when appropriate educational support is provided. In contrast, the comments made by Sandra, aged 9, and David, aged 8, display a sense of helplessness:

> I want to write but I'm the only one who can't write.

> I don't like reading to the teacher – I try not to be noticed.

A publication originating in the USA has amply demonstrated the perceptiveness of the children involved (Kavanaugh, 1978). The book grew out of 'roundtable' discussions of a range of topical issues, led by the teenage editors of a magazine.

One of the issues discussed by a group of dyslexic children related to their own difficulties as perceived by them retrospectively. The following quotes, part of longer accounts, are taken from that work:

> My mother's read up on it. She didn't think it was anything. 'So what? You have a reading disability. You've got to conquer it yourself.' I think she was right. (Jon, 15)

> It just scared me. I thought I'd never be able to do anything for myself. Other kids told me that too ... I get by. Sometimes I like doing things, and other times I just don't want to be bothered with it. (Diane, 13)

> I felt 'why me?' for some time. It just didn't make sense. I could follow the action of a TV show, but I couldn't understand school assignments until the teacher went over them. (Cathy, 12)

A recent detailed description of the emotional reactions to the consequences of dyslexia experienced by eight boys aged from 16 to 17 reveals the pupils' extremely adverse experiences of education (Edwards, 1990). The boys are currently attending a residential special school for dyslexic pupils. In their previous education elsewhere, they are reported as having experienced four groups of adverse responses from teachers: *violence*; *unfair treatment*/discrimination; inadequate help and *humiliation*. A failure by teachers to accept the existence of dyslexia was coupled with a readiness to label the pupils as disruptive and/or 'dim'. The pupils' emotional reactions included truancy, psychosomatic pains, isolation, alienation from peers, a failure of communication within the family, lack of confidence, self-doubt and denigration, competitiveness disorders, sensitivity to criticism and behaviour problems (ibid, p. iv). The case studies reveal in clinical detail the pressures and the pains experienced. The importance of consistent help from competent teachers with a genuine interest in the individual and his learning difficulties is emphasized. The value of contact with other dyslexic pupils is stressed, but the disadvantage of reinforcing social isolation as a consequence of a residential school education is also acknowledged. The importance of capitalizing on pupils' strengths is crucial. The adverse consequences of 'rubbing the students' noses in their weaknesses', was coupled with great resentment at being labelled and treated as if they were unintelligent or abnormal. This account reveals the horrific emotional costs, to individuals and their families, of professionals not acknowledging and alleviating the pupils, specific learning difficulties (Edwards, ibid.).

Consideration of specific learning difficulties should take account of the views of the learner not only with regard to initial feelings but also in relation to ongoing methods of intervention. Pupils' preferences for different organizational arrangements in secondary schools have indeed been investigated (Payne, 1991). Further research, based on the emotional and social factors discussed in this chapter, would seem essential.

Cognition and emotion

Socio-emotional approaches examine learning difficulties in the context of personal and interpersonal meanings and relationships. These difficulties, and any neurological dysfunctions associated with them, are not regarded as developing solely within the individual but from the individual's interactions within social relationships (Coles, 1989).

Recent British cognitive research into specific learning difficulties (dyslexia) seems remarkably devoid of mention of social and emotional factors (see Ellis, 1984; Snowling, 1985; Seymour, 1986; Coltheart, 1987a). Meanwhile, there is strong evidence that socially induced anxiety results in performance decrements (see Zatz and Chassin, 1983, 1985). Furthermore, working memory capacity is regarded as the locus of the effects of anxiety on cognitive task performance (Eysenck, 1979, 1982; Darke, 1988). It is argued that anxious subjects have effectively smaller working memory storage or processing capacity to devote to the task. Since working memory is also central to the investigation of reading difficulties (see Baddeley, 1979; Daneman and Carpenter, 1980; Shankweiler and Crain, 1986), and such difficulties are often associated with a range of emotional correlates as reviewed by Tansley and Panckhurst (1981), it is indeed surprising to find the apparent lack of reference to the links between cognition and emotion in cognitive research concerned with specific learning difficulties (dyslexia).

Material written for educational practitioners, however, makes more recognition of social interaction and emotional reactions as contributors to the causes and effects of specific learning difficulties (see Young and Tyre, 1983; Reason and Boote, 1986; Miles, 1988). Furthermore, as quoted above, letters received from parents in the context of this inquiry are particularly convincing in illustrating the personal frustration, anger and anxiety experienced by their children and themselves.

A clearer understanding of these social and emotional influences and ways in which their effects can be alleviated, or turned to advantage, is needed. This chapter, therefore, reviews some relevant theoretical perspectives. It then considers the implications of these views for the identification of pupils who might need additional support. Finally, a review is made of the evidence for the efficacy of intervention which concentrates on emotional support of various kinds.

Theoretical perspectives

The socio-political context

While acknowledging the anguish and embarrassment of persistent learning failure, Coles (1987, 1989) argues that educational difficulties are shaped by political, economic and cultural factors. According to Coles, schools, as organizations embedded in social and economic contexts, have a tendency to 'explain away' failure by labelling the child 'learning disabled', a term used in the USA to denote problems similar to those described in Britain as specific learning difficulties (dyslexia). In Coles's view, the over-individualized cognitive and neuropsychological work associated with learning disability research has significantly detracted attention from a consideration of the interactive context of children's learning.

Sigmon (1989) traces the historical developments in the USA that have resulted in the term LD (learning disabled) becoming by far the largest special needs category, providing children so labelled with a variety of 'special programmes', that might not be in the best interests of the children themselves. Statistics about special provision for children for ethnic minority communities reflect these trends (Tucker, 1980; Finn, 1982). According to Adelman (1989), the effect has been to trivialize learning difficulties and seriously confound the research and practice of those whose purpose it is to broaden the focus of intervention at school.

These kinds of views are not unfamiliar in Britain. With regard to children from ethnic minority communities, statistics are provided by the DES (1981b) and, more recently, by Verma and Pumfrey (1988). With regard to the effect of overall school organization and ethos, evidence is available in relation to primary and secondary schools (Rutter *et al.*, 1979; Mortimore *et al.*, 1988). The American experience, however, is particularly relevant to those involved in making additional provision for pupils identified as having specific learning difficulties. It warns against the pitfalls of allowing labels, limited to within-child variables, to detract attention from policies and organization that take account of the full social and interpersonal context in which both general and specific learning difficulties arise (Sigmon, op. cit.).

Self-concept and motivation

Self-concept, broadly defined, relates to the individual's perceptions of her or himself. These perceptions are formed through personal experiences and interpretations of the environment and are especially influenced by reinforcements, evaluations by significant others and attributions for one's own behaviour (Shavelson and Bolus, 1982). The construct of self-concept has further been defined as multifaceted and hierarchical (Shavelson, Hubner and Stanton, 1976; Wylie, 1979; Burns, 1986). These authors provide comprehensive reviews of the self-concept literature and the conceptual and methodological problems associated with the research and evaluation of it. For the purposes of educators, Lawrence's slim volume on self-esteem in the classroom describes the main constructs in an easy and readable way (Lawrence, 1987).

This chapter is limited to an examination of the possible causal relationships between self-concept and achievement, particularly with regard to literacy. While reference is made to research linking self-concept with 'poor reading' or 'retarded reading', we have only found one recent research report relating these aspects to specific learning difficulties (Somerville and Leach, 1988). Even in that case, however, the subjects participating in the study were drawn from pupils referred to an agency for assistance because of 'problems with reading at school'. The point to note, therefore, is that findings relate to the slower development of literacy in general and are not limited to the kinds of additional methodological considerations resulting from a need to define specific learning difficulties or subgroups of pupils with such difficulties.

While there is evidence of a link between self-concept and academic achievement, it is not clear from this literature whether a low self-concept and negative perceptions of self are causes, effects or both of low levels of academic functioning (see Wood and Burns, 1983; Burns, 1986). Studies directly examining these issues have been reviewed by Butkowsky and Willows (1980) and Lawrence (1985) and support all three possibilities. Consequently, Lawrence takes the view that it is not a unidirectional phenomenon and that, in practice, attention should focus equally on both self-concept and achievement skills.

Butkowsky and Willows (1980) comment on the lack of specificity regarding the self-perceptions that comprise an academic self-concept. They examine the relationship of certain specific self-perceptions to motivation and competence by comparing children operationally defined as manifesting reading difficulties with relatively average or good readers. This type of group comparison has limitations (Bryant and Goswami, 1990). Despite these, the work is relevant to the emotional concomitants of learning difficulties. Two types of task were used, one involving reading and the other line drawings. The results of this experimental study are listed in more detail below as they point to the clinical and remedial implications of such work.

(i) Children of relatively poor reading ability were found to have lower initial expectations of success with both types of task. Furthermore, they showed greater decrements in their expectations of success following failure; thus, their confidence appeared to be more easily shaken.

(ii) Poor readers gave up more easily in the face of difficulty. Butkowsky and Willows argue that such children may not have had the opportunity to discover that they have the capacity to achieve outcomes that exceed their expectations. Their lack of persistence provided evidence in support of the notion that eroding motivation and confidence increases the probability of future failure.

(iii) Average to good readers tended to attribute their success to the presence of ability. In contrast, poor readers attributed their success to external causes such as luck, and their failure to self-perceived lack of competence. This particular attributional style was similar to the kind of causal inference that has been shown to relate to low achievement motivation (Weiner, 1979, 1985). Butkowsky and Willows comment, however, on the need for empirical confirmation with larger populations of children with reading difficulties.

The poor readers' lack of persistence, limited expectations of success and attribution of success to external factors is consistent with the notion of 'learning helplessness' (Abramson, Seligman and Teasdale, 1978; Diener and Dweck, 1978; Miller and Norman, 1979). While studies of learned helplessness have involved pre-training procedures to induce that 'state', it seems that learned helplessness occurs naturally in the population of children with reading difficulties. Similar parallels can be found with research relating to locus of control theory (Rothbaum, Wolfen and Visintainer, 1979; Lefcourt, 1981; Morgan, 1986), although none of this research is directly concerned with literacy. Finally, the development of avoidance of those situations that bring about negative self-concepts is described by Bird et al. (1981). This then completes the downward spiral linking personal perceptions and interpersonal relationships with continued learning difficulties at school.

Lest these conclusions be seen as too melodramatic, mention needs to be made to the work of Hammill and McNutt (1981). Their meta-analysis of 30 years of correlational research, consisting of a total of some 322 studies mainly in the USA, showed that the correlates of reading were confined to academic aspects, phonic knowledge, intelligence, 'readiness' and spoken language. Measures of affect, such as anxiety and self-concept, were not found to be significant. Bearing in mind that only a very small proportion of the studies were directed at learning difficulties, it should be emphasized that serious emotional reactions are not inevitable, an aspect returned to in the section on Identification and Incidence.

A recent longitudinal study of some 3000 children in Bergen, Norway provides data for the whole cohort and for a subgroup of pupils with specific learning difficulties (Gjessing and Karlsen, 1989). The children's abilities in reading, spelling and mathematics are the key dependent variables. In relation to the whole cohort, regression analyses demonstrate that the best predictors of achievement are of a linguistic–cognitive nature, explaining between 26 per cent and 42 per cent of the variance, depending on the school subject. The socio-emotional factor explains only 1.2 per cent to 2.7 per cent of the variance, but the researchers describe the dyslexic and retarded pupils as having poor self-concepts, lacking self-confidence and being poorly accepted by peers. Dyslexic pupils respond differentially to the same types of instruction, some making above average progress while others 'continue their pattern of slow growth' (Gjessing and Karlsen, 1989, p. 283). These results illustrate the need for individual approaches and more refined research designs that take account of the interaction between aptitude, temperament and instruction and do not make blanket assumptions about social and emotional influences.

The family context

When children do not achieve educational progress as expected, members of the family, in particular parents and the child concerned, need to accommodate the tensions and conflicts that can arise.

These kinds of family interactions have been described by Ravenette (1979), who discusses the negative effects of the label dyslexia. According to him, the family might place the child in a permanent role of 'disabled', which stands in the way of the child's progress. The label can also lead to misunderstandings between the family and the school if discussion centres around the existence of a condition rather than agreed and shared methods of intervention.

Miles (1988) takes a different view. For him the term dyslexia assists parents and the child to make sense of occurrences they know to exist. They know the child has difficulty with reading and spelling; they need explanations which remove the sense of self-blame. Miles sees this as the cornerstone for counselling children and their parents.

Similarities might be found in the case of obesity: 'serious overweight' can imply indulgence with consequent guilt while 'hormonal imbalance', as a causal explanation, exonerates the sufferer. Then, however, there may be a tendency to look for cures administered by experts instead of self-regulated diets based on well-researched knowledge. In relation to specific learning difficulties, Somerville and Leach (1988) warn against the perpetuation of programmes, including counselling, that receive favourable reports from consumers but lack objective evidence of effectiveness. Families concerned about their children's learning difficulties might indeed be particularly vulnerable to the marketing of unproven approaches.

Cunningham and Davis (1985) describe a model of the process of adaptation undertaken by parents whose children have been diagnosed as disabled. Drawing on Kelly's personal construct theory (Kelly, 1955), they see parents as having to construct a framework for understanding their child in relation to the label. Inherent in the model is the notion that parental reactions, such as self-blame, denial or hostility, should not be regarded as maladaptive but part of the exploration and reconstruction that they need to undertake.

It may seem insensitive to draw parallels between a lifelong disability such as Down's syndrome and specific learning difficulties, although serious literacy problems also effectively result in disability. Knusson and Cunningham (1988) argue, however, that parental distress is not proportionate to the extent of the disability but relates to values, aspirations, hopes and knowledge. They refer to the extensive body of research undertaken by Lazarus and his co-workers which shows that stress depends on personal appraisal of the relationship between environmental causes and the demands they make on available coping resources (Lazarus et al., 1985; Lazarus and Smith, 1988).

Fundamental to all these views is a need to take account of the sense the child is making of the situation and the perceptions of family members. Consequently, learning difficulties are explored by looking both beyond psycho-neurological explanations and the immediate teacher–child interaction to other interactions that might not be as readily apparent. The cases of Dibbs and Lesley are well-known examples of children whose learning difficulties have been attributed to social and emotional circumstances and not to psychoneurological factors (Axline, 1964; Martin, 1986, 1989).

Stress and learning

Gentile and McMillan (1987, 1988) focus on the concept of stress in relation to learning difficulties in literacy. Drawing on the work of Selye (1976), they define stress in terms of physiological responses manifesting themselves in fight or flight reactions which range from hostility to subdued behaviour. Previous research linking emotional disturbance with reading difficulties is interpreted within this paradigm. In addition, instructional conditions, such as requiring pupils to read aloud or complete innumerable workbooks to overcome skills deficits, are regarded as stressors inhibiting successful learning.

Methods of goal-setting, self-incentives and self-monitoring, all based on social learning theory, are described as ways of stress reduction (Bandura, 1977). An inventory differentiates between 'fight' and 'flight' coping strategies in helping pupils with difficulties in literacy acquisition. Whilst the authors do not offer evaluative evidence of their own, they provide many useful suggestions for educational practitioners.

Identification and incidence

The Bullock Report referred to evidence that boys retarded in reading were more than twice as likely to show anxiety or lack of concentration (GB.DES, 1975). Studies reviewed by Tansley and Panckhurst (1981) similarly mention an increased incidence of emotional problems associated with poor reading. In the USA Spache (1976) cites some 64 studies which relate emotional maladjustment and reading difficulties to a wide range of problems such as aggression, anxiety and depression. Focusing on the concept of stress, Gentile and McMillan (1987) refer to some 17 studies that describe a connection between emotional disturbance, the resulting loss of concentration and reading difficulty. However, few of the studies cited by the British or the American authors are of recent origin and none are clear about causal relationships. Consequently, definitions of specific learning difficulties, which exclude primary emotional disturbance, become equivocal. The problem of deciding whether the disturbance is the cause, effect or the consequence of other variables remains.

If, as has been argued here, a variety of interrelated factors contribute to a child's difficulties in a complex and incremental way, then teasing out particular social or emotional measures, for the purposes of identification, becomes problematic. Furthermore, research attempting to clarify the relationship between specific learning difficulties and emotional aspects is complicated by the methodological problems of having to operationalize the definitions of both concepts. A lack of consistency then prevents the generalization of findings.

Research by Rourke and his colleagues questions the inevitability of learning difficulties leading to anxiety, low self-esteem and further difficulties (Rourke, 1988). While the evidence is linked to the American term 'learning disabilities' rather than 'specific learning difficulties', the two can be regarded as similar.

Clinical scales specifically designed to evaluate socio-emotional functioning were administered to a sample of 100 learning disabled pupils (Porter and Rourke, 1985). An analysis of results for the whole sample suggested that learning disabled children were not particularly prone to socio-emotional difficulties. However, a multivariate analysis of variance revealed significant differences across four subtypes: 50 per cent of the subjects showed no disturbance; 25 per cent exhibited a profile suggestive of depression and anxiety; approximately 15 per cent were characterized by descriptions related to aggression; 10 per cent exhibited roughly normal socio-emotional functioning accompanied by a variety of somatic complaints.

Similar results, using different measures of socio-emotional functioning, were reported by Speece, McKinney and Applebaum (1985). In their study, one-third of the subjects exhibited completely 'normal' profiles. Finally, an investigation of social competence, conducted by Ackerman and Howes (1986), demonstrated that a significant proportion of learning disabled pupils were regarded as popular with their peers and active in after-school interests.

Taken together, these three studies provide convincing evidence that learning difficulty does not necessarily lead to socio-emotional disturbance. Furthermore, results emphasize the fallacy of assuming that the children are relatively uniform in their socio-emotional functioning. It needs to be noted, however, that the measures used in these studies were in the form of inventories. Results did not draw on clinical assessments or the kinds of detailed observations undertaken in the Butkowsky and Willows (1980) study, described earlier in this chapter in some detail, in which the children showed a lack of persistence and limited expectations of success. Although these 'poor readers' were not necessarily 'disturbed', their approach to learning tasks was adversely affected by their difficulties.

Effectiveness of intervention

It may be possible to increase persistence, expectation of success and motivation by modifying what poor readers say to themselves about their performance. The effectiveness of such techniques, however, needs empirical validation in terms of measured progress.

Interventions typically consist of counselling and self-esteem enhancement (Lawrence, 1973, 1985; Cant and Spackman, 1985). Lawrence's oft-quoted first study suggested that counselling can be undertaken by any sympathetic adult who can create an uncritical atmosphere, provide opportunities for the child to talk about family, friends, anxieties and aspirations and so build up the child's self-esteem. Lawrence provided evidence that the intervention could result in enhanced progress in reading. A searching critique was, however, written by Pumfrey (1979). While being attracted by the use of counselling with children who had reading difficulties, he suggested that Lawrence had overstated his case.

Research evaluating self-esteem enhancement or stress reduction procedures has generally been equivocal. While some studies, not necessarily concerned with specific learning difficulties, have resulted in improved reading test scores (Wooster and Carson, 1982; Hadley, 1988), others convincingly demonstrate superior gains through direct instruction (Sharpley and Rowland, 1986; Somerville and Leach, 1988).

Lawrence's subsequent study goes some way towards resolving this issue (Lawrence, 1985). He postulates that children who receive remedial help with the skills of reading will show higher gains if this help is supplemented by a therapeutic approach aimed at enhancing self-esteem. He then provides results to demonstrate that retarded readers allocated to treatment groups involving Distar (Engelmann, Osborn and Engelmann, 1969) plus counselling or Distar plus drama produce higher gains in reading and in self-esteem when contrasted with those who receive Distar only or no special treatment. The conclusion will seem obvious to applied practitioners: you learn to read through reading and appropriate emotional assistance enhances that learning. The assistance might not require additional drama or counselling sessions but plenty of opportunity for discussion with a sympathetic adult who supports the learner in reading and writing; that is, a 'top-down' approach as described in the first chapter of this section. This is clearly an important area for further research. Its application to that subset of pupils with severe and prolonged literacy difficulties, which may differ qualitatively as well as quantitatively from those of 'poor readers', would be central to the work.

It can be argued that the effectiveness of parental help with literacy is dependent on the warmth and intimacy created between the parent and the child (Young and Tyre, 1983; Miller, 1987). Successful studies illustrate the importance of providing sufficient advice and support to parents, particularly when they become involved in helping their children with learning difficulties. If parents and children are not clear about what they are to do or cannot perceive progress, then the tensions and anxieties described earlier in this chapter easily become exacerbated. Of particular interest is a pilot project in Calderdale, UK, consisting of a summer school for parents and children with specific learning difficulties. It focuses on shared reading for enjoyment and a wide range of other activities not necessarily involving literacy (Poole, 1989). On a broader front, the DES has funded the UKRA to carry out a study of family reading groups (Stuart, 1990).

None of the studies of intervention reviewed in this section have attempted to select subgroups of children with specific learning difficulties and identified emotional problems. As Rourke (1988) points out, simple contrasting group designs ignore the heterogeneity of the population of children both with respect to patterns of cognitive strengths and weaknesses and with respect to particular forms and manifestations of emotional difficulty. If only a proportion of children exhibit marked emotional problems associated with specific learning difficulties, then future studies of intervention should be targeted more carefully to involve them. Meanwhile, of course, sympathetic and supportive instruction should continue to underpin all aspects of education.

Summary

This chapter has considered social and emotional influences from a wide range of theoretical viewpoints. These include socio-political considerations where labels, limited to within-child variables, can detract attention from policies and organization that take account of the full social and interpersonal context in which the learning difficulties arise.

Whilst research has examined the relationships between self-concept and achievement, there is no separate body of work relating to specific learning difficulties. One study of 'poor readers' shows lower expectations of success, a tendency to give up more easily in the face of difficulty and a tendency to attribute success to external causes such as luck. A longitudinal Norwegian study of dyslexic pupils demonstrates the need for more refined research designs which examine the interaction between aptitude, temperament and instruction.

Theoretical aspects of stress management are considered briefly. Fundamental to these approaches is the need to take account of the sense the child is making of the situation and the perceptions of family members. Several American studies show that learning disabilities do not necessarily lead to socio-emotional disturbance. Like the Norwegian research, they emphasize the heterogeneity of the population of children with literacy difficulties. Furthermore, causality is a complex issue. It is often not possible to decide whether emotional disturbance is a cause or effect of the literacy difficulty or a consequence of other variables.

Research evaluating intervention in terms of self-esteem enhancement or stress reduction has generally been equivocal. But the studies reviewed have not attempted to select subgroups of children with identified emotional problems and specific learning difficulties. Such work is, however, complicated by the methodological problems of having to operationalize definitions of both concepts. There is much scope for future research that attempts to involve targeted subgroups and examine processes and outcomes in more detail.

Recommendations

4.1. Specific learning difficulties be examined in the context of personal experiences and interpersonal relationships, recognizing the emotional impact of a prolonged struggle with literacy.

4.2. Educationalists be mindful of the pitfalls that allow labels limited to within-child variables to detract attention from instructional conditions, organizational aspects and general policies.

4.3. No simple dichotomies be drawn between cognitive and affective research.

4.4. The interactions between aptitude, temperament and instruction be examined both in daily practice and in undertaking research into the effects of social and emotional factors on literacy acquisition.

4.5. Aspects such as self-esteem, stress management and the emotional support afforded by more general language experience approaches to literacy be studied.

4.6. Those involved in clinical treatment make available the time to undertake that work thoroughly.

Chapter 5

Cognitive Aspects of Word Recognition

Introduction

This chapter presents a selective overview of recent cognitive research into children's specific literacy problems. This field of research reflects interests of cognitive psychologists and, consequently, gives particular views about the reading and spelling process. Much emphasis is placed upon areas such as 'phonological processing', 'working memory' and 'lexical access'. As outlined by Bertelson, learning to read is regarded as an explicit manipulation of the units that the written symbols stand for: 'the word is where the action is' (Bertelson, 1986).

The term 'psycholinguistic' usually refers to global 'top-down' approaches to reading development (see Chapter 3). Its use has been criticized by Smith (1988), who argues that the term cannot properly be restricted to the areas of contextual prediction and the meaning-getting process (semantics). Ironically, perhaps, the term is probably more appropriate to describe the way cognitive psychologists now perceive the links between language and literacy acquisition. There is growing support for the view that children with specific learning difficulties (dyslexia) have difficulties with language. The focus is on phonology and, possibly, syntax, but not semantics (Vellutino 1979, 1987; Stanovich, 1986). The contribution of within-child variables that are non-language based has suffered significant criticism (Vellutino, 1979, 1987; Bradley, 1990; Bryant, 1990).

The emphasis on phonological processing can be no accident. Intuitively this is the area of language least associated with 'intelligence' as it is typically understood (Stanovich, Cunningham and Freeman, 1984; Ellis and Large, 1987).

The major non-linguistic construct influencing current research is probably 'working memory', which refers to the immediate mental workspace sharing its limited resources between the functions of processing and storage. However, to suggest that children with specific learning difficulties have problems with the higher control processes of working memory can create a dilemma if this is seen in terms of the construct of 'general intelligence' (Oakhill, 1984). A plea can be made for the 'specificity' inherent in the term specific learning difficulties (see Stanovich, 1986).

Specific learning difficulties and immediate verbal memory are presumed to be linked through the nexus of phonological memory, processing and awareness, which can thereby affect the higher processes of working memory (see Jorm, 1983; Shankweiler and Crain, 1986). Several aspects of phonological processing have been put forward as being significantly associated with literacy difficulties. These are phonological awareness, phonological recoding in lexical access (such as naming) and phonetic recoding to maintain information in working memory (such as immediate rehearsal). A useful review and introduction to the concepts and terminology of this field are provided by Wagner and Torgeson (1987).

Developmental models of the acquisition of literacy have been adopted by a growing number of cognitive psychologists. The problems of children with specific learning difficulties are considered in terms of the kind of developmental sequence described below.

Models of development

The developmental aspects of reading and spelling have been modelled by Frith (1985). Notable alternatives are provided by Marsh *et al.* (1981) and Ehri (1985). Although basically similar, the models differ in detail. A comparative review is provided by Snowling (1987).

Both reading and spelling are thought to have fairly independent sequences of development, with reciprocal influences occurring at different stages. The major stages of development are referred to as the 'logographic', the 'alphabetic' and the 'orthographic' (Frith, op. cit.).

The *logographic stage* is basically one in which children recognize words holistically. This would appear to be far more significant for reading than for spelling, since alphabetic information is required for recognizable spelling. The model explains the phenomenon that young children are capable of reading what they cannot spell and spelling what they cannot read, indicating that two separate strategies are involved (Bryant and Bradley, 1980).

The *alphabetic stage* describes the development of letter–sound knowledge, thus allowing reading by grapheme–phoneme correspondence to take place. Much of the development here would seem to be driven by spelling (Mommers, 1987; Cataldo and Ellis, 1988, 1990).

At the *orthographic stage* children read and spell by a more direct route based on an automatic knowledge of the associations between grapho-phonic elements, syntax and semantics. Some children have been labelled 'dysgraphic' because they display difficulty in spelling, not reading. They are presumed to have difficulty at the orthographic stage in that they are only capable of spelling on the basis of letter–sound correspondences (Frith, 1980).

Both Frith and Snowling consider that specific learning difficulties are largely associated with the alphabetic stage. This is where phonology has a major part to play.

The developmental sequence can be regarded as mirroring a traditional progression of teaching in this country from 'look and say' to 'phonics'. Such a teaching approach has probably evolved from assumptions about the simplest way to teach children. It could be argued, however, that the teaching process itself imposes a developmental sequence upon the children. On the other hand, it has also been suggested that the sequence mirrors the evolution of the writing script (Marshall, 1987).

Alternative routes to word recognition

The 'dual route' model has had a major influence on the way readers are thought to approach their task. There are said to be two major forms of access to the printed word: firstly, through the 'direct' route and, secondly, through the

'phonological' route. When a word is processed through the 'direct' route, phonology is not involved. The word is linked directly to semantic processing, that
is the meaning-getting aspects of reading. When a word is processed through the
alternative 'phonological' route it has to be phonemically parsed (sounded out) in
order to be accessed.

The dual route model is increasingly receiving criticism, particularly with
regard to literacy development. A basic separation between the routes may be
untenable (Bertelson, 1986); for example, grapho-phonic (letter–sound) knowledge is probably one of a cluster of cues used by the child. Evidence suggests
that it is a particularly important form of cue for young readers, or for readers at
an equivalently early stage of development (Stanovich, 1980; Reitsma, 1984;
Stuart-Hamilton, 1986).

Links are commonly made with types of 'acquired dyslexia', the 'acquired'
referring to adults who, through some form of neurological damage, have lost
their ability to read and write. For example, some of the adults have difficulty in
reading phonically regular non-words. This is suggestive of an impairment to the
'phonological route'. A case of acquired phonological dyslexia may in this case
be diagnosed.

Parallels have been drawn between subtypes of acquired dyslexia and children
considered to have specific learning difficulties or 'developmental dyslexia'
(Coltheart, 1987a). These approaches have been criticized on at least two
grounds. Firstly, the origins of the 'impairments' may be different: whilst the
adults have achieved literacy and lost it, the children have not acquired literacy
in the first place. Secondly, and perhaps more fundamentally, it cannot necessarily be assumed that children have neurological 'defects' similar to those identified in the adults. As argued by Bryant and Impey (1986), children's difficulties
range from mild to severe and are most constructively regarded as developmental 'delays' rather than permanent 'defects'.

Further analogies have been made between the stages of reading development
drawn up by Frith (1980), types of acquired dyslexia and forms of developmental
dyslexia. Detailed reference to this integrated developmental model is found in
Ellis (1984).

A sophisticated, empirical approach to describing route models of the reading
process has been provided by Seymour (1986, 1987). Seymour describes the difficulties of each individual in his study over a series of assessment tasks. The term
'strategic options' is put forward as a useful alternative to 'dyslexia'. Results for
the whole sample are fairly heterogeneous except that all display some degree of
'impairment' to the 'grapheme–phoneme converter route'; that is, they have problems in encoding letters into sounds and blending them appropriately.

Seymour's research demonstrates that individuals designated as dyslexics may
display a number of cognitive 'impairments', both phonological and visual, that
may range from mild to marked in terms of severity. Visual impairments, for
example, involve the failure of visual analysis at various stages of the reading
process. A comparison is made with children at the orthographic stage of literacy
(see Frith, 1980, earlier in this section). Such children are thought to construct
spellings via phonology and letter–sound associations. The failure of a detailed
visual word analysis is suggested as the cause for specific spelling difficulties.

Seymour does not suggest that the empirical investigations of his research are
suitable for use in assessment by applied practitioners. Nevertheless, some of his
measures, such as those involving reaction time, may eventually prove valuable
in the applied field. The methodology has great potential.

Phonological awareness

An approach concentrating on children's problems in reading, however sophisticated its level of empirical observation and analysis, is essentially descriptive. It does not readily explain causation. The use of younger reading and spelling age-matched control groups can begin to address these issues (Goswami and Bryant, 1990).

Dyslexic and poor readers have been shown to display difficulty with phonologically regular non-words when matched with controls of an equivalent literacy level (Snowling, 1980; Baddeley *et al.*, 1982; Frith and Snowling, 1983; Seymour, 1986, 1987; Holligan and Johnston, 1988). Similarly, those designated as being dyslexic have shown a lower use of phonology (rhyme) in a cued recall task when compared to younger readers (Rack, 1985).

Detailed longitudinal studies are needed to elaborate and explain the more subtle relationships between variables. The most notable predictors of young children's literacy development have been found to be those involving phonological processing or awareness. For example, correlations of 0.53 and 0.75 have been obtained between phoneme reversal tasks given to kindergarteners and first grade readers, a year later (Lundberg, Olafsson and Wall, 1980; Mann, 1984; Wagner and Torgeson, 1987). Similarly, a combined rhyme/alliteration awareness and letter knowledge measure at four years of age accounted for 73 per cent of the variance of reading and 64 per cent of spelling at age six years (Bradley *et al.*, submitted).

All measures of phonological awareness are highly intercorrelated, suggesting that they are measuring a common factor (see Wagner and Torgeson, 1987; Yopp, 1988). Measures of syllabic awareness, although an aspect of phonological awareness, did not make any unique contribution to reading development in the Swedish study. The two uniquely independent contributions were made by the phoneme reversal task and less strongly by the skill of rhyme production. The former is clearly a very explicit measure of phoneme segmentation skills (Lundberg, Olafsson and Wall, 1980).

A re-analysis of the data suggests that measures of rhyme production and syllabic awareness may be distinguished from other measures of phonological awareness (Wagner and Torgeson, 1987). Rhyme awareness has been conceptualized as a form of 'intra-syllabic awareness' based on two phoneme segments (Trieman, 1985; Bryant *et al.*, 1990). The awareness of alliteration is more clearly related to phonemic awareness and segmentation skills. In itself it has been shown to be a powerful predictor at four years of age of phoneme segmentation skills and, more importantly, of reading and spelling (Bryant *et al.*, 1990). Similarly the production and awareness of rhyme from three years of age has been shown to display independent effects upon literacy development (Maclean, Bryant and Bradley, 1987).

A cluster of variables has been distinguished that are directly associated with the acquisition of literacy, but are independent of variables that appear to be closely associated with IQ in their effects on literacy acquisition. For example, the *WISC-R* subtest of Coding appears as an IQ-loaded associate of literacy. In contrast, rhyme awareness, phonological skills and memory span load on the IQ-independent factor of literacy (Ellis and Large, 1987).

The above correlational studies, though impressive, can only prove an association between phonological awareness and literacy attainment. Training studies, such as that of Bradley and Bryant (1983, 1985) and its follow-up by Bradley

(1989), have begun to provide added weight to the view that auditory categorization (phonological awareness) is one of the causal predictors of later reading and spelling.

The significance of rhyming as causal variable has yet to be demonstrated with the use of more stringent criteria; the suggested influence of rhyming remains correlational (Maclean, Bryant and Bradley, 1987). The production of nursery rhymes may be associated with aspects of early phonological sensitivity as yet unmeasured. An interactionist view is that early phonological awareness and sensitivity are part of a language acquisition device with a critical development period (Mann, 1986).

An emphasis on the importance of nursery rhymes links comfortably with the 'top-down' approach to reading development described in Chapter 3. The essentially aesthetic pleasure of engaging in playful speech may result in increased cognitive skill. Similarly, the activity of reading, which follows a little later in the developmental sequence, is thought to have significant effects on children's cognitive development (Stanovich, Cunningham and Freeman, 1984; Stanovich, 1986).

Evaluating the connections

In investigations of Portuguese 'illiterate' adults, it has been shown that they lack phonological awareness, particularly with regard to phonemic segmentation and deletion. This has led to the conclusion that phonemic awareness is achieved as a *consequence* of being literate in an alphabetic and basically phonetic script (Morais *et al.*, 1979, 1986; Bertelson *et al.*, 1985). This is in contrast to the conclusions of the previous section, that phonemic awareness is a *prerequisite* of becoming literate.

A subtle reciprocal interaction between variables seems likely (Stanovich, 1986). If certain cognitive abilities develop as a consequence of the growing reading skills of the child, it may be not only the underlying cognitive functions that dictate the course of reading development but the language experiences associated with the processes of learning to read. The implications are that learners not only learn to read by reading but that many apparently underlying competencies also develop through reading.

This reciprocal interaction between prerequisite and consequent abilities must include the other crucial influences of social, cultural and emotional variables considered in the previous two chapters.

Attempts have been made to evaluate the different phonological variables involved. Two alternative paths of development, extending from the early sensitivity to rhyme, have been suggested. The first, and probably more well known, is that of early rhyming ability influencing the development of phonemic awareness and skill, exemplified by children's use of alliteration. The development of grapheme–phoneme (letter–sound) conversion skills is consequently encouraged. It probably begins with the integration of first and last letter cues to a basically 'logographic' approach to reading.

The alternative path leads directly from rhyme to the use of analogies in reading and spelling. Children are able to take advantage of units of sound larger than phonemes, such as 'beak' and 'peak'. It has been suggested that such use of analogies belongs to the orthographic stage of development (Marsh *et al.*, 1981). However, children at very early developmental stages in reading and spelling also display this ability (Goswami, 1986, 1988). A conception of literacy development in terms of stages may be too rigid. A conception in terms of waves of influences may be more appropriate (Cataldo and Ellis, 1990).

Visuo-spatial knowledge and memory may have a small part to play in the very earliest logographic reading (Ellis and Large, 1988). A more significant effect is that of the immediate visual sequential memory, though the purely visual nature of this measure must be doubted. It is very much a measure involving verbal mediation or encoding (see Vellutino, 1979; Hicks, 1980; Jorm, 1983).

The most crucial influences upon the development of *reading* are ascribed to the following aspects: firstly, phonological awareness, including phoneme segmentation, syllable segmentation and sound blending; secondly, knowledge and recognition of the letters of the alphabet; and thirdly, verbally mediated immediate visual memory span. The higher processing verbal skills, such as vocabulary and syntax, have a reciprocal influence upon the final orthographic reading stage (Ellis and Large, 1988).

Studies of *spelling* have investigated its links with other aspects of development, including literacy. The variable phonemic awareness has been separated into 'implicit phonemic awareness' and 'explicit phonemic awareness'. The former involves the ability to sound match using rhyme and alliteration, assessed by the *Auditory Categorisation Test* of Bradley (1984). The latter, 'explicit' awareness, involves the ability to find and detach individual phonemes, assessed by a phoneme segmentation task (Cataldo and Ellis, 1988, 1990).

'Implicit' phonemic awareness begins as a reciprocal interaction between reading and spelling. 'Explicit' phonemic awareness, however, has an independent effect on the early alphabetic stages of spelling. Spelling would appear to be the mediator for phonological strategies in the acquisition of reading (Ellis and Large, 1988). This is perhaps not surprising taking into account that spelling, unlike reading, begins in earnest mainly from a phonological basis.

Short-term memory

The development of short-term auditory memory span is largely paced by the development of reading itself (Ellis, 1988, 1990; Ellis and Large, 1988). It has not been possible to distinguish poor readers or dyslexic children from equivalent ability younger readers on measures of memory span (Hulme, 1981a, b; Johnston, 1982). A relatively poor memory span does, however, appear to be strongly associated with reading ability in reading retarded children (Johnston, Rugg and Scott, 1987).

Short-term visual–sequential memory appears to be associated more with sound blending and phonological skills than does auditory short-term memory (Ellis, 1990). At first glance this seems surprising; however, phonological ability may determine the extent of verbal mediation and the rehearsal of visual symbols. With auditory presentation, phonological storage is obligatory (Salame and Baddeley, 1982); with visual presentation phonological storage is under strategic control. Children need to develop an appropriate strategy for rehearsing the names of a sequence of objects (Keeney, Canizzo and Flavell, 1967).

Another, related influence on visual memory span is the speed and ability to name stimuli (Spring and Capps, 1974; Ellis, 1990). Naming difficulties have been implicated as a problem for dyslexic children, particularly since Denckla and Rudel's (1976) study of rapid automatized naming. In an excellent review of the relationship between short-term memory and reading retardation, Jorm (1983) suggests that the difficulty can be accounted for in terms of the retrieval of phonological codes stored in long-term memory.

Bryant and Bradley (1985) suggest that most of the phonological memory problems described by Jorm could be due to the lack of literacy skill. A replication of the name-finding study found that naming speed was directly related to the phonological complexity of the words and that poor readers had relatively more difficulty than better readers (Katz, 1986). It is easy to see how naming speed may be interpreted as being a product of reading. A simple explanation for such naming speed deficits is that 'dyslexic' children have less practice in speech–motor encoding than do normal readers (Spring and Capps, 1974). Consequently, the best practice of 'articulatory encoding of visual stimuli' (naming) may be provided by the activity of reading itself.

'Auditory memory span' has been related to the topic of 'developmental dyslexia' (Rugel, 1974; Thomson, 1982; Lawson and Inglis, 1985; Ellis and Large, 1987). It has often been regarded as one of the identifiers of specific learning difficulties (Naidoo, 1972; Miles, 1983a, b; Thomson, 1989). It should be noted, however, that the reciting of number sequences, the measure commonly used for assessing 'auditory memory span', does not distinguish between the various phonological aspects of memory described above.

There is a small amount of evidence relating to the independent effects of sentence memory span on literacy development. A correlation of 0.36 has been found between pre-school memory span and later reading comprehension (Jorm et al., 1984). However, any effects of possible early literacy development were not taken into account.

The association between memory span and reading comprehension would appear to be more robust than that between memory span and reading accuracy. Once decoding difficulties have been taken into account, it may be that measures of sentence memory span and literal reading comprehension are probing equivalent activities. Recently, correlations as high as 0.57 have been obtained between sentence memory span and comprehension with a sample of older primary-aged children (Hulme, 1988).

Speed of articulation of words has been linked with the memory span of young children (Hulme et al., 1984). Explanations are based on the 'working memory' model. It is argued that the 'articulatory rehearsal loop', through repetition, extends the time limit of the short-term phonological store (Baddeley et al., 1975). The speed at which a child can covertly or overtly articulate words is consequently related to memory span. Auditory memory span thus appears to develop in association with reading (Johnston, Rugg and Scott, 1987).

Part of the difficulty of those designated as dyslexic is revealed in tasks requiring non-word repetition. Dyslexic children have been shown to display more difficulty with such tasks than reading age-matched younger children (Snowling et al., 1986).

This returns the discussion to the link between linguistic and immediate verbal memory deficits. Language disordered children are known to display specific difficulty in immediate auditory memory span. Their difficulties cannot be explained away as being the consequence of general verbal ability, speed of articulation or reading ability. It is thought that they have a capacity limitation in the phonological short-term store of working memory. Consequently, it is assumed that young language disabled children suffer from a lack of sufficient opportunity to establish 'phonological representations' through repetition (Gathercole and Baddeley, 1990).

The extent of shared variance between phonological memory and vocabulary growth has been demonstrated in a longitudinal study by Gathercole and Baddeley (1989). They also suggest a critical period for the influence of phonological memory (Gathercole and Baddeley, 1990). Thus it seems that vocabulary, speech and phonology must be closely interlinked in the study of 'short-term' or 'working' memory associated with the early stages of literacy development.

Sequencing

Sequencing difficulties are associated with traditional notions of dyslexia. It is not clear whether sequencing is a problem in the acquisition of literacy. One study has shown that between 4 per cent and 19 per cent of the errors made by young, poor readers can be ascribed to reversed sequences (Liberman *et al.*, 1971). Terms such as auditory or visual sequential memory abound in the literature. According to many researchers both can be accounted for by the notion of immediate verbal memory span (Velluntino, 1979; Hicks, 1980; Jorm, 1983). Even a phenomenon as extreme as mirror writing has been explained as due simply to inadequate learning of the directional skills of literacy (Velluntino, 1987). A study by Hulme makes pertinent observations. He considers memory for individual phonological items to be the source of difficulties previously ascribed to sequencing (Hulme, 1981a, b). A clear account of why short-term auditory or phonological storage is subject to sequential errors is provided by Frick (1988).

There have been suggestions that children with specific learning difficulties (dyslexia) have a more basic and central sequencing deficit (see Singleton, 1988), and that such problems can be displayed motorically through irregular eye movements (Pavlidis, 1981a, b, 1990a). It would seem, however, that the most parsimonious explanation for typical errors would be inadequate learning experience and limited auditory memory span.

Comprehension

Children with specific learning difficulties are not usually regarded as having problems with comprehension. It is possible, however, to have both (Bishop, 1989a).

An 'interactive–compensatory' view suggests that readers use any available resource in order to read a given text. These resources include visual, graphemic, phonological, syntactic and contextual information. If children with specific learning difficulties have problems with one aspect, say phonology, they will attempt to compensate by using other resources, such as context (Stanovich, 1980; Potter, 1982; Harding, 1984). A detailed review is provided by Stanovich (1986), who also criticizes approaches recommending contextual guessing alone.

Various aspects of short-term memory impinge on comprehension (Hulme, 1988). Long sequences of text involving multiclausal sentences make obvious demands (Kleiman, 1975; Glanzer, Fischer and Dorfman, 1984; Yuill and Oakhill, 1988). Problems with decoding create major problems with comprehension, affecting attempts at the short-term storage of words (Perfetti and Lesgold,

1977). Although there is clearly a link between decoding skills and comprehension, it should be noted that the association is far from perfect (Mommers, 1987).

Views have been put forward implicating the higher control processes of working memory. Those with poor comprehension are not reported as having difficulty with simple memory tasks, such as reciting digits (Perfetti and Lesgold, 1977; Daneman and Carpenter, 1980; Baker, 1985). It has been suggested that learners with poor comprehension and adequate decoding skills may have difficulty in the constructive aspects of thinking and remembering (Oakhill, 1982). It is difficult, however, to distinguish between causal factors linked to thought and understanding, and those involving complex working memory processes (Yuill, Oakhill and Parkin, 1989).

Profiles and the identification of subtypes

Some subtype conceptions have already been described in this chapter. They relate to the 'dual route' models where analogies are sought between 'acquired dyslexia' and 'developmental dyslexia' (Ellis, 1984). More traditional subtype groupings, tending to stress auditory/visual differences, are reviewed by Thomson (1989). In both approaches to the identification of subtypes, the visual group forms a minority of the specific learning difficulty (dyslexia) population. Furthermore, there is a developing trend to relate such groupings not to difficulties with the visual system but to difficulties at the orthographic stage, described previously.

Although Seymour (1986) could find no clear subtype groupings amongst his small number of subjects, despite identifying a variety of 'impairments', larger surveys have found 'clusterings' using a range of statistical techniques. One study, involving the Aston Index, found two factors in groups of poor reading and dyslexic children, an auditory factor and a verbal labelling factor (Hicks and Spurgeon, 1982). The utility of this distinction was unknown. The verbal labelling factor was simply a new name for some of the subtest items initially regarded as representing visual channel difficulties.

More recently, three subgroups of 'dyslexic' children have been identified on the basis of their test results on the *British Ability Scales (BAS)* (Elliott and Tyler, 1987; Tyler, 1990). The largest grouping was that referred to as having a 'sequential processing deficit' where the children's performance was relatively weaker on the scales of Information Processing, Recall of Digits, Basic Arithmetic, Immediate Memory for Visual Recall, and Delayed Memory for Visual Recall. The last two scales were assumed to assess skills associated with verbal mediation (Elliott, 1983). An interesting facet was that the subscale of Recall of Digits stood out as the weakest correlate of this cluster. The other two groupings were designated as the 'holistic retrieval of information' and the 'mixed' groups. The problem with the former group was that only two subscales, Word Definitions and Recall of Designs, stood out as problematic for the 'holistic dyslexic' children. Further work is in progress in assigning poor readers to each of the above subtypes (Tyler and Elliott, in preparation). Whilst the research is of interest, it does not currently have any direct implications for intervention.

A difficulty with statistical techniques that search for factors or clusters in a collection of subtests is that the results depend on what has been included in the calculation; the variables defining the subtypes have to be there in the first place. Consequently, an analysis of the normative data of the *Revised Wechsler Intel-*

ligence Scale for Children (WISC-R) resulted in a replication of the general structure of the test (Lawson and Inglis, 1984, 1985). There were two bipolar factors, one loading on Full Scale IQ and the other on the Verbal Performance continuum. The high loading subtests for the verbal factor were Digit Span, Arithmetic, Coding and Information, those subtests children with specific learning difficulties commonly have difficulty with. This was seen to support the notion of a verbal processing deficit. The researchers concluded that the children had a left hemisphere deficit (see Chapter 9). Their evidence was, however, only correlational.

A 'sequencing factor' involving the subtests of Arithmetic, Coding and Digit Span was also shown to be predictive of later reading difficulties (Bannatyne, 1974), but it did not distinguish between 'slow starters' and 'long-term failures' (McKay, Neale and Thompson, 1985). The direction of the effect was also unclear: did the sequencing problems cause a difficulty with literacy or did a difficulty with literacy cause children to perform badly on the particular subtests? Twin study evidence has indicated that there may be a genetic basis (Ho, Gilger and Decker, 1988). As discussed earlier in this chapter, these subtests might largely reflect problems regarding auditory memory span and inadequate learning experiences.

Identification in terms of 'subtypes' or 'profiles' is only useful to the child if some form of curricular advantage follows. This is not typically the case. At present, the results of the statistical approaches described in this section are more important to the researcher than to the practitioner (see Chapter 9).

Identification of the 'specifically reading retarded' child

Attempts have been made to distinguish between the 'specifically reading retarded' child and those who are more generally 'backward readers'. The Isle of Wight Study is regarded as a 'classic' in this field (Rutter, Tizard and Whitmore, 1970). Significant marking characteristics have been found to involve linguistic abilities rather than motor abnormalities (Rutter and Yule, 1975).

A replication in Dunedin, New Zealand, with a younger and smaller cohort, did not fully duplicate the findings of the Isle of Wight Study. At the ages of three and five years the specifically reading retarded child did not display the verbal disabilities predicted by the Isle of Wight Study. Only with pupils aged seven and, more significantly, nine years, were the verbal deficits identified (Share and Silva, 1986; Share *et al.*, 1987).

The Dunedin study provides support for the view that a general verbal or language deficit is a consequence of and not a cause of the acquisition of literacy (Stanovich, 1986). At the pre-reading stage 'specifically reading retarded' children have difficulty only with early literacy skills, such as letter naming, and the ubiquitous phonological deficits (Jorm *et al.*, 1986).

More controversially, no basic differences are suggested between 'specifically reading retarded' and 'reading backward' children. It is argued that all of the supposed marking characteristics of 'specifically reading retarded' children are statistical artefacts (Share *et al.*, 1987). These include the even higher ratio of boys to girls and their poorer prognosis of attainment in literacy (Yule, 1973; Rutter and Yule, 1975).

It has further been suggested that typical test profile differences between 'specifically reading retarded' and reading backward children are psychometric selection effects. Thus verbal subtest deficits on the *WISC-R* are ascribed to correlations of verbal intelligence with school achievement. The difference between groups is posited as being totally due to the expected large variance on the Performance subtests. The viewpoint may become even more controversial when applied to the ACID profile on the *WISC-R* (relatively low scores on Arithmetic, Coding, Information, and Digit span subtests) commonly associated with specific learning difficulties. It could again be argued that the profile is merely a correlate of school achievement (van der Wissel, 1987). Cogent arguments against the views of van der Wissel have been made (Tyler and Elliott, 1988; Elliott, 1989). If children with specific learning difficulties can be considered in relation to 'subtypes', research may eventually suggest different paths towards the acquisition of literacy.

The Isle of Wight Study indicated that there was a 'hump' at the lower end of the normal distribution of reading achievement suggesting a distinct reading retarded group of children (Yule *et al.*, 1974). More recent studies have not replicated that finding and have concluded that the 'hump' is a statistical artefact (Rodgers, 1983; van der Wissel and Zegers, 1985; Share *et al.*, 1987). However, a 'tiny hump' was noted in a recent large survey (Dobbins, 1988). Much current research is now predicated on the assumption that continuous cognitive influences on the process of literacy acquisition are being observed (Seymour, 1986). The concurrent existence of both commonalities and differences between pupils with and without specific learning difficulties is to be expected.

Identification of the 'clumsy' child

In this chapter it has been assumed that specific learning difficulties are largely associated with the areas of language and speech. The problems of clumsiness, considered a marker of dyslexia by neurologists such as Critchley (1970), have not appeared as significant. It is, of course, likely that motor difficulties predict handwriting and spelling difficulties (Jorm *et al.*, 1986). It can be argued that the apparent success of multisensory teaching has been due to a reliance on motoric memory as opposed to a reliance on deficient phonological memory (Hulme, 1981a, b). Automatization is important (Fawcett, 1989; Lamm, 1989).

There is a clear overlap of problems associated with 'clumsy' children and those of speech disordered children. Comparisons can therefore be made between children labelled 'dyspraxic' (clumsy) and children labelled 'dyslexic' (Snowling and Stackhouse, 1983; Snowling, 1987). The production of speech is a motoric function. However, simple motoric problems cannot be regarded as the primary problem with regard to literacy (Bishop and Robson, 1989).

Clumsiness itself has a conceptual 'specificity' although it is a heterogeneous condition. A discussion of relevant approaches to assessment is provided by Henderson (1987). Clumsiness is often found to be an associate of more generalized learning difficulties (Rutter and Yule, 1975; Silva, McGee and Williams, 1985; Jorm *et al.*, 1986; Share *et al.*, 1987; Lam and Henderson, 1987). Nevertheless, the concept of 'specific' motoric disorder seems appropriate in that some clumsy children are of superior intelligence (Losse *et al.*, 1991).

A claim has been made for the primacy of visual perceptual factors (Lord and Hulme, 1988). This is supported by lower scores on the Performance scales of the *WISC-R* (Hulme *et al.*, 1982). There is also some evidence for verbal or vocabulary decline (Losse *et al.*, op. cit.). This can be explained as being a consequence of general educational and literacy difficulties.

Evidence indicates that the problems of the seriously clumsy child are persistent and pervasive, and may also involve specific learning difficulties. The prognosis is not too optimistic with regard to maturation and remediation. Early identification is nevertheless important in promoting positive labelling, as behavioural difficulties and low self-esteem are often associates of 'clumsiness' (Losse et al., op. cit.).

Identification of children with phonological difficulties

For the purposes of cognitive research, tests have been designed to refine the observation of the inferred underlying processes, such as compound phonemic awareness (Yopp, 1988). This, in turn, may be related to the notions of implicit and explicit phonemic awareness described earlier in this chapter (Ellis, 1990).

The simplest form of test of auditory discrimination is probably that devised by Wepman (1975), in which the child decides whether words such as 'sip' and 'tip' sound the same or different. More complex tasks are represented by the *Auditory Categorisation Test* (Bradley, 1984) in which the child selects the odd one out from three words, such as 'hat, mat, fan'. The complexity of the task is also influenced by the working memory load required (see Wagner and Torgeson, 1987). A recent adaptation of this test has therefore included the use of pictures to lighten the memory load. In typical tests of phonemic blending the tester utters phonemes such as 'c-o-l-d' and the child blends them orally to make the appropriate word. The range of tests used suggests a developmental progression associated with the development of word recognition itself.

Other aspects, such as the ability to repeat phonologically regular non-words, or even a series of non-words, may be assessed. This type of test is now commercially published (Gathercole and Baddeley, 1990). A diagnostic comparison can also be made between the reading and spelling of regular and irregular words (Boder and Jarrico, 1982).

In the context of educational practice, however, phonological difficulties are best identified through a series of criterion-referenced assessments to determine which learning targets have been achieved. These range from alliteration and rhyming to the use of complex phonological cues. Such methods are described in the psychoeducational section of this book. Difficulties with phonological processing may also be observed informally, involving the recognition of miscues in reading, 'bizarre' spelling, immature or deviant speech patterns, difficulties in word recall or the observation of rhyming and alliteration while enjoying the content of the story or rhyme.

Implications for teaching

It was suggested earlier in this chapter that spelling could be a major factor deciding the pace of development of word reading (Mommers, 1987; Cataldo and Ellis, 1990). Children would need to attend to both alphabetic and orthographic aspects of reading in order to write words correctly. Spelling practice can thus be regarded as a form of multisensory teaching, involving motoric memory as well as auditory and visual input, particularly if words are sounded out in the process. That way of teaching is indeed emphasized in the 'simultaneous oral spelling' suggested by Bradley (1981) (see Chapter 7 for details of the procedure).

Psychological theory related to word recognition does not match educational practice in any clear way. Indeed, different implications can be drawn from the same evidence depending on the educational preferences of the teacher. It is, for example, quite reasonable to assume that phonological awareness can be achieved through the enjoyable experience of nursery rhymes and stories. Alternatively, however, it can be argued that at least some children require carefully planned and repetitive practice of that 'awareness'. These issues are discussed in more detail in Chapters 3 and 6.

A developmental view, limited to print recognition and reproduction, would imply a sequence of teaching aims roughly related to the age of the child. It would tend to ignore the broader linguistic aspect of literacy. Oral and rhyming activities would be recommended at the earliest pre-school stage. Prior to the onset of literacy, around the age of four years, alliterative activities would be required in combination with other activities emphasizing the development of phonemic awareness. At age five years, children would start to develop a 'sight vocabulary' (the logographic stage) and would be taught to recognize letter sounds. At around the age of six years children would begin to map independently their phonological representations. At this stage spelling would be taught by a combination of verbal/phonological and handwriting/motoric approaches. Fully independent reading would be expected to begin at age seven years and onwards.

Children failing at any particular stage, due to lack of appropriate intervention or to more organic reasons, would be regarded as having special educational needs. Further enrichment at the problematic stage would be required, together with more systematic and repetitive practice.

The instructional sequence outlined above does not take account of the range of educational methodologies. As described in Chapter 3, it would be regarded by some as presenting a very narrow view of literacy. It should be noted, therefore, that research into the cognitive processes involved in print recognition and reproduction is not the same as research into methods of teaching reading. Many cognitive psychologists do not think of their research from an educational standpoint. Their first aim is a conceptualization of the underlying processes themselves.

Summary

This chapter has focused largely on psychological aspects of print recognition and reproduction and, of necessity, it has only been possible to give short summaries of the extensive work that has been undertaken. Nevertheless, it is hoped that the references provided will enable interested readers to acquire a more thorough knowledge of the field.

The research reported here has covered the following main areas:
- developmental stages associated with the acquisition of word recognition and reproduction;
- models of the reading process drawing on work concerned with 'acquired dyslexia';
- different aspects of phonology, particularly phonological awareness;
- the effects of 'short-term' or 'working' memory on word recognition;
- attempts to link possible subtypes with the results of normative testing.

None of the research has been conclusive and further work is essential in these important areas. Currently, therefore, it should be recognized that cognitive research does not yet offer agreed methodologies for identifying different kinds of deficits that relate directly to specific forms of educational intervention.

It appears, however, that children with specific learning difficulties have particular problems at the level of phonological processing. What is known of the origins of these problems is both complex and limited. It is thought that learners' capacity may be limited in the phonological short-term store of working memory. Educational implications would emphasize the provision of sufficient opportunity to establish phonological awareness and phonological representations through repetition, or using alternative compensatory strengths.

Far more work is needed to investigate the relationship between linguistic difficulties and literacy. In particular, the onset and interaction of the differing forms of phonological and language difficulties require further research. Relevant training studies are also needed, both to illuminate presenting characteristics and to assist with the development of teaching approaches.

Some have regarded specific learning difficulties to be caused by relatively minor cognitive problems that are exacerbated by lack of appropriate opportunities to learn. Others have assumed, in contrast, that the difficulties mirror cognitive impairments that can only be alleviated or circumvented, but not overcome or 'cured'. These viewpoints reflect different conceptions of the relative roles played by 'nature' and 'nurture'. Currently, however, cognitive research into children's literacy problems provides little evidence in either direction, and it would seem logical to suggest an interactionist perspective. Those struggling with what will seem to them a lifelong disability would certainly emphasize constitutional aspects. They may represent the extreme of what might be regarded as a continuum of specific learning difficulties ranging from mild to severe. They might also have qualitatively distinctive but varied patterns of intra-individual differences that may respond differentially to various pedagogic interventions. The search for aptitude × intervention interactions should continue.

Recommendations

5.1. Teachers and other adults engaged in pre-school work place an increasing emphasis upon oral activities, emphasizing rhyme, rhythm and repetition in playful speech with all pupils.

5.2. Educational psychologists and teachers continue to develop skills and methods to effect the early identification of children who are at risk of poor literacy development.

5.3. Further techniques be developed to assist with the cognitive and linguistic weaknesses of children with specific learning difficulties, involving educational psychologists, teachers and speech therapists.

5.4. Educational practitioners keep up to date with, and contribute to, psychological research concerning specific learning difficulties, always questioning underlying assumptions and paradigms.

5.5. The search for aptitude × intervention interactions be actively pursued.

SECTION C: PSYCHOEDUCATIONAL RESPONSES

This section includes descriptions and discussions of the theoretical aspects of specific learning difficulties (dyslexia) and links these with the educational responses to such learning difficulties. The issues addressed include identification, interventions and their evaluation, and the organization of support services for pupils with learning difficulties and with specific learning difficulties. The financial implications of provision in an LEA, in relation to the incidence of specific learning difficulties, are also considered. The views of Her Majesty's Inspectorate concerning the organization and efficacy of support services at primary and secondary stages are outlined and discussed. Consideration is given to the importance of INSET in better equipping teachers to address the special educational needs of individuals and groups of pupils within the context of a whole-school philosophy aimed at optimizing access to the National Curriculum for all pupils.

Chapter 6

Psychoeducational Literature: Theory and Identification

Introduction

> My child has problems in learning how to read, write and spell. There's no reason that I can see. He's unhappy. He needs help. I don't care what you call this problem – specific learning difficulties, dyslexia, or whatever. We all know it's a very real misery-making monster. Please do something to help, and quickly.

For better or for worse, many professionals involved with pupils having SpLD, and parents whose children have such learning difficulties, are less concerned with the theoretical and technical niceties of incontrovertible assessments, incidence estimates and diagnoses. In the interests of their pupils and children, they typically consider that they must not become immobilized, impaled on the spears of professional indecisiveness. Their inclination is to do something constructive, and to do it as soon as a difficulty is noticed. The argument that good practice will drive out bad theory has a strong appeal. Their entirely legitimate concern is that something is done for the child. If some action is taken, it might be effective. If nothing is done, hope is lost. The difficulties become compounded. To wait until the experts have agreed methods of diagnosis and fully effective means of intervention is to condemn many children to illiteracy. The perfect is seen as the enemy of the better. Such understandable imperatives must be acknowledged and responded to by professionals. These imperatives must not, however, undermine a commitment by professionals to develop better models and identification techniques that will be of assistance in devising increasingly effective interventions. To engage in this venture, it is essential to know what work is in hand in both these areas. It is towards this end that Chapters 6 and 7 are presented.

Much has been written on the theoretical basis and identification of SpLD from a psychoeducational perspective. A detailed description of recent work would be a book in its own right. Consequently, this chapter aims to provide only an outline of the field. It will also provide pointers to some of the identification techniques used and to the theoretical issues relating to their uses and limitations.

Theoretical considerations

The identification of SpLD is contentious for the reasons outlined in previous chapters. It follows that, in the absence of an agreed theoretical model of SpLD, estimates of its incidence will inevitably vary. Even if there *was* an agreed conceptual basis of SpLD, its operational definition would still present difficulties as such empirical techniques involve cut-off points that are typically arbitrary.

There are many supporters of a lexical encoding deficiency hypothesis as a basis for conceptualizing and alleviating SpLD (Ellis and Miles, 1981; Miles and Ellis, 1981; Miles and Miles, 1990). Other workers who are equally actively involved in the assessment and teaching of pupils with SpLD disagree (Brown, 1990). Many workers consider that groups and individuals with qualitatively different learning abilities and styles exist (Carbo, Dunn and Dunn, 1986; Gjessing and Karlsen, 1989; Tyler, 1990). Identifying these groups is considered essential. Because of such differences, it is argued that the nature and content of learning materials, and the ways in which these are presented to and are interacted with by children, are important contributors to their progress towards literacy. Others see predominantly quantitative differences (Bryant, 1990). Some workers consider both qualitative and quantitative inter- and intra-individual differences to be important in conceptualizing and identifying SpLD.

In the absence of a conceptual consensus at either the psychological, educational or neuropsychological levels, explorations will continue into various approaches to construing the issues involved, operationally defining identification techniques and estimating the incidence of SpLD.

Given the present state of knowledge, dogmatic assertions concerning either the conceptual basis or the incidence of SpLD should be treated with caution.

In its wisdom, the law in the UK (and elsewhere) recognizes the existence of SpLD and the need to identify and alleviate such learning difficulties. The challenging task of implementing such a policy in England and Wales lies with LEAs and their professional staff. This is possible only to the extent that the 'syndrome' of SpLD has a valid theoretical basis and its aetiology, presenting characteristics, prognosis and response to interventions meet the criteria discussed in Chapter 1.

Reading acquisition

From the undoubted inter- and intra-individual differences in both the underlying processes and the manifestations of attainments in literacy and numeracy, the downward slope to deviations, difficulties and deficits is an ever-present danger and temptation. Difficulties with written language are seen as central to the problems of SpLD. The understanding and identification of these difficulties are best approached in the context of current theories of language development in general and of reading acquisition in particular. The acquisition of language skills is generally acknowledged to be a developmental process. 'Bottom-up' theorists see reading as the 'sequential processing of information from print to meaning' (see Chapter 3). They call for the development of subskills, favour phonic teaching and consider both the implicit and the explicit awareness of the phonemic structure of language to be essential. In contrast, 'top-down' theorists view reading development in terms of hypothesis generation and testing in which 'letter and word perception is controlled by linguistic context'. They emphasize language experience methods and draw attention to the differences between spoken and written language (Forness and Kavale, 1983; Pumfrey, 1991) (see Chapter 3 for a more extensive discussion).

More recently, syntheses of these apparently opposing views have been emerging in interactive models of information processing (Rummelhart and Speaker, 1985; Reason et al., 1988; Reason, 1990b; Pumfrey, 1991). Snowling (1987) presents a model of the interaction between decoding (phonological and whole word) and semantic processing. Frith (1981) considers information processing models as a theoretical breakthrough giving rise to new suggestions for helping pupils with SpLD. Holistic and serial information processing can be integrated within cognitive-development models of literacy development.

The International Reading Association has produced one of the most helpful compendiums in the above field entitled *Theoretical Models and Processes of Reading*, now in its third edition (Singer and Ruddell, 1985). This book is an essential antidote to oversimplified assumptions concerning the complexities involved.

Reading disability

Theories of reading disabilities follow from acquisition theories. 'Top-down' theorists consider that breaking down a language process, such as reading, into its constituent subskills actually thwarts acquisition, making it unnatural and meaningless. The suggestion that '...the cure for dyslexia is to learn to read' (Smith, 1973) may well be questionable both logically and theoretically, but it has a popular appeal and a theoretical basis in psycholinguistics.

'Bottom-up' theories have a somewhat longer history in connection with the alleviation of SpLD. The function-deficit models represent one strand of development. These aim to develop, for example, visual or auditory perception, discrimination, memory and other skills deemed to underpin language attainments and progress. For example, the educationally oriented work of Frostig in this field was extremely influential some 30 years ago. Because visual perception was seen as an important underpinning process that could be assessed, and it was also seen as amenable to improvement, specialized training programmes were devised. The Frostig–Horne Perceptual Development Programme was one such system (Frostig, Lefever and Whittlesea, 1964, 1966). A number of diagnostic tests are given to identify visual–perceptual strengths and weaknesses. After this assessment, a series of up to 359 worksheets could be prescribed with the aim of improving a pupil's visual–perceptual skills. Later research cast doubts on the validity of the theoretical basis of the associated identification procedures and the subsequent interventions. Such improvements in visual–perceptual skills as were made did not transfer to improvements in reading or learning disabilities. Had they done so, the materials would have increased in popularity and would have been in common use today. This is not to say that either the avenue, or the specific materials, have no utility.

The parents and teachers of pupils having SpLD have often turned to this and other similar identification and training programmes. The results were not encouraging. The American Academy of Pediatrics, the American Academy of Ophthalmology and Otolaryngology and the American Association of Ophthalmology were severely critical. They issued a joint statement asserting that visual training was ineffective in treating learning disabilities and could even cause a delay in the provision of adequate treatment (Dreby, 1979).

It is a field in which research continues. The development of a technique for identifying dyslexia *before* a child has started to read was researched at the University of Manchester in the UK and has been further developed at the George Washington University in the USA (Pavlidis, 1990a, b), and now in Greece at the University of Saloniki. Based on the child's ability to track patterns presented by an array of light-emitting diodes, Pavlidis is currently studying the modifiability of such patterns of eye movements. Whether this will prove to be a cul-de-sac or a Royal Road to the diagnosis and alleviation of dyslexia remains to be determined (see Chapter 10 for a fuller consideration of psycho-ophthalmo-logical issues) (Pavlidis, 1990b).

Set within a broader theoretical framework that accepts the existence of both visual and auditory dyslexias, work on the identification of poor visual memory and its effects on children's reading and writing continues. A stimulating account of work carried out in this field at an American reading centre was presented at the 1990 UKRA Conference (Huston, 1990). At the reading centre, where Huston is director, this work is linked to individualized programmes that are shown to have beneficial effects. It is clear that the field cannot be ignored, but must be considered within the context of language development in general. Her book describing the wider work of the centre contains valuable suggestions concerning the identification of dyslexias and their alleviation (Huston, 1987).

The research by Kirk and his co-workers leading to the development of the Illinois Test of Psycholinguistic Abilities has come under serious criticism (Newcomer and Hammill, 1976). This led to a continuing debate concerning Kirk *et al.*'s theorizing and its applications in the identification and alleviation of SpLD. Indeed, Kirk's involvement in the field has been seminal, and continues (see Chapter 1). The ideas for alleviation that Kirk and his colleagues advocated have been shown to be of considerable value in work with underprivileged pupils with severe reading difficulties (Kirk and Kirk, 1971). Pupils' psycholinguistic abilities and reading attainments improved significantly, despite an apparent gap between Kirk's theorizing and his educational interventions (Naylor and Pumfrey, 1983).

Nowadays, work emphasizing the importance of phonological awareness in the development of literacy abilities is commonplace (see Chapter 5). Many earlier workers, including the Kirks, were well aware of this issue. Whilst the model of communication which the Kirks's developed and tested has many weaknesses, its recognition of (a) channels of communication (auditory–vocal, visual–motor); (b) processes (reception, organization, expression); and (c) levels of organization (automatic, representational) and their integration in a single framework had much to commend it, despite inadequacies that have subsequently been identified.

The nature and identification of specific learning difficulties

In assessing children suspected of having SpLD, it is essential that a variety of possible sensory causes be investigated. If this is not done, a misdiagnosis may occur and an inappropriate intervention may be prescribed. Help in the alleviation of the sensory difficulty may be disastrously delayed as a consequence. An excellent introduction to this important aspect of assessment has been written by a teacher who has carried out research and diagnostic work at the Learning Difficulties Clinic of St Thomas's Hospital, London, for over ten years (Quin and MacAuslan, 1986).

The importance of having such a child's hearing and speech tested when hearing impairment is suspected cannot be overemphasized (Markides, 1983). At a basic level, one-sided hearing, partial or intermittent hearing losses, infections of the middle ear in early life, 'glue ear' and other auditory problems may adversely affect learning. The educational implications of impaired hearing have been well-considered in a recent book in the extensive series *Special Needs in Ordinary Schools* (Webster and Wood, 1989).

Similarly, sight should be tested. Poor eyesight, squinting, 'wobbly' eyes and the identification of the reference eye can have important diagnostic implications for interventions (see Chapter 10). To provide an adequate education for the visually handicapped child will require full use of the considerable body of expertise that exists in this field (Chapman and Stone, 1988).

As noted earlier, responses to SpLD are strongly influenced by opinions concerning the nature of the condition itself. There is no disagreement about the existence of children experiencing unusual and unexpected difficulties in becoming literate. The severe, long-standing and intractable nature of these difficulties in many cases is well documented by professionals and by individuals who have experienced such learning difficulties (see Chapter 1). Equally, it is agreed that such children (and adults) need help. Differences arise concerning how the need for such help can be identified. Whether the disability is part of a continuum of attainments ranging from, for example, a competent reader to semi-literate or illiterate (Bryant, 1985; 1990), or whether pupils with SpLD are qualitatively different from other readers (Ellis and Miles, 1981; Frith, 1985; Temple, 1986; Snowling, 1987, 1990). Bryant argues for early interventions that will help all children and '...will take a step towards the eradication of dyslexia before it develops' (Bryant, 1985).

Many who support the contention that children with reading difficulties do not differ qualitatively from each other would affirm the argument presented in the

Tizard Report (*Children with Specific Reading Difficulties*) that, whilst recognizing the existence of a subgroup of pupils with specific reading retardation who have particular characteristic and specific difficulties and instructional needs, *all* children with reading difficulties should receive remedial teaching and no one group can benefit more, or is in greater need (Fredman, 1989). A move away from such classifications towards a more process-oriented approach, with emphasis on reading strategies and individual prescriptions, has many advocates (Fredman and Stevenson, 1988). Others support the view that '...the kinds of teaching procedures used for slow learners and generally backward readers are not particularly appropriate' for the dyslexic child (Thomson, 1984).

There are a number of special schools and centres whose entire work involves the assessment and teaching of pupils with SpLD. Some of these establishments have been formally recognized as efficient by the DES. Many of the schools are independent. LEAs will, in certain circumstances, use these facilities. Although there is considerable overlap, the diagnostic techniques, teaching methods and programmes used in specialist schools tend to vary in their focus, intensity and kind from that taking place in most mainstream schools for such pupils, unless the LEA has a specially trained and well-resourced support service for this purpose (see Chapter 8). Thus it has been asserted that dyslexic children need *special* help with phonological processing, whereas the general population of poor readers needs all-round help (Ellis and Large, 1987). (Information on specialist teaching programmes is presented in Chapter 7.)

If a child is identified as having SpLD and a Statement is prepared in agreement with the interested parties recommending that the child should be educated at, say, a residential school specializing in the education of pupils with SpLD, the LEA will be faced with important financial consequences (see Chapter 8). Many parents who believe that their child has SpLD would like such provision, although most could not afford the cost. In a number of court cases, LEA 'within-school' support has been portrayed as a less effective, even inadequate, form of provision whereby the authority meets its legal obligations under the requirements of the Education Act 1981, or has failed to meet them. In view of the inherent uncertainties in identification indicated earlier, this point highlights a continuing concern that parents and voluntary bodies are likely to come into conflict with LEAs on issues concerning the identification of SpLD (Chasty and Friel, 1991).

Despite the apparently opposing quantitative and qualitative positions concerning the nature of SpLD, there is considerable scope for synthesis. Bryant and Bradley have suggested the existence of continua for each component of the reading process, with every child varying in its position on each of the continua, thus recognizing the uniqueness of the individual. Children can be considered not only along an extensive continuum of reading skills, but also along a continuum of *evenness* of relative levels of cognitive processing. Some of these cognitive processes will, to varying degrees, be important in learning to read. For example, these could include the components of language studied by Bryant, Bradley, Ellis, Snowling, Miles and others in their attempts to conceptualize the condition and to develop techniques that can be used to identify pupils with such difficulties.

At the even end of the continuum of the evenness–unevenness profile would be found backward readers. At the uneven end would be found the pupil with SpLD. The SpLD pupil merges with the backward reader as the number of relatively weak cognitive processes increases: the child no longer has one or two weaknesses, rather the child has isolated strengths, and eventually no particular strengths, thereby showing an all-round relative developmental delay. This type of synthesis allows for a slow learning child to show additional SpLD – a mixture of moderate delays and more severe difficulties. Such children have traditionally been excluded from the dyslexic category. This is almost certainly because teaching methods suited to slow learners have been considered to meet their paramount need.

The Bryant and Bradley synthesis combines both a quantitative distribution of difficulties and a qualitative aspect that is infinitely more complex in its distributions than a simple categorization of dyslexic and backward readers, or even of dyslexic subgroups and other poor readers (see Chapters 2 and 5). Deciding which pupils have SpLD remains an arbitrary decision. Where should the cut-off points be made?

Whilst professionals disagree concerning the nature of SpLD and its identification, there is little doubt that sufficient is known about pupils' attainments, abilities and progress at school to identify pupils with unusual, unexpected and intransigent difficulties in becoming literate and numerate. Further, enough is known about pupils' motivations and the range of methods and materials available to help virtually all such pupils to improve their attainments. As noted in Chapter 2 and above, a key issue is 'Who pays for what?'. The values and priorities of our society underpin the answers to the central questions of professional and financial resources. This is a political and financial issue, rather than solely an educational one.

Pupils are often identified as having SpLD if there is an unusual and unexpected discrepancy between some measure of general intellectual ability and their levels of attainment (Hammill, 1990). Most children learn to read, spell and write; some take longer than others. Typically, the more intellectually able a child, the more rapidly will they become literate. This is a well-validated prediction. However, a number of pupils who would be expected to learn to read fail to do so. Their failure is unexpected and unusual. As such, it is a cause of concern to parents, pupils and professionals. This concern is also a reflection of our tolerance, or intolerance, of individual differences between pupils in their rates of progress towards, and standards of, literacy.

Although there is no universally accepted definition of SpLD, a child who fails to reach a level of achievement in, for example, reading or spelling that is predicted on the basis of measured intelligence, chronological age or grade placement in the absence of adverse exogenous factors, is often labelled as SpLD or dyslexic. The definitions presented in Table 1.1 reinforce this point. There is considerable disagreement about the theoretical basis of such discrepancies (Stanovich, 1991). And even where there is a conceptual basis, measurement of the discrepancy remains controversial (Shepard, 1980; Wilson, 1987).

Incidence

Identification can be conducted on an individual basis, as in clinical work, or across groups of children. The impetus of single case clinical work can lead to epidemiological studies in which the incidence of SpLD in populations can be estimated. Incidence figures would provide valuable information for the planning of provision and the allocation of resources. Such studies are, none the less, based on theoretical models of SpLD that do not command the acceptance of all professionals. Thus the interpretation of whatever incidence figures are derived is open to debate, and the assumptions on which the figures are based can be questioned. Despite these reservations, large-scale studies based on specified populations have, on balance, been helpful despite the variations in figures that they produce (Davie, Butler and Goldstein, 1972; Rutter and Yule, 1975; Clark, 1979; Dobbins; 1990a).

On the basis of a discrepancy of at least 28 months between reading test scores and scores predicted using children's age and ability, Rutter and Yule used regression equations to identify a group of children labelled as 'specifically reading retarded'. They established incidence figures of 3.5 per cent of 10-year-olds and 4.5 per cent of 14-year-olds on the Isle of Wight and 6 per cent of 10-year-olds in an area of London as falling into this category. These figures, and those quoted in the studies noted above, suggest that both the conceptual models, and the operational definitions of identification techniques associated with them, contribute to incidence figures of various categories of pupils with literacy difficulties.

Rutter and Yule's work has been criticized on the grounds that their score distributions were distorted by ceiling effects resulting from an insufficient range of possible scores on the reading test (Rodgers, 1983; Share *et al.*, 1987). Other workers question the appropriateness of using IQs in the definition of learning disabilities (Siegal, 1989; Stanovich, 1991).

In relation to incidence estimates, two Scottish surveys merit attention. Both focused on pupils of average or above average intelligence who were experiencing difficulties in reading and other aspects of literacy. A community study of specific reading difficulties involving more than 80 professionals over various periods was carried out with the aid of a grant from the Scottish Education Department during the period 1966–68 (Clark, 1970). The aims of the study were:

- To examine the incidence of severe reading disability in a normal school population. (Potential utility: estimating the resources required to address the issue.)
- To identify the pattern of disabilities characteristic of pupils with severe reading difficulties. (Potential utility: identifying the type of provision required.)
- To suggest means of identifying such pupils as early as possible (Potential utility: preventing the development of severe reading disability.)

The study was not planned to prove the existence, or otherwise, of dyslexia. Clark accepted that the terms specific reading disability, dyslexia or word blindness are all used to describe pupils '...who fail to learn to read in spite of normal intelligence, intact senses, proper instruction and normal motivation'(Clark, 1970, p. 20).

One of the great strengths of Clark's research was the operational definition of all the categories used. Each is specified in terms of scores on particular tests. What was done, the results obtained and their presentation could not have been more explicit.

The two-year study was carried out in three phases. The first involved assessing the reading level and a large number of home, school and pupils' attributes related to reading level, of all the pupils in the community. One year later, all the backward readers were identified and studied. In stage three, another year later, *all children of average intelligence and above* who were still backward readers, were identified.

Thus, all the children born in the county of Dumbartonshire in a five-month period were tested after they had completed two years at school and were aged about seven years ($N = 1544$). Clark found that about 15 per cent of these pupils still had no independent reading skill. In view of the 1990/91 concern and controversy about standards in reading in England, it is interesting that Clark noted in 1970 that 'More recent evidence from annual surveys mentioned above would indicate that in the last few years there has been an increasing incidence of non-functional readers at the age of 7' (p. 129). In stage 2 of the study, 230 backward readers were identified. They were all pupils who obtained reading quotients of 85 or less. The majority of these pupils were of low average intelligence. In stage 3:

> When all the children who had been severely backward in reading at the age of 7 and who were of average intelligence were re-tested at 9 years of age, it was found that few such children were two or more years backward in reading, in fact, about 1 per cent of the total population, mainly boys. These 19 children represented the incidence of severe reading disability in children of average intelligence *whatever the cause of the difficulty.* (Clark, 1970, p. 127)

In order to explore their characteristics, an extensive battery of 12 tests was administered, as follows:

- Bender Gestalt Test.
- Illinois Test of Psycholinguistic Abilities.
- Birch and Belmont Tapping Test.
- Wepman Test of Auditory Discrimination.
- Neale Analysis of Reading Ability.
- Monroe Visual–Auditory Learning Test.
- Analysis and synthesis of words and common phonic units.
- Test of visual discrimination and orientation.
- Identification of first and last letters in words.
- Differentiation of right and left.
- Matchbox Test.
- Attitude to reading.

(For details of each test see Clark, 1970, pp. 86–7.)

In this group of 19 pupils, 15 were boys and 4 were girls. Speech defects and difficulties in auditory discrimination were common. Many showed poor visuo-motor coordination. 'The striking finding was the *diversity* of disabilities and *not* an underlying pattern common to the group which could have provided the basis for one single remedial method for all these children' (ibid., p. 128).

Some twenty years later, the Grampian Region Psychological Service carried out a survey of children with SpLD during the academic year 1985–86. In evaluating its eventual incidence estimates, it is important to consider the position adopted in defining the syndromes of specific developmental dyslexia and specific learning difficulties.

> Specific Developmental Dyslexia refers more particularly [than dyslexia] to difficulties in learning to read occurring essentially in the absence of significantly low ability, serious illness, emotional disturbance, cultural or materi-

al deprivation, or shortcomings in the educational process itself. Some or other of these factors may be found in association, as aggravating causes, but are not primary in causal significance.

Specific Learning Difficulties incorporates specific developmental dyslexia but, by definition, acknowledges that reading itself is unlikely to be the only disability. Spelling is almost always implicated (sometimes much more severely than reading) and problems with certain fundamental aspects of number learning are also likely to be impaired. Again, as in 2 (above), low intellectual ability is not a primary factor, nor are adventitious disadvantages such as ill-health or poor stimulation. (Grampian Region Psychological Service, 1988)

The weaknesses of identification by negative criteria, by the absence of particular circumstances, have often been criticized (Thomson, 1989). Such a procedure is logically flawed. In part, this criticism is offset by the specification of certain positive indicators concerning the relationship between abilities and attainments that operationalize the definition of the condition.

One of the aims of the survey was to record all pupils referred to the psychological service in the academic year 1985–86 who were:

- suspected in the referral of having dyslexia *or* specific learning difficulties (the abbreviation SpLD being used henceforth);
- referred as having scholastic attainments substantially below perceived potential;

[The Scottish Report uses the initials SLD. In England these have a very different connotation. Hence, in the interests of clarity, the abbreviation SpLD has been substituted to stand for specific learning difficulties.]

The survey involved all psychologists employed by the Grampian Education Authority. The survey reports that it set out clear criteria for identifying SpLD. The psychologists are reported as having found little difficulty in using the criteria consistently. The region has a primary school population of about 43,000 pupils and a secondary school population of some 32,000 with just over 1000 pupils attending special schools and units.

In the year in question, three of the four psychological teams in the region returned a total of 32 cases. Three-quarters of the referrals took place in the upper primary school years. The average age at referral was 8:08 years for primary school pupils and 9:07 years for all referrals, respectively. In the survey, boys referred outnumbered girls by 2:1. Over 80 per cent of referrals were made by schools. Of these, one-third were made at the parents' request. Three of the 32 referrals were made directly by the parents. 'These proved to be the sole instances judged not to be SpLD' (Grampian Regional Psychological Service, p. 50). (This comment is not to be taken as a criticism of the policy of direct access to psychological services by parents.)

The number of returns received represents approximately 5 per cent of new referrals made to the psychological service in 1985–1986. New referrals, in turn, constitute annually between 1 and 1.5 percent of the school population. From ten to 15 percent of all children are referred to the regional psychological service at some time during the period from 2:00 years to

18:00 years and it can be estimated that from 5 to 7.5 children in every 10,000 of this population are referred annually because of SpLD or suspected SpLD, suggesting an approximate incidence of *identified SpLD in the school population of one percent*. This implies that many cases remain unidentified. (ibid., p. 49)

The children were all of *at least normal intellectual ability*. In contrast, their attainments in both reading and spelling were, on average, some two years below chronological age. Their arithmetic skills were also impaired. It is worthy of note that the incidence figures obtained earlier in the Strathclyde region with a somewhat similarly defined population, but based on a more clearly specified population, was also approximately one per cent (Clark, 1970).

It was also noted in the Grampian survey that the types of miscues made by the pupils were not characteristically different, with rare exceptions, from those found in other pupils with learning difficulties. The significant ability–attainment discrepancy in the presence of no immediately apparent environmental cause points towards 'within-child' causes.

The survey concludes by confirming '...the existence, in a small proportion of otherwise normal, healthy children, of severe specific learning difficulties... Such pupils merit long-term assistance and follow-up...'

Whether or not there are children with SpLD or dyslexia who have qualitatively different learning characteristics has been a long-standing issue. In one study of 570 grade 2 pupils, 80 were identified as 'disabled readers' (Taylor, Satz and Friel, 1979). Of these, about half were deemed dyslexic. Tests between the dyslexic and non-dyslexic groups of disabled readers showed non-significant differences. 'The search for more meaningful sub-groups of poor readers would seem to require either a substantial revision of the concept of developmental dyslexia, or alternative means of classification' (ibid.).

Profile analysis as a means of identification has already been mentioned in Chapter 5. The *WISC-R* test has been extensively used in the diagnosis of learning disabled children (Dudley-Marling, 1981). The issues of diagnosis/identification, and the techniques that should be used, remain contentious.

Dobbins (1986, 1990b) has posed and addressed three questions of concern to all interested in the incidence of children manifesting various types of reading difficulty. Firstly, 'Do those pupils who present with a specific reading difficulty differ, in any educational sense, from those whose reading problem is part of a general failure to grasp the curriculum?' Dobbins argues that low achievers are typically reading 'as well as can be expected'. Those with a specific reading difficulty will be 'reading at a level below their expected level'. On the basis of research findings supporting the view that low achieving readers differed from underachieving readers in various ways, Dobbins accepts that the answer to the first question is 'Yes'.

For him, the second question necessarily is: 'Can LEAs assign low attaining readers to the specific or to the general sub-groups?' Arguing for the use of predictions of reading attainment made from scores on a test of general ability using regression equations, his answer is, given an adequate support service, 'Yes'.

His third question is: 'Are those pupils who have been identified as belonging to a specific reading difficulty sub-group, dyslexic?'

A population of some 5000 fourth-year junior school pupils in an LEA was tested using *Raven's Standard Progressive Matrices* (Raven, 1958) (assumed to be a test of general intellectual ability) and the *Reading Test BD* (National Foundation for Educational Research, 1970). Expected reading test scores (ERS) were estimated on the basis of the relationship between intelligence test score and reading test score for the entire group using a regression equation. On the basis of this information, seven groups in Table 6.1 were formed.

Table 6.1: Groups as operationally defined by Dobbins (1990b)

1. *Poor readers*. Reading quotient 85 or less on a scale with a mean of 100 and a standard deviation of 15 ($N = 744$; 14.8 per cent)
2. *Low achievers*. Poor readers whose actual reading test score equalled their expected reading test score, plus or minus 8 RQ points ($N = 216$; 4.3 per cent)
3. *Underachievers*. Poor readers whose actual reading test score was more than 8 RQ points below that predicted ($N = 528$; 10.5 per cent)
4. *Moderate underachievers*. Poor readers whose actual reading test score was between 9 and 17 points of RQ below their predicted score ($N = 314$; 6.3 per cent)
5. *Severe underachievers*. Poor readers whose actual reading test score was more than 17 RQ points below their predicted score ($N = 210$; 4.3 per cent)
6. *Anticipated underachievers*. Severe underachievers whose poor reading attainments can be understood ($N = 98$; 1.7 per cent)
7. *Unanticipated underachievers*. Severe underachievers whose underachievement cannot readily be explained (N = 82; 1.4 per cent)

By comparing the characteristics of group 7, the unexpected underachievers, with definitions of 'the dyslexic pupil', it should be possible to answer his third question. Dobbins shows characteristic Delphic caution. 'If the emphasis is on *reading* only, and spelling and writing are disregarded, the "unexpected under-achiever" meets the definitions of the "dyslexic pupil"' as described by three well-known experts because 'these definitions identify dyslexic pupils without reference to cause. If this is acceptable, it is argued that what is proposed here is also an acceptable working definition of dyslexia. However these three defi-nitions are themselves "exclusionary" so it is not surprising that they should fit together' (ibid., p. 35). If a definition implies a cause or an aetiology, then it is clear that '...no claim can be made to identify unexpected underachievers as dys-lexic' (ibid.).

The approach has conceptual limitations in its instrumentation, its cut-off points and its interpretation. It also has many strengths, not least its replicability, and the equity with which educational resource decisions can be made concern-ing systematically identified pupils with unanticipated reading difficulties. In a further study, it has been shown that there is considerable stability in the identifi-cation of underachieving readers even when different measures of intelligence and reading are used (Dobbins and Taffa, 1990).

Early identification is often seen as providing the best chance of effective intervention (Tansley and Panckhurst, 1981; Forness and Kavale, 1983; Simm, 1986). Considerable interest was generated in identification procedures for pre-dicting children 'at risk' of future difficulties in literacy. Considerable efforts have been expended in developing screening procedures. The perennial problem of considerable numbers of false negative and false positive predictions has led to a reduction in this type of work.

The use of ability–achievement discrepancies, grade placement–achievement discrepancies and *WISC-R* Verbal IQ – Performance IQ discrepancies represent three approaches in current use. One American report presents 14 ways of using these to define learning disabled pupils (Epps, Ysseldyke and Algozzine, 1983). Unsurprisingly, they found that the various operational definitions identified significantly different proportions of children in their sample of learning disabled pupils. Comparisons of cut-off and regression based definitions of reading disabilities have also recently been reviewed (Fletcher *et al.*, 1989).

Frequently, attempts to assess such discrepancies have used only single measures of ability and attainment. It is easy to be misled by discrepancies that appear considerable, but may be no more than artefacts of the instruments used. For example, estimating the statistical significance of the difference between scores on two correlated tests requires the simultaneous consideration of their reliabilities and intercorrelation. Whether or not a statistically significant finding is psychologically significant from the point of view of the identification of SpLD is a further and sometimes neglected issue (Pumfrey, 1977). Even this approach fails to take into account the variety of cognitive functions that may be involved in SpLD.

Despite this, the use of discrepancy formulae continues in the identification of SpLD. The psychological and psychometric legitimacy of certain of these strategies appear more valid and equitable than others (Newman, Wright and Fields, 1981; Hessler, 1987; Kavale, 1987; Mastropieri, 1987; Mellard, 1987; Wilson, 1987). For example, regression equations can be used to determine the difference between expected reading attainments based, for example, on a measure of intellectual ability, and a child's actual reading attainment. This approach is likely to lead to more informed and fairer decision-making concerning the degree of an individual's difficulty, and the subsequent allocation of additional help, compared to a less complex approach based on, say, the simpler discrepancy between mental age and reading age. Considering more than a single ability–achievement discrepancy for each child can improve the likelihood that discrepancies are valid.

The Linbury Research Project is a longitudinal study initially involving over 1300 pupils attending state primary schools in rural and urban areas in England. Testing of the pupils takes place in the school setting. One recent report involving 462 pupils having a mean chronological age of 8:07 years has examined their reading and spelling skills in relation to the children's intellectual abilities, as measured by the *WISC-R* (Newman, Wright and Fields, in press). A series of neuropsychological tests was also used. These measured various aspects of memory, perception and laterality. The pupils' emotional and behavioural adjustment was appraised using Rutter's *Children's Behaviour Questionnaire*. The pupils' parents and teachers were also interviewed concerning the children's reading and spelling development. Five hundred children were identified as overachievers, normal achievers and underachievers based on discrepancies between mental age and reading and spelling ages, respectively. This is a somewhat crude approach, but it is explicit.

The method of data analysis used was a form of cluster analysis. The authors see this as having the advantage of avoiding the use of arbitrary cut-offs between ability and achievement in defining dyslexia and identifying pupils. In addition, a multivariate technique such as cluster analysis allows a concurrent examination to be made of a number of ability–attainment discrepancies. The authors report the identification of five groups of children. Two of these groups, comprising 26 per cent of the sample, were performing above the level of reading or spelling predicted by both verbal and performance IQ. None of these had received remedial help. Two other groups, comprising a further 63 per cent, were achieving at or just below the level predicted by their intellectual abilities. Thirty-eight per cent had received or were receiving remedial help.

In the third group comprising the remaining 11 per cent of the sample, reading and spelling were considerably poorer than predicted by the pupils' intellectual abilities. Ten of these pupils (93 per cent) were boys. Of the group, 62 per cent had received or were receiving remedial help. An examination of the results from the neuropsychological tests showed that this group also had the poorest performance on many of these. In addition, the group showed a number of other features associated with dyslexia, such as a relatively high reported familial incidence of difficulties in reading (48 per cent) and spelling (56 per cent). Does this mean that we have, at last, an accurate estimate of the incidence of dyslexia in the population?

Unfortunately, the answer is 'No'. As with all such studies, a considerable number of questions are raised bearing on the validity of the model of cognitive functioning on which their work is based, the assumptions underpinning the analytic techniques adopted and the interpretation of the findings. Despite such caveats, work of this nature is to be welcomed. The Linbury Project is of considerable importance. Equally unfortunately, longitudinal studies in this, or any other, country are either far too small, short or few to allow detailed identification of the patterns of children's developmental characteristics to be validly mapped. Fortunately, some countries do rather better (Gjessing and Karlsen, 1989). The identification of the variance of literacy related abilities and attainments and their change over time is essential if the nature of SpLD is to be clarified and valid estimates of incidence obtained.

From incidence to policy

The combination of a policy that is seen as socially desirable (mainstream education for the majority of pupils with special educational needs) and economic (mainstream education is typically less expensive than small groups, units or special schools) has an almost irresistible appeal to politicians and administrators. Parents, pupils and some professionals are more cautious.

However, there are examples where it appears that the mainstream education of pupils with SpLD can be effective and efficient. Therefore an explicit and public means of identifying SpLD is essential. The method will almost certainly have weaknesses, but it must be defensible theoretically and in terms of public policy. Unsurprisingly, the specialist training of teachers, coupled with the availability of non-teaching assistants, is involved. The selection of pupils with SpLD is essential. Extra resources are required to help with their education. This strategy may still prove more equitable and cost-effective than the other alternatives open to an LEA.

At Eggars School in Hampshire, it is reported that 21 pupils out of 560 have been diagnosed as 'severely dyslexic' (Kirkman, 1990). These pupils receive specialized teaching and intensive support. About a quarter of their time is spent in small groups of no more than four pupils working with a teacher who has been trained to help pupils with serious literacy difficulties. For the rest of their timetables, the pupils attend mainstream classes. The support they receive, if required, is from non-teaching assistants.

Members of the School Psychological Service are reported as having helped to pioneer this approach. Hampshire now has four comprehensive schools with similar facilities for children with 'severe dyslexia'. Until 1986, the LEA's educational option for such pupils was to send them to independent boarding or day schools. The cost to the county of the former was approximately £15,000 per pupil per annum. This is about ten times the cost of educating a non-special needs pupil in mainstream secondary school.

Eggars School apparently acts as a 'magnet' school in that it draws pupils at the age of 11:00 years with 'severe dyslexia' from a catchment area larger than that from which it draws its majority intake. Approximately 14 pupils apply for the five or six places available annually. What happens to those who are not accepted? What happens to pupils with similar special educational needs who do not apply? These are challenging questions that must be addressed concerning many people both within Hampshire and elsewhere. They are not a new concern. They underline the need for an explicit LEA policy concerning the identification and resourcing of all special educational needs. If, as has been argued earlier, all children are special, how should this issue be addressed?

Acceptance at Eggars School requires that the pupil be in the lowest ten per cent of their age group for *both* reading and spelling, and in the lowest five per cent for *either* reading *or* spelling. In addition, they must have had a minimum of two years' special help whilst attending primary school. *They also have to be of at least average intelligence.* An admissions panel, which includes the head of special needs at the school, the headteacher and an educational psychologist, considers the applications early in the Lent term each year.

When it comes to the issue of whether help should be given to the Johns, James or Jacks identified in Chapter 2, it appears that the Johns are favoured by the school's (and the LEA's) policy. The notion of investment in the 'most salvageable', to use Collin's earlier phrase, namely those pupils of higher general ability, has reappeared. The validity of both the assumptions and the values underpinning such a policy will continue to be a matter of debate. Without doubt, the policy can be defended in terms of the DES policy stated in Appendix 1.

Hampshire has approximately 592 primary schools attended by 112,980 pupils and 109 secondary schools with 97,310 pupils. It also has 48 special schools and 17 special education units attached to mainstream schools. It is a very large LEA. If, as is reported above, there are four comprehensive schools in Hampshire with similar intakes of pupils with 'severe dyslexia', the number of pupils that are accepted is but a minute proportion of those falling within the Eggars's definition.

The British Dyslexia Association considers that the incidence of dyslexia is about four per cent in the population. If this estimate (and it can only be that for reasons discussed in Chapter 2) is correct, some 4500 primary and 3900 secondary pupils experience SpLD. (The British Dyslexia Association advises clients to use this term when communicating with LEAs concerning dyslexia because of its professional currency.)

The Education (Special Education Needs) Regulations 1983 define the procedures that the LEAs have to follow when assessing special educational needs. The LEAs have a legal duty to seek written advice, which includes the professionals' judgements on the provision required to meet the child's needs. The provision currently available in policy and resource terms within an LEA is not relevant to the professionals' considerations. Critics argue that, because of the lack of consensus on the identification and incidence of SpLD, this legal provision represents an open-ended demand on LEAs who have to work within controlled budgets. A legally immovable object meets an unstoppable force.

Managing such a system could become impossible. Proponents see the interests of the individual pupil as paramount.

Justification of any cut-off point is difficult. However, it can be argued that such operational definitions of special educational needs have a degree of equity and openness in their favour. The decision-making process, whereby a subset of pupils receives extra support, is explicit. It can be costed, managed and its efficacy assessed. It can also be challenged.

During the first years at Eggars, one of the major aims is to improve the dyslexic pupils' literacy skills. To this end they undertake an intensive literacy-related programme. This includes computer programmes, plus a range of less expensive and esoteric motivational devices aimed at encouraging experiences of success and thus improving self-esteem. Because of the difficulties that many dyslexic pupils experience with fine motor control, they are taught to use cursive handwriting. Additionally, there is a special maths programme. Most teachers would recognize the elements involved in this type of programme. It is not esoteric. It involves a policy decision on selection, resource allocation and time-tabling. It can be accommodated within a 'whole-school' philosophy and approach to addressing special educational needs, provided that resource allocations to pupils with other special educational needs are considered and provided for satisfactorily. This is an exceedingly difficult, if not impossible, task by virtue of its ill-defined and unconstrained nature.

Despite this, SpLD will continue to be identified and alleviated, albeit imperfectly.

Identification – why bother?

The clinical and educational usefulness of the distinction between reading backwardness (RB) and specific reading retardation (SRR) has been called into question by a number of workers (such as Fredman, 1989). In her review, Fredman questions researches describing different reading disability syndromes on the grounds that the existence, or otherwise, of similar characteristics in normal readers has not been adequately investigated. With a colleague, Fredman found that, in so far as the phonological and whole-word attack strategies of 13-year-old pupils were concerned, the reading characteristics of the SRR group did not differ from those of the RB group (Fredman and Stevenson, 1988). Bruck (1988) came to similar conclusions about the reading and spelling of a group of dyslexic children (mean age 10:07 years) who were compared with normal readers matched for reading age.

It is now better appreciated that studies using chronological age or mental age matched controls, as opposed to reading age matched controls are confounded by intractable 'chicken and egg' problems of interpretation concerning causality. Proposed symptoms and deficits could just as likely be a consequence of reading inexperience as a cause of reading difficulty. Directional confusion, for example, has frequently been included as an important symptom of the SpLD syndrome. Recent evidence suggests that confusions such as b/d, are attributable to reading experience and skill levels (Young and Tyre, 1983; Bryant and Bradley, 1985; Bryant and Goswami, 1990: Cataldo and Ellis, 1990). Such argument and evidence apparently leaves little with which to identify SpLD.

This issue was earlier addressed by Bryant and Bradley (1985). They found no evidence for the assumption of a variety of proposed deficits. This view implies that all children with, for example, difficulties in learning to read are, to various degrees, merely less mature or capable than the majority of children of the same chronological age in the development of the competencies underpinning the development of literacy. The possibility of identifying SpLD is called into question. If this is the case, is the study of SpLD a pseudo-science? (Kavale and Forness, 1985).

Identification can be justified as essential for the estimation of incidence and as necessary for the provision of appropriate interventions. If individually pre-scribed teaching is advocated, the necessity of identifying SpLD, as distinct from other reading difficulties, might be considered to be precluded (Singleton, 1988). However, individualized instruction does not dispense with the professional responsibility for identifying the child's strengths and weaknesses, if these are likely to be helpful in devising an individualized programme. In the interests of efficient education, the search for approaches relevant to more than one individual is also a valid endeavour. There is also the legal position that SpLD exists and can be identified. If professionals cannot agree, the courts will decide whether or not the evidence presented establishes the case for such classification of a pupil (Chasty and Friel, 1991).

In practice, identification of SpLD is regularly undertaken and is advocated by those who consider that qualitative differences between pupils in their text-processing strategies do exist. The quest for these leads into cognitive psychology, which is not the central focus of this chapter (see Chapter 5).

The means of identification

Because the conceptualization of SpLD is contentious, the means of identification vary. Normative tests, criterion-referenced tests and informal reading inventories can be used in a variety of combinations. Normative tests are widely used in identification procedures when discrepancies between scores are considered central to the identification. Criterion-referenced instruments and check-lists of what are claimed to be the distinctive characteristics of SpLD are also available. Yet again – *caveat emptor*!

There are many tests available to help professionals make explicit and reliable assessments of pupils' abilities and attainments. For example, Pumfrey (1985) provides details of 199 reading tests and assessment techniques classified by objective, type of test and the age level for which it is appropriate. By following a ten-step sequence of decisions, a range of tests potentially suited to a particular assessment need can be rapidly identified and summaries of them compared (Pumfrey, 1985). There are other compendia in the field of language and reading (Vincent et al., 1983; Vincent, 1984). Other major sources provide useful information on a much wider range of psychological tests and assessment techniques (Levy and Goldstein, 1984; Sweetland and Keyser, 1984, 1985; Mitchell, 1987).

The importance of selecting instruments that are capable of providing valid information to improve the decision-making process requires that test users be adequately trained in the administration of tests and assessment techniques. Users must also be aware of the strengths and limitations of such instruments. This requires that users are able to judge whether the test or technique they propose using itself measures up to explicit, acceptable criteria (American Psychological Association, 1985; British Psychological Society, 1989). Against such criteria, many tests and assessment techniques have significant shortcomings.

The *Bangor Dyslexia Test* (Miles, 1983a) was the result of many years of clinical work with children, generally of above average ability, who had experienced severe and prolonged difficulties with various aspects of literacy and numeracy. The work was carried out at Bangor University (Miles, 1983a, b). The instrument is offered as a way of advancing the understanding of such pupi's' difficulties. It tests the following ten diagnostic indicators:

- Left–right (body parts).
- Repeating polysyllabic words.
- Subtraction.
- Tables.
- Months forward.
- Months reversed.
- Digits forward.
- Digits reversed.
- b × d confusion.
- Familial incidence.

The test is not intended as a '...means of definitive diagnosis'. Despite the considerable reputation of its author, the test has been severely criticized on technical grounds. Much further work needs to be done before it can be used with confidence (Pumfrey, 1985; Singleton, 1988).

The *Aston Index (Revised)* was devised as part of a research and development project carried out at the University of Aston (Newton and Thomson, 1982). It has two levels of use. Level 1 is intended for use after the child has been at school for about six months. Its major focus is to diagnose potential language problems, thereby assisting classroom teachers in the early identification of children who are at educational risk. It can be used as a screening device for this purpose. The index enables teachers to assess a range of skills shown by earlier research as necessary for literacy (Newton, Thomson and Richards, 1978, 1979). Level 2 is designed for use with older pupils who do not appear to be coping with reading, spelling and writing as adequately as the teacher might have expected. It is claimed that the index can be used to '...predict possible "barriers to learning" in the individual child ' (Handbook, p. 1). The nature of a child's particular learning pattern can be *indicated* by the profile of results that represents the summary of the diagnostic testing. The profile of 'General underlying ability and attainment' uses chronological age plus subtests 2, 3, 6 and 7, together with measures of mental age and attainment. The 'Performance items' profile uses subtests 12, 13, 14 and 15. It is suggested that eight types of learning patterns, four prefaced by the adjective 'specific', may be identified. A list of materials designed to develop skills in the areas assessed by the index is provided, thereby linking testing and teaching. Evidence of the efficacy of this strategy is not provided in the Handbook. The index represents '...a beginning in awareness that certain neuropsychological correlates of "language and the brain" would need to be taken into account when trying to understand the individual difference in learning style of our schoolchildren' (personal communication).

Related to the index, the *Aston Portfolio Assessment Checklist* is an attempt at making the diagnostic teaching of reading a classroom reality (Aubrey *et al.*, 1982). The system is designed for mainstream classroom use for children '...with specific reading, spelling and writing problems (e.g. dyslexia)' (Manual, p. 4). The portfolio is packaged in a box containing a 26-page manual, assessment cards, assessment checklists and teaching cards. Using the materials requires that the teacher identifies children who, for no apparent reason, are underachieving in reading and spelling. A rule-of-thumb means of locating such children is provided, based on the teacher's knowledge of the child's verbal and non-verbal ability to grasp new concepts quickly. Of major concern are attainments markedly below the child's intellectual ability. Using the assessment cards enables the teacher to identify skills that the child may not have mastered. These skills are linked directly to subtests contained in the second part of the checklist. If the child fails to meet the criterion of mastering any of these, the teaching cards linked to that subskill may be used. The validity of the assessment card checklist identification procedure merits further investigation. Reservations have been expressed because the reliabilities and validities of the subtests are not reported in the manual. The issue of false positive and false negative identifications is not addressed (Pumfrey, 1985; Singleton, 1988). Both the *Bangor Dyslexia Test* and the *Aston Index* and *Portfolio Assessment Checklist* require considerable further research and development. A major issue is how well these approaches differentiate between various groups of pupils experiencing SpLD. Despite such strictures, both command a degree of popularity with teachers, according to the sales figures. By themselves, these figures should not be taken as a valid index of diagnostic worth. They do, however, represent professional concern over identification and a willingness to experiment with approaches that appear to hold some promise of improved practice. The key question is whether these, or any, approaches to identification lead to improved institutional and individual decision-making. In simpler terms, does it help the teacher to help the pupil with SpLD minimize the adverse effects on attainments?

The *Boder Test of Reading–Spelling Patterns* is based on extensive clinical work by a paediatric neurologist and a research psychologist (Boder and Jarrico, 1982). The authors claim that the test enables subtypes of reading disability to be identified. 'Specific reading disability, or developmental dyslexia' can be differentiated from non-specific reading disability. This is achieved by comparing a child's reading and spelling performances on words that are 'known' and 'unknown', phonetically regular or otherwise. The test looks at both successful performance and errors. The grade and age-related materials include 13 word lists graded for both reading and spelling. In each list of 20 words, one half of the words are phonetically regular. If further information is required to clarify an assessment, an additional eight diagnostic indicators are described. The record forms and summary sheets are well designed and easy to use. Adequate administration of the test requires training and considerable practice.

The reading–spelling patterns obtained enable three subtypes of developmental dyslexia to be identified. These are called 'dysphonetic', 'dyseidetic' and 'mixed dysphonetic–dyseidetic'. Differential diagnosis is determined by empirically derived cut-off performance scores on the tests. Evidence for the validities of the test's differential diagnostic power includes work from four PhD theses. The implications of the results for remedial instruction are presented.

The test has been criticized technically in relation to both item selection and cut-off criteria, on both of which little information is provided. Despite such legitimate reservations, the approach developed by Boder and Jarrico has aroused considerable interest among clinicians, research workers and teachers specializing in the SpLD field (Reason, 1984; Pumfrey, 1985).

Clay's individual *Diagnostic Survey* is integrated with what she describes as 'recovery procedures' (Clay, 1979a). The purpose of the survey battery is the

early identification of children who are not making satisfactory progress in learning to read. It is designed for use with children aged six years. Additionally, it is
suggested that the instrument can be used with older pupils experiencing difficulties in learning to read. This is because it is mainly (but not entirely) a criterion-
referenced oriented procedure in which normative considerations are not central.
The skills tested include those shown in Table 6.2.

Table 6.2: Diagnostic survey (Clay, 1979a)

- A record of reading behaviour on books
- Letter identification test
- Concepts about print (Sand and Stones tests)
- Word tests
- Other reading tests
- Writing samples
- Writing vocabulary

Initially, a running record of the child's reading behaviour on books at three
levels of difficulty is required. An error (miscue) analysis is carried out and various categories of errors noted. The test of letter identification is accompanied by
normalized scores, into which the raw scores can be converted. The stan-
dardization is based on 320 urban children aged from 5:00 to 7:00 years and on
282 aged from 6:00 to 7:00 years tested in 1968 and 1978, respectively. In a
sample of 100 urban 6:00-year-old pupils, a split-half reliability of 0.9 and a
correlation with word reading of 0.85 are reported. [Ages given as
years:months.]

The *Concepts about Print Tests* called Sand and Stones require the child to
demonstrate an appreciation of concepts such as book, page, letter, front, back,
etc. Normative information, as for the *Letter Identification Test*, is presented and
test–retest and internal consistency reliability coefficients in the ranges of 0.73 to
0.89 and 0.84 to 0.88, respectively, are reported from small samples of kindergarten children.

Details are provided of the *Reading Recovery* procedure likely to be required
by between 10 and 20 per cent of children. The programme integrates all four
aspects of language. The results of a three-year research programme capitalized
on the skill of competent teachers to develop suitable teaching strategies. The
results presented show the extensive field trials to be effective.

A somewhat similar approach to early identification has been produced in the
UK (Reason and Boote, 1986). Four stages in learning to read are described: pre-
reading; beginning to read; intermediate; and basic reading skills have been mastered. At each of these levels three related aspects of language development are
considered: concepts and approaches; visual word recognition; and phonics. The
theoretical basis of the model is clear. It integrates both top-down and bottom-up
approaches to the teaching of reading in an interactive framework. A series of
criterion tests are indicated. Thus, in relation to 'concepts and approaches', the
equivalent to Clay's sand and stones tests, include the checklist of the vocabulary
of reading shown in Table 6.3.

Both of the above popular approaches recognize the importance of metacognitive processes and of inter- and intra-individual differences in identifying children with difficulties in learning to read, spell and write. Both approaches have

associated teaching programmes. Both can be used to develop programmes responsive to the needs of pupils with SpLD. Metacognitions matter.

Table 6.3: Vocabulary of reading (Reason and Boote, 1986)

- Show me the *first* page of the book
- Show me the *last* page of the book
- Show me the *top* of this page
- Show me the *bottom* of this page
- Show me the *front* of this book
- Show me the *back* of this book
- Where does the story begin?
- Show me a *word*
- Show me the first word on this *line*
- Show me the words *under* the picture
- Show me the words *over* the picture
- The child points word by word as the teacher reads

This section concludes with a reference to the most recently developed individual diagnostic test in the UK. This is known as the *British Ability Scales (BAS)*. It was developed, and subsequently revised, at the University of Manchester School of Education by a team of researchers led by Dr Colin Elliott (Elliott, Murray and Pearson, 1983). Currently it is the only general cognitive abilities battery developed and standardized in the UK that meets certain key requirements of the 1981 Education Act. It is of particular value in relation to the assessment of a pupil's learning difficulties, whether general or specific. The *BAS* has been used in several important research projects concerned with the learning characteristics of pupils with reading difficulties (Elliott and Tyler, 1986; Tyler and Elliott, 1988; Elliott, 1989; Tyler, 1990). The *BAS* enables a vast range of diagnostic hypotheses to be examined. The profiles of an individual child's abilities and attainments has the potential to provide pointers to interventions likely to reduce specific learning difficulties. This assertion is controversial (see Chapter 5).

The *BAS* consists of 23 scales, all of which are available in long and short form versions. The scales cover a variety of perceptual and cognitive skills grouped by stimulus mode, process and response mode. The six major process areas and the subscales associated with them indicate the flexibility of the *BAS*. They are given in Table 6.4.

The *BAS* is a well-constructed and sophisticated instrument. The scales have been standardized on nationally representative samples of subjects aged from 2:06 to 17:06 years, although not all of the scales cover the entire age range.

Availability of the *BAS* is currently restricted to qualified psychologists. Elliott has argued for the instrument to be made available to teachers who have undertaken an appropriate course of training in the theory, practice and interpretation of the data yielded by the *BAS*.

The *BAS* is being used in the individual assessments associated with the requirements of the Education Act 1981 and with Circular 22/89 in the preparation of Statements of special educational needs (Farrell, Dunning and Foley, 1989).

Table 6.4: Six major process areas of the BAS

1. Speed
   - Speed of information processing
2. Reasoning
   - Formal operational thinking
   - Matrices
   - Similarities
   - Social reasoning
3. Spatial imagery
   - Block design
   - Rotation of letter-like forms
   - Visualization of cubes
4. Perceptual matching
   - Copying
   - Matching letter-like forms
   - Verbal–tactile matching
5. Short-term memory; and
   - Immediate visual recall
   - Delayed visual recall
   - Recall of designs
   - Recall of digits
6. Retrieval and application of knowledge
   - Basic number skills
   - Naming vocabulary
   - Verbal comprehension
   - Verbal fluency
   - Word definition
   - Word reading
   - Conservation

There is a strong case for extending the availability of this instrument to a wider group of professionals concerned with the assessment and the alleviation of general and specific learning difficulties.

Summary

There is a plethora of educational tests that claim to differentiate between children with SpLD and other pupils with severe and prolonged reading difficulties. From the viewpoint of practitioners, problems of identification and incidence are important. Their complexities must be acknowledged. The strengths and limitations of various approaches to assessment must always be carefully considered. Informed professional judgements have to be made concerning which approach or approaches to identification, if any, one is to adopt. That is why all LEAs require an explicit and clear policy concerning the identification of pupils with SpLD (see Chapter 13). In this respect, the perfect is the enemy of the better.

Identification and incidence are, of course, only starting points. Effective interventions are the Holy Grail. We consider promising practices in Chapter 7.

Recommendations

6.1. Given the present state of knowledge, dogmatic assertions concerning either the conceptual basis or the incidence of specific learning difficulties be treated with caution.

6.2. It be recognized that cut-off points with regard to additional provision remain to a large extent administrative and financial decisions dependent on political will.

6.3. Identification procedures and operational definitions include consideration of the child's previous learning history and present development.

6.4. Both normative and criterion-referenced assessment of specific learning difficulties be supplemented by the observations of pupils, parents, teachers and psychologists.

6.5. In identifying pupils with specific learning difficulties, attention be given to the strategies, strengths and weaknesses that children bring to their attempts to read and write.

6.6. There be further research into similarities and differences between children with specific learning difficulties and younger normal readers in their information processing.

6.7. There be rigorous research into individual differences amongst children considered to have specific learning difficulties; in particular, the existence, nature and incidence of various subgroupings of educational relevance.

6.8. In assessing children suspected of having specific learning difficulties, a variety of possible sensory causes, particularly hearing and vision, be investigated.

Chapter 7

Intervention and Evaluation

Introduction

The great investment of time and energy by professionals over many years in research, development and daily practice in the classroom and the clinic have resulted in a pedagogic cornucopia. However, the existence of this cornucopia does not imply that a panacea to the alleviation of all learning difficulties is either known or available. As noted earlier, whether or not this potential resource can be drawn on and further developed, to the benefit of pupils with SpLD, is largely a political and financial issue. It is not an educational one.

Psychologists and teachers know a great deal about children's abilities, attainments, attitudes and motivations. Some 18 books have been published since 1987 and more are in preparation in an important series for professionals entitled *Special Needs in Ordinary Schools*. The series was conceived and edited by Peter Mittler, Professor of Special Education and Head of the School of Education at the University of Manchester. The contributors address an extensive range of differing special needs and cover age levels from the pre-school to 18 plus. (It must never be forgotten that SpLD represent but one aspect of the questionable legal and administrative term 'special educational needs' for the reasons discussed in Chapters 1 and 2.)

Despite the undoubted expertise exemplified by the many contributors to Mittler's series and by the other contributions listed in Table 7.1, psychologists and teachers are far from complacent about their knowledge and skills. Both points should be neither forgotten nor neglected. Who knows more about the conditions for effective teaching and learning? Who is more experienced in identifying and alleviating learning difficulties? Who is at the sharp end of the shortage of resources in terms of equipment, materials, trained and experienced staff and time? Who else is simultaneously dealing with the demands of implementing the National Curriculum? Despite such pressures, whilst much remains to be learned by professionals, it is asserted that enough is already known to improve the attainments in literacy and numeracy of virtually all pupils.

From the psychoeducational viewpoint, assessment and intervention set in a particular theoretical context are Siamese twins in providing help for pupils perceived as having SpLD: each depends on the other. As has been noted in Chapter 6, there are many ways of identifying SpLD. There are also many educational interventions that have been devised to alleviate SpLD. The conceptual and empirical complexities discussed in previous Chapters underline the point that much is known about inter- and intra-individual differences between pupils in terms of their attainments and progress in the skills of literacy and numeracy, and in the inferred abilities that underpin such performances.

Approaches with wide applicability

Some well-known teaching approaches, originally developed for either normal learners or undifferentiated poor readers, have also been used with SpLD pupils. These include Paired Reading (Morgan, 1976; Topping, 1991), Relaxed Reading (Lindsay, Evans and Jones, 1985), Shared Reading (Greening and Spenceley, 1987), Pause, Prompt and Praise (Wheldall, Merrett and Colmar, 1987) and Peer Tutoring (Topping, 1988).They are all variants on a common theme: the importance of participant modelling. Paired Reading involves the alternative uses of both simultaneous and independent modes of reading. Shared reading focuses on modelling and the simultaneous mode. It is recommended where children find difficulties in deciphering text. Relaxed Reading and Pause, Prompt and Praise concentrate more on the independent mode. Advice to professionals and to parents on supporting learning at home are given in Wolfendale (1987) and Cicci (1987), respectively. Emphasis on supervisor training and monitoring to maximize constructive support and to minimize negative reactions by the tutor is required by all the approaches mentioned earlier in this paragraph. The theoretical orientation of these is psycholinguistic; the pedagogy is 'top-down' rather than 'bottom-up'.

Direct instruction aims to maximize the engaged contact time between pupil, task and teacher through active participation and group response (Engelmann, Osborn and Engelmann, 1969). Programmes are suited to teaching to objectives and follow a sequence of model, lead, test and review. Direct instruction is essentially a method rather than a programme, although many commercially produced direct instruction programmes exist. These include whole-word, phonetic and morphemic strategies that are phased in at appropriate levels. They are typically well structured and sequenced and have in-built revisions of earlier learning. These characteristics meet the criteria advocated by many organizations involved in alleviating SpLD, such as the British Dyslexia Association. The National Association for Remedial Education publishes a helpful compendium of phonic resources (Herbert and Jones, 1984) in addition to their valuable list of reading materials (Atkinson, Gains and Edwards, 1991). Both publications have a wide applicability in the teaching of literacy skills.

A key issue is whether the considerable range of teaching/learning methods, techniques and materials currently available are differentially effective with pupils having identifiably different learning characteristics. In terms of their ability to become literate, pupils with SpLD have much in common with other pupils; but they also manifest a number of differences in their abilities and attainments that are pedagogically important. If such pupils are not a homogeneous group, but can be validly subdivided, we then need to investigate which methods, for which group, at which stage in the development of particular aspects of literacy, are most helpful. The search for these aptitude × instruction interactions (AII) is a continuing challenge to professionals.

That search cannot be adequately addressed and better answered without a considerable investment in basic and applied research. Blind empiricism can never produce satisfactory answers (Kavale and Forness, 1985; Hammill, 1990). We need to know why particular AIIs are effective, when they are found. Theory helps one to search systematically.

The purpose of this chapter is to present brief descriptions of promising lines of development in alleviating SpLD. References are provided so that details of the materials and methods and their evaluations can be followed up.

Interventions

The last decade has seen a revolution in learning/teaching opportunities for those suffering from learning difficulties in general and SpLD in particular. This revolution owes something to new teaching materials, but rather less than it does to the advent of the microcomputer. The possibilities that the combination of both has opened up, are dramatic. Basic research into the nature and alleviation of SpLD has been more rigorously carried out than hitherto possible (see Seymour, 1986; Coltheart, 1987a).

Computer assisted learning (CAL) is a method of presentation that appeals to many children. It is typically seen as 'different', perhaps because it provides opportunities for active engagement in game situations, the provision of emotionally neutral informational feedback, the absence of adult-associated adverse comment on performance and the sense of coping successfully with modern technology. Its value lies in the range and quality of the software available (Sawyer and Flann, 1983). The text processing and print-out facilities can be used creatively to aid the child with writing and spelling difficulties.

In terms of applications in classrooms and clinics, the range of hardware and software that has been developed and disseminated is of growing importance (Blanchard, Mason and Daniel, 1987; Moseley, 1990a; North West SEMERC, 1990). As programmes become increasingly interactive, so our understanding of the ways in which children with SpLD deal with and produce symbolic materials, such as texts, will become increasingly clear. The repertoire of software resources able to facilitate pupils' progress towards literacy will expand exponentially. The pioneer work of the five LEA consortia-supported Special Education Microelectronics in Education Resource Centres (SEMERCs) at Oldham, Doncaster, Bristol, Newcastle and Redbridge is to be applauded.The Department of Psychology at the University of Hull, in collaboration with the BDA, have produced a guide to the use of computers for facilitating literacy development in dyslexia and other learning difficulties (Singleton, 1991).

Teaching arrangements

In the past, children experiencing problems with aspects of literacy in particular were seen as in need of remedial teaching. Many studies attested to the significant short-term beneficial effects on pupils' progress and attainments. Despite this, by the 1970s doubts had been cast on the efficacy of the long-term effects of the short-term remedial teaching of reading. The way was laid for the current vogue for in-class support to facilitate curricular access (see Chapter 8). The advent of the National Curriculum has contributed to this development, particularly at the secondary school stage.

As has been pointed out, the disenchantment with the remedial teaching that took place was arguably somewhat hasty and unjustified (Payne, 1989, 1991). The well-established, short-term gains could equally support an argument for longer-term intervention. Indeed, a long-term need would be consistent with information processing deficit models of reading disability. The concept of 'cure' is almost certainly misplaced (Wilsher and Taylor, 1987). Simm's long-term study of the effects of the remedial teaching of reading criticizes earlier studies showing only short-term gains by virtue of limitations in sample size, brief interventions, short follow-up periods, uncontrolled 'Hawthorn Effects' and control groups obtaining unscheduled help (Simm, 1986). His own study looked at a large number of children referred to an LEA remedial service over a period of several years. He claims valuable long-term effects from the remedial help provided. Children with dyslexic symptoms apparently benefited as much as others. However, the means used to assess progress in his work involved measures of *rates of progress* in reading attainments. This is a complex index that has an appealing simplicity. Coupled with this are a number of hidden weaknesses that can mislead the unwary reader. Simm's claims are not as clear-cut as he assumes.

A case exists for a variable balance of in-class support and special tuition. This is what appears to be happening in practice (see Chapter 8). An example of how, using such a combination, it has been possible to help pupils with severe dyslexia at the Eggars School in Hampshire, was earlier outlined in Chapter 6.

Teaching responses

The uniqueness of each child's pattern of abilities, attainments and difficulties is well accepted. The need for individual programme prescription, monitoring and adjustment has long been recognized (Tansley, 1981; Thomson, 1984; Hinson and Kelly, 1986; Fredman, 1989; Jackson, 1989; Miles and Miles, 1990).

A variety of approaches in which the instruction for children with literacy difficulties has been determined on the basis of individual assessments has been described in an article entitled 'Integrating the testing and teaching of reading' (Pumfrey, 1990c). The sources and approaches listed are not specifically designed for use with children having SpLD. Despite this, it is clear that many pupils likely to have SpLD will be involved in such integrated programmes of assessment and teaching at various levels of sophistication. An *indicative* list of the vast range of materials available is shown in Table 7.1.

Teaching through assessment and its reciprocal, assessment through teaching, are modern concepts with a very long history in education. They embody valid pedagogic principles. In practice, their relationship is similar to that of the chicken and the egg. Arguing as to which comes first, or is the most important, is a highly suspect endeavour.

Some specialized approaches

Practitioners often tend to become wedded to a restricted number of teaching approaches. Various teaching programmes for SpLD pupils have been used with apparent success. Many of these have been the fruits of '...work by gifted individuals who were influenced little or not at all by the findings of experimental psychologists' (Miles and Ellis, 1981). Not all would agree with this claim. There are many approaches that owe much to psychological principles and there are many such systems in regular use.

Some of the approaches listed have a relatively narrow focus on particular aspects of literacy skills. Others have a far wider coverage. As might be expected from the discussion in Chapter 1 on Kirk's seminal involvement in the learning disabilities movement, he sees that term as preferable to many others including 'dyslexia' (Kirk and Chalfant, 1984). He also provides a wide coverage including:

- Attentional disabilities;
- Memory disabilities;
- Perceptual disabilities;

- Thinking disabilities;
- Oral language disabilities;
- Reading disabilities;
- Handwriting disabilities;
- Spelling and written expression disabilities;
- Arithmetic disabilities; and
- Self-esteem, social behaviour and delinquency.

Table 7.1: Linking the assessment and teaching of literacy skills

*Early Detection of Reading Difficultie*s (Clay, 1979a)

Preventing Classroom Failure (Ainscow and Tweddle, 1979)

Educational Applications of the WISC-R (Nicholson and Alcorn, 1980)

Development of Reading and Related Skills with Pupils of Secondary Age (DORRS) (ILEA, 1981)

Barking Reading Project (Barking and Dagenham LEA, 1982)

Classroom Observation Procedure (ILEA, 1982)

Aston Index (Revised) (Newton and Thomson, 1982)

Aston Portfolio (Aubrey *et al.*, 1982)

Cloze Procedures and the Teaching of Reading (Rye, 1982)

DATAPAC (Akerman *et al.*, 1983)

Linguistic Awareness in Reading Readiness (Downing, Ayers and Schaefer, 1983)

QUEST Screening, Diagnosis and Remediation Kit (Robertson *et al.*, 1983)

Special Needs Action Programme (SNAP) (Ainscow and Muncey, 1984b)

Making Sense of It (Miscue analysis) (Arnold, 1984)

Direct Instruction (Science Research Associates, 1985)

Teaching with Precision (Raybould and Solity, 1985)

Special Needs in the Primary School: Identification and Intervention (Pearson and Lindsay, 1986)

Learning Difficulties in Reading and Writing: A Teacher's Manual (Reason and Boote, 1986)

The Primary Language Record (Barrs *et al.*, 1988)

Early Identification of Special Needs (Wiltshire County Council Eucation Department, 1988)

Bromley Screening Pack (Bromley LEA, 1989)

Touchstones (NFER, 1989)

Computer-assisted Learning Programmes with Speech Enhancement (Davidson, 1990)

Twenty specialized approaches are listed in Table 7.2. They are only a sample of the available methods but include most of the major approaches associated with institutions specializing in the identification and alleviation of SpLD. Ten of these specialist approaches to helping pupils with SpLD have been described in some detail, together with evidence concerning their efficacy (Pumfrey, 1991).

The effects of function training on children's progress in reading were some-what disappointing (Hicks, 1986). This heralded a shift of interest to the 'surface' behaviours of spelling and reading tasks themselves. Subskill deficit models prompted identification procedures and teaching to remedy gaps in knowledge or skills related to actual literacy tasks and materials (such as letter sounds, sound blending, selected words). More recently, attention is being paid to the ways in which individual children process the information in texts (Seymour, 1986; Coltheart, 1987a). The focus of this work tends to be the processing of individual words rather than the running texts that are a dominant concern in education.

Increasingly, it is argued that teaching programmes for pupils with SpLD should be individualized, should aim to identify and improve a pupil's relatively weak information processing skills and to capitalize on alternative strategies and strengths where possible. This is a laudable aspiration, but much more research is required before such an ambitious objective is effectively achieved (see Chapter 5). The differential efficacies of the methods and materials listed in Table 7.2 are not unequivocally established.

Table 7.2: Some specialized approaches

Fernald Multisensory Approach (Fernald, 1943)

Orton–Gillingham Method (Orton, 1967; Vickery and Reynolds, 1987)

Gillingham–Stillman Alphabetic Method (Gillingham and Stillman, 1956)

Alpha to Omega (Hornsby and Shear, 1975; Hornsby and Farrer, 1990)

Edith Norrie Letter Case (Norrie, 1960; Arkell, 1970)

The Bangor Teaching Programme (Miles, 1982)

Bannatyne's Colour Phonics (Bannatyne, 1967)

The Hickey Method (Hickey, 1977; Augur and Briggs, 1991)

Peabody Rebus Reading Programme (Clark and Davies, 1979)

Aston Index (Revised) (Newton and Thomson, 1982)

Aston Portfolio Assessment Checklist (Aubrey et al., 1982)

Spelling Made Easy (Brand, 1984)

Academic and Developmental Learning Disabilities (Kirk and Chalfant, 1984)

Alphabetic Phonics (Cox, 1985a)

Children's Written Language Difficulties: Assessment and Management (Snowling, 1985)

Tactics for Teaching Dyslexic Students (Dinsmore and Isaacson, 1986)

Dealing with Dyslexia (Heaton and Winterton, 1986)

The Bangor Dyslexia Teaching System (Miles, 1989)

The Icon Approach (Brown, 1990)

Dyslexia: A Teaching Handbook (Thomson and Watkins, 1990)

NB: Although the above references are arranged in chronological order, this does not necessarily indicate the sequence in which the systems were developed.

Secondary sources of information on some of the 20 somewhat specialized approaches listed in Table 7.2 are available (Johnson, 1978; Naidoo, 1981,1988; Tansley and Panckhurst, 1981; Thomson, 1984, 1988b, 1990; Augur, 1986; Miles and Miles, 1990; Pumfrey and Elliott, 1990; Pumfrey, 1991). Readers intending to use specialized materials could, to advantage, read the summary accounts contained in the secondary sources before deciding which of the primary sources to consult. This should be backed up by finding out where the particular approach is in regular use, observing it in practice and discussing its strengths and limitations with those involved.

The majority of the specialized approaches concentrate on improving the child's ability to develop and use the phonic skills in which many pupils with SpLD are at a serious disadvantage. The theoretical orientation towards alleviation tends to be 'bottom-up'. Pupils with SpLD have to be taught to master the many elementary skills that most children acquire with relatively little difficulty in their progress towards becoming literate and numerate. Other practitioners work to strengths in, for example, visual or semantic aspects of language. Many combine simultaneous work with both the weaknesses and strengths of the pupil. The majority of practitioners stress the importance of a multisensory approach.

A moment's reflection suggests that these approaches have many principles in common with the teaching of literacy to *any* pupil. The important differences appear to be in the degree of structure, detail, assessment, systematic teaching, record-keeping and overlearning that characterize the specialized approaches for pupils with SpLD. Their time-consuming nature is apparent. There is no 'quick fix', no magic method, no panacea to alleviate SpLD.

Most of the specialized programmes are highly structured. Teachers are trained to use these, whilst emphasizing discovery learning and cueing. It is often intended by those who have created programmes in specialist facilities that they can be applied in ordinary classrooms (Cox, 1983, 1985a, b). Naidoo (1981) has noted their common features, most of which help the child to decipher print through a phonic (or in the case of Fernald, an alphabetic) approach. Most 'eschew whole word methods which leave the child to deduce the coding system for themselves' (ibid.), a process considered extremely difficult for the SpLD pupil. To greater or lesser extents, they are multi-sensory, if only 'by virtue of their integrated reading, writing and spelling schemes of teaching' (ibid.). *It is considered essential to teach virtually everything*, with little reliance on deduction or generalization. Programmes tend to be comprehensive and detailed, often specifying or recommending a teaching order. The work is typically cumulative, starting with the smallest sound–symbol unit (letters) and building up to words. Some rote learning and a great deal of overlearning are considered necessary in order to achieve the automaticity that is the hallmark of the competent reader and writer. Such programmes meet the characteristics recommended by the British Dyslexia Association that teaching should be structured, sequential, cumulative and thorough.

To many teachers unfamiliar with such systems, their content, detailed structure and pedagogy can be a considerable challenge. As a consequence, one often-raised criticism is that the materials are tedious, boring and involve a massive amount of overlearning by the pupil. An important counter argument is that other less structured pedagogies have signally failed to help pupils with SpLD to become literate.

In 1980 Hornsby and Miles reported a series of investigations into the effects of dyslexia-centred teaching programmes to assess whether or not the specific processes were effective in alleviating dyslexia. The study involved recording the progress made by 107 children who were identified as experiencing SpLD and were receiving tuition by means of a dyslexic-centred programme. Forty-one clients were under the care of a programme organized and implemented by a hospital's learning disabilities clinic. A further 44 were involved with a unit attached to a university department. The remaining 22 clients were being assisted by a voluntary organization. All three centres accepted the existence of dyslexia and were committed to identifying and alleviating the condition. The results were presented in terms of the pupils' reading and spelling ages. On the basis of these, it was claimed that the programmes were effective in helping the pupils, even though the three programmes varied from one another. Before accepting the validity of the conclusions, it is essential to read the original account and to bear in mind the complexities in assessing 'improvement'. A follow-up study reported later also merits critical consideration (Hornsby and Farrer, 1990).

A study of the use with dyslexic pupils of a multisensory technique known as simultaneous oral spelling involved a comparison with the effects of the visual inspection of words (Thomson, 1988b). He reports that the first of these techniques resulted in a significant differential improvement in the spelling of dyslexic pupils. From this and other studies, Thomson concluded that dyslexic pupils showed significant cognitive deficits, namely in phonological coding, phonemic awareness and alphabetical skills. Equally importantly, he asserted that these could be overcome by appropriate pedagogic interventions. It was, however, shown that the non-lexical phonological spelling of the dyslexic pupils was particularly resistant to pedagogic interventions.

The same worker reports findings from a study of the spelling of 68 pupils attending an independent school at which he is the co-principal (Thomson, 1990). All of the pupils involved were of at least average intelligence as measured by the WISC or the British Ability Scales, falling in the range of 105–140. 'The results show that the children are not only doing better than dyslexics not given help, but are bettering the "norm", and appearing to be catching up' (ibid., p. 162). These comments are based on the use of achievement ratios to measure rates of progress. For example, a child making 12 months of progress in reading age in a year has an achievement ratio of 12 months of reading age progress to 12 months passage of time (= 1). Achievement ratios greater than 1 are deemed 'better than expected'. The converse applies to achievement ratios that are less than 1.

Thomson acknowledges the problems of interpretation that these statistics present. For example, a child who is one year of reading age behind his chronological age at 8:00 years is further below the average in reading for that age-group than a child who has a reading age of 12:00 years at the chronological age of 13:00 years. This is because the spread of reading ages in a year group increases over time. Thus two different amounts of progress can produce apparently identical improvement ratios. In practice, such equal ratios do not indicate equivalent progress.

The same author has also presented results from a study of 58 8:00 to 13:00-year-old dyslexic children's spelling of regular and irregular words. Children with lower reading ages are better at regular words. With increasing reading age, the performance on regular and irregular words becomes more and more similar, until a ceiling is reached. In relation to spelling age, the spelling of regular and irregular words starts at similar levels, diverges and then converges at a test ceiling level. Thomson sees these findings as consonant with Frith's model of the development of reading and spelling (see Chapter 5).

Dyslexic pupils have considerable difficulties with phonological structure and the segmentation of words in both reading and spelling. A third study by Thomson involved the teaching of syllabification skills to 20 dyslexic pupils. The teaching system used with the training group ($N = 10$) was based on 'syllable analysis'. This involved teaching the pupils that words in English can be divided into six basic syllable types. 'Children are encouraged to tap out words into their beats or units, and to recognise how many beats there are in a given word. They are then taught how to divide the words up into syllables and to assign them to one of the above six categories of classification' (Thomson, 1990, p. 166). The results presented indicate that whilst both the treatment and the control groups were at the ceiling for single syllable words, the training had resulted in significantly superior performances in two and three syllable words by the training group.

Thomson considers his work to show the possibility of improving the written language skills of dyslexic pupils by particular teaching programmes. The gap between chronological age and attainments that can increase, can also be narrowed. Although spelling is more resistant, considerable progress can be achieved.

A programme entitled 'Reading Recovery' has been developed at the Ohio State University (Pinnell, Lyons and Deford, 1988). It is included in the 14th edition of a book entitled *Educational Programmes that Work* published annually in the USA by Sopris West Inc. in cooperation with the National Dissemination Study Group. It aims to reduce reading failure by early identification and intervention. The aim is to help children to improve their attainments through individually tailored 30-minute teaching sessions. The programme supplements the normal reading programme in a classroom. A specially trained teacher works with the child every day on reading and writing experiences. The Reading Recovery programme focuses on enabling children to make their own links between reading and writing, thereby capitalizing on the importance of semantics. The elements of the lessons are reported as being the same for each child although the content differs so as to meet each child's instructional needs.

A series of techniques, rather than full programmes in themselves, has also been recommended for use with SpLD pupils, although the approaches may not have originally been designed for such pupils. Nor is there necessarily any convincing statistical evidence of their long-term efficacies. There are some systems that claim to be effective, but the evidence is relatively limited (Branwhite, 1983; Cornwall, Hedderly and Pumfrey, 1984; Andrews and Share, 1986; Hicks, 1986; Pumfrey, 1991). They are mentioned to indicate the type of materials available. Excellently organized summaries of teaching materials that are helpful to all teachers of all pupils are produced by the National Association for Remedial Education (Atkinson, Gains and Edwards, 1991). The British Dyslexia Association, Dyslexia Defined, Learning Development Associates and the Remedial Supply Company are just four of the many groups disseminating information concerning the assessment and alleviation of literacy difficulties (Brett, 1990).

A comparison of the effects of using a direct instruction programme to assist pupils with SpLD with the effects of self-esteem enhancement and a psychomotor programme has been carried out (Somerville and Leach, 1988). Pupils were randomly allocated to the three treatment groups and a control group. Those involved in the teaching were predisposed towards the intervention to which they had committed themselves. 'Blind' conditions of testing and teaching did not apply, but the teachers, parents and children felt the control treatments to have been successful. In the event, the measured success did not support their estimates. The direct instruction group made significantly greater gains. The study does not make clear whether it is the direct instruction principles of teaching or the programme content that is responsible for the success. It can be argued that such a distinction is analogous to considering which constituent in a cocktail determines the cocktail's unique effect on taste buds.

The *English Colour Code Programmed Reading Course* (Gessert, 1976) uses a system related to, but far less elaborate than, that specialized programme listed earlier and developed by Bannatyne (1967). Baldwin's (1968) *Patterns of Sounds* is helpful in promoting sound blending. It also includes pictures which pick out the outstanding features of the various letters, blends and diagraphs. These pictures are, at the same time, associated with the sound of the various letters and letter clusters. A similar set of embedded pictures was devised by Forrester (1985). This material was used in an LEA unit for SpLD pupils (Jackson, 1989). The notion of 'symbol accentuation' has a long pedagogic pedigree. A recent and stimulating description of the use of this technique with pupils having severe learning difficulties shows considerable promise (Jeffree and Skeffington, 1985). Wendon (1973) has devised a set of pictures created from letter shapes in her *Pictogram System*. These are part of a more comprehensive programme for teaching the structures of language. Characters drawn onto the letter shapes are accompanied by mnemonic stories and rhymes to help the pupil recall the sounds of symbols and the rules governing their use. Pollock's (1978) *Signposts to Spelling* also uses mnemonic drawings as *aides-memoire* for spelling rules.

The technique of simultaneous oral spelling (SOS) forms part of the approach developed by Gillingham and Stillman (1956). It was devised for poor spellers who could read. The technique was used to enable them to learn to spell words that were not studied in the context of 'rules' and 'generalizations'. They suggested that the sounds and symbols of English be introduced in a systematic way, starting with letters. Beginning with the phonograms a, b, f, h, i, j, k, m, p and t, the students then learn to read and spell words that can be composed from these elements (such as 'bat', 'fat' and 'hat'). There are many series of graded readers that have been constructed on a similar systematic phonic basis.

As developed by Bradley, SOS combines various pedagogic approaches. As advocated by proponents of a language-experience approach to literacy, the Bradley version of SOS uses words that the pupil has selected from his or her own vocabulary, even if the pupil is unable to read or write many words and has little appreciation of the sound–symbol relationships of letters.

I have found that when students work with words they want to learn, are helped to work out each word using plastic script letters, and then record and practice it using this SOS adaptation they do learn words successfully. However, the student then has to be taught to generalise from the words learned to others which have similar sound and orthographic patterns, again using the plastic script letters. This method of generalising from one word to another has proved outstandingly successful in other controlled training studies. (Bradley and Bryant, 1983, 1985)

Detailed descriptions of the technique are available (Bradley, 1985). Readers will recall that Bradley and Bryant consider that the differences between children in their reading abilities are quantitative and not qualitative. Hence the technique is seen as of general utility with pupils having literacy difficulties, whether the pupils are categorized as having SpLD, being dyslexic or having literacy difficulties.

The steps given by Bradley are shown in Table 7.3. It is claimed that the whole procedure requires only 30 seconds per word and that it works equally well for students at all levels of literacy from non-readers to undergraduates, and in learning other alphabetic languages.

Table 7.3: Simultaneous oral spelling (Bradley, 1985)

1. The student suggests a word he wants to learn.
2. The word is written correctly for him (or made with plastic script letters).
3. The student names the word.
4. He then writes the word himself, saying the alphabetic name of each letter of the word as it is written.
5. He says the word again. He checks to see that the word has been written correctly. This is important, as backward readers are often inaccurate when they copy (Bradley, 1983).

Repeat steps 2 to 5 twice more, covering the stimulus word as soon as the student feels he can manage without it.

6. The student practises the word in this way for six consecutive days. The procedure is the same whether or not the student can read or write, and whether or not he knows the sound/symbol relationships. But it must not deteriorate into rote spelling, which is an entirely different thing.
7. The student learns to generalize from this word to words with similar sound and orthographic patterns, using the plastic script letters.

Goulandris (1985) advocates the use of tape recording equipment to aid memorizing. The child's voice is recorded and played back (self-voice echo). Listening to their own voices is thought to be more effective than listening to recordings made by others. This approach has been further developed by Lane (1990) under the aegis of the University of Exeter School of Education in his Aural–Read–Respond–Aural–Written (ARROW) technique. The method has its origins in infant teaching/learning approaches and was originally developed as a technique to help in the education of hearing impaired pupils with marked difficulties in language skills attending a unit attached to a mainstream school.

Children using the system will use at least one, and probably all, of the five components of ARROW:

Aural. The pupil listens to speech on a headset. The content can range from single words to complex sentences. The speech can be from any source, live or recorded. Typically the speech is produced by a teacher, assistant, parent or volunteer helper.

Read. The child simultaneously listens to the voice and refers to a text of it. With non-readers, visual support material can be provided.

Respond. Following simultaneous listening and reading, the pupil is encouraged to imitate the words given on tape or presented live by the teacher.

Oral. The pupil repeats the utterance presented by the teacher. The pupil then listens to a replay of his or her own recorded speech. The teacher's voice can be switched off when this is done.

Written. When listening to a replay of their own voice, the pupil may be asked to write down what they have heard. Non-readers may be asked to arrange visual materials in a sequence mapping the recorded material.

'The basic ARROW method for improved reading and spelling lends itself to many variations dependent on the needs and ability of the child ...the techniques

are based on the author's work as a mainstream Infants/Junior teacher and clinical experience with Special Needs children...' (Lane, 1990, p. 239).

A particular tape recorder is recommended for those who wish to use all of the
possibilities of the approach. A specially designed two-track machine is required.
In addition, the recorder has a rapid rewind facility and the headset boom micro-
phone provides high fidelity speech recording. A pause control allows a high
standard of edited recording and is required for certain techniques recommended
for the teaching of reading and spelling. The machine does not erase any pre-
recorded material and also allows the pupils to record their own voices if a gap is
allowed on the tape following the permanent pre-recordings. Pre-recorded
material can be prepared by the teacher or can be purchased.

There is evidence of the efficacy of the ARROW approach to the improvement
of children's language abilities, both receptive and expressive. Improvements in
listening skills, short-term memory, speech, reading accuracy, reading comprehension and spelling have been reported (Lane, 1990). The considerable support given by the School Psychological Service and the LEA in the development
and dissemination of Lane's ideas indicates that it has considerable promise. The
use of the equipment is rapidly learned and the pupils soon become adept at
operating it whilst the teacher assumes a supervisory role.

A group of teachers taking an Advanced Diploma in the Education of Pupils
with Specific Learning Difficulties (Literacy) considered that the system had
possibilities and, inevitably, limitations. Currently ARROW is being tried with a
small group of pupils with SpLD. The results are awaited with interest.

There are some materials and suggestions that seem particularly useful to
teachers attempting to match instruction to needs as indicated by the child's
pattern of functioning. The *Aston Teaching Portfolio* mentioned earlier potentially offers such flexibility. It presents ideas and materials for use and adaptation
as appropriate to the child's particular learning characteristics. Its use allows a
continuing assessment of the child's development. It has been suggested that the
materials can be used in conjunction with other programmes in order that
sequential teaching is not lost in using 'bits and pieces' from the portfolio
(Thomson, 1984).

A number of techniques and suggestions relate to sequencing skills and the
awareness of word structure. Montgomery (1981) considered that dyslexics were
less aware of how they articulated the range of phonemes, when compared with
reading age controls. If this is so, and already a number of other lines of investigation support the contention, there are implications for remedial treatment.
(Evidence presented in Chapters 5 and 6 bear on this.) It could indicate the need
for closer collaboration with speech therapists to develop activities that would
make children more aware of how they use their speech organs (Montgomery,
1981). The pioneer work of Edith Norrie (1960) comes to mind in this respect.

Bryant and Bradley (1985) describe a technique using plastic letters '...to
make children more aware of the sounds shared by quite different words' and
'...to give children the idea that words with common sounds often shared the
same spelling patterns too' (see p. 122). Hirsh-Pasek (1986) suggests that finger
spelling could be used as a supporting strategy for helping dyslexics in segment-
ing words into component sounds. A list of potentially helpful tasks abstracted
from various programmes, including Lewkowicz's (1980) review of phonemic
awareness training, has been published by Leong (1987). 'Attack-a-Track' deals
with alphabetic order and syllable segmentation (Lewis, 1976). The importance
of syllabification is also emphasized as a means of improving reading skills by

Scheerer-Neuman (1981) although he points out the sometimes conflicting results of segmentation by articulatory syllables and by morphemic divisions. Articulatory syllable segmentation was easiest and was used the most. Snowling (1987) also recommends teaching children to segment words in order to highlight orthographic clusters. Other workers favour morpheme segmentation by virtue of differing theoretical positions concerning the roles of visual–semantic processing and the importance of teaching to children's strengths (Brown, 1981, 1990).

Difficulties in verbal labelling are attributed to the SpLD syndrome by many workers (Ellis and Miles, 1981; Miles and Miles, 1990). Hulme (1981a, b) considers how this can impair the recall of letter strings. He recommends tracing to aid recall and the use of multi-sensory techniques including writing activities. The influence of the earlier work of Ferland (1943) is still clear in many contemporary approaches. The study of phonological deficits and the availability of alternative compensatory strategies including visual or semantic competence is seen as relevant to advancing understanding and control in the identification and alleviation of dyslexia. The importance of studying both inter- and intra-individual differences in dyslexic pupils, and the need for longitudinal case studies, are also seen as vital (Gjessing and Karlsen, 1989; Snowling, Hulme and Goulandris, 1990). The demands on the resources of skilled research workers and practitioners to carry out such programmes unfortunately exceed availability.

Cursive script is recommended for pupils with SpLD (Thomson, 1984; Brown, 1990). Both authors describe how this can be effectively introduced. It has also been suggested that cursive writing is simpler in terms of starting and finishing strokes, in its lack of straight lines and confusable forms. Its connectedness helps in the assimilation of word patterns as gestalts (Phelps and Stempel, 1987). These authors have also developed an evaluation scale for children's handwriting which aims to identify qualities in need of additional teaching attention.

A plea for children experiencing segmentation and reversal problems has been made by Yule (1988). She criticizes publishers of children's books and readers for failing to provide print that is carefully spaced and uses typefaces which maximize differences in letter shapes. Layouts are typically designed for pleasing overall appearance and not for close examination. This does not help the young reader and may unnecessarily confuse a child with SpLD. It follows that considerable care is needed in the selection of books in relation to their typefaces and other presentational attributes.

Another worker has considered reading comprehension skills and suggests steps and strategies for their promotion (Maria, 1987). She considers some traditional higher order reading skills and uses story plans to develop an awareness of organization and implications. Often comprehension *per se* (as opposed to comprehension derived via text) is not considered a prime cause for concern in certain definitions of SpLD. Such metacognitive skills, rather than the mere extraction of utterances and literal meaning from text, can be sources of difficulty. Instructional strategies used with a college student who was having such organizational and metacognitive difficulties, in addition to problems with spelling, have been described and the means of help that were used discussed (Ganschow, 1984). Case studies can often provide valuable and promising insights. Strategies for managing written work, which included exploration, planning and drafting and complement the suggestions made by Maria, are also available (Moulton, 1985).

Teaching quality

In relation to SpLD, the 'within-child' nature of the problems is usually high-lighted in contrast to possible environmental causes of a child's difficulties. A closely related issue is that of variabilities in 'within-teaching' approaches. Valu-able advice concerning the quality of teaching and on the management of in-struction is available (Tansley and Panckhurst, 1981; Young and Tyre, 1983; Bellan, 1986; Payne, 1991).

One important aspect of teaching quality is the knowledge, ability and willing-ness to look critically at the evidence adduced in support of particular methods and materials claimed to be effective in alleviating SpLD. An appreciation of the strengths and limitations of various research methodologies is required if one is to make informed critical comment on particular claims. Such problems have been discussed by many authors (Kavale and Forness, 1985; Wilsher, 1990). Considerations include matters such as: the selection of subjects (criteria, defini-tions); the instruments used; the presence or absence of controls; assignment to groups for comparative purposes; teacher variables; variations in the content, form, frequency and length of remediation and the context in which it is delivered; Hawthorne effects and statistical considerations such as group size and errors of measurement; and regression effects. Wilsher discusses the strin-gent conditions he considers essential to remedy any weaknesses in research design. Thus, in methods experiments, subjects should be selected from a clearly specified population and allocated to intervention and control groups on a ran-dom basis to avoid bias. Controls are important, but most types of controls have drawbacks. Matched pairs cannot be controlled for all variables. *Post hoc* con-trols have differing bases of selection; historical controls are subject to Hawthorne effects and 'dummy' treatments cannot be considered to be placebo controls when the treatment is evidently a 'dummy' for experimenters, parents and possibly subjects to see. Double blind conditions are therefore recommended by Wilsher, but recognized as not always possible, especially in the real world of the classroom or clinic as opposed to the laboratory. The importance of using appropriate methods of statistical analysis and the need to replicate studies are also vital.

If such a counsel of perfection seems daunting and demotivating to the teacher interested in carrying out a classroom-based study, a previously mentioned point bears reiteration: the perfect is the enemy of the better. If you have an idea on how to alleviate SpLD, try it out. The vast majority of studies into the efficacy of interventions on SpLD fall considerably short of the ideal of a classical methods experiment. Despite this point, awareness of that ideal may help in moderating claims for efficacy based on suspect research designs.

There can be little doubt that professional development in this field is depen-dent on a continuing involvement by teachers and psychologists in the theoreti-cal and practical day-to-day aspects of work with pupils. Collaboration between these two groups is also required. Being a competent professional, effectively alleviating pupils' SpLD, *is not enough*. It may, at one very important level, satisfy teacher, parent and pupil, but by itself such highly valued competence in a professional is insufficient.

It is equally essential that a profession be able to articulate, communicate and discuss its concerns, initiatives and discoveries. This is not done in isolation. Active membership of professional organizations concerned with the area is essential. From the crucibles of the classroom and clinic will gradually emerge the increased ability to identify and help pupils with SpLD. Reporting detailed and systematic feedback on both successes and failures to informed and interested colleagues is of the essence. Individual clinical case studies and large-scale methods experiments can make their distinctive contributions to discourse. Attendance at, and contributions to, local, regional and national meetings concerned with SpLD are vital. Currently, these attendances are unfortunately rather low, unless the programme is linked to the contemporary and time-consuming National Curriculum related demands on teachers. To this we briefly turn.

The delivery of the National Curriculum to pupils with SpLD represents a tremendous challenge. The heightened awareness of the importance of literacy and numeracy, not only by virtue of their inclusion in the core curriculum, but because of the importance of attainments in these fields, has been accepted in Western society since long before the advent of popular education in the 19th century.

Having Statements of Attainment, Profile Components, Attainment Targets, Programmes of Study and Standard Assessment Tasks will heighten the attention of all concerned with pupils who have SpLD. So too will the requirements for a School Development Plan. The financial consequences of Local Management of Schools will additionally come to bear on this issue of how to help pupils with SpLD, not necessarily to the advantage of the pupils involved. In the midst of these developments, pupils with SpLD will continue to arrive at and work their way through the educational system. They must not be overlooked.

Summary

SpLD are not 'cured' or completely rectified by any means currently at our disposal. Such difficulties can be alleviated and their adverse effects reduced. There is no simple recipe to attain even this end but there are many promising lines of methodological development. The pursuit of literacy by the pupil with SpLD is demanding of the pupil, the parent and the professional. It is expensive psychologically and financially. It remains an eminently worthwhile objective.

The earlier stated aims of professionals concerned with the phenomenon of SpLD merit reiteration. They are to conceptualize, predict and control the phenomena such that individuals are helped to develop key communications skills related to literacy and numeracy. There has been a great deal of research into the efficacy of a variety of educational interventions intended to alleviate SpLD. Most of the studies have methodological weaknesses that preclude simple generalizations either to pupils with SpLD in general or to clearly specified subsets of that population.

Studies carried out from ostensibly antithetical theoretical positions concerning the nature of symbolic thinking and its development into various forms of language, such as the 'top-down' and 'bottom-up' theories, hold hope. Their opposition is more apparent than real (see Chapter 3). The Hegelian dialectic process of hypothesis, antithesis and synthesis is operative in this field, albeit slowly and hesitantly. Apparently conflicting findings may be construed as sustaining a compensatory approach to the alleviation of SpLD.

Thus task analysis research sustains a large body of opinion supporting teaching methods that aim to develop decoding skills at either phonetic or orthographic levels. Similarly, research and teaching based on psycholinguistics has generated much discussion concerning the importance of more holistic approaches. The polarized and controversial positions of the advocates of the 'real book' versus those favouring the use of phonics and graded series in the teaching and learning of reading represents a tension that, in practice, is resolved by a variety of syntheses, not by a single one. The pragmatic syntheses are largely context-specific.

For pupils with SpLD, it is essential to identify the instructional needs that they have in common with their peers who become literate without undue difficulty. It is equally essential to establish whether SpLD pupils have additional differentiated instructional requirements. If they do not have these, it is difficult to accept that they should have undue difficulties in becoming literate.

Evidence suggesting the existence of subtypes of SpLD is not incompatible with the existence of common quantitative differences between all pupils in certain key processes underpinning the acquisition of literacy. The search for aptitude × instructions that are differentially effective with dyslexic pupils compared with others of similar reading ages must be pursued. The particular focus in interventions on the individual's strengths and/or weaknesses in attainments, and the processes that underpin these, will continue as a focus of activity. Whilst what is not known about alleviating SpLD is considerable, it must be emphasized that a great deal is known about how individuals can be helped to become literate and numerate.

For conceptual reasons, there is unlikely ever to be an educational panacea to SpLD. Some promising avenues have been, and are being, developed. The question 'What materials and/or methods can be used with a child having SpLD to help him/her become literate?' can be answered simply – but only by the cavalier. Complex questions such as this can rarely be adequately answered with simplistic answers.

Recommendations

7.1. The symbiotic relationship between assessment and teaching be appreciated by all professionals involved with pupils identified as having SpLD.

7.2. There must be rigorous research into the short-, medium- and long-term efficacy of various methods of teaching the skills of literacy to pupils with SpLD.

7.3. Claims for the efficacy of any intervention be subject to critical and informed examination, and its procedures to systematic replication.

7.4. Through INSET, teachers and psychologists be encouraged to become aware of a wider range of methods and materials likely to be of value to individual pupils with SpLD.

7.5. Professionals collaborate in devising and evaluating interventions for alleviating the SpLD of individuals.

7.6. The communalities between all pupils learning to read and the distinctive characteristics of those with SpLD be explicated and their instructional implications both considered and investigated.

7.7. The search for effective aptitude × instruction interactions for groups of SpLD pupils having specified common attributes be intensified.

Chapter 8

Support for Pupils with Specific Learning Difficulties

Introduction

How can specialist teaching be efficiently and effectively directed at children with specific learning difficulties? This question has exercised professionals for many years. If pupils' learning difficulties have not been met by schools using their own staff, a case could be made for the establishment of a separate LEA service. The demonstration of a highly effective remedial education centre at Selly Wick House, Birmingham, by Schonell and Wall of the University of Birmingham School of Education, was seminal (Schonell and Wall, 1949). Pupils who were 'underachieving' in reading and other basic skills were identified and helped.

Before the Warnock Report, published in 1978, and the passing of the Education Act 1981, the majority of LEAs provided peripatetic teaching services largely as a consequence of the influence of the work of Schonell and his colleagues (Sampson, 1975; Pumfrey, 1980). These remedial services were designed to help pupils with particular learning and adjustment difficulties. The majority of the clients they served attended mainstream schools. The commonest form of provision was known as 'remedial education'. Its primary focus was on identifying and alleviating underachievement in literacy in general and in reading in particular.

The remedial teaching was usually carried out in small groups, or individually, elsewhere in the school or at a local remedial education centre. Initially these services were organized under the aegis of the LEA Schools Psychological Service. Increasingly the Remedial Education Services became autonomous, although cooperation with the Schools Psychological Service was always maintained, albeit to varying degrees.

These services provided excellent examples of accountability. Their costs were clearly identified. Their efficacy was measured by the attainments and the progress in reading made by individuals and groups with whom they worked. Their results were regularly published. The short-term effects of the remedial teaching of reading were generally very favourable. They provided valuable help for very many pupils.

Not surprisingly, the post-intervention follow-up studies of effectiveness that were carried out showed little long-term differences in the subsequent mean scores on reading tests of children who had been given remedial teaching of reading and comparable groups who had not. This finding disappointed many local politicians, and some professionals, who had earlier believed the remedial teaching to be an efficient means of reducing underachievement in the long term after a short-term intervention. (Their faith in the long-term efficacy of a limited intervention was analogous to the efficacy of the 'short, sharp shock' as a means of modifying the long-term behaviour of delinquents; that is, misconceived.) Whether or not the remedial teaching of reading was effective depended on the cause of the underachievement. Where this was lack of educational opportunity, the prognosis was good. Where the cause lay within the child, the likelihood of rapid progress was lower, irrespective of how bright the pupil was.

When it was appreciated that there were limitations in the effectiveness of such peripatetic remedial services, a number of LEAs required that the remedial services modify their work. In the event, they were often encouraged to widen the scope of their activities. The excellent work that they had done could not be ignored merely because they failed to achieve the impossible. This led to the provision of an advisory support team capable of providing a much broader range of help than that formerly given. In many LEAs the remedial service was restructured to comprise a special educational needs advisory and support service of the kind recommended in the Warnock Report.

Instead of concentrating on individual pupils, subsequently attention became increasingly focused on schools as systems that could be improved to the benefit of all pupils involved. Considerable tensions existed within and between services. Some professionals considered that concern with the individual pupil was the central focus of professional activity. Others considered that intervention at the systems level was, on balance, the more effective strategy in improving children's attainments. The synthesis of these two approaches was evolving until the advent of the statementing procedures under the Education Act 1981 refocused attention on the individual pupil. It has been argued that the 'systems' and 'whole-school' orientations to helping pupils with specific learning difficulties led to the loss of the benefits to individuals of the more traditional approaches (Bradshaw, 1990).

Remedial education services were seen as concentrating on reducing failure (and not doing it too well, in the long term). In contrast, support services focused on the positive; on developing sound practice. The former was seen as reactive; the latter as proactive. In practice, the former services regularly carried out objective evaluations of their efficacy. This was rarely done to the best of the authors' knowledge, by support services and their advocates in relation to their expanded roles.

Changing practices

The Warnock Report (GB.DES, 1978) followed by the 1981 Education Act set the context for thinking about children with special educational needs and also for gradual changes in the provision that has been made for these children up to the present (1991). Education services are now facing the challenges involved in combining the ideals of 1981 with the possibly competing demands of the National Curriculum and its assessment, and Local Management of Schools arising from the Education Reform Act, 1988 (GB.DES, 1988e).

Withdrawal

At the time the Warnock Report was written almost all special provision for children with learning difficulties, including that made for children with specific learning difficulties, involved withdrawal from the normal classroom. This might be a full-time special class organized separately from the normal school, part-time attendance at a centre, a special class within the pupil's own school or with-drawal from the normal class for specific tuition (Brennan, 1979). Where both separate classes and withdrawal existed in one school, separate classes were regarded as being for dull pupils and withdrawal for more able pupils with read-ing difficulties. A third form of organization or 'non-organization, mixed ability without support', was noted. Brennan (1979) produced evidence of restricted curricula and impoverished opportunities, since those with learning difficulties had less access to specially equipped rooms, out-of-school resources and equip-ment within school than had other pupils. The dangers of a 'sink class' devel-oping were recognized. Clunies-Ross and Wimhurst (1983) found that most provision was made through slow learner classes, sets, options or withdrawal, but also mentioned 'the floating support teacher'. Raybould, Roberts and Wedell (1980) also referred to joint support teaching but again did not develop the idea.

A 1984 HMI report, *Slow learning and less successful pupils in secondary schools*, reported that '...the standard of work from pupils of broadly similar aptitudes and abilities was markedly better when the variety and range of work was wide, with pupils using the skills they had to complete interesting and imaginative work rather than over-practising their weak points' (GB.DES, 1984, p. 16). This was linked to pupils following a subject-based curriculum rather than to the work of the remedial department, 'too much of which was limited in range and rarely called for the skills and knowledge so laboriously acquired' (ibid.). This report also recognized that pupils in remedial classes can become isolated and eventually be incapable of rejoining the academic mainstream of the school. In examining the work of withdrawal groups they reported that '...there is rarely any organisational framework to ensure links between group and mainstream work... Reading is seen as a separate skill which having been acquired will transfer to any context' (ibid.). Remedial teachers were often physically and pro-fessionally isolated from their colleagues, though there were some interesting examples of remedial teachers working in the classroom with subject teachers and acting as consultants to a subject department.

In relation to pupils with SpLD, the following comment is made by HMI in the report: 'Specific learning difficulties in reading, writing and spelling, and perhaps other subjects also, [which] require careful assessment and special teach-ing programmes in those areas, though they may be associated with reasonable general ability in other aspects. Such difficulties may be amenable to special help in the short term but may sometimes need such support over a long term' (ibid., p. 4).

Despite such criticisms and comments, Moses, Hegarty and Jowett (1987) report concern among headteachers that special needs were not being met because of a reduction in the number of part-time teachers who had previously provided withdrawal work and concluded that 'withdrawal is undoubtedly popu-lar with junior school teachers and they would like more of it'.

Nevertheless concern at the possibly damaging effects of withdrawal was growing. Payne (1989), in a survey of some 60 articles and books, found little hard evidence of the damaging effects of withdrawal on pupils, 'Yet many authors were quite happy to cite them as obvious fact'. Poor self-esteem or social isolation arising from attainment difficulties, or from personal characteristics associated with those difficulties, is not easy to distinguish from that caused or exacerbated by the way in which schools respond to special educational needs.

Pearl, Donahue and Bryan (1986) surveyed the research on the social relationships of learning disabled children in the USA. They found widespread evidence
of social difficulties despite the fact that most definitions of 'learning disabilities'
explicitly exclude social or emotional maladjustment as a primary characteristic.
Attitudes towards learning disabled pupils by fellow pupils, teachers and parents
were less favourable than for other pupils. Learning disabled fourth grade pupils
viewed on short video clips were judged less positively than their non-learning
disabled classmates, but this distinction did not apply with younger pupils. This
research does not identify the causes of the differences in attitudes to these
American pupils, and if it did the relationships identified would not necessarily
be the same in England and Wales.

In Britain there was also concern that the curriculum was restricted in order to
allow for extra practice in basic subjects. Sometimes a subject would be dropped
altogether, at other times some lessons would be missed, leading to a loss of continuity and making successful performance unlikely. French was the subject most
often affected, but geography, history, science and English literature were also
restricted or omitted. The social and curricular impoverishment of much remedial education was a cause of dissatisfaction, though the strength of the personal relationships between remedial teacher and pupil was recognized and
valued.

The results of research that sought to measure the improvement in reading
skills resulting from various regimes were disappointing. Reading and other literacy difficulties did not regularly show a marked long-term improvement in
response to short-term interventions (Gittleman, 1983; Hicks, 1986; Wilsher,
1989). Small-scale studies often gave more promising results, though as pieces
of action research they may not have been able to meet the highest standards of
design. Some, for example Gregory, Hackney and Gregory (1981), which used
both contemporary and historical control groups, showed real improvement in
reading levels following a corrective reading programme.

Support

By the mid-1980s there was considerable dissatisfaction with most of the existing models of remedial education, whether this provision had been for children
whose learning difficulties affected most aspects of the curriculum, or for those
whose difficulties were restricted to areas dependent upon literacy. At this time
also, pupils with more clearly identified special educational needs, often physical
or sensory disability, were entering mainstream schools. These pupils made extra
demands on their teachers but, when good quality support was provided, teachers
acquired the skills and knowledge required and their pupils thrived (Millar, 1986;
Booth, Potts and Swan, 1987). If pupils with disabilities like these could be supported in mainstream classes what of the old 'remedial' group? 'Special educational needs in ordinary schools' was listed by the DES as one of the priority
areas for the in-service training of teachers, and college-based special educational needs in ordinary schools (SENIOS or SENOS) courses were established in a number of colleges to prepare teachers to work as special needs
coordinators in mainstream schools or as members of a support service. Lloyd-
Smith and Sinclair-Taylor (1988) describe one such course, while Butt (1986)
outlines one local authority's initial training programme to introduce changing
practice. The edition of *Support for Learning* in which Butt's article appears, also
included a further five articles on support service developments.

Later surveys show increasing diversity of provision. Brennan (1987) found 14 different forms of support for learning available in mainstream secondary schools: advice from remedial, subject or visiting specialists, the provision of teaching materials, modification of the child's timetable, withdrawal for remedial teaching, preparatory or follow-up work, curriculum modification, a special class or unit and non-teaching support. Outside consultation and support teaching could be provided by an area special needs centre, special school head or out-reach teacher or educational psychologist. Mills (1988), in a survey of 26 urban secondary schools in one authority, found the use of a varying mixture of sets, withdrawal, support teaching and special classes. The two most widely used were withdrawal (23 schools) and support teaching (20 schools). Gipps, Gross and Goldstein (1987), using a survey of LEA practices, reported on the diversity of systems being used in both primary and secondary schools. Pearson and Lindsay (1986) surveyed the problem-solving models used in primary schools as part of whole-school approaches to meeting pupils' special educational needs.

Many local authorities developed special educational needs support services. The progress of such services, their strengths and the difficulties they were encountering, was surveyed by HMI in 1987/88 and reported in 1989 (GB.DES, 1989h). This report is considered in more detail later in this chapter.

In 1985 the National Association for Remedial Education published - *Guidelines 6: Teaching Roles for Special Educational Needs*, and in 1986 changed the name of its journal to *Support for Learning*. 'Access to the curriculum', 'the whole-school approach', 'support for learning' and 'differentiation' became positively loaded phrases in the educational world. Reports of relatively small projects by committed teachers describe progress, but these are not changes that can readily be introduced, as a whole-school approach makes demands on all staff. These changes depend on a climate in which schools have moved away from a rigid ability setting and in which all staff accept a commitment to all pupils. Additionally there has to be a willingness to examine aims, objectives and methods. Such a climate depends upon an atmosphere of trust and professional confidence within the staff and between staff, pupils and parents. Its advocacy is easy: its realization in practice presents many challenges.

Dessent (1987) examined the philosophical and policy issues involved in integrating children with special educational needs into mainstream education. The meaning and implications of positive discrimination are considered. Positive discrimination does not necessarily mean that children with SEN should receive something different, one aspect is that in some respects they should be treated equally; in particular they should be treated as being of equal value. Resource allocation policies will need to concentrate on improving that which is normally available. Positive discrimination is an ethical issue. Like many ethical matters it is also essentially political.

Twenty years ago, once qualified, a teacher rarely observed or was observed by another teacher, so many found accepting another teacher into their classroom somewhat threatening. Other recent developments have helped to break down teacher isolation. Teacher appraisal, as described in an HMI report (GB.DES, 1989i), is likely to take the process further, when it is introduced.

The difficulties involved were recognized along with the demands made on the interpersonal skills of teachers who were now working with adults as well as, or even instead of, children (Visser, 1986; Lloyd-Smith and Sinclair-Taylor, 1988), the importance of support and involvement from a senior member of the school staff and training for the whole staff (Butt, 1986).

Descriptions of support teaching or the whole-school approach do not differentiate between pupils whose learning difficulties are specific and those for whom the difficulties are more general. The commitment is that all the pupils shall have access to the full curriculum. Dyer (1988) writes, 'It is a recognition of the right of pupils to a common education even if some find the going tough'. Lavers, Pickup and Thompson (1986) describe how they came together to share their experiences and to find solutions to problems within their Devon secondary schools. They record the adaptations they made and their conviction that 'much is to be gained by further developing and extending our supportive role in preference to a system of extraction'. The significant changes in special education provision that are taking place have profound implications for all involved (Ainscow, 1989).

Butt (1986), an LEA adviser, looks at the advantages of a resource base, support teaching, whole-school approach, one of which was that it 'might be more acceptable to the dyslexia lobby', and describes the training programme his county was following to facilitate such developments.

What is support teaching?

LEAs and individual schools in various parts of the country examined their practice and published descriptions of their actual or intended practice, problems and successes. Some of these were circulated as internal or consultative documents. Others were published more formally in educational journals or newspapers. These considered the reasons for change, types of change and the demands change makes on both support and subject teachers (Visser, 1986; Davies and Davies, 1988; Dyer, 1988; Mills, 1988; Ainscow, 1989).

Support teaching is a relatively new concept and the pattern chosen in one school will not necessarily be the same as that chosen in another, nor will a particular school's pattern necessarily remain the same over a number of years. Some schools depend mainly on resources provided by an authority-based service. In others, all resources are managed within the school. Dyer (1988) presents a detailed analysis of support that includes many of the following points: support may be given at a systems level in organizing teaching groups, planning curricula, pastoral care or examining and adapting teaching materials which will be used by large groups of pupils (Kemp, 1986). Support may also be given to a teacher colleague to help adapt or prepare materials, advise on objectives or some other aspect of management. Support can also include two teachers working together, though there are many different ways of managing this. The extra person may work only with the identified pupil, or with a group that includes that pupil, or may move around the room assisting the subject teacher in any relevant way, so that either teacher is available to assist the special needs pupil(s) as required. Sometimes the support can be given through careful observation so as to assist future programme planning. Substitutional support occurs when the support teacher takes the class and so frees the class teacher to observe or work with a particular pupil or group of pupils. There may be a need to provide additional or specialized equipment and ensure that the pupil has the skills to use it. Support may also involve organizing non-teaching resources, possibly parents or other pupils, and will certainly require liaison within the staff and between school, the parent and outside agencies.

Fish (1989) looks at the major dimensions of special education and at the level of intervention that may be required on each dimension. Almost all the education dimensions may be relevant to pupils whose learning difficulties appear to be specific, but not exclusively so.

Bringing the above sources together, the types of interventions that might be provided for pupils with specific learning difficulties include the following.

- Specially prepared or highlighted work sheets.
- Teaching the technical vocabulary prior to a lesson.
- Providing a tape recording of literature being studied.
- Providing a photocopy of notes to save note-taking at speed.
- Facility to tape-record notes or 'written work'.
- Teacher time to transcribe or to help the pupil transcribe the above tape recording.
- Word processor for extended pieces of written work.
- Tuition to help the pupil learn to use the word processor effectively.
- Tuition to help the pupil organize their work more effectively.
- A remedial programme for specific areas of skills weakness.

Most of these suggestions also have relevance to pupils whose learning difficulties are general, rather than specific. Until we have a more adequate understanding of which interventions at which stage of literacy development are most helpful to pupils, until we understand aptitude × instruction interactions (AIIs) more fully, this situation will continue.

These interventions depend on skilled teachers assessing pupils' needs in relation to the curriculum, keeping records, liaising with colleagues, parents and other professionals. It is to be hoped that as skills are being learned by pupils in relation to the general curriculum they will be used and generalized.

These types of intervention do not preclude the direct teaching of literacy skills, though the materials used may be ones that arise from the general or subject curriculum rather than a previously freestanding but structured programme. This places greater demands on the skills and knowledge of the support teacher who has to understand the principles of learning well enough to adapt them to changing subjects. The advantages to the learner should be access to the full curriculum with differentiation only of delivery and/or recording. Programmes which can be incorporated into such a structure have been described (Begley, Brown and Cameron, 1989; Mason, 1989). There may be a place for withdrawal teaching but this would not normally form an extended part of the special provision, rather it would be designed to overcome a specific difficulty. Evidence on the extent to which this policy (a) is applied and (b) is effective, is awaited.

Some teachers have used peer tutoring with pupils with a wide range of reading attainments. A well-known example is its use in Paired Reading (Pumfrey, 1991; Topping, 1991). Medcalf (1989) used a variant system known as Pause, Prompt and Praise (McNaughton, Glynn and Robinson, 1987) with ten 9- to 11-year-old pupils all in need of reading help. Three of the four better readers acted as tutors and the others were assigned to either a tutee or a tape-assisted reading programme. All pupils showed improvement in reading, and after six months the gains were still evident and most marked for the tutors. Conway and Gow (1988) look at the use of peer tutoring, reciprocal teaching and cooperative learning to develop the academic and social skills expected of a mainstream student. Moore (1988) describes the work of Palinscar and Brown in using reciprocal teaching and scaffolding to develop reading comprehension with pupils who could decode print. This area of research is particularly interesting because it appears that it may help pupils in a number of ways, through increased literacy skills and increased social skills. It is also possible that through supportive involvement with an academically more successful class member, pupils with specific learning difficulties (and others) may be less likely to be the victim of critical comments and become incorporated into the social fabric of the class rather than suffer the social isolation described by Sabornie (1989). An extensive 'paired reading' project has been carried out in Kirklees LEA (Topping, 1991). The findings underline the appeal of the strategy to professionals, parents and pupils. Teachers of pupils of all abilities consider it worthwhile. In combining participant modelling, a psycholinguistic model of reading acquisition, self-selection of materials, positive reinforcement and the involvement of significant others, such as parents and peers, motivated time on task is enhanced. The evidence of the effects of the approach on improving pupils' relative reading attainments is less convincing at present. In part, this is due to poorly designed studies and suspect methods of measuring progress. The value of 'paired reading' with pupils having severe and prolonged specific learning difficulties is yet to be determined.

Word processing also offers opportunities to pupils who have become dispirited through continuing failure to produce written work which looks good and contains no spelling errors. Simmons (1988) reports on its acceptability to pupils, 'It looks a lot nicer. There's no scribbling out'. Davidson (1988) found that a group of boys with specific learning difficulties responded well to the opportunities the word processor gave them to redraft their work, which improved in its breadth of vocabulary, its variety of sentence structure and general interest, as well as in technical accuracy. The pupil with SpLD will frequently read, spell and write poorly. One way of reducing the number of 'errors' identified by a teacher is to write *less*. Another is to write *illegibly* so that, for example, uncertainties about the positions of 'i' and 'e' in words such as 'perceive' are not visible. A further strategy is to avoid the frustration presented by too demanding educational tasks by *avoiding* lessons. All of these actions reduce motivated time on task and increase the probability of compounding specific (or general) learning difficulties with secondary emotional ones (see Chapter 4). The use of technology as described above can help to change this downward spiral of a pupil's poor reading, writing and spelling, many errors, many corrections and increasing frustration.

Good classroom management is important; having two teachers or a teacher and an assistant working together does not necessarily lead to more time on task and more effective learning. The use of room management techniques in classes for children with severe learning difficulties led to an increase in the time children were actively engaged (Thomas, 1985). Thomas (1986) looked at the possibilities of using similar forms of role definition in a mainstream class. Shepherd *et al.* (1990) showed that changes in teacher behaviour could increase the academic engagement of previously disengaged pupils. The principles also apply to helping pupils with specific learning difficulties.

The aims of the whole-school approach to special needs or learning difficulties are wider than are those of 'remedial teaching'. Remedial teaching was judged mainly by the progress pupils made in their measured reading and spelling skills and, in most studies, these are the only areas assessed. Hudson and Clunies-Ross (1984) suggest that in evaluating a wider approach to special needs one would consider pupil achievement, pupil adjustment, peer acceptance, teacher attitude, parent attitude, school organization and curriculum. Pupil achievement can be assessed in terms of literacy skills and also in relation to the rest of the National Curriculum, which pupils are now required to follow. Pupil adjustment can be assessed through a behaviour rating questionnaire (Mitchell, 1985), through school attendance rates (Gregory, Hackney and Gregory, 1982) and through recourse to school records. Peer acceptance can be assessed through sociometry (Sabornie, 1989), or through other questionnaires, observations or interviews.

Thomas (1990) examines the purposes of evaluation in various situations and shows how a primary school might evaluate its own changes in practice. Bibby (1990) evaluates in-class support in a secondary school in terms of perceived pupil progress, attitude to support by both the target pupils and the rest of the class, and the impact of support teaching on teachers. The outcomes of both these evaluations are positive enough to encourage the schools concerned to continue to develop support teaching and for other schools to move in that direction. They do not provide a clear comparison with other forms of intervention as, for example, the only approximation to a control group is the subject's previous performance and self reports. An evaluation of this type is a large-scale project beyond the resources of an individual school, but reports of smaller projects do help to clarify important issues and ways of assessing them. This is particularly important if informed judgements about the right use of expensive resources are to be made.

Education Reform Act 1988 and the National Curriculum

Curriculum-based intervention is supported by the National Curriculum Proposals for English as the following points indicate (NCC, 1988, 1989a).

12.3 Pupils with special educational needs, like all other pupils, should have the opportunity to experience the full range of the English curriculum. For example, pupils with reading problems (including dyslexic pupils) should not be deprived of literature, but should have the opportunity of experiencing it through listening to others reading aloud, whether live or recorded, and through seeing plays and films, as well as through reading suitably simplified texts.

12.10 ...They may however have particular difficulty with attainment targets concerned with secretarial skills and in this respect may benefit particularly from using word processors including spelling checkers.

The National Curriculum with its many attainment targets may help pupils with specific learning difficulties for it provides a framework in which the skills they have in oral and aural work can be explicitly recognized and credited. The speaking and listening component in English has equal weighting with the reading and writing components up to the end of Key Stage 3 (14 years). The secretarial aspects of spelling and handwriting account for 30 per cent of the writing component, 10 per cent of the whole of National Curriculum English.

17.26 ...The reason for separating these two aspects [composing and secretarial] in attainment targets is that they are independent abilities: people with good spelling and neat handwriting are not necessarily good writers and vice versa.

Similar support is given in Curriculum Guidance 2 (National Curriculum Council, 1989b, p. 8):

> Pupils with specific learning difficulties will benefit from teaching approaches which make best use of their oral strengths and avoid difficulties with written communication, through appropriate use of tape recorders and guidance on note taking for instance.

The possibility of modifying Standard Assessment Tasks is also discussed.

The above consideration of one aspect of the Education Reform Act 1988 presents an optimistic view of its impact on children with special educational needs. As yet we do not know what will be the overall impact of the manifold pedagogic and administrative components of the National Curriculum, its assessment and the public reporting of this, together with the resource implication for pupils with specific learning difficulties of the Local Management of Schools (LMS) and the operation of support services.

Fish (1989) sets SEN in the context of education in general and recognizes that the changes resulting directly and indirectly from the 1988 Act will present a major challenge to those working in special education:

> The nature of the educational and social situations an individual has to face may play a major part in determining how far disabilities are handicapping. An underlying belief that a set of performance criteria can be found to grade children...presents a profound challenge to the objective of according equal worth to all children within the education system...together with an equal entitlement to high quality education. (Fish, 1989)

The emotional impact of specific learning difficulties upon pupils and their self-esteem is covered in Chapter 4. However, the following comments from one pupil with a specific difficulty in writing have been echoed by many others, some of whom may have given up the struggle to become literate in the face of long-standing and severe learning difficulties.

> My English teacher did not seem to like me or my writing. One day she happened to see some of my work in my history book and commented 'Oh so you write badly for him too'. It was as if she thought I had a personal vendetta against her. Primary school was 'the pits' because of my writing, it was untidy and I could not write fast enough, also my spelling was poor. Each teacher had their own theory. I did not like writing, especially letters or anything special. In secondary school priorities changed. I would always have to write 'intelligent' things using long descriptive knowledgeable language to prove that I was at all capable. If teachers hadn't given me praise for the content of my work, I would have given up. [There was a time when she nearly did.]

Support service costs

Support services for children with specific learning difficulties are expensive. They can, however, represent a considerable saving to an LEA over the expenditure that would be incurred if such pupils were dealt with in other ways, such as attending either residential or day special schools.

In several major LEAs there are support services that have been developed to enable the authorities to meet their legal obligations to provide for such pupils within the authorities' own schools. In at least one court case a parent argued that the LEA could not fulfil its legal responsibilities of making suitable education for a statemented pupil within its own schools as it did not have available teachers who held specialist qualifications in the education of children with specific learning difficulties. The parent won the case. The child involved was placed at an independent residential school where the staff were suitably qualified. The cost to the LEA was some £15,000 per annum for a provision that had not been considered the most appropriate by its officers. The parents were delighted at the decision. A number of LEAs responded to this judgement by ensuring that they did have suitably qualified teachers, enabling them to support such pupils within the LEA's own schools in the vast majority of cases.

In order to demonstrate that they were capable of providing the teaching expertise that such pupils require, a number of LEAs have ensured that they have a body of suitably qualified teachers. These are qualified and experienced teachers who have undertaken appropriate further training in the identification and education of children with specific learning difficulties. Many support teachers have completed advanced diplomas and higher degrees as part of such professional development. A part-time Diploma in Advanced Studies in the Education of Pupils with Specific Learning Difficulties (Literacy) was established at the School of Education of the University of Manchester. Similar developments have taken place at universities, polytechnics and colleges across the country. The Royal Society of Arts and the British Dyslexia Association have developed in-service courses. A registered charity, Dyslexia Defined, also helped in sponsoring teachers to take further training.

Support services with a brief focused on pupils with specific learning difficulties began to appear. The following example indicates how this currently operates in a large LEA. It also highlights the resource implications of such developments.

The authority's policy is integrationist. Its long-term aim is that the vast majority of children with special educational needs will be educated in its own mainstream schools, with the necessary support being provided. The LEA's policy for pupils with specific learning difficulties is identical in its integrationist aspirations. The LEA has an official document entitled 'Provision for Pupils with Specific Learning Difficulties (Dyslexia)'. The work of teachers appointed to the service:

...consists essentially of direct teaching, together with appropriate related activities as directed by the District Education Officer. These related activities may include:

i   liaison with teachers, parents and other agencies;
ii   cross-curriculum support; and
iii diagnostic assessment and evaluation.

The teachers are appointed *solely* for all activities related to meeting the needs of children with specific learning difficulties who *are the subjects of statements of special educational needs*. Wherever possible, the teachers are based in a single school. They are supported by a reading and language service that itself has a staff of 77 working in 12 centres throughout the LEA.

In 1990 the Specific Learning Difficulties Support Service was staffed by 94 specialist teachers. They were working in some 300 schools. The teaching undertaken was with groups of between 4 and 12 pupils. Overall, the service was supporting about 928 statemented pupils with specific learning difficulties. Forty-one other pupils attend 'out-of-area' boarding schools and four attend 'out-of-area' day schools. The average cost per annum for these out-of-area pupils was quoted as £10,000. The additional 'within-area' costs were estimated at about £2000 per annum per pupil. Pupils without statements attending mainstream schools cost about £1175 and £2000 per annum at the primary and secondary stages, respectively.

The estimated annual cost of the support service for statemented pupils with specific learning difficulties was £2,000,000 per annum. To make sense of this figure, it needs to be set in a demographic context. The total population of the LEA is about 1,380,000. The school population is some 196,000. The current rate of provision for statemented pupils with specific learning difficulties is approximately 1 in 200, namely about 0.5 per cent. To make provision for the British Dyslexia Association's current estimate of an incidence of dyslexia of four per cent would mean that the support service would have to expand eightfold. Its costs would rise in tandem to about £16 m. per year. Put in terms of the pre-Community Charge rating system, the costs would represent a rates rise of about 5p. in the pound. It should also be born in mind that there are estimates of the incidence of specific learning difficulties that are far higher than four per cent. There are also other pupils competing for limited resources. What are tax and ratepayers prepared to support? What priority should be accorded to pupils with specific learning difficulties? There are no easy answers.

In 1990 the Department of Education and Science issued a draft circular concerning staffing for pupils with special educational needs. Section 2(4) of the Education Act 1981 requires LEAs to keep under review their arrangements for special educational provision. They are also required to ensure that, subject to considerations of the views of the parents, all pupils for whom they maintain statements of special educational needs should be educated in mainstream schools, provided that this is compatible with the pupils receiving the special education they require, with the provision of efficient education for the other pupils and with the efficient use of resources. A major purpose of the draft circular was to encourage '...the more cost-effective use of staff and other resources to meet the needs of pupils with SEN whether it is appropriate to educate them in county or voluntary schools or in special schools' (GB.DES, 1990b, para. 2).

In the draft circular, Section 4 concerns support services. 'LEAs should take account of the nature and extent of external services required to support teachers in their work. These will vary according to the type of provision, the numbers of children involved and the range and complexity of their special educational needs' (GB.DES, 1990b, para. 7).

From observations of classroom work seen to be effective for pupils with differing degrees of learning disability, a 'model' for assessing staff time required by such pupils was developed. Account was taken of group size and the number of staff required. The intensity of demands made on staff was also given some consideration. By relating the complexity of pupils' learning difficulties to their needs for a balanced and broadly based curriculum, judgements are made concerning the appropriate staffing levels.

A table is presented in the circular giving staffing levels for primary and secondary school pupils grouped under five bands of learning difficulty. In so far as one can judge, children with specific learning difficulties would come under group 5. The teacher/pupil ratios specified are 0.1 teachers and 0.1 special support assistants at the primary level and 0.1 teachers and 0.05 special support assistants at the secondary level. A key question is how is this to be funded?

HMIs' survey of support services for special educational needs

In a survey based on visits to ten support services, plus additional documentary evidence from a further six, HMIs of schools appraised the aims of support services, their resourcing and the effects of the latter on the achievement of the former (GB.DES, 1989h). The majority of the visits were carried out by teams of two or three HMIs who collectively observed some 180 lessons and 12 in-service sessions. LEA officers, headteachers, pupils, parents and members of support service teams were involved in discussions with HMIs. The quality of the work carried out in classrooms by support teachers, and the ways in which the endeavours of support services affected the standards of teaching in schools, were of central interest.

The major focus of seven of the ten services visited was on general learning difficulties. The remaining three were concerned with pupils having visual and hearing impairments. Of the six other support services contacted, five were mainly involved with general learning difficulties and the remaining one with pupils suffering from visual impairments. It is not claimed by HMIs on the basis of such a limited sampling that the evidence and judgements represent an 'accurate or comprehensive picture of support services nationally'. Despite this, in the same paragraph, the report claims that '...the issues and trends identified are considered to be fairly typical'.

Although the survey was not focused on pupils with specific learning difficulties, its findings have implications for the means whereby LEA services address their responsibilities for the identification and education of such pupils within the context of a whole-school approach to meeting special educational needs.

At the time of the survey, support services were in a period of reconstruction, having evolved from the earlier remedial services. Support services were typically expected to develop their range of activities and the roles of their staff. The main thrust in most LEAs was towards the development of a '...unified and coherent service, capable of flexible deployment across special and ordinary schools, and across a range of learning difficulties and types of special needs' (ibid., para. 8). The distances between such rhetoric and the realities of present provision and practice are currently yawning chasms rather than readily bridgeable gaps.

In passing, the advent of LMS and the delegation to schools of an increasing degree of financial autonomy has important implications for the future of such services. Whether the services are centrally retained by the LEA, or whether their costs are delegated to schools who then 'buy in' what the schools consider necessary (and the law requires), are key issues. This is also the case with other LEA services, such as school psychological services, concerned with pupils having general and specific learning difficulties. There is already evidence that certain LEAs, because of limited budgets and the resource implications of LMS, are dramatically reducing what is provided centrally by their support services. The legal responsibilities of LEAs and schools to meet the educational needs of pupils will increasingly determine the nature of provision, as the effects of delegated budgets impact on the LEAs and schools. There is a real danger that, because of the extra resources typically required by pupils with special educational needs, such pupils may be perceived by some schools as an undue drain on limited resources unless the LEA takes such resource issues fully into account in its funding formulae. Government funding policy is crucial.

The importance of support services working to a clear LEA policy and pattern of organization was emphasized in the HMIs' report. Unfortunately, in few of the LEAs was such a clear brief operative. Lacking central direction, several services were working to establish their own code of practice. Too many support services worked in isolation from the other aspects of the LEA's advisory services. This lack of coordination led to classroom teachers reporting confusing and contradictory advice being given by different advisory groups concerning '...for example about oral work, the grouping of pupils and the adaptation of teaching methods. Several schools reported that many of the tasks identified by the special needs support services were additional to those promoted by other interests, despite the fact that most pupils and organisational needs had common requirements' (GB.DES, 1989h, para. 22). The autonomy of such support services from the psychological services, which had stimulated and developed the former remedial education services, has not been an entirely beneficial evolution.

Most support services are based on peripatetic teams of teachers. Training for their new responsibilities was considered inadequate by HMIs in five of the services visited. Cutbacks in the funding of in-depth INSET for such specialist teachers are increasing. On reflection, the dramatic reduction in full-time, long courses of advanced study and training for qualified teachers in relation to pupils with special educational needs is a case in point. This is not to argue that the significant expansion of INSET for all teachers is not of value. Both are required.

One worrying example has recently come to light. Members of a support service had been admitted to a two-year, part-time course of advanced study and training in a field central to their developing responsibilities in relation to pupils with specific learning difficulties and *undertaken in their own time*. At the end of the first year of the course (September 1990) they were informed that the LEA was no longer willing to continue this funding of INSET undertaken during teachers' own time. The administrative reasons given had a somewhat hollow ring. The implications of such a policy are extremely disquieting.

According to the HMIs' report, the 'whole-school' approach to meeting special educational needs was not well addressed in the practices of the support services. The quality and range of practice also varied considerably from service to service. Little of the work done in withdrawal sessions observed was related to the context of the school's curriculum. In only five per cent of the sessions did the help provided either follow up, or prepare for, a classroom lesson. On a more positive note, in two-thirds of the services, the support service teachers were involved in other working arrangements including team teaching and shared lesson planning. The 'best practice' in such a situation was represented by a classroom so arranged that both teachers could interact with a full range of pupils and in which support given to individuals was a common but unobtrusive aspect of teacher–pupil contact.

The new pattern of support service provision has led to a reduction in the amount of time spent by support teachers on teaching pupils individually or in small groups. Reciprocally, more time was being spent on advisory and INSET work on the assumption that this represented a more effective way of developing and providing services for all pupils. This is not a development universally welcomed by support service teachers, headteachers and their staffs, parents and pupils. The HMIs' report notes that 'All forms of direct teaching by the support services did lead to improvements in the performances of the pupils...each service could point to some sources of evidence indicating progress by most of the pupils involved...with overall results spanning the range from marginal improvements to substantial gains' (GB.DES, 1989h, para. 36).

It will be hard to convince the parents of pupils with specific learning difficulties that their child is likely to benefit from changes in resource allocation that reduce the time available for individual and small group instruction. Eight of the ten services visited carried out formal evaluations of their in-service work with teachers. The current absence of empirical evidence of the efficacy of such changed practices on *children's attainments* does not engender confidence in any disinterested observer. Observers of the scene whose children do have specific learning difficulties are far from disinterested. They will almost certainly continue to seek highly specialized and very expensive support for their child paid for from the public purse.

> The general picture is one of support services for special needs undertaking some promising developments in school-based practice and in-service training. About one half of those visited had well qualified staff with considerable experience of working with children and teachers in a variety of contexts. An equal number were experiencing difficulty in moving from a traditional role, of dealing mainly with literacy and numeracy, and into fulfilling a broader set of expectations. (ibid., para. 46)

The overall impression presented by the report is one that is critical of many aspects of support services' current policies and practices. A number of basic issues that must be addressed by support services, if they are to be effective and be seen as effective, are identified.

For example, the following points are quoted from the conclusions to the HMIs' report.

- Policies which direct the work of support services are explicit in only a few LEAs.
- Only a few LEAs provide clear and co-ordinated leadership for their services.
- The number of pupils directly helped by the support services varies considerably between authorities.
- A central topic of debate in many LEAs is the issue of where best to concentrate the efforts of the support services.
- Collaborative arrangements with class teachers need to be further refined.
- Few support services have the accommodation, resources and clerical support necessary for their work.
- Most services recognize this kind of provision as not a proven best arrangement for meeting special needs.

- Evaluative procedures are not yet widespread...and more attention needs to be given to the method and means by which the efficacy of a service is to be determined.

Additionally, growth-points based on the expansion and development of current good practices by support services are identified and promoted.

- Some services have made a good beginning towards evaluating the effectiveness of their contribution.
- The general impression is that service provision does make a difference to the schools and the pupils receiving it.
- The better support services are helping schools across a broad front make more effective provision for all pupils.

Teaching and specialist expertise and time can never meet the demands that are made of them. Parental expectations understandably rise when effective approaches to helping children with specific learning difficulties are indicated.

In certain respects, support services are analogous to a rope in a very active tug-of-war. They are subject to the conflicting pulls of their history of effective work with individuals and specified groups and the somewhat contrasting (but not entirely incompatible) expectations aroused and demands made, by a whole-school approach towards identifying and alleviating special educational needs.

Pupils with special educational needs in ordinary schools

A further HMIs' report entitled *A Survey of Pupils with Special Educational Needs in Ordinary Schools* was published (GB.DES, 1989b). This survey involved single day visits by HMI to 55 primary and 42 secondary schools in 38 LEAs.

About 50 per cent of the primary and 25 per cent of the secondary schools had whole-school policy statements concerning SEN. A further quarter of the secondary schools had policy documents developed by the SEN departments. The importance of the support of the senior management of the school in such endeavours, and for the coordination of policy planning and development to be carried out by a qualified member of staff, were seen as essential to the development of adequate policies.

Focusing on top junior or first year secondary school pupils, up to three pupils with special educational needs in each school were tracked for one day.

In just over half of the 269 lessons seen in primary schools the standard of work from pupils with SEN was judged to be satisfactory or better. In secondary schools the standard of work was judged to be at least satisfactory in half of the 218 lessons seen. The main features of practice which resulted in work of at least satisfactory standard among pupils with SEN also constituted good practice for all pupils. (ibid., para. 2)

The report describes various organizational systems used to group pupils with SEN. At both the primary and secondary levels, three-quarters of the schools extracted pupils from mainstream classes for differing periods weekly. Typically, these pupils worked in small groups usually on a restricted range of language and computational skills. The materials used were frequently unrelated to the pupils' ongoing classroom work, thereby contributing to discontinuities in the curricula of some of the pupils. In contrast, the provision of support teaching for these pupils within the mainstream classes was found in about half of the primary schools and in a quarter of the secondary schools. This practice was particularly valuable where the teachers had received some joint training and had clarified their respective roles. Responsibilities for monitoring and recording their work with pupils with SEN were also previously agreed. Such collaborative planning often involved other members of the LEA support service as well as teaching colleagues in the school and also the pupils' parents.

Only two per cent of primary schools used a class designated as a remedial class for pupils with SEN. Nine per cent of schools had at least one pupil with SEN being taught in an off-site special class. This arrangement is reported as being particularly poorly balanced and coordinated in relation to the requirement of the National Curriculum. Extraction from the mainstream class took place in about three-quarters of the pupils tracked. They worked in small groups with an average size of about six and with a range of from 1 to 15 pupils. Extraction time ranged from half an hour to two and a half days a week.

In secondary schools the pupils were involved in more than one system of grouping each week. Twelve per cent of schools adopted mixed ability classes. Designated remedial classes were used in one-third of secondary schools.

The best class group organization in both junior and secondary schools exhibited similar attributes. These included the careful identification and assessment of pupils with SEN and also informing parents of their children's weekly timetables. In addition, work programmes were differentiated to ensure a match with pupils' performance levels. Positive self-images were supported and realistically high performance expectations set.

The effective use of additional teachers in mainstream classes to support pupils with SEN required that both the support and the mainstream teachers be trained in preparation for such teamwork. Readers will note that this finding concurs with the findings of the survey of support services outlined earlier.

Some two-thirds of primary schools had designated members of staff with responsibility for the coordination of provision to meet SEN. In only one half of the schools had these teachers received some specialist training. The duties were typically carried out by class teachers without any non-class contact time being allowed for the additional responsibilities involved.

Support service teachers worked in three-quarters of the primary schools that the HMIs visited. In half of the schools the priority of such peripatetic teachers was on teaching pupils with SEN. In contrast, in a quarter of primary schools, priority was given to providing advisory support. In just under one-fifth of the primary schools visited, supply or temporary teachers were taking pupils with SEN. Problems of curricular discontinuity were exacerbated by such arrangements.

In contrast, in relation to staffing, nearly all secondary schools had a designated coordinator or head of department of SEN. Three-quarters of schools had staff who had undertaken training, usually a short, non-award bearing course, for the responsibilities. Despite this, there were frequently discontinuities in the pupils' work programmes.

Over fifty per cent of secondary schools in the sample used specialist subject teachers in teaching classes, sets or groups of pupils with SEN, albeit for only a few periods weekly. Very few of these subject specialists had undertaken training in identifying and meeting pupils' SEN. Input to schools from peripatetic teachers employed by LEA support services was minimal. Supply and/or temporary teachers were teaching pupils with SEN in 30 per cent of the secondary schools visited for some or all of the day. This further confounded problems of curriculum discontinuity for the pupils concerned.

On a more positive note, over the previous two years a quarter of the secondary schools had involved all staff in school-based INSET on SEN. The staff from LEA support services and advisory services had contributed to this INSET. The extent, quality and effects of this INSET on pupils or staff are neither described nor evaluated.

The report states that the majority of the pupils tracked were following a curriculum that met the suggested plan for the National Curriculum (NCC, 1989b). There was, however, a substantial minority of about one-third of both primary and secondary pupils with SEN who were following curricula showing limitations in one or more of breadth, balance, differentiation, continuity and progression.

Examples of inadequate education were seen in both primary and secondary schools. This work was characterized by insufficient differentiation to match the individual pupil's abilities. In some cases the readability levels of worksheets and texts were far too high for some pupils to understand what was required of them. An oral explanation by the teacher at the start of a lesson typically failed to result in the necessary differentiation.

At this stage it is important to ask what is actually meant by such relatively imprecise terms as 'breadth, balance, differentiation, continuity and progression'. Unless operationally defined, they can act as a smokescreen rather than as an illumination of how well a child is responding to educative processes. It is equally important to consider how pupils with specific learning difficulties manifest, for example, in an apparently intractable inability to read, write or spell, can be given access to the National Curriculum.

Overall, the survey indicates that the education of pupils with SEN has received considerable attention from schools and their staffs. It is claimed that this has had beneficial effects (though these claims are not supported by quantified information concerning pupils' attainments, attitudes or adjustment). As can be deduced from the previous paragraphs, much more remains to be done if the entitlement curriculum is to be delivered to pupils with SEN, including those with specific learning difficulties.

Summary

The evolution of remedial education services into support services as one means of meeting pupils' special educational needs has led to a broadening of the responsibilities of such services. This broadening has been underpinned by a 'whole-school' philosophy concerning the identification and alleviation of pupils' SEN. There still remains much heterogeneity in the aims, organization and approaches adopted by support services in different LEAs. An even greater heterogeneity exists between the characteristics and special educational needs of the individual pupils that the combined efforts of schools and support services must address. Pupils with specific learning difficulties are but one of many groups claiming additional resources.

Most services are inadequately resourced both materially and in terms of staff training. There are many uncertainties concerning the efficacy of support services in relation to pupils' attainments in the basic subjects of the National Curriculum. The advent of LMS may well lead to a curtailment of activities deemed of lower priority than the legal obligation of LEAs and schools to meet pupils' special educational needs in general and specific learning difficulties in particular. With LMS and the current upsurge in applications for the preparation of statements on individual pupils, there could well be a reversal of the trend to reduce the direct teaching of pupils who experience such intractable problems.

Recommendations

8.1. All children with specific learning difficulties should follow the whole curriculum.

8.2. Differentiation of the delivery and/or the recording of the curriculum, but not the content, be provided for pupils with specific learning difficulties.

8.3. Suggestions for differentiation made in the National Curriculum guidelines be evaluated and developed.

8.4. Maintaining the self-esteem of pupils with specific learning difficulties be considered an essential component in achieving literacy.

8.5. Teachers provide help across the curriculum where the specific learning difficulties are causing problems in areas other than literacy.

8.6. The value of cooperative learning for pupils with specific learning difficulties be further explored.

8.7. Pupils' views about the nature and quality of the support they receive or consider desirable be sought.

8.8. Differentiation of the curriculum, and access to it, requires consideration of the inter- and intra-individual differences of all pupils.

8.9. Participation in the National Curriculum by pupils with specific learning difficulties be ensured by encouraging good practice for all pupils.

SECTION D: PSYCHOMEDICAL RESPONSES

This section presents selected aspects of the psychomedical research literature bearing on specific learning difficulties (dyslexia). An awareness of the contributions of colleagues working in other disciplines is important if we are not to become immured in the conceptual concrete of our own specialisms. The material presented makes no claim to being comprehensive, but the references provided will enable readers to follow up the summaries.

Chapter 9

Review of the Neuropsychological Literature

Introduction

In reviews of the concept of specific developmental dyslexia, Singleton (1975, 1976) argued that research in the area was in a state of conceptual and methodological disarray. He pointed to the existence of confusion resulting from vague and idiosyncratic diagnostic criteria, to the unreliable figures of incidence, to confusion as to whether it is a unitary condition, and to the existing understanding of aetiology being based upon guesses, speculation and tenuously related findings. However, in later articles (1987, 1988) Singleton argued that recent neuropsychological research was enabling the development of more robust and sophisticated models of the reading process.

Currently, no comprehensive theory of the neuropsychological processes underlying SpLD exists. This is not really surprising. However, the number of studies and the influence of the findings in this area have increased significantly since the late 1970s. This has been enabled by the development of increasingly more sophisticated non-invasive neuroradiological, electrophysiological and other neurodiagnostic procedures. The gathering evidence, if not conclusive, is certainly thought-provoking and is increasing our understanding of the relations between brain function, behaviour and learning (Pavlidis, 1990a, b).

This 'gathering evidence' is important for practitioners to note. In the search for an effective educational response to SpLD, practitioners who have unconsidered objections to the use of a 'medical (or neurological) model' may incur an increasing ignorance of related evidence within the fields of neurology, neuropsychology, neurochemistry and allied medical sciences. Hynd and Cohen (1983) suggest that few practising psychologists or reading specialists can be considered to be up-to-date in their familiarity with such literature. Hynd, Quackenbush and Obrzut (1980) argued that many practising psychologists have an inadequate background in the physiological and neurophysiological bases of behaviour within their preparatory training. This assertion has some validity in so far as many educational psychologists are concerned.

Post-mortem studies

There has been a limited, but increasing, number of autopsy studies of the brains of individuals considered to be developmental dyslexics (see Drake, 1968; Galaburda, 1979; Galaburda and Eidelberg, 1982; Galaburda *et al.*, 1985; Galaburda, Signoret and Ronthal, 1985; Obrzut and Hynd, 1986). The reports of these studies suggest that bilateral anomalies are found but that there is a significant predominance of anomalies within the left hemisphere. Galaburda *et al.* (1985), reporting on a series of autopsy studies on male individuals with SpLD, found hemispheric symmetry of the planum temporale in all cases. It is, it should be noted, normal to find a degree of asymmetry. Histological examination also showed varying degrees of ectopias (mislaced neurons), cytoarchitectonic dysplasias (focal abnormalities in the cortical cytoarchitecture consisting usually of a displacement of cells and disordered layering) and brain warts. These anomalies predominated around the left perisylvian region. A smaller number of such anomalies was present in the right hemisphere, particularly in the temporal, parietal and frontal cortical regions.

Masland (1990), reports that Galaburda has now performed autopsies on nine children (seven boys and two girls) diagnosed as dyslexic. A predominance of the anomalies described above was found in the auditory areas of the brain within the seven boys. In the two girls scar tissue was found suggestive of injury in late pregnancy or early infancy. These findings are particularly interesting and demand further research to clarify possible aetiological factors as well as, and perhaps of more importance, their implications for learning and teaching.

The findings from such studies need to be considered with the utmost caution. The numbers involved are very small and the types of anomalies described are not unique to people with SpLD. Neuronal ectopias, for example, are found in 5–30 per cent of brains in autopsies where no known or documented history of any disorder exists (Brun, 1975; Veith and Schwindt, 1976). Brain warts have been reported in about 26 per cent of brains (Schulze and Braak, 1976). Focal dysplasias have been reported to be linked with epilepsy (Taylor *et al.*, 1971) as well as with SpLD. It is not clear, therefore, just what comparison can be made given the undocumented variability of the 'normal' control population. The results from post-mortem studies are clearly inconclusive as yet in determining whether neuropathology is the cause of SpLD. However, the evidence from these early studies is highly suggestive of this. Galaburda *et al.* (1985) argued that the probability of finding symmetrical plana and the other anomalies in four consecutive cases was of the order of 4×10^{-7}.

Much 'soft' evidence is available from the use of increasingly more sophisticated neurodiagnostic procedures such as those described below.

Developments in neurodiagnostic procedures

There is a vast array of possible neurodiagnostic procedures available today. The information gleaned from any particular procedure will be interpreted in the light of information gained from a battery of tests that might include neurological, psychometric and behavioural tests. It is usual for neuropsychologists to use psychometric and behavioural measures to enable inferences about neurologic differences to be made. The procedures highlighted here are those that are relatively recent developments or ones that are, perhaps, more likely to be used within research relevant to SpLD due to their relative non-invasive character. Bergleiter (1985) has argued that the use of these procedures enables an interface between neurophysiological and behavioural sciences.

Computed axial tomography (CAT)

CAT has had a very significant effect upon clinical neurology and research because it has been considered to be relatively risk-free, apart from exposure to limited radiation. Such a view might be reconsidered in the light of the development of MRI (described below). CAT is a technique used to visualize the soft tissues of the brain and spinal cord, ventricles and subarachnoid space. CAT scans employ beams of X-rays which are rotated around 180 degrees. According to the relative absorption of the rays at different coordinates, a computer defines the relative density upon a visual display. An injection of a water-soluble, iodinized contrast medium is often employed to enhance the attenuation of the X-rays. The use of such a medium has its own limited risks.

Regional cerebral blood flow (rCBF)

The assessment of rCBF has proved useful to investigate alterations in brain metabolism relating to cognition. Typically two measurements are taken: one where the patient is at rest and another where the patient is involved in a set cognitive activity. The patient inhales xenon, a radioactive isotope, for a short period of time. Measures are taken as the isotope circulates throughout the blood by detectors placed near the scalp. Subcortical and cortical blood flow varies according to metabolic demands, and by comparing rCBF patterns at rest with patterns during activities, pictures of brain activity can be established (see Hagberg, 1978). These procedures have been used with children but some concern is felt about the levels of radioactivity that they may be exposed to.

Electroencephalography (EEG) and event-related potentials (ERPs)

Procedures involving ERPs make use of EEG, within which electrodes are placed on the scalp so as to measure the brain's electrical waveforms. ERPs are the measurement of the late components of a waveform whilst the patient is actively involved in a perceptual or cognitive task. Topographical mapping of EEG and ERP measures through the use of computers has enabled researchers to record more easily electrical activity as it evolves throughout the brain.

Magnetic resonance imaging (MRI)

This procedure enables very clear visual definitions of the soft tissues of the brain and spinal cord. It involves the computerized mapping of the resonance of hydrogen (protons) in the brain. Hydrogen protons resonate within a magnetic field at specific frequencies and their resonance following a brief pulse of magnetic energy decays differentially depending upon their density. A computer is used to produce an image based upon the rates of decay. The resulting images are considerably clearer than those obtainable by CAT scans (Hawkes *et al.*, 1980). This procedure is also superior in the sense that it does not involve any exposure to radiation; it is completely safe and may therefore be repeated as often as required (Oldendorf and Zabielski, 1984). The procedure is a recent development that appears to be ideally suited to the study of developmental issues. It is to be expected that it will encourage a significant increase in neuropsychological research related to SpLD.

Ultrasonography

In this technique high-frequency sound waves are directed into the skull. The sound waves create echoes that are variable according to the tissue involved. The varying echoes are converted into a picture upon an oscilloscope. These procedures are becoming increasingly popular as they are non-intrusive, have no side effects, can be portable and are relatively inexpensive in comparison with other procedures (Babcock and Han, 1982).

Three types of scanners are available. 'Real-time scanners are portable but the quality of the images obtainable is not as high as with other scanners. Water-delay scanners involve the use of a number of sources of sound waves from within a water container. The patient lies on a membrane covering the container and images similar to CAT scans are obtained. The best images are obtainable from contact scanners that involve the manual movement of the scanner upon the head.

Theory and research

Around the turn of the century a number of authors (Pringle-Morgan, 1896; Bastian, 1898; Hinshelwood, 1900, 1902, 1909) reported on individuals who appeared to have a congenital inability to learn to read. Hynd, Connor and Nieves (1987) argue that in these early reports, and with the benefit of hindsight, a number of observations were made that are consistent with present-day conceptualizations. They noted that: (1) 'congenital word blindness' was evident in children of normal ability; (2) it was more prevalent in males; (3) the actual problems manifested were variable but related to an underlying inability to read; (4) normal teaching methods did not seem to be effective; (5) a genetic component appeared to exist and express itself in a variable fashion; (6) the disorder could be diagnosed using a variety of procedures; and (7) the region of the angular gyrus in the left cerebral hemisphere appeared to be implicated.

An influential theory was put forward by Orton (1925, 1926, 1937), who suggested that incomplete cerebral dominance was the major cause of developmental reading difficulties. Orton proposed a single causative factor theory of dyslexia. Many other authors have since suggested alternative single or dual cause theories, such as a maturational lag of cerebral organization (Bender, 1957; Delacato, 1959), hemispheric differences (Bakker, 1984a,b), perceptual-motor deficiencies (Drew, 1956; Kephart, 1960; Frostig and Maslow, 1970), temporal-order recall (Bakker, 1972), cross-modal integration (Birch and Belmont, 1964), language deficits (Vellutino, 1979) and deficits of the parietal region (Jorm, 1979). Whilst such single factor theories propose alternative causes, they have a number of common features. Each suggests a neurological dysfunction in terms of deficit or delay. Methodologically or theoretically each views dyslexic children as an homogeneous group within which individuals may or may not display characteristic difficulties or deficits. In many of these single or dual factor theories a view of brain function as highly localized is held. Lashley (1938), however, provided convincing evidence that brain function is not strictly localized. This led to mass-actionist theory and the concept of equipotentiality where complex cognitive skills are seen as dependent upon the equal participation of all areas of the brain.

The theory of incomplete cerebral dominance is not supported by research (Hynd and Obrzut, 1977; Moseley, 1988). The evidence to date suggests that neither a strict localizationist or mass-actionist perspective is completely correct. ERP and evoked-potentials research points to the view that the neurological activity underlying some basic sensory functions tends to be relatively more localized than the activity underlying higher cognitive processes, such as reading (see Duffy et al., 1980). Supportive evidence is available from post-mortem studies (Masland, 1990). Such topographical and histological studies suggest that, rather than being localized, higher cognitive processes are dependent upon a number of cortical areas and the interactions between them (Euler, Lundberg and Lennerstrand, 1989).

Correspondingly, since 1970 the majority of authors have put forward theories and cognitive models based on a multiplicity of possible causes (Boder, 1973; Denckla, 1977; Marcel, 1980; Morton, 1980; Shallice, 1981; Ellis, 1984; Hynd and Hynd, 1984; Seymour and MacGregor, 1984; Mayeux and Kandel, 1985; Seymour, 1986; Coltheart, 1987a,b; Singleton, 1987). Many of these authors suggest models of functional interactive cognitive systems. The system for reading is seen to include the occipital cortices, the region of the angular gyrus, Wernicke's area, the left planum temporale, the arcuate fasciculus, Broca's region and the supplementary motor area (Hynd and Hynd, 1984). Any weak point in the interaction of the system or in particular important cortical areas would affect the performance of the whole system; each part of the system being interdependent for the effective performance of complex skills. Weak points, or dysfunctions, might be indicated by dysplasias, ectopias or the hemispheric symmetry of the planum temporale as suggested by the post-mortem studies and from MRI studies (Rumsey et al., 1986). Further, given that the number and site of such anomalies might be random between individuals, any given individual's actual behavioural performance might be unique.

Such structural anomalies could result from a range of physical or viral insults, could be genetically determined or could result from a number of other causes. Some authors suggest that such anomalies occur during the fifth to seventh month of gestation (Geschwind and Behan, 1982; McBride and Kemper, 1982). They argue that the location of the majority of anomalies provides evidence that they must have occurred during this period (the latter part of neuronal migration to the cortical plate), as the areas involved are the last to complete this process. Such anomalies can be experimentally produced in animals only in this period

(Dvorak and Feit, 1977). Obrzut and Hynd (1986) suggest that, given the slower rate of growth of areas of the left hemisphere in gestation, there are a number of possibilities as to why the left hemisphere is more susceptible to insult. An area growing more slowly may have a longer time within which it may be susceptible to any random insult or may be affected for a longer time by a causative agent. Another argument might be that the causative agent involved is directed at particular biological features present predominantly in the left hemisphere. Immunological and chemical studies would support such a view (Renoux *et al.*, 1983; Oke, Keller and Adams, 1978). Exactly what the causative agent or agents are for the observed anomalies is as yet not known.

Given the notions of interactive cognitive systems, of anomalies that may have a variety of possible locations, aetiologies and effects, and of possible genetic determinants (DeFries, 1991), then it is possible that SpLD may be caused by a number of structural anomalies or may result from an expected normal range of genetically determined individual differences. If this is the case, then it would appear to be inappropriate to use theoretical, methodological or intervention approaches that treat all individuals with SpLD or dyslexia as having the same disorder. It is necessary to look more closely and to classify the types of structural anomalies or differences in relation to the types of difficulties experienced. Indeed there is a growing consensus amongst researchers about the existence of subtypes. This consensus has arisen from the neurological evidence concerning the different possible aetiological factors involved, increasingly sophisticated experimental investigations arising out of the conflicting results of studies which treat 'dyslexics' as an homogeneous group, from research with adults who have 'acquired dyslexia' as a result of some trauma and from the results emanating from the use of the more sophisticated, non-invasive neurophysiological investigative techniques referred to above (Duane, 1991).

Acquired dyslexia: the search for subtypes

Obrzut and Hynd (1986) argue that researchers have sought to delineate different subtypes from a number of approaches and that the majority of those who have attempted to draw conclusions on the basis of measures of reading or from psychological measures have failed to integrate their findings with psychoneurological variables. They also suggest that the majority of studies based upon measures of reading make use of diagnostic tools that look at simplistic skills, such as sight reading or phonological word building, and thereby fail to take a comprehensive view of all the possible phonological, graphological, motor, semantic, syntactic and schematic aspects to reading. Despite the different approaches and limitations of design they argue that there is still a striking similarity of results. Early models of subtypes (Boder, 1973; Pirozzolo, 1979) suggested three types: one, which Boder described as 'dysphonetic', involving difficulties with sound–symbol relations; a second, termed 'dyseidetic', involving difficulties with visuo-spatial aspects; and a third type in which both types of difficulties are observed.

Other researchers, such as Marshall and Newcomb (1973, 1980) and Singleton (1987), have put forward more complex models that are more suited to dealing with the observed variety of difficulties experienced by children. These models make use of evidence gleaned from studies of adults with acquired dyslexia where observed difficulties can be directly related to the sites of lesions in the neurological system. The models are built up using a psycholinguistic-information processing approach to encompass the range of literacy difficulties observed. Different authors propose different numbers of subtypes, which are seen as 'ideal forms', and it is recognized that there is considerable overlap concerning the actual difficulties experienced by any particular individual.

Subtypes of acquired dyslexia

1. *Deep dyslexia*. Individuals with deep dyslexia have difficulty with phoneme–grapheme conversion and with more abstract words. They have characteristic errors in their reading that show common or semantic substitutions. They can usually read familiar words, particularly concrete nouns, but more abstract nouns, adjectives and verbs are found difficult. Non-words are found almost impossible (Coltheart, Patterson and Marshall, 1980). It has been suggested that such people show an over-reliance upon visualization, word frequency and contextual cues. Saffran *et al.* (1980), and Coltheart (1984) argue that such people may not be able to use the reading systems within the left hemisphere at all. Rather, they use right-hemisphere processes to aid global and pictorial recognition in conjunction with semantic and contextual cues. The characteristic semantic errors and difficulties with abstract words would be explained by such an hypothesis.

2. *Phonological dyslexia*. Individuals in this subtype have similar difficulties with phonological analysis but do not show evidence of semantic errors or of being affected by the concreteness of words (Shallice and Warrington, 1980; Patterson, 1982). They have difficulty with non-words and great difficulty in sounding out words. In some cases difficulties are also shown with multisyllabic words where prefixes and suffixes are omitted, added or substituted (Funnell, 1983). Such individuals appear to be able to avoid the semantic errors characteristic of deep dyslexics by using a strategy of visual similarity. For example the non-word 'rale' may be read correctly through analogy with a known word, such as pale (Kay and Marcel, 1981). This type of strategy enables the avoidance of semantic errors but gives rise to visual errors where errors are visually similar substitutions.

3. *Surface dyslexia*. This subtype includes individuals who display ability in reading phonetically regular words and non-words but have difficulties in reading irregular words, whole-word recognition and the use of contextual cues (Patterson, Marshall and Coltheart, 1985). Apparently such individuals cannot make use of visual analysis to recognize whole words. The reading of irregular words results in errors that show that the reader is over-relying upon phonological strategies. Reading can be painfully slow, involving the deliberate sounding out of words. If asked for the meaning of words the response is often based upon pronunciation, and homophones are often guessed incorrectly. Not surprisingly, the comprehension of text is poor. Understanding appears to depend upon a phonological pathway and cannot be accessed via visual analysis.

4. *Direct dyslexia*. This subtype is often termed 'hyperlexia'. Typically, individuals display competent accuracy in oral reading skills but have very poor comprehension of the text read. They are often able to read material beyond their normal vocabulary usage. It appears that while they are able to read print via phonological and whole-word recognition strategies, their semantic analysis seems to be unable to make sense of the text read (Schwartz, Saffran and Marin, 1980; McClure and Hynd, 1983; Shallice, Warrington and McCarthy, 1983).

The comparison of acquired and developmental subtypes

A number of authors have attempted to draw comparisons between subtypes of acquired and developmental dyslexia (Jorm, 1979). Whilst such comparisons may be productive in the building of models of developmental dyslexia and its subtypes, caution needs to be exercised. There are a number of issues that need to be addressed in attempting to generalize adult-based research to children. It cannot be assumed that the relationships between neurological structures and cognitive performance are the same in children and in adults. A major variable that demands consideration is that of ontogenetic development. The relationship between brain, learning and behaviour in developing children has to be viewed in the light of research into the notions of genetic predetermination, continuities and discontinuities in development and plasticity. Research into the development of neuropsychological organization in children such as functional brain organization, information processing and lateralization needs to be integrated into theoretical perspectives of developmental dyslexia subtypes (Hynd and Willis, 1988). This area of research is a large and complicated one that is beyond the scope of this text, but a number of texts give informative outlines of the area and how the findings relate to developmental dyslexia (Hynd and Cohen, 1983; Hynd and Hynd, 1984; Hynd and Willis, 1988).

Hynd and his co-workers (op. cit.) argued that comparable difficulties were evident in developmental and deep dyslexia. Difficulties within phonological processes and in reading non-words were seen to be prevalent in developmental dyslexia. Supportive evidence of difficulties with the reading of non-words is available (Snowling, 1980, 1981). Baddeley *et al.* (1982) have shown that children with developmental dyslexia can be taught these skills although not to the same levels of skill as other children. Individuals with deep dyslexia are unable to master this skill. Johnston (1983) reported a case study of apparent developmental dyslexia that exhibited the characteristic semantic errors of deep dyslexia.

A number of authors have reported case studies of developmental dyslexia that display the profile of skills and typical errors associated with phonological dyslexia (Bradley and Bryant, 1983; Temple and Marshall, 1983; Bradley and Bryant, 1983; Seymour and McGregor, 1984; Temple, 1985). Similar comparisons have been made for surface dyslexia (Ellis, 1979; Coltheart, 1981, 1982; Coltheart *et al.*, 1983; Seymour and McGregor, 1984) and direct dyslexia (Richman and Kitchell, 1981; Healy, 1982; Seigel, 1984).

The comparisons of acquired and developmental subtypes appear to be growing in number. As authors suggest differing numbers of 'pure form' subtypes, it is important that such research is placed within a conceptual framework or model of the functional reading system. Within the research on adults, the recorded profiles of skills and difficulties in individual cases show considerable overlap across the pure forms of subtypes. Given the range of possible causes of developmental dyslexia it would be expected that overlap across pure forms and the variety of observed profiles would be greater. The performance of individuals with developmental dyslexia may well be unique. For models to be useful they need to be sufficiently robust to include the psychoneurological evidence from histological and modern non-intrusive methods, the evidence from developmental psychoneurology and that from the variability of difficulties observed. Future research needs to integrate the findings from each of the approaches. Comprehensive assessment within a case study approach or large-scale studies that take account of subtypes would seem to be appropriate rather than studies that use heterogeneous groups. The assessments need to ensure that cognitive and psychoneurological measures are assimilated with a comprehensive view of linguistic performance rather than simplistic phonological or whole-word reading measures.

Implications for educational intervention

A neuropsychological approach to educational intervention with children with SpLD depends upon a knowledge of brain structures, functions and processes. The evaluative research of traditional methods of intervention has been beset by empirical and methodological confusions (Gaddes, 1985). The evaluation of different remedial approaches has tended to treat children with SpLD as an homogeneous group. Teachers, schools and LEAs often espouse particular favourite approaches, such as whole-word, phonic or language experience and attempt to apply these, in the name of good practice, to all children regardless of the type of SpLD, or individual profile, a child may have. Other teachers may attempt a number of approaches with children in the hope of finding an approach that seems to work with a given child. While the latter approach attempts to match teaching to learning style, neither stance is particularly helpful for increasing our knowledge of the effectiveness of given approaches with particular subtypes.

A psychoneurological approach suggests that to attempt to remedy directly skills that are dependent upon damaged or deficient cortical structures by practice in the deficient skill is a fruitless and demoralizing task for all concerned. Arguments for plasticity of function within which surrounding cortical tissue can take over the functions of impaired areas with minimal residual deficiencies (Wilson and Wilson, 1980) only relate to incidences of severe trauma, not to cases of genetic or mild developmental deficiencies (St James-Roberts, 1981; Rapin, 1982). Genetic or developmental neural anomalies will not go away. A frequently suggested approach, is a compensatory one based on a comprehensive assessment of the pupil's relative strengths and weaknesses and where teaching is directed by the strengths, not weaknesses, of the child. The children are helped to compensate for their difficulties via strategies based on strengths. Cognitive approaches to neuropsychological rehabilitation are receiving increasing attention (Seron and Deloche, 1989). Alleviating SpLD is one aspect (Bakker, 1990a,b).

Assessment may include psychological, neurological and behavioural measures, and involve inferences based upon current knowledge of functional cortical systems. The approach would involve inferences based upon current knowledge of cortical structure and function and, conversely, inferences upon possible cortical anomalies based upon measures of performance. A teaching programme is then constructed to match instruction to the learning style of the child, bearing in mind an analysis of the learning task and social and emotional factors. The approach does not rule out remediation of deficient skills but suggests that complementary processes and skills need to be taught to enable compensation and integration of the specific skills into the complete process. Hynd and Hynd (1984) point out that many teachers have experience of pupils who spend years unsuccessfully attempting to learn phonics and of children who over years have managed some limited success in this area, but are unable to use the skills effectively when reading texts.

A knowledge of both the various subtypes of SpLD and a variety of teaching approaches would enhance the possible successful match of teaching approaches to pupil learning needs. Teaching approaches based primarily upon visual recognition would not be appropriate for children with surface dyslexia. If a multisensory approach was adopted to word recognition, then compensatory skills might be attempted. Variations on the multisensory theme would seem to be a catch-all for all subtypes and Hulme and Bradley (1984) have provided evidence that such approaches are most effective for undifferentiated groups of dyslexic children. Evidence is not available as to whether multisensory approaches are as effective for particular subtypes as other more specific approaches. Phonetic approaches would not be seen to be appropriate for phonological and deep developmental dyslexia – the subtypes regarded as the most prevalent (Pirozzolo, 1979). Developmental direct dyslexia may respond to either word recognition or phonetic approaches depending on whether auditory or visual pathways are disconnected from semantic analysis in the functional system.

Teaching strategies based on linguistic patterns would not be appropriate for deep or phonological dyslexia as they require prior phonological knowledge. Cloze-procedure with its emphasis on context cues and meaning would not be seen to be appropriate for surface or direct subtypes (McClure and Hynd, 1983). Language experience approaches may not be helpful for developmental direct dyslexia. There are innumerable teaching approaches and their adoption in any given case needs to be made with a knowledge of the characteristics of the various subtypes.

The point being made is that it is the profile of strengths and weaknesses that should direct the teaching approaches adopted. It is not suggested that a particular rather than a range of approaches should be adopted, only that some approaches will not be helpful in given cases. Factors relating to motivation and self-esteem are seen as important and the psychoneurological approach is essentially one of ensuring success and avoiding failure. The implementation of the National Curriculum together with the current moves towards an entitlement model and support within the classroom necessitates that such support is directed towards access of the curriculum. Knowledge of the variety of SpLD and characteristic profiles of subtypes will enable appropriate differentiation of teaching for varying needs rather than simplistic global responses. Action research in this area needs to be supported.

When a child is learning to read, perceptual considerations are important (Gibson and Levin, 1975; Gibson, 1985). The meaning of letters is in large measure determined by the letters' orientations in space. For example, rotating a letter 'd' can lead to b, q or p in English text. Simultaneously, changes in the shapes of letters may have to be discounted when they do not necessarily affect the meaning attributed to the letter, as when a 'd' becomes 'D'. As crossword enthusiasts appreciate, the sequence of letters in text also contributes significantly towards meaning, for example mate/tame/meat. The preceding points highlight the importance of the many and various perceptual features of text. Because both spatial orientation and shape discrimination are typically linked to right hemisphere functions, it could be argued that the initial stages of learning to read are linked with the right hemisphere. When the perceptual analysis of the features of text becomes automatized, as in the competent reader's performance, the reader's focus is on semantic and syntactic analyses. These processes are, in the main, controlled by the left hemisphere. In moving from the initial stages of learning to read to the level of skilled performance, the hemispheric mediation moves from an emphasis on right hemispheric functions to the left hemisphere functions.

On the basis of such theorizing, Bakker (1990a) has hypothesized the existence of two distinctive types of dyslexia. Some pupils may fail to make progress in learning to read because they do not make the hemispheric shift. They continue to rely on reading strategies dependent on right hemispheric functions. Such pupils are called 'P' type by Bakker: 'They tend to read relatively slowly and in a fragmented fashion, albeit rather accurately because they remain sensitive to the perceptual features of text.' Other children begin learning to read by using left hemisphere strategies. These are called 'L' type. They '...read in a hurried fashion and produce many substantive errors (omissions, additions, etc.)' (ibid., p. 12). On the basis of the lateral distribution of electrophysiological activity evoked by words to be read, differential performances in predicted directions on selected cognitive tasks and differential responses to interventions, Bakker considers the L–P classification to be valid. He claims that approximately 60–70 per cent of dyslexic children can be classified in this way.

These findings have implications for interventions. The simplification that the left visual field and the left-hand project to the right hemisphere contains an important element of fact. The reverse linkage obtains for the right visual field and the right hand. Hemisphere-specific stimulation (HSS) is achieved by presenting textual materials to the left and right visual fields, or to the left and right hand of L and P types, respectively.

Both visual HSS and tactile HSS have been studied by Bakker. He reports promising results. Visual HSS involves the child sitting in front of a computer monitor at the centre of which is presented a small square. Using a joystick, a small × can be directed across the screen by the child. When the × and the square coincide, a word that is to be read is presented for a specified brief period either to the left or right visual field, dependent on whether the child is L or P type dyslexic. According to Bakker, visual HSS has been shown to be more effective in increasing the reading accuracy of L dyslexic children than of control treatments.

Using the visual HSS technique with P type dyslexic children produces mixed results. A parallel technique for tactile HSS appears to hold more promise for them. This involves presenting the child with plastic letters that they are required to handle. The letters are fixed onto a board inside a tactile exploration box. Children palpate the letters, out of sight. L type dyslexic children use the left hand in order to stimulate the right hemisphere and P type dyslexic children use the fingers of the right hand in order to provide stimulation of the left hemisphere. A field study involving over 50 remedial teachers is reported as showing that P type dyslexic children who received tactile HSS read more fluently than a control group of P type dyslexic children who received control treatments (Bakker, 1990). Tactile HSS is also cheaper and easier to develop in classrooms as it does not require sophisticated IT equipment. Its replicability across classrooms is less easily achieved.

A recent development of HSS is known as hemisphere alluding stimulation (HAS). This approach utilizes classroom materials and adapts them for use with P and L type dyslexic pupils. The principle is that texts are made more perceptually demanding for L type dyslexic pupils. This is achieved by mixing lower and upper case letters in text. When sentences are read, textual information is projected to the rear of both hemispheres, from whence it travels to other parts of the brain. It is claimed that, because of the perceptual complexity of the texts, the right hemisphere becomes more activated in the processing involved.

For P type dyslexic pupils; demands in phonetic, semantic and syntactic aspects of text are created. All three allude to left hemisphere functioning.

Activation is achieved by emphasizing the use of rhymes and semantic puzzles in texts. The latter uses a form of 'cloze' procedure.

The HAS approach has not been as extensively investigated as HSS. It is claimed that HAS is more effective in promoting the reading efficiency of L and P type dyslexic pupils than children under control treatments.

There have been single case studies of the effects of HAS with two P type dyslexic boys that suggest promise (Bos, 1988; Kappers, 1988). Aged 11:00 and 13:00 years, respectively, both boys had reading ages of 7:06 years at the start of the studies. The treatments given were in three phases: HAS 1, HAS + HSS, and HAS 2, over a period of three weeks, with three treatment sessions of about 30 minutes each session. HAS consisted of phonemic and semantic text training through the use of rhymes, word finding and other left hemisphere-activating tasks. HSS comprised channelling the child's reading to the right ear whilst, simultaneously, music was taken to the left ear. The purpose was to stimulate the left hemisphere.

At the start of the studies, following the final treatment session and at a follow-up one month later, standardized word, sentence and passage reading tests were taken by the boys. Further, at the end of each treatment session, word and sentence reading tasks were given. The reading miscues identified were classified as either fragmentation or substantive errors.

It is reported that the two pupils showed significant falls in the number of fragmentation errors in both word and sentence reading. There were also important differences in the progress made. One boy showed treatment-induced improvement in reading fluency, accuracy and reading age; the other only showed improvement in reading fluency (Bakker, 1990a).

Clearly, this type of work is in its infancy. Important questions bearing on the validity and utility of the theory underpinning both HSS and HAS remain to be explored. It continues the quest to identify aptitude × instruction interactions pertinent to the alleviation of specific learning difficulties in reading (Bakker, 1990b; Bakker, Bouma and Gardien, 1990; Kappers, 1990).

Summary

This chapter has given a brief outline of developments within the field of psychoneurology in relation to SpLD. Evidence from a limited number of post-mortem studies on individuals with documented developmental dyslexia is now available. This evidence suggests that cortical anomalies are present in the brains of such individuals and that these anomalies are most prevalent in areas long considered to be involved in the development of literacy processes.

An increasing amount of supportive evidence is also emanating from research making use of more sensitive and sophisticated neurodiagnostic procedures, such as magnetic resonance imaging and CAT scans. To date the evidence for a neuropathological aetiology of SpLD is not conclusive but is very persuasive.

Many researchers and practitioners are attempting to differentiate subtypes of developmental dyslexia based on the variety of difficulties observed. Comparisons with models of subtypes suggested in the research on acquired dyslexia are being made with some caution due to possible ontogenetic and developmental differences. The search for subtypes is being integrated with cognitive information-processing models enabling robust models that are more able to incorporate the wide variety of difficulties observed.

The implications of a neuropsychological approach to intervention are that learning programmes should be directed by a comprehensive assessment of the learner's strengths and weaknesses. The use of a compensatory approach based upon the learner's strengths rather than weaknesses is frequently advocated. Essentially such an approach seeks to ensure success and avoid failure. Other neuropsychological interventions aim to alleviate weaknesses in hemispheric functions in order to improve reading attainments. Such work is still in its infancy.

Recommendations

9.1. Initial training and in-service training include opportunities to introduce and update professional knowledge of current neuropsychological research findings and methodologies.

9.2. Pactitioners ensure that their assessments of children with specific learning difficulties be undertaken with an awareness of possible neuropsychological factors and be based on a comprehensive view of literacy skills.

9.3. Neuropsychological insights be drawn on to provide more precise descriptions of specific learning difficulties so that intervention strategies can be better matched to individual needs.

9.4. The advice and guidance given to teachers, parents and pupils should not only focus on learner's weaknesses but should encourage compensatory approaches.

9.5. Further case studies and action research be carried out directed towards increasing knowledge of the effectiveness of different teaching approaches for possible neuropsychological subtypes of specific learning difficulties.

9.6. Psychological services collate and disseminate evaluative research data related to neuropsychological insights and interventions.

9.7. Practitioners differentiate schemes of work within the National Curriculum so that children with specific learning difficulties are not treated as a homogeneous group.

Chapter 10

Psycho-ophthalmological Literature

Introduction

To be able to see is usually considered a prerequisite of normal reading development. Teachers are sensitive to the importance of this point when trying to understand *why* a pupil experiences difficulties with textual materials. Professionals appreciate that visual perception, SpLD and their interrelationships are complex. Simplifying the apparently complex is one aspect of advancing understanding in a given field, usually at the conceptual level. Avoiding the danger of unjustified oversimplification is the concomitant challenge.

In the study of specific learning difficulties there has always been a hope that there might be a relatively simple diagnosis and solution. Consequently much effort has been spent on the investigation of the role of vision in the reading process. Vision is a major sensory channel used in reading by most children and therefore it is highly probable that some poor readers will have defective vision. It is equally true that some very fast readers can have defective eyesight, as at least one of the authors can testify. For example children with myopia are thought to learn to read relatively easily. The problem of short-sightedness is not necessarily a handicap.

At an early stage in the history of 'dyslexia' much attention was focused on the development of a dominant eye and, of course, the dyslexic phenomenon was originally described as 'word *blindness*' (Critchley, 1970).

Eye dominance

Many psychologists writing reports on individual children continue to state that a child is 'cross lateral' with a dominant eye that is on the opposite side to their dominant hand. The 'dominant hand' is usually taken to mean the one with which the pupil writes. Some tests of dyslexia include items that ask for evidence of mixed laterality. For example the Webster test of dyslexia includes questions implying that poorly established hand or eye preference and crossed laterality are 'dyslexia' indicators (Webster, 1971).

Several theories suggest that eye dominance is important. Masland argues that the brain of the dyslexic child is different from that of the normal person. The visual pathways and neural transmission become important when the brain acquires meaning from print (Masland, 1990). Other theories centre around the fact that, when looking at a distant object, the sight from each eye follows a parallel line but, when looking at something close to the eyes, they must converge and one eye then becomes dominant.

Stein and Fowler (1982) argued that dyslexia is associated with a failure to de-velop consistent dominance of one eye's 'ocular motor' signals and that this leads to confusion about precisely where words and letters are on a page. Their work was discussed in the previous DECP working party report. Several articles have been produced since 1983 suggesting that their original finding, that more than half of the dyslexic population had an unfixed reference eye on a binocular vision test when compared to only one per cent of controls, needs further investi-gation (Newman *et al.*, 1985). The Stein and Fowler studies have been difficult to replicate. There has also been criticism of the fact that the dyslexic sample had been referred to an ophthalmologist in the first place and therefore one would ex-pect ophthalmological problems (Wilsher, 1990). Wilsher also pointed out that the Dunlop test used by Stein and Fowler is a visual/verbal test on which a child with learning difficulties may easily make two or more inappropriate responses out of ten (the criterion for determining unfixed reference)(Dunlop, 1972).

In the Newman *et al.* (1985) study, 323 unselected schoolchildren were tested with a reading test, an IQ test and the modified Dunlop test as used by Stein and Fowler. The same high incidence of unfixed reference eye was found amongst the poor readers as in the Stein and Fowler study but Newman and colleagues also found the same percentage of excellent readers to have the condition. In an earlier study, Bishop, Jancey and Steel (1979) also found that the Dunlop test failed to discriminate good from poor readers.

A further study by Stein and Fowler (1985) concluded that some dyslexic children may be helped by the occlusion of one eye. The experimental design of this study was extensively criticized by Wilsher and a re-analysis of the data by Bishop suggested that there was 'no evidence that monocular occlusion in chil-dren with unfixed reference eye results in improved reading scores' (Bishop, 1989b; Wilsher, 1990). Work on the nature of disordered vergence control in dys-lexic children continues (Stein and Riddell, 1988; Stein, 1991).

There are further problems for teachers and educational psychologists wishing to pursue the crossed laterality or eye dominance factor, because the currently available tests for eye dominance may not be reliable or comparable to the more sophisticated tests used by Stein and Fowler. Most tests of eye dominance in-volve static conditions but reading is essentially a dynamic task involving eye tracking. The muscles controlling fine eye movement may be far more important than the simple measure of eye preference so commonly used by psychologists. Also, a number of studies of whole populations and large samples of dyslexic groups have cast doubt upon the commonly held view that crossed laterality or left handedness is more common in the dyslexic population.

Clark (1970) compared 69 children with specific reading problems with a con-trol group of 42 primary aged children and she found that on none of the lat-erality measures was either group significantly different from the total measured population of 1544 children. Similarly, in the Isle of Wight study it was claimed that handedness and eyedness measures failed either singly or in combination to distinguish between children with specific reading retardation and controls (Rut-ter, Tizard and Whitmore, 1970). The National Child Development Study found no differences in reading comprehension between groups of children showing consistent or inconsistent patterns of handedness and hand/eye laterality and, as in the Isle of Wight study, mixed handedness and crossed hand/eye laterality were not associated with reading problems (Whittington and Richards, 1987). Where a *change* of hand dominance was reported between the ages of 7 and 11, there was also generally reported lower than average reading comprehension scores and this was associated with 'underachievement'. This finding may be of little relevance to a clinical population because of the different method of collecting data. The finding may be associated with the lower reliability of data for people who have problems with a written comprehension task administered to a group.

Moseley (1988) asserted that if firmly established left handedness, left eyedness or crossed laterality were in any way important in the causation of specific learning difficulties then associations would have appeared in the Isle of Wight or the National Child Development studies and in other similar studies. He conducted a study that involved a much wider range of tests given to a sample of London junior school pupils. His conclusion was that, while many of the measures might have needed refinement, 'it is reasonable to state that eye dominance (as measured by conventional sighting tests) and crossed hand-eye laterality are completely irrelevant to the assessment and treatment of reading and spelling problems'. He suggested that many of the apparent laterality problems reported from clinic samples may be explained in terms of selective referral bias or as consequences rather than causes of learning difficulty and that theories linking cerebral dominance and dyslexia were at present little more than speculation (see Chapter 9).

Some EEG studies suggest that there are neurophysiological differences between children who learn to read easily and those who do not. One example of a measurable EEG difference in a dyslexic sample was the relative delay in reduction of theta activity on eye opening, as compared to a normal control group. This was said to suggest differential cortical activity (Pinkerton, Watson and McClelland, 1989).

EEG studies generally add weight to Vellutino's theory that in dyslexic subjects there is a different left hemisphere functioning. Pinkerton and her colleagues in Northern Ireland also suggest that their EEG findings are consistent with the view that there is an impairment of the processes which mediate the focusing of attention. They point out the difficulty of knowing whether the learning difficulty causes the differential response to the EEG or whether the different information processing, as a result of the delayed acquisition of skills, is responsible for the different findings. They suggest that the right auditory pathway assumes dominance in normal children and therefore there is a dominant connection between the right ear and the left (normally language) hemisphere. In the dyslexic group it appeared that the loss of asymmetry observed may not be due to a defective right pathway but to a more efficient left one. This view seems to concur with Flynn and Deering's (1989) analysis of dyseidetic or visual dyslexic subjects. They suggested that their neurophysiological analysis pointed to the theory that visual dyslexic subjects *over used* linguistic abilities rather than that they were deficient in visual spatial skills (Flynn and Deering, 1989).

The theories considering that eye dominance is important often explain this in terms of a difference between the dyslexic person's brain and the normal brain. It is hypothesized that the dyslexic person has a weaker verbal centre (usually the left brain) or that somehow the spatial right brain becomes dominant. There are proponents of the theory that in dyslexic individuals this difference in brain configuration also affects the fine motor movements of the eyes, the muscles affecting speech and the fine finger movements. Geschwind (1983), for example, suggested that high levels of exposure to testosterone, the 'male' hormone, during foetal life produce a shift towards left handedness and a slowing of left hemisphere growth. Others have suggested from post-mortem evidence that the left hemisphere functions are somehow taken over by the right hemisphere in some dyslexic persons (Witelson, 1977; Galaburda *et al.*, 1985; Bakker, 1990a,b).

Eye tracking

Clinicians have also reported on the high incidence of right to left tracking of information among the dyslexic population. This is often measured from pictures drawn by dyslexics or from the speed of coding or tracking tasks in the two directions. The reliabilities of such measures are not known and neither are the validities. The assumption that right to left scanners or visual trackers will start to draw pictures from the right is not necessarily correct and studies have indicated that about 70 per cent of the population draw more than half of their figures facing towards the left and that this percentage is repeated in the dyslexic sample (Moseley, 1988). In an unpublished study, Hedderly (1981) has noticed that more than 50 per cent of dyslexic children start to draw faces from right to left as compared with less than 13 per cent of a control group. Since the controls were tested in different circumstances this observation may have been an artefact of the presentation of the task.

If dyslexic children naturally track visual information from right to left while being taught by a teacher who assumes the child is following from left to right, it would be understandable that habit interference may occur and children may develop a learning block to the visual print. This problem would also explain reversals and the misreading of one word for another. It would also add to the explanation of the success of schemes, involving paired reading because the child has to follow from left to right fairly rapidly and therefore practises the skill.

Long ago, Zangwill and Blackmore (1972) noticed an increased likelihood of right to left scanning in a dyslexic group. It could be inferred from this observation that if the page was turned upside down so that print could be scanned from right to left, then the task should be easier. Several studies have looked at this approach. One compared good readers with poor readers on two tasks. The first involved reading a word list that was upright and the second involved reading an inverted list. The control group read the upright list three times faster than the dyslexic group but the two groups were very much the same on the inverted task (Larson and Parlenvi, 1984). This study has been severely criticized (Wilsher, 1990), but, even if there was a difference, it is difficult to see how society could provide effective remedial treatments. Although there would be no problem reading a book or newspaper upside down, apart from comments in the tube train, it would not be very easy for dyslexic people with this problem to cope with road signs, advertising material and general written information. It is also likely that by the time the child is referred for remedial help he or she would have seen enough print the right way up to cause problems if it was inverted.

Moseley pointed out that one of the problems with research in this area is that few researchers are experts in both fields of visual function and dyslexia. Nevertheless he indicated that some findings are now accepted and are not artefacts of poor research design or misunderstandings or a result of placebo effects. The most obvious of these is that children should be examined for visual acuity at the normal reading distance if they have reading problems and then appropriately treated for any vision defects (Moseley, 1990b). Moseley also suggested that dynamic binocular function at the reading distance should be assessed and any necessary treatment evaluated carefully by both specialists in vision and by teachers or psychologists. In a follow-up study of dyslexic boys, Moseley proposed that his findings were consistent with the view that the right eye has an important part to play at the stage of learning to read where there is a transition from single word reading to a more fluent reading, which is increasingly dependent on the use of linguistic context. He reported that competent readers have an asymmetrical visual scan taking in about 14 characters to the right and only about 7 to the left of the fixation point (Rayner, 1983). This is thought to be a learned effect but children who are diagnosed as 'dyslexic' might not have learned this skill. Moseley asserted that it is possible that the right eye is important to enable the child to lead the left to right scanning process. He expressed hope that further work designed to improve the knowledge of the process of visual instability will enhance the development of methods that would enable children to improve their reading ability.

In a review of the clinical features and management of dyslexia, Helveston (1987) argued that there was no valid scientific confirmation of most of the benefits claimed for 'eye exercises' designed to improve reading or learning ability. It is probably more important to train left to right scanning incidentally as part of the process of teaching a child to read. This of course occurs naturally in 'paired reading' as reported in the previous DECP inquiry and in Topping and Wolfendale (1985). Bilingual children, however, can learn to read from left to right and right to left according to the text.

It has even been suggested that dyslexics would learn to read better if they had both eyes occluded. Blau and Loveless (1982) taught subjects to handle three-dimensional letters without seeing them. They attempted to show that one hand was better than the other at learning the names of letters and their experimental group achieved some success. This approach to therapy is still being developed (Bakker, 1990a,b).

Another approach has been taken by Pavlidis who postulates a difference in higher order cognitive processes that leads to differential eye movements or 'defective oculomotor control' (Pavlidis 1979, 1981a, 1983, 1990b; Pavlidis and Miles, 1981). The general finding reported by Pavlidis is that when reading, the eyes of the dyslexic population make more fixations and regressions, often fixate for longer and make less efficient saccadic movements. He suggested that his light tracking task provides a differential and objective diagnosis of dyslexia.

Many researchers have since cast doubt on Pavlidis's conclusions. Stanley, Smith and Howell (1983a) pointed out that there is little dispute that the reading eye movements of dyslexic readers differ from those of normal readers but there is considerable doubt about the non-reading tracking movements. The work by Brown and his colleagues in San Francisco and further work by Stanley and others leads to the conclusion that eye movements do not hold the key to dyslexia (Brown *et al.*, 1983a, b; Stanley, Smith and Howell, 1983a,b). Furthermore, the concept of faulty oculomotor control as a mechanism leading to dyslexia seems not to stand the test of experimental evidence, although one cannot rule out the possibility that for *some* individuals such a problem exists. Olsen, Kliegl and Davidson (1983) reported that less than one per cent of dyslexic people have a faulty oculomotor control system. A considerable range of eye movement patterns were noticed in experiments, which were unrelated to reading or linguistic factors. Faulty eye movements or faulty oculomotor control do not seem to be credible explanations for an underlying cause of most specific reading problems (Olsen *et al.*, 1983; Rayner, 1985).

Much of the recent experimental evidence supports the hypothesis that dyslexia and the 'faulty' reading eye movements are primarily problems associated with differences in processing linguistic text and that the problems lie with the verbal mediation process rather than with general perceptual processing (Vellutino, 1979, 1987; Miles and Miles, 1990).

Practising educational psychologists and teachers may take some comfort from this finding because some were concerned that Pavlidis seemed to have put forward a diagnostic process but without a simple portable way of measuring the eye movement phenomenon or modifying it. Sequential problems when reading or writing can be measured and observed through the use of fairly traditional pencil and paper tests, albeit not with the precision of the laboratory.

Lenses and filters

One interesting development not mentioned in the previous DECP inquiry, but which does have an easy, portable assessment and remedial technique, is the use of coloured filters and overlays when reading. There have been many reports in the popular media about the success of the technique propounded by Helen Irlen, which involves dyslexic subjects wearing tinted lenses (*Sunday Times*, 22 December 1985; *BBC Television News*, 31 March 1987; *Times Educational Supplement*, 18 September and 4 December 1987). Winter (1987) also refers to the publicity received in a variety of popular journals, including those designed to appeal to the mass market. The Irlen Institute originated in America and now has a London base that claims to offer an approach 'which is based on widespread research during the past five years into perceptual and learning problems involving several thousand individuals'. A scrutiny of the only independent study referred to in the press cuttings provided by the Irlen Institute revealed that word reading was not reported to have improved with the use of filters (Robinson and Miles, 1987). Essentially the claim of Helen Irlen is that there is a syndrome called the 'scotopic sensitivity syndrome'. This involves an array of perceptual anomalies that allegedly cause visual dyslexia. The scotopic sensitivity syndrome allegedly consists of visual distortions in four categories. These are:

*   Light sensitivity: the ability to accommodate high contrast and glare.
*   Visual resolution: the ability to see print clearly and without distortions.
*   Span of focus: the ability to perceive groups of words at the same time.
*   Sustained focus: the ability to do tasks with the eyes in a relaxed state with objects in focus.

Claims have been made that between 50 and 75 per cent of learning disabled people suffer from this syndrome and therefore learning to read is affected (Irlen, 1983; Clayton, 1987). The appeal of the diagnosis is that it readily leads to treatment since the sufferers can have personal tinted lenses through which they are able to read because the offending light wavelengths can be filtered out or reduced. The disadvantage of the approach is that it is difficult to assess the validity of the scotopic sensitivity syndrome. This is partly because of the lack of an opportunity to consider the original research findings. Many psychologists have difficulty accepting that there is a major visual component to dyslexia because of the increasing evidence that most cognitive disabilities are essentially linguistic in nature (Snowling, 1987; Miles and Miles, 1990).

Scotopic sensitivity has been described as being the ability to see at low levels of light (Millidot, 1986). This results from the functioning of the rods and the sensitivity is normally measured in terms of the minimum level of light intensity that can be detected. However, Irlen does not seem to be referring to, or measuring, the same thing since she is essentially referring to sufferers being affected by particular wavelengths of light, which then have to be screened out. Sufferers are said to report that when they attempt to read, the letters on a page jump about, blur or spiral. Again there is little evidence in the scientific literature that dyslexic people report this phenomenon, although the popular press frequently quotes this aspect of dyslexia, usually in individual cases. In a previously unreported study, Hedderly asked 200 children aged between 7 and 15, referred between 1983 and 1987 to a Dyslexia Institute in Yorkshire, a number of questions relating to visual problems. Only six (three per cent) reported upon questioning that words 'jumped about on a page' and these were mainly older children. This contrasted with an incomplete control group of 'normal' children matched for age, but not ability or scholastic attainment (except that it was 'normal'), where 13 of the 121 controls reported that words jumped about when reading. There seemed no point in pursuing this line of inquiry in view of the preliminary data. There is also a high level of suggestion in the questions. It was concluded that 'naïve' dyslexic children do not report visual problems or word blindness and they do not usually interpret their reading problem as 'words jumping all over the place'. This is possibly an adult or media interpretation of the puzzling situation occurring when otherwise intelligent people have reading difficulties.

In the same clinical population there were 18 children who subsequently received the Irlen tinted lenses. In almost all cases the children and their parents reported an improvement in the ability to read and most of the children were quite enthusiastic. All had received a colour vision test and a test similar to the Irlen test as part of their diagnostic assessment when referred to the Dyslexia Institute and only 3 of the original 18 had expressed any preference for reading with a filter at the time of initial referral.

Congdon (1990) also reported that in a clinical sample of 160 cases he found that: 'a small percentage of these children reacted positively to the lenses.'

One of the problems for psychologists appraising Irlen's work is that many of the unpublished studies have serious flaws.The test for the scotopic sensitivity syndrome, for example, is not described adequately in the literature and therefore results cannot be easily replicated. Clinicians have found no greater incidence of an improvement in dyslexic children's reading levels when using coloured overlays than when reading in the normal population. This seems to be the case, despite the media publicity about the treatment.

Rosner and Rosner (1987) reviewed the majority of known studies of the tinted lens treatment and commented on the extremely unsatisfactory experimental designs in use. There are other flaws in the way in which evaluative questions are posed in some of the unpublished studies and in the way that tests are carried out; there is a high level of direction and suggestion. Irlen, for example, suggests that parents should be present throughout the testing of children. It is thought that adults are more suggestible than the young child would be if tested alone, and therefore a belief in the 'treatment' may be instilled even when there is no scientific proof of a change. This process has been observed and noted in a different context in the treatment of behaviour problems (Hedderly, 1978).

Reeves (1988) also reviewed the literature and drew attention to the short-comings of most of the existing studies. He referred to the small-scale study by Gregg (1988), which reported improved reading in a group of children using coloured overlays. In this study there was no control group and the gains were not particularly good when compared to those reported in many paired reading studies (Topping and Wolfendale, 1985). A further problem could have occurred because the reading gains were measured using the *Neale Analysis of Reading Ability* (Neale, 1966). These tests were carried out by a reading teacher independently from the remainder of the experiment as is appropriate in good experimental design. However, no mention was made of the fact that the *Neale* (1966) test involves three parallel versions of which two are printed on a blue or yellow background. If coloured overlays were used on top of these, the background colour would presumably have an effect. Similarly if the tests were read without the overlays then children with the scotopic sensitivity syndrome could perhaps respond to the test differently, thus confusing the data. The revised version of the *Neale Analysis of Reading Ability* avoids this problem of background colour (Neale, 1989).

There are further problems with the theoretical basis of this treatment. The Irlen Institute claims that: 'Irlen lenses are spectrally modified to meet your individual requirements. There are over 140 possible variations, and it is only through an intensive diagnostic process that the correct prescription can be determined. By eliminating specific wavelengths of light and letting in those rays which your eye can handle we slightly shift the focus on the retina to produce a sharper, clearer and more stable image.'

However, Moseley (1990b) and Mitchell (1987) found, for both overlays and lenses, from a spectrophotometric analysis of the light absorption characteristics, that these acted primarily as an overall absorber of visible light. There was no evidence that specific spectral wavelengths were cut out. Moseley claimed that in any case it was impossible to sharpen the retinal image by such means. If pure colour wavelengths were allowed through to the retina, it is possible that depth perception would alter because of the different refractive index of the light received. There might be a danger here of subjects reacting inappropriately to the alternating conditions with and without spectacles if these were involved, since they may become more prone to accidents through errors of judgement of visual depth. It seems to follow from Moseley and Mitchell's analysis that the most significant effect of the Irlen lenses is to reduce light overall rather than affect specific colours (Moseley, 1990b).

If this is indeed the case, it is misleading to give the syndrome a name that is a meaningless phrase in layman's terms. It would probably be more appropriate to call the syndrome a 'light sensitive syndrome' or even a 'photopic sensitivity syndrome'.

Another review was carried out by Howell and Stanley (1988) in the wider context of the history and use of colour in remedial treatment for children with a learning disability. They quoted unpublished studies indicating cases where improvement had been made by children using the lenses, but again the design and number of subjects involved seemed unsatisfactory or insufficient to make valid conclusions. These authors were prepared to accept that the Irlen treatment works in some way, but they do not believe that a special syndrome of scotopic sensitivity needs to be postulated.

Winter (1987) tested dyslexic pupils under four conditions with a letter identification visual search task. The four conditions were: with an Irlen lens; with an untinted lens; with a plain grey lens; and with no lens at all. He found that none of these conditions was associated with superior performance on the task, but nevertheless several children reported that the grey lens or the untinted lens actually helped them with the task. He concluded from the evidence that the Irlen lenses did not improve performance in any way. His experiment was criticized by the Rosners because he used a visual tracking or 'proof reading' task (Rosner and Rosner, 1987). This, they suggested, did not parallel the reading task. However, it is in fact a good test of Irlen's hypothesis that the lenses produce a more stable image. If this were the case, a sufferer's performance on a proof reading task should improve dramatically and the improvement should be relatively easy to measure. In Winter's sample only 22 children had 'scotopic sensitivity', and 7 of these he could not test. Five just forgot to bring their glasses to school on the day of the test. This observation also casts some doubt about the children's acceptance of the validity of the lens treatment.

Richardson (1988) conducted a study of ten dyslexic boys' reading skills using a red filter. This student's study was well designed and controlled in most respects. She used Irlen's screening test procedure before selecting her subjects. Her conclusion was that subjects performed better on a word reading (but not in a word matching) test with the red filter as compared to control overlays. This, of course, militates against the placebo effect interpretation of the improvement. She concluded that her research supported Helen Irlen's thesis. This conclusion is a little surprising because the Irlen Institute emphasizes the need for individual diagnosis and prescription, also emphasizing the need for repeat assessments because of sensitivity changes. This is incompatible with the finding that one colour, red, can help all scotopic-sensitive dyslexic subjects. The red filter is usually the one that restricts more light than other filters, and in view of Moseley's claims that Irlen lenses simply restrict about 55 per cent of the light, there may be some indication that glare is a problem for some people when reading. One interesting inconsistency of the Richardson study was that the blue filter was frequently identified as the preferred colour in the subjective reports of the children (Richardson, 1988). The evidence from the reading test to some extent contradicted the subjective report of the children. This effect was also noted in the Winter study (Winter, 1987).

O'Connor and Sofo (1988) studied six groups of children with reading difficulties. Four were diagnosed as having the scotopic sensitivity syndrome and two were found not to be sensitive. The groups used clear filters, selected filters or a random coloured filter, for one week. The results reported strong confirmation of the value of the selected filters. This study has not yet been replicated and only involved small numbers.

A more recent study has been carried out by the Medical Research Council in the Applied Psychology Unit at Cambridge (Neary and Wilkins, 1989). Here Neary and Wilkins tested 20 people who were selected by the Irlen Institute as successful long-term wearers of the tinted lenses. The subjects were tested under four conditions. One test included random strings of between one and seven letters designed so that the visual aspects of reading could be assessed in isolation from understanding. Another included a visual discrimination test involving very small shapes. The researchers claimed that there were significant improvements in a few subjects and modest improvements in the group as a whole in acuity and muscle balance when the subjects used the tinted lenses when compared to the alternative conditions with neutral and untinted lenses (Bald, 1990). This experiment suffered from the difficulty that the sample was selected by the Irlen

Institute. Conventional statistical analysis would not be appropriate because the subjects could hardly be regarded as being naïve to the aims of the experiment. Also the subjects had presumably had time to accommodate the lens situation and therefore practice effects would occur. Alternatively, deficits would occur in the 'strange' conditions thus accounting for the apparent 'gains' in the condition when the subject was wearing 'their' tinted lens. Wilkins (1990) argued that the differences recorded in the improvement of muscle balance could not be explained by motivational effects because the subjects were unaware of the purpose of the tests or of the way that measurements were made.

In other publications Wilkins and his co-workers have suggested that certain styles of text resemble a pattern of stripes under some light conditions and that this can have adverse effects. These, he suggests, are similar to the 'dazzle' effect that many of us notice when viewing a series of close, black parallel lines on bright white paper. He pointed out that many combinations of shapes or flickering lights produce reactions in people with epilepsy and therefore by analogy he suggests that it is possible that visual discomfort when viewing print could contribute to developmental dyslexia. Wilkins concluded from work over a long period that for people who are susceptible to the 'dazzle' effect, text can usually be made clearer in two ways (Wilkins, 1989). The first is to cover the lines that are not being read, thereby reducing the 'stripe' pattern. (Reading aids designed to achieve this are marketed by Engineering and Design Plastics, Cambridge.) The second is to use tinted lenses, especially those that absorb green light. Since these lenses will usually be various shades of red, the Richardson study may be worth repeating with a larger sample.

Although Irlen hardly mentions colour vision, there has been some research indicating that there is a difference in the retinas of dyslexic persons, which might explain the frequent 'failure' of colour screening tests even though more sophisticated testing fails to find a colour vision defect *per se*. Grosser and Spofford (1989) used a method of 'retinal periphery' to map colour-sensitive zones of the retinas of 14 dyslexic individuals and 14 control individuals. Dyslexic subjects reported colours at more peripheral positions and the authors inferred that dyslexic individuals had an anomalous distribution of retinal receptors (rods and cones). In particular they inferred from their results the presence of cones in the peripheral retina. The authors suggested that their findings explained the erratic eye movements noted in dyslexic people and they indicated that their tests could be used in a battery of tests for dyslexia (Grosser and Spofford, 1989).

The evidence from a number of other sources already discussed in this chapter indicates that visual problems do not seem to be a major cause of dyslexia. The Vellutino experiments are well known but other workers, such as Ellis and Miles (1978), have compared control and dyslexic individuals on their ability to process verbal information (letter pairs) and non-verbal, highly reversible nonsense figures. Even though the nonsense figures were presented in rotation and reversed, dyslexic persons had no more difficulty than the controls in discriminating between the figures. When dyslexic persons had to discriminate between letter pairs on the basis of the names of the letters, their performance was considerably inferior to that of the controls. This seems to confirm that, as a rule, dyslexic individuals have minimal problems with visual perception but that they do have a difficulty recalling names and with 'naming' language. The studies of Bradley and Bryant (1985) have shown that young children who have difficulties in reliably classifying speech sounds and in producing rhymes often go on to have reading problems.

If the Irlen lens treatment is succeeding, one hypothesis is that it might be due to a placebo or 'Hawthorne' effect. It is possible that attention is increased in the experimental situation and the subject is motivated and tests out the lenses, therefore obtaining more practice. In a school situation the Irlen spectacles help to identify a pupil as handicapped and it is possible and indeed likely that teachers will be less critical of failure and more supportive of progress by the child. Psychologists still need to know more about the syndrome and whether it relates to something that can be generally measured and replicated. Wilkins's research at the Applied Psychology Unit in Cambridge does not give enough information to evaluate whether good readers also produce similar results in the same conditions. Many non-dyslexic pupils are also diagnosed as having 'scotopic sensitivity'. We need to know the relevance of this syndrome to learning difficulties.

It remains an open question whether the syndrome operates on the theoretical basis put forward by the Irlen Institute. This raises other questions about the ethics of administering a test and treatment for which there is no agreed scientific theoretical framework, although workers like Wilkins and Neary seem to be developing this. It might be reasonable to test a child with and without overlays to see whether there is any improvement in reading or tracking speed, and it might be worth using an overlay or lens in remedial programmes if the child or the parent thinks it will help. Selling the treatment as a solution to an incorrectly named syndrome may not be appropriate. On the other hand it might be this very part of the process which leads to an improvement. It is perfectly reasonable to follow up a valid observation with a treatment even if scientists are not clear why it works. If the client believes in 'scotopic sensitivity' and accepts the lens treatment as a solution, then this could contribute to an improvement. This is a motivational aspect of applied psychology. The issue relating to the proposal of treatments based on an explanation acceptable to a client, even though the psychologist might have a completely different explanation, or indeed no explanation, was discussed earlier, in relation to treating children's behaviour and learning problems, by Hedderly (1979). The resolution of the issue is complex and complicated because the efficacy of orthodox remedial treatments is often no better or just as doubtful and the prognosis for an *individual* on any remedial programme is nearly always uncertain.

Drugs and eye movements

One other area of research that merits consideration is the effect of drugs on eye movements, which may help to develop the theoretical situation by analogy. It is well known that anti-epileptic drugs impair memory and psycho-motor skills. Richens (1989) pointed out that the subject's eyes are a very good channel/ mechanism for examining the effect of drugs. Drugs can reduce the ability of people to follow or track moving lights or to distinguish flashing lights. It has been found that both normal control groups and epileptic subjects perform badly on all kinds of psycho-motor skills and intelligence measures when under the influence of anti-epileptic and other drugs. Even quite low doses of some anti-epileptic drugs effect saccadic eye movements and smooth tracking. In many situations the impairments noted in dyslexic individuals mirror those of normals when under the influence of carbamazepine or phenytoin (Dodrill and Troupin, 1977). The theory that some dyslexics have an impaired cerebellar vestibular system might gain some support by analogy from drug studies. The cerebellar is responsible for integrating and regulating fine movements initiated by the frontal lobes. Damage to this system is caused by, for example, heavy metal poisoning, and impairment can be caused by some drug treatments. One feature of cerebellar injury is nystagmus (rapid, uncontrolled eye movements). Levinson (1989) suggested that the cerebellar vestibular system determined fixation and tracking movements but that this was impaired in dyslexics and therefore they were predisposed to make errors of letter order and direction when reading or writing. Psychologists still speculate whether the rapid eye movements caused by drugs or damage is an artefact of the reduced learning ability or the cause of it. Since neuro-transmission is a two-way process, the resolution of this issue will continue to be difficult. (For other psychopharmaceutical issues related to SpLD, see Chapter 11.)

Summary

This chapter has considered the role of vision and visual perception in the diagnosis and treatment of dyslexia. It seems fairly well established that although poor vision might inhibit a child's progress in literacy it is not in itself an explanation for the dyslexic or specific learning difficulties that most teachers and psychologists have encountered. The various explanations which relate to dominant eyes have little everyday use, for either treatment or diagnosis. It is now also well established that in the reading task there are significant differences between the eye movements of dyslexic and normal children. Current thinking seems to accept the explanation that this may be an artefact of the delayed acquisition of the literacy skill. The finding that most dyslexic children have well established visual/spatial ability also seems to point to the conclusion that the problem is with the link between the language centre, which holds the 'naming' skill, and the visual centre. Essentially the problem is in the pupil's ability to encode phonologically or decode rather than in their ability to see or visualize the words.

Scotopic (and photopic) sensitivity diagnosis and treatment should also be regarded with some caution, although there is evidence that the treatment works for some children and adults. The original theoretical framework now seems implausible. The placebo effect probably accounts for much of the reported improvement. If the 'treatment' leads to more reading practice, then gains are likely to be made anyway. There is some evidence that visual discomfort can be reduced with the use of coloured lenses and that some people may be helped by treatment of this kind.

It is likely that psychologists and other specialists will continue the search for a range of psycho-ophthalmological causes even though many workers argue that dyslexia is not one condition but many (Yule, 1988). Enough is known about the errors made by children with specific learning difficulties and their attention problems to suggest that there may be some potential in looking further at the issues of colour perception, light intensity and the reading process. The general conclusion of this chapter is that the eyes no longer have the answer. A concentration on the visual function is unlikely to help most dyslexics.

Recommendations

10.1. Clinical cases be documented with a view to considering patterns of abilities and difficulties in specific learning difficulties.

10.2. Children with reading difficulties, who may also have visual disabilities, be referred to the appropriate specialists.

10.3. Awareness of research on the role of visual factors in the diagnosis and treatment of specific learning difficulties, and advice to clients on the significance or otherwise of such findings be developed.

10.4. Collaborative research be conducted on perception and learning and on the role of vision and learning with reference to pupils with specific learning difficulties.

Chapter 11

Psychopharmaceutics and Specific Learning Difficulties (Dyslexia)

Introduction

The prescription of drug treatment is usually resorted to only when techniques of behavioural management have failed. The daunting scope and complexities of this field can be appreciated by consulting any major text concerning the pharmacological basis of therapeutics (for example Goodman *et al.*, 1985). This particular publication is in its eighth edition and comprises 67 chapters in 18 major sections. Of these sections, numbers I, II and III are of particular help in relation to the subject of the present book. Section I consists of four chapters outlining general principles. Section II contains seven chapters focusing on drugs acting at synaptic and neuroeffector junctional sites. Section III comprises 11 chapters concerned with drug actions on the central nervous system. See also Vess, 1990.

The medical considerations of learning disorders comprise a vast field. Shea (1987) gives a classification of learning disorders and current views on the possible physical and chemical factors that cause, contribute to or maintain such disorders. The neurodevelopmental requirements for learning literacy skills and indications for the use of medication are also briefly discussed.

Learning and behaviour are related to brain function. Children show great inter-individual variability in their genetic and neurophysiological characteristics. Understanding why some intelligent children find extreme difficulties in becoming literate has concerned, and still concerns, a range of specialisms in medicine. Does the apparent underachievement of pupils mean that specific learning difficulties (dyslexia) is explainable, in part, in terms of neurophysiological structures and functions?

There is much evidence to support the hypothesis that dysfunctions in the individual's ability to receive, analyse, synthesize, store and retrieve sensory information, and dysfunctions in symbolic operations, are implicated. If this is the case for some children, is it possible that psychopharmacological interventions – drug treatments – might facilitate learning? The answer must be 'in principle, yes'.

The established effects of pharmaceutics on various types of symptoms, functions and behaviours is a major strength of medicine. Matching the treatment to the patient's condition is of the essence, even though a degree of 'trial and error' inevitably remains. It must also be remembered that in developing knowledge in this field, irreversible damage has been done to individuals involved in drug trials. Are the potential benefits worth the inevitable risks involved?

The four major classes of psychotropic medication are: stimulants, tranquillizers, anticonvulsants and antidepressants. These include many of the drugs most commonly prescribed for children with behavioural and/or learning disorders. A helpful introduction, written for teachers, is available (Forness and Kavale, 1988).

As differential diagnosis develops, it is possible to conceive a time when the neurophysiological symptoms and/or causes of various types of specific learning difficulties (dyslexia) can be alleviated by psychopharmaceutical interventions. Such a state of understanding and control of human behaviour represents a somewhat distant horizon. Despite, or because of, this, considerable efforts have been and are being devoted to the endeavour (Humphries, 1981; Rentel, Corson and Dunn, 1985; Herson, 1986).

A critical consideration of a range of treatments of dyslexia has recently been reported by a psychologist who has been involved in the field for a considerable period (Wilsher, 1990). Studies ranging from individual clinical cases to double-blind studies of the effects of interventions are reported in the literature. Wilsher pinpoints the weaknesses in a number of such treatment studies, and thus the limitations in the validity and generalizability of the results obtained. 'Although some of the so-called "treatments" for dyslexia have serious faults in the methodology used to research them, this does not mean that they could never be shown to be effective' (ibid., p. 3). The planning of treatment evaluations requires considerable expertise if valid conclusions are to be obtained.

Many people would like a cheaper, environmentally friendly alternative to the use of petrol in cars. It is possible to argue that water can be used as a fuel to run a car. The argument is based on combining the principles of electrolysis of water with that of spark ignition. The gullible can be persuaded of its utility. The case collapses when the energy equations involved are made explicit (or when tried in practice). The theoretical basis of such a water-driven vehicle is shown to be invalid. The parents, and teachers, of children with specific learning difficulties (dyslexia) search for ways of helping them to overcome their difficulties. New suggestions for identification and intervention are always appearing. Snake-oil panaceas are still as saleable as they ever were, and likely to remain so. Informed criticism of treatments claimed to be effective is essential. This demands a considerable knowledge of research methodology.

Before turning to more specific psychopharmacological interventions, brief mention will be made of the effects of vitamins and trace elements, of antihistamines and of food additives on pupils with learning difficulties in general and specific learning difficulties in particular. There are lessons for both professionals and parents.

Vitamins and trace elements

If something is 'good' for you, is not more likely to be better? A recent report states that vitamin and mineral supplement manufacturers in the UK sold £135m. worth of their products during 1989. The market is growing. The National Association of Health Stores has some 700 members in the UK. If the present rate of increase continues, sales in the market will have risen by nearly 50 per cent by 1993. Currently 1 in 4 adults in the South East and 1 in 8 in the rest of the country take daily supplements. Herbal extracts, minerals, trace elements and amino acids sit side by side on the shelves with familiars such as vitamins A, B, C, D and E in a proliferation of health shops. Their offerings include '... boron (to help you retain calcium), biotin (regulates yeast infection), co-enzyme Q-10 (increases the body's utilization of oxygen), ginko-biloba (improves concentration, moods, brain functions), guarana (for fatigue, allergies), lapacho (a natural antibiotic), selenium (immune system booster, anti-oxidant) or silymarion (keeps the liver healthy)' (Rich, 1990). In addition there are many fashionable elixirs, such as evening primrose oil, garlic, kelp, ginseng and royal jelly, to mention but a few. As the range and variety of such supplements increases, so do confusions concerning precisely what these supplements do, as opposed to what it is claimed that they do. They are not classified as drugs and are governed by the Food Acts. Because of this, they do not require the long-term scientific evaluation required of drugs. Despite this, the Department of Health has recently withdrawn at least two supplements because of adverse effects discovered in other countries (germanium, a trace element; and tryptophan, an amino acid). The claims that some manufacturers make for their products frequently have inadequate scientific backing (Rich, 1990). The professor of nutrition and dietetics at King's College, London, is reported as saying, 'In this country, a good, balanced diet provides all the vitamins, minerals and nutrients that the body needs – frequently in excess of the recommended amounts ... any excess beyond the body's needs, whether eaten as a pill or obtained from natural dietary sources, does more good to organisms in the sewer than to the consumer' (ibid.). *Caveat emptor!*

Can the taking of very high doses of vitamins enable children with learning disabilities to function more effectively? Wilsher cites three of many studies that have been carried out. The first, by Rimland, was reported at a conference of the Association for Children with Learning Disabilities held in Atlanta, USA, in 1981. In this study, interested doctors identified learning disabled pupils and prescribed large doses of the combination of vitamins considered necessary. According to a subsequent telephone survey, a considerable number of the children showed improved performances at school. Only a minority showed toxic side-effects. Rimland concludes 'solid, incontestable research, as well as an enormous amount of clinical evidence, shows megavitamin therapy ... to be the treatment of choice for learning and behaviour disorders' (ibid., p. 10). Rimland's study lacked controls, objective measures and double-blind procedures. Wilsher notes that 'There appears to be no medical basis for the idea that taking several times the recommended daily dose will help learning; in fact some vitamins are toxic and must not be taken in excess' (ibid., p. 10).

In 1988 Benton and Roberts presented a study of the effects of the daily recommended dose of multivitamins on schoolchildren's intellectual functioning. The work received widespread television and press coverage in the UK. The study was well-designed, double-blind and placebo-controlled, involving 30 secondary school pupils treated for eight months. Significant improvements in nonverbal IQ scores were obtained (Benton and Roberts, 1988). Naismith *et al.* (1988) subsequently failed to replicate this result using a much larger sample of 154 pupils. In that both of these studies were with normal pupils, rather than with children with specific learning difficulties (dyslexia), the major lesson is that small group studies can produce positive (or negative) results by chance.

There were direct beneficiaries of Benton's original research work. The widespread publicity that it received led to chemists' shops running out of vitamins.

Subsequent work by Benton, presented in a paper given at the 1990 Annual Conference of the British Psychological Society, claims that children showed increases of up to nine points in their IQ when given vitamin supplements. This latest study was based on the results obtained from more than 160 twelve-year-old pupils attending seven schools in Belgium. The pupils kept records of their diet. Half were given vitamin supplements for five months and the rest took pills containing no active ingredients. In contrast, a report in the *Lancet* dated 30 March 1990 by Crombie, a senior lecturer in epidemiology at Dundee University, finds no such effects in a sample of 43 pupils assessed on six IQ tests following a nine-month period of vitamin supplementation.

The controversy concerning the existence and nature of a relationship between nutrition and intelligence continues unabated. The Dietary Research Foundation, established in 1989, considers, on the basis of existing knowledge, that pupils who take pills containing the recommended daily amounts of certain vitamins and trace minerals ('Vitachieve' is one such product) are at an advantage in terms of subsequent scores on non-verbal IQ test scores. Whether this effect will help enhance the attainments of children with specific learning difficulties remains, understandably, far from clear.

Originally it was planned that a study to test the supplementation hypothesis would take place in five countries. In the event, 1200 children in Cumbria and California were involved. The results recently published are based on tests given to 410 of the 615 pupils in the American sample. The workers involved in this recent study have taken considerable care in its design, analysis and interpretation. The British results have not, at the time of writing, been published, though it is indicated that these are broadly similar to those in California.

The Californian pupils on such treatment for one term scored 3.7 points higher than a group receiving placebo pills. Other groups receiving 50 per cent and 200 per cent of the dose achieved no significant improvement. The pupils in this study did not keep daily records of their nutritional intakes.

The Medical Research Council has noted that children's diets can differ widely between countries. This could affect the interpretation of the results of the supplementation study. Additionally, it has been suggested that because vitamins and minerals are used in the metabolism of other nutrients, if the latter are either absent or in short supply, the effects of the supplements could vary.

Dr D. Conning, Director-General of the British Nutrition Foundation, is reported as commenting that 'Most children will show no improvement and some will perform worse. A few children will do exceptionally well, but we do not know which. We do not know if the changes represent real changes in intelligence or an improvement in the ability to concentrate, and we do not know what effect any of the changes will have on educational standards' (Abrams, 1991).

Blood samples from the children are currently being assessed to explore 170 combinations of factors that might contribute to the effect identified.

One of the American members of the Dietary Research Foundation research team has suggested that the recommended daily intakes of certain vitamins and minerals are too low in the UK. He recommends vitamin and mineral supplements (Schoenthaler, 1991). The saga is likely to run far longer than *The Mousetrap*. If there is a link, it would be of particular interest to many readers if it were established whether, amongst the pupils taking part in such studies, some had previously been identified as having specific learning difficulties (dyslexia). The incidence figures from various studies suggest that this is highly likely to have been the case. If such pupils could be identified, were they *differentially* helped, or not, in relation to their progress in literacy skills by vitamin supplementation? On the surface, it would appear that *only* pupils on vitamin-deficient diets would be likely to benefit.

The only people who actually need to take regular vitamin supplements are those not eating sufficient of the normal daily foods. These *may* include children who refuse to eat fruit or vegetables, are on medication, have an illness, have a metabolic disorder or are known to need extra vitamins.

The importance of a range of trace elements as possible causes of specific learning difficulties (dyslexia) is a closely related field. Some workers consider that, in certain cases, a mild, sub-acute form of zinc deficiency is implicated, and that this has implications for treatment (Grant *et al.*, 1988). An insufficiency of essential fatty acids (EFAs) has also been suggested as a potential cause of learning difficulties. The damaging effects of varying levels of lead pollution on children's intellectual functioning in general has also been an area of concern (Quin and Macauslan, 1986). Whilst the identification of associations between such dietary and environmental variables and specific learning difficulties is possible, causality is less readily established. It follows that the evaluation of interventions is equally complex.

Antihistamines

In the USA, Levinson (1980) has advocated the therapeutic use of antihistamines in the treatment of dyslexia. The therapy is based on the assumption that some dyslexics suffer from a cerebellar-vestibular disorder. This makes them prone to feelings of motion-sickness. Associated with this are problems in processing textual materials, which appear to move. Treatment involves providing a course of one or more anti-motion sickness drugs (trade names are presented in parentheses). These include ' ... cyclizine (Marezine), meclizine (Antivert), dimehydrinate (Dramimine), diphenhydramine (Benadryl), methylphenidate (Ritalin), etc.' (Levinson, 1980, p. 236). It is claimed that 88 per cent of dyslexics show 'some clinical measure or degree of favourable therapeutic response' (p. 237).

Professor Richard Masland, Emeritus Professor of Neurology of Columbia University and currently President of the World Federation of Neurology, has argued that the theoretical basis of the treatment is without substance. The existence of individuals with severe vestibular disorders, but no problems with their reading, is one empirical challenge. An examination of a group of developmental dyslexics compared with a control group showed that the groups did not differ in the incidence of vestibular difficulties (Brown *et al.*, 1983a). Levinson's methodology is severely criticized by Wilsher (1990). It does not include control groups. Efficacy is assessed objectively by testing the speed of fusion of moving pictures plus the subjective reports of parents. It is only the latter that supports the 88 per cent success claim. It is not known whether similar subjective impressions of improvement or benefit would have been obtained in a placebo control group.

Despite such comments, the theoretical and treatment issues will still run for some time. Current studies of the importance of automaticity in becoming literate make the first point. It is argued that reading and spelling deficits are the surface consequences of a more general learning deficit, the relative inability to automatize skills. The performance of a group of 12- to 13-year-old dyslexic pupils was compared with that of a control group on eight tests of motor skills ranging from gross skill, such as beam balancing, to fine motor skills, such as tapping. The test of automaticity used a dual task paradigm. Subjects performed each motor test twice, once as a single task and once as a dual task concurrently with a simple counting task. The prediction that, regardless of performance level on the single task, performance on the dual task would be significantly worse for the dyslexic pupils was upheld for all eight motor tests. A major point is that such findings are interpreted as questioning the validity of the lexical skills-deficit hypothesis. It is also claimed to have important treatment implications (Fawcett, 1989). The existence of pupils with severe motor disorder who have no difficulties in literacy skills has yet to be adequately incorporated into the model proposed. At the same conference, a complementary paper on work in Israel entitled 'Failure in achieving automatic performance of psychomotor skills' took the theoretical issues much further (Lamm, 1989). The possibility exists that drug treatment might improve the development of automaticity in children with specific learning difficulties (dyslexia).

Food additives

The use of food additives has for some time been commented on as a potential cause of hyperactivity and learning disabilities in children (Feingold, 1975). The importance of an additive-free diet is emphasized in such circumstances.

Cases of individual pupils who react adversely to particular food additives are known to the author. If such effects occur, one can understand why these could adversely affect children's literacy skills. However, it is difficult to accept that the effect is specific to aspects of language. It is equally difficult to accept that there is likely to be an effect specific to the somewhat heterogeneous group comprising pupils with specific learning difficulties (dyslexia).

According to Wilsher (1990), there have been many studies in this field. He cites the example of a small-scale research by Mates and Gittleman (1981) using a double-blind procedure. A number of children on an additive-free diet were identified. A pilot study placebo trial excluded any children who responded markedly to a placebo. Subsequently, the researchers administered high doses of additives that had been approved by the USA Food and Drug Administration Agency. The research design was a double-blind cross-over model in which each subject acted as his or her own control. Eleven children were assessed on a battery of 19 hyperactivity rating scale tests by five different groups of assessors. These included mothers, teachers, psychiatrists, psychologists and children. 'No differences whatsoever were seen between the behaviour of those children on food additives and of those on placebo. It would appear that the reaction to additives proposed by Feingold may not be easily demonstrable' (Wilsher, 1990).

Such small-scale evidence is important, but not conclusive. Possible adverse individual effects, as opposed to group effects, of food additives identified in clinical settings cannot be ignored. For example, in recent work in one nursery school known to the author, four individual cases merit mention. Mention is made not because of the specifics of the cases, but because it is unlikely that the nursery school and its pupils are atypical. The first case was of a girl aged four years. When she ate food containing certain additives, she developed a fine rash and became difficult in her behaviour. By elimination, the additives to which she reacted adversely were identified. When these were removed from her diet, the symptoms disappeared. To enable the girl to keep to the diet, her mother sent the girl's lunch to school. The girl's health and application at school are reported as having improved. The second case is of a two-year-old boy. He was affected by a smaller range of additives and was consequently not allowed to eat certain convenience foods containing these identified substances. His difficult behaviour decreased and his application to activities at school improved. He was able to eat the school meals that were provided. A change in the school meals system took place. The kitchen was provided with 'pre-prepared' vegetables. The boy began to develop a rash and his behaviour again deteriorated. It was found that a readily identified and specific preservative additive used in the preparation of the vegetables was apparently responsible for this effect on this particular pupil. Two other pupils were not allowed foods containing tartrazine because of dramatic adverse effects on their behaviour consequent on their ingesting any food containing the additive. Here we are moving into the field of allergic responses. It is one in which much work remains to be done. This work must be kept in perspective in that it concerns all children and not only those with specific learning difficulties (dyslexia).

Psychostimulants

A review of eight long-term studies of the effects of stimulant drugs on the academic attainments of hyperactive and learning disabled pupils reports that, in seven of them, the drug treatments did not enhance academic attainments (Gadow, 1983).

A study of the effects of methylphenidate (Ritalin) in combination with reading remediation involving 66 children randomly allocated to placebo or methylphenidate conditions has been carried out. The pupils were tested on 22 basic reading skills at the start of the study, after treatment and on two follow-ups. Immediately after treatment, a significant advantage favouring the methylphenidate group was found in reading initial consonants. A trend in favour of the group was also found in respect of spelling and comprehension. Post-tests held at 2 and 18 months after treatment demonstrated no significant differences between the groups on reading achievement and academic tasks. This is interpreted by the authors as suggesting that the stimulants may not enhance learning or the acquisition of new skills, but may help improve the ability to apply mastered tasks (Gittleman, Klein and Feingold, 1983).

According to Wilsher (1990), methylphenidate and dextroamphetamine are two psychostimulant drugs that have been shown to improve the attention of hyperactive learning disabled pupils. The effects on their educational performances show no gains due to the drugs. Experiments with non-hyperactive children in double-blind controlled trials also showed no benefits in reading attainments. 'Stimulants do not appear to address themselves specifically to the central problem area of the reading disabled child, i.e. reading performance' (ibid.).

Attention deficit disorder is a clinical syndrome related to reading disability. Two frequently used medications are methylphenidate and dexedrine. Despite earlier promising indications with hyperactive and learning disabled children (Lerer et al., 1979), the effects of the former on reading performance in the classroom appears to be less than satisfactory (Cooter, 1988).

Piracetam and dyslexia

Piracetam is a drug that was first used 24 years ago in the treatment of memory problems in the elderly. It is known by the trade names of Nootropil, Nootropyl, Nootrop and Noostan. The drug is structurally related to a naturally occurring neurotransmitter known as gamma-aminobutyric acid (GABA). It has been claimed that the drug selectively improves the efficiency of cognitive functions. Wilsher (1990) reports that piracetam is structurally similar to GABA. However, its precise action is unknown. Evidence exists suggesting that piracetam ' ... increases the turnover of ATP (adenosine triphosphate), which would increase the energy of cells ... work so far suggests that the drug seems to improve left hemisphere functioning' (ibid.). The drug is also reported as not having significant side-effects (Chase *et al.*, 1984; Wilsher, 1986; Wilsher *et al.*, 1987).

The use of this drug in the treatment of children with learning difficulties has a more recent history (Wilsher, 1980; Wilsher *et al.*, 1987). A clinical study using 16 male dyslexic adolescents and 14 normal student volunteers took part in a double-blind trial lasting three weeks. Both groups treated with piracetam required fewer trials to reach criterion in a rote verbal learning task (Wilsher, Atkins and Manfield, 1979).

The initially promising results led to another study using a further 14 learning disordered boys. The study was based on a four-week, double-blind, cross-over study. Significant improvements in the learning of cognitive tasks were not identified. Subsequent re-analyses of the findings using EEG results showed that piracetam reduced left-hemisphere delta power and that this was related to improvements on neuropsychological measures of verbal/sequential performance.

Wilsher also reports further work based on the effect of piracetam or placebo treatments on 257 boys for 12 weeks by DiIanni *et al.* (1985). Associated with this were special studies by Rudel and Helfgott (1984), Chase *et al.* (1984) and Connors *et al.* (1984). The findings from these researches are complex, far from conclusive, but promising (Wilsher *et al.*, 1987).

A subsequent multi-centred, large-scale, long-term study of the effects of piracetam on dyslexia is of considerable importance because of both its scope and results. It comprised five investigative teams following a common protocol and initially involved 225 dyslexic children (153 boys and 72 girls) of above average intelligence aged between 7:06 and 12:11 years. On average, their reading skills were 3.4 years below their expected reading age. Children with abnormal results on audiologic, ophthalmologic, neurologic, psychiatric and physical examinations were excluded from the research. So too were emotionally disturbed or educationally deprived pupils. None of the participants had recently been treated with psychoactive medications. The study was based on a 36-week, double-blind, placebo controlled design. Two hundred pupils completed the 36-week study. Both the placebo and the piracetam groups were comparable on a number of demographic characteristics including sex, race, full-scale IQ, performance IQ, verbal IQ and reading quotient. The piracetam group was, on average, slightly younger than the placebo group by about four months.

The *Gray Oral Reading Test* (Gray, 1963), the *Gilmore Oral Reading Test* (Gilmore and Gilmore, 1968) and the single-word reading test from the *Wide Range Achievement Test – Revised (WRAT-R)* (Jastak and Wilkinson, 1984) provided attainment indices.

Summarizing the complex results, 'Children with developmental reading disorder (dyslexia) who were treated with piracetam showed improvement in reading ability (*Gray Oral Total Passage Score*) and reading comprehension (*Gray and Gilmore Comprehension Scores*). These improvements were evident over a 36 week period, which is one of the longest controlled trials of its kind. The medication was well tolerated' (Wilsher *et al.*, 1987, p. 237). These are challenging findings. Inevitably one wonders what has happened in the longer term to the pupils' progress when the medication had ceased?

In conclusion, Wilsher reports that in various studies dyslexic pupils given piracetam have shown improvements in a range of performance indicators. These include reading skills, verbal memory, verbal comprehension, verbal conceptualizing ability, feature analysis and the ability to process letter-like stimuli (Wilsher *et al.*, 1987, p. 230). The field is clearly one in which developments will continue.

Summary

Nutrition, vitamins, trace element imbalances, allergies, heavy metal toxicities and the effects (including side-effects) of psychopharmaceutics command the attention of a large and broad audience. Considerable media and public attention is devoted to such issues. Claims for dietary and/or psychopharmaceutical means of preventing or 'curing' complex illnesses or alleviating their symptoms are commonplace. The majority of such claims are typically not scientifically well-established.

Complex biochemical and neurophysiological functions interact. They underpin cognitive processes supporting the development and maintenance of a range of literacy-related performances (and other behaviours). This chapter has selectively indicated a number of issues that are currently the subject of increasing professional interest and activity, and of parental concern in relation to pupils with specific learning difficulties (dyslexia).

The fields are clearly ones in which explorations will continue. History has shown vividly that there can be unanticipated and disastrous consequences for individuals when scientific understanding is being developed. Despite this, the simplistic appeal of 'snake-oil' solutions to children's specific learning difficulties will continue to be exploited. The armour of informed scepticism is an important protection for professionals and parents against exploitation by the unscrupulous. It will be a long time before the dietary and/or drug control of specific learning difficulties will be fully achieved. This does not mean that nothing of value has been learned or that the avenues should be abandoned. A balance between informed scepticism and an openness to new ideas and practices is essential. This state is one of dynamic, rather than unstable or stable, equilibrium.

Recommendations

11.1. Those evaluating the efficacy of psychopharmacological treatment of specific learning difficulties have a thorough technical appreciation of research design and methodology.

11.2. Claims for causal relationships between vitamin supplements, trace elements, food additives, pharmaceutics and specific learning difficulties be treated with caution.

11.3. Attention be paid to the ethical issues involved in psychopharmacological research and experiments.

11.4. More multidisciplinary research be undertaken in psychopharmaceutics and specific learning difficulties.

SECTION E: SURVEY RESPONSES

This section presents the results of surveys in five important fields. The first briefly summarizes the aims, structure and scope of the inquiry initiated by the Division of Educational and Child Psychology of the British Psychological Society into Specific Learning Difficulties (Dyslexia). An overview of the policies and practices of local education authorities is presented in the second chapter. This is followed by an analysis of the views of educational psychologists concerning professional practice and development. The views of a selection of major organizations involved in specific learning difficulties (dyslexia), including those of the Department of Education and Science, are then presented in the fourth chapter. The section concludes with a survey of the policies and practices of examination boards concerning dispensations for pupils with specific learning difficulties (dyslexia).

Chapter 12

Aims and Structure of the Inquiry

Introduction

The Education Act 1981, the Education Reform Act 1988 and their associated circulars and regulations provide the central legal and administrative contexts within which most teachers and educational psychologists function in England and Wales. Their work includes professional and legal responsibilities concerning children experiencing a wide range and variety of learning difficulties. The field is both complex and controversial. It affects pupils, parents and professionals.

'Specific learning difficulties' is a descriptive label used to designate one group of children having special educational needs under the provisions of the Education Act 1981. Specific developmental dyslexia is also interpreted as being included under Section 1 of that Act. Despite the existence of official guidance in the form of circulars and regulations, LEA policies concerning the identification and provision to meet the special educational needs represented by both of these groups vary considerably. So too do the identification procedures, interventions and resource provisions that derive from these policies.

In part, these variations are due to legitimate disagreements between professionals concerning the validity of the constructs and the procedures whereby a child is deemed to exemplify the requisite characteristics of either or both terms. Some professionals consider the two terms to be synonymous. Others have reservations as to the validity of one or the other, or both. Most parents of children experiencing specific learning difficulties are unconcerned about the label used to designate their child's status: they want action to alleviate the child's learning difficulties. Parents become impatient with what appear to them irrelevant, arcane and time-wasting arguments between professionals concerning the name given to their child's condition. Increasingly, where parents consider that their child has not rightfully been accorded the educational resources from the public purse that will alleviate the learning difficulty, the law is invoked. Parents are legitimately challenging the opinions of administrators, psychologists and teachers in the courts (Chasty and Friel, 1991).

Such situations can become emotionally highly charged. Educational psychologists are frequently at the centre of the turbulence in such cases. Often they contribute to it. Their knowledge, expertise and interpretations are open to detailed examination. It is the profession's informed disinterest (the antithesis of lack of interest) in the issues that is one of its major strengths. The maintenance of such qualities requires that the educational psychologist remains abreast of the latest developments in theory and in basic and applied research. The present report represents a contribution to that process by raising issues, providing information and making recommendations.

Background

The Division of Educational and Child Psychology of the British Psychological Society (DECP) has a long-standing tradition of carrying out inquiries into controversial topics of major importance to its members and the clients that they serve. Educational and child psychologists' duties and opinions concerning their work and its development formed the basis of one inquiry (Wedell and Lambourne, 1980). Procedures for the identification of children requiring special education and the assessment of their needs were introduced by Circular 2/75 of the Department of Education and Science (GB.DES, 1975a). Concern about these proposals led to a DECP inquiry into the role of the educational psychologist in this field. This inquiry provided data of value when the regulations for the Education Act 1981 were under discussion (Cornwall and Spicer, 1982). The finding that the educational psychologist was the LEA's main coordinator of advice on pupils requiring special education helped considerably in modifying the DES's earlier view that the educational psychologist was merely a member of an assessment team, providing 'psychological' advice on pupils with special needs.

Some LEAs and their psychologists have been, are being and will continue to be criticized because of alleged inadequacy of provision, or their apparent lack of concern, for pupils who were described variously as 'dyslexic', having 'specific reading difficulties' or 'specific learning difficulties'. The issues involved are not simple ones. Identification of a specific learning difficulty involves an understanding of the nature of children's normal physical, emotional, social and cognitive development in particular contexts. It is against this that the possibility of specific learning difficulties (dyslexia) has to be considered. Physiological, psychological and pedagogic analyses are involved. The causes of

learning difficulties have to be explored. The contingencies that maintain and reinforce difficulties must also be analysed. Both can only be done within a theoretical framework, even if that is an eclectic one.

At present, in relation to specific learning difficulties (dyslexia), no single
level of analysis, no single theory, no means of identification commands general
acceptance. That is why equally competent and qualified psychologists are rightly cautious. Even if agreement on identification did exist (and there are many
cases where this does occur), it does not follow that accurate identification of a
condition means that necessarily it can be rapidly treated. The conceptual controversies have a long history. These issues have been, in turn, fuelled or dampened
by legislation, DES reports and research findings.

The Chronically Sick and Disabled Persons Act 1970 included a section on
'special educational treatment for children suffering from acute dyslexia'. This
required that each LEA provide the Secretary of State with information on the
provision of special educational facilities for children '...who suffer from acute
dyslexia'. The subsequent debate led the Advisory Committee on Handicapped
Children, chaired by Tizard, to produce a report. This cast doubts on the validity
of the concept of 'dyslexia' and proposed that a more usefully descriptive term
'specific reading difficulties' should be used (GB.DES, 1972). For a period, the
topic of dyslexia appeared to lose the impetus afforded it by the 1970 Act,
although voluntary associations, such as the British Dyslexia Association and the
Dyslexia Institute, continued to press the case for its recognition. The Bullock
Report also rejected the term 'dyslexia'. It chose to recommend 'specific reading
retardation' instead (GB.DES, 1975b). Chaired by Warnock, the Committee of
Enquiry into the Education of Handicapped Children and Young People opted for
the more inclusive descriptive term 'children with learning difficulties'. Its report
recommended that this term be used to describe both pupils then categorized as
educationally subnormal and those with learning difficulties who were the concern of various remedial services. It also recommended that children with
'specific reading difficulties' might be described as having 'specific learning difficulties'. Additionally, the report accepted that there are other children '...whose
disabilities are marked but whose ability is at least average and for whom distinctive arrangements are necessary' (GB.DES, 1978).

The subsequent Education Act 1981 and Circular 8/81 made it an LEA responsibility to identify and alleviate learning difficulties (GB.DES, 1981). Dyslexia, despite the controversies surrounding the concept, is deemed to be one
group of such learning difficulties. Circular 1/83 on the 'Assessment and Statements of Special Educational Needs' established procedures whereby such responsibilities could be administratively discharged (DES, 1983). The legal status
of a statement under the provisions of the Education Act 1981 underlined important resource responsibilities for LEAs. The role of the educational and child
psychologist, in collaboration with the teacher, parents and other professionals,
in preparing statements highlighted controversial theoretical and technical issues
concerning how valid assessments of specific learning difficulties (dyslexia)
could be carried out. Unavoidably, in the background lurked the ethical challenge of equitable resource allocation in a situation where demands outstripped
resources. In effect, the concept of special educational needs raised parental expectations considerably. Unfortunately, no additional funds were allocated by
central government to meet these. Linked to legislative imprecision, this made
the task of professionals charged with administering the system exceedingly difficult: many would say impossible.

Such developments indicated the desirability of the DECP making an examination of these issues. Towards the end of 1981 a working party was established. In December 1984, its findings were published in a report entitled 'Specific Learning Difficulties: The "Specific Reading Difficulties" versus "Dyslexia" Controversy Resolved?' (Cornwall, Hedderly and Pumfrey, 1984). The question mark in the title was both deliberate and important. The report was a substantial piece of work comprising 121 pages. It included recommendations concerning the uses and limitations of labels, inter-professional cooperation, cooperation with parents, the improvement of the work of School Psychological Services, assessments, interventions and examination dispensations. The report was well received by a wide readership. It was influential in developing understanding between voluntary and statutory groups. An index of its success is that the report was reprinted, and sold out. A third impression was made in response to continuing requests for copies from various individuals and organizations.

Since 1984, problems in the identification, prevention and alleviation of special educational needs (SEN) in general, and of specific learning difficulties (dyslexia) in particular, continue to concern many professionals, parents and pupils.

The passing of the 1981 Education Act, its implementation in 1983 and the subsequent numerous related circulars and regulations have highlighted many issues concerning policy and practice in the field of specific learning difficulties (dyslexia) (GB.DES, 1989a, b). The evaluation of the working of the Education Act 1981, carried out by a Select Committee of the House of Commons and published in 1987, identified a number of important concerns. The Education Reform Act 1988, introducing a National Curriculum with Programmes of Study, Attainment Targets and regular assessments of standards and progress, also has important implications for LEA policies and practices concerning children with specific learning difficulties (dyslexia). The introduction of Local Management of Schools, as set out in Circular 7/88, further highlights financial and staffing resource issues that could adversely impinge on non-statemented pupils with special educational needs (GB.DES, 1988c). The revision of the advice in Circular 1/83 concerning 'Assessments and Statements of Special Educational Needs: Procedures within the Education, Health and Social Services' is now completed in Circular 22/89 (GB.DES, 1989f). This was a direct consequence of dissatisfactions expressed in their report by a Parliamentary Select Committee on the implementation of the Education Act 1981 (House of Commons Education, Science and Arts Committee, 1987). Advice concerning the school curriculum and assessment for all pupils is presented in Circular 5/89 (GB.DES, 1989c). Modifications and disapplications concerning pupils with special educational needs, including pupils with specific learning difficulties (dyslexia), are detailed therein (ibid., paras 55-64).

Controversies concerning the nature, incidence and alleviation of specific learning difficulties (dyslexia) continue. Research also continues its advances in conceptualizing the nature, predicting and controlling these phenomena. There are still many marked disagreements between workers. These frequently concern aetiology and interventions. Agreement on presenting characteristics is greater, though far from unanimous. In summary, although there are individuals and groups who are, at times, intemperately critical of other workers, there is clear evidence of more constructive dialogues than previously in the UK and elsewhere (Hammill, 1990).

The right to, and means of, financing interventions is one of the major focuses of current concern. The administrative procedures for allocating additional resources from the public purse in a democratic system is a continuing 'battle' between competing priorities. It is not a psychological issue, but a financial/political/values one for society. In contrast, whether such conditions as specific learning difficulties (dyslexia) actually exist, and (if they do) their natures and relationships, are key psychological, educational and medical issues.

In 1988 the Committee of the Division of Educational and Child Psychology of the British Psychological Society decided to examine current challenges and responses, and to make recommendations. The Association of Educational Psychologists (AEP) accepted an invitation to be associated with the inquiry. In combination, the overlapping memberships of the DECP (1989 membership = 889) and the AEP (1989 membership = 1605) comprise the vast majority of educational and child psychologists employed in the UK.

Peter D. Pumfrey, currently Professor in Education at the Centre for Educational Guidance and Special Needs of the University of Manchester and Rea Reason, Associate Tutor to the course of professional training for educational psychologists and Senior Educational Psychologist in the same Centre, were appointed to coordinate the work and prepare the final report. A group of 11 educational psychologists,* with particular interest in the field, was involved. These were drawn from eight LEAs and carried out extensive preparatory work during the autumn term of 1988. During 1989–90 the same team collected, analysed, interpreted and wrote up the very considerable body of information collected during the inquiry.

Aims of the inquiry

The aims of the current inquiry include the following:

- in so far as is possible, to provide a wide-ranging, disinterested and objective report of current thinking, policies and practices;
- to outline the background to current challenges and controversies concerning the nature of specific learning difficulties (dyslexia);
- to identify key issues in furthering our ability to understand the challenges under consideration;
- to review the literature on identification and interventions from complementary psychological, psychoeducational and psychomedical viewpoints;
- to make available to members of the DECP, AEP, LEAs, other interested groups of professionals and lay persons, a description of LEA policies, practices and future plans concerning specific learning difficulties (dyslexia);

---

* Betty Allan, Lancashire LEA; Robin Bartlett, Oxfordshire LEA; John Coleman, Rotherham LEA; Mary Dean, Oxfordshire LEA; Ann Forrester, Tameside LEA; Margaret Gregory, Salford LEA; Robin Hedderly, Kirklees LEA; Peter Pumfrey, Manchester University; Rea Reason, Oldham LEA and Manchester University; David Webster, Lancashire LEA and AEP representative; John Wilkins, Liverpool LEA.

- to present the views of practising educational psychologists concerning identification, intervention and provision;
- to present the views of statutory bodies, voluntary organizations, and individuals;
- to review the policies and practices adopted by examination boards;
- to make recommendations.

Structure of the inquiry

Beginning in January 1989, the following actions were taken. They provided the data on which the report is based. The actions specified also indicate the structure of the inquiry.

LEA policies. A letter (marked for the attention of the principal educational psychologist), outlining the purposes of the inquiry was sent to all 104 Chief Education Officers in England and Wales, together with a brief questionnaire concerning LEA policy.

Educational psychologists' practices. A letter outlining the purposes of the inquiry was sent individually to all members of the DECP and AEP in January 1989, together with a short questionnaire. Many educational and child psychologists are members of both organizations. Distribution was organized so that no one received duplicate questionnaires.

The views of a wide range of voluntary and professional groups were sought concerning:

- the concept of specific learning difficulties (dyslexia);
- identification and assessment;
- prevention;
- teaching methods;
- provision of resources.

The views of professional psychologists in other countries on the issues that were being addressed, as represented through their national professional associations, were solicited.

Other perspectives. The 11 members of the working group volunteered for specific tasks related to the collection and analysis of information and the writing up of preliminary drafts of sections of the report. Manual and computer literature searches were carried out reviewing the literature from three complementary perspectives: psychological; psychoeducational and psychomedical. Letters were sent to the editors of a number of national papers and periodicals. The purposes and scope of the inquiry were outlined, and readers invited to write to the inquiry coordinators concerning the concept of SpLD (dyslexia) identification and assessment, prevention, teaching methods and provision of resources.

A survey of Examination Board policies and practices on dispensations for pupils deemed to have specific learning difficulties was carried out. This extended the related survey carried out in the earlier (1983) inquiry. A letter was published in *The Psychologist* informing all members of the British Psychological Society of the inquiry and asking for their views on specific points.

Conclusion

The inquiry focused on children who are described as having specific learning difficulties (dyslexia). The natures of, and relationships between, these two terms are controversial and theoretically important. In addition, their uses have significant practical consequences for pupils, parents and professionals. The scope of the inquiry is considerable. It is much larger than the earlier report published in 1984.

This research and review builds on the previous DECP report. It is intended to increase public and professional awareness of current policies and practices as they affect children with specific learning difficulties (dyslexia). It is written by educational and child psychologists, but is also intended for that much larger group of teachers, administrators, voluntary groups and parents who are equally interested and involved. Whilst it is unlikely that children with specific learning difficulties (dyslexia) will consult this report, its preparation is an acknowledgement of the importance of their education.

The completion of this report has been dependent on the cooperation and goodwill of an extensive range of organizations and individuals. The reactions of readers to the challenges and responses described and discussed, and the recommendations presented, are awaited with interest.

Summary

- Controversies surround the concepts of specific learning difficulties and Dyslexia. These controversies impinge on LEAs' institutional and individual decision-making policies. They also affect the procedures and provision to which they give rise under the requirements of the Education Act 1981 and the Education Reform Act 1988. The issues concern and affect pupils, parents and professionals.
- In 1988 the DECP Committee decided to take further its previously published report 'Specific Learning Difficulties: The "Specific Reading Difficulties" versus "Dyslexia" Controversy Resolved?' (Cornwall, Hedderley and Pumfrey, 1984). The AEP agreed to cooperate in the venture. The intention was to take into consideration subsequent theoretical, research and administrative developments.
- The inquiry was to be a national one entitled 'specific learning difficulties (dyslexia): challenges, responses and recommendations'.
- P. D. Pumfrey and R. Reason of the Centre for Educational Guidance and Special Needs, within the School of Education at the University of Manchester, were invited to organize the inquiry and prepare the report. A group of 11 qualified and experienced educational and child psychologists from eight LEAs comprised the team.
- In so far as was possible, the inquiry aimed to provide a wide-ranging, disinterested and objective report of current thinking, policies and practices in the specified area.
- In order to place the role of LEAs and educational and child psychologists in context, it was considered essential to identify key controversial issues. It was also necessary to review the pertinent literature on assessment and interventions from three complementary viewpoints: psychological, psychoeducational and psychomedical.

- The policies and practices of LEAs were solicited, the views and practices of educational psychologists were also obtained and both sets of data analysed.
- A wide spectrum of information and opinion was sought. Respondents included the Department of Education and Science, other statutory bodies, voluntary associations and individuals in the UK. The views of psychologists in other countries was sought via their professional associations.
- The policies of examination boards were sought on dispensations for pupils deemed to have specific learning difficulties (dyslexia).
- The following four chapters provide a summary of the investigations carried out into the above issues.
- Recommendations concerning the development of policies and practices are presented.

Chapter 13

Local Education Authority Policies and Practices

Introduction

This inquiry was aimed at updating our knowledge of current policies and practices in relation to children with specific learning difficulties (SpLD) within local education authorities (LEAs). Aspects of policy and practice that were of particular interest were the approaches LEAs took to: providing statements of special educational needs, identification, provision, in-service training (INSET) and their plans for any future developments.

Relevant information was gathered through a questionnaire survey. It was felt appropriate that such information would be sought from principal educational psychologists with the permission of chief education officers. In the event, 85 per cent of the responses were provided by principal psychologists, the remainder being provided by education officers. The questionnaire addressed the five broad areas: overall policy, identification, provision, INSET and future plans. The findings are outlined in the remainder of this chapter. They should be viewed in the encouraging light of the response rate, which was relatively high for such a questionnaire survey. Responses were received from 79 of the possible 106 LEAs (this includes the Isle of Man and Isles of Scilly), giving a return rate of 74.5 per cent (Table 13.1).

Table 13.1: LEA responses

Overall return rate: 74.5 per cent
Post of respondent: principal psychologist, 85 per cent; education officer, 15 per cent

Type of LEA	Returned no. (%)	Possible returns	Percentage returned by type of LEA (N=79)
County council	28 (35.9)	39	71.8
Metropolitan districts	26 (33.3)	36	72.2
London boroughs	18 (21.8)	20	90
Welsh counties	6 (7.7)	8	75
Other	1 (1.3)	3	33.3

Overall policy

Q.1: 'Has your LEA a formulated policy on SpLDs?'

Yes: 42 (53.2 per cent)   No: 37 (46.8 per cent)

Q.2: 'Is there a document specifying this policy?'

Yes: 24 (30.4 per cent)   No: 55 (69.6 per cent)

The returns suggest that around half of the LEAs have a formulated policy. This finding is a little less than that suggested by the 1983 survey (58.2 per cent). Of the 42 LEAs who reported that they had a policy only 24 (57.1 per cent) of them said that the policy was a written one. However, in addition to this information 32 supporting documents were returned from 26 LEAs that described policy or practice. These documents provided a wealth of information about the variety of responses LEAs have made to cater for children with SpLD.

These supporting documents may be described as:

Reports to the Education Committee	13
LEA policy statement/circular	6
Guidelines for schools	3
Educational Psychology Service statements/circulars	2
Description of Reading Support Service	1
Guidelines for parents	3
Assorted letters/minutes/recommendations	4

The 13 LEA reports to the Education Committee were particularly interesting. Twelve of the thirteen addressed the issue of SpLD (dyslexia) specifically rather than addressing the issue of special educational needs in general, although many comments within the documents and responses suggested that SpLD were and should be, identified and provided for in the same way as any other form of special educational need. Perhaps it is for this reason that a number of responses suggested that no policy was formulated for children with SpLD. Further, it was interesting to note that the majority of reports to the Education Committee had arisen as a result of similar causes and purposes. The cause for the majority of the reports made was the increasing demands upon resources since the Education Act 1981 came into force in April 1983. The purpose of the reports, quite obviously, was to recommend increasing the available resources.

The number of requests for assessment and additional support by parents, often supported by dyslexia units or consultants, was seen to be increasing. So too was the number of children identified by teachers within schools as a response to duties under the Act. This increase was seen to be due not to integration, but to a heightened awareness on the part of teachers. The Education Act 1981 seems to have enabled many children to have their special educational needs recognized and, perhaps, addressed.

The general structure of the reports was also very similar: an introductory section outlining the issues and what the difficulties are, followed by a report of current provision and recommendations for action. An introductory section might describe the apparent conflicting views within the literature and amongst the 'experts'. They pointed out the lack of consensus upon terminology, characteristics, incidence, identification and ways of dealing with SpLD.

Although all of the reports recognized both of the terms SpLD and dyslexia, the majority tended to recommend SpLD. Two reports tended to make use of both terms together. The one report that used the term dyslexia in its title argued that the policy for identifying, assessing and meeting the educational needs should be the same for dyslexia as for other special educational needs. Many of the reports referred to the Bullock Report and the Joint Schools' Council and the BMA statement. The general trend was to support the use of the term SpLD rather than dyslexia but to acknowledge that dyslexia was an increasingly familiar term.

The details of the current and recommended future plans outlined in those reports will be discussed later in this chapter. In most cases the adopted strategy in providing for SpLD was to make a continuum of provision. This range of provision was seen as necessary to correspond with the continuum of needs based on the degree of severity of a child's problems. It was the degree of difficulties that is related to additional or alternative provision rather than the existence of SpLD. The incidence of SpLD was acknowledged as difficult to ascertain but there was a general agreement that the vast majority of children with SpLD will continue to receive their education within mainstream classes. It appeared from the reports that it was the county councils rather than the smaller metropolitan districts that tended to make use of special schools. As in the previous inquiry, a 'filtering' approach to providing for children with SpLD is in evidence:

- increasing the ability of classroom teachers to identify and deal with SpLD;
- provision within the school's own resources;
- provision of limited individual or small group teaching provided by the LEA;
- provision of advice from a peripatetic support service;
- provision of direct teaching support from a peripatetic support service, individual and/or small group (some);
- provision full-time or part-time within a unit (a few);
- special school provision (very few, usually for pupils with additional difficulties, such as emotional or behavioural problems);
- provision at out-of-community residential schools, some of which may specialize in dealing with SpLD (very few).

The policy statements and remaining variety of documents provide guidelines for schools, parents and professionals. They make suggestions as to how identification, assessment, teaching and monitoring may be effectively achieved. In all cases SpLD are viewed as but one form of special educational need and guidance is given on how the 'staged' process of assessing special educational needs under the 1981 Act should be undertaken.

The list below was provided originally by a large South of England County as outlined in the 1983 survey report. It has been adopted fully or in part by a number of authorities as evidenced by its inclusion on policy statements and reports to council. It is suggested that children with SpLD have one or more of the following characteristics:

- extreme and persisting difficulty in learning to read, write or spell in children who otherwise appear able and well motivated, who have not suffered from protracted absence or ill-health, or from unfavourable environmental conditions;
- extreme and persisting difficulty in remembering and dealing with sequences, such as the letters in written or printed words, or the sounds of oral words, or the sequence of words in a sentence;
- similar difficulties with sequences of numbers, or with arithmetical operations;
- problems with the recognition or retention of patterns, particularly where the factors of sequence, direction or orientation are important;
- spelling errors which are particularly bizarre, unusual or distorted, and which may be wholly inconsistent and irregular or marked by systematic errors, with letter sequence (such as reversals) or which had high levels of skill that represent consistently phonetic versions of words whose correct spelling is regular;
- reading errors that are characterized by the persistence of frequent omissions and tabulations of words and part of words, hesitations and repeated amendments;
- writing that continues to be very much slower than average or to be marked by extreme irregularity of layout and presentation, or very unusual letter formation;
- a wide, often growing gap between the child's level of 'conceptual' understanding, or the sophistication of his or her oral language, and his or her level of performance in 'technical' skills such as reading, writing, spelling, drawing, interpreting maps and diagrams, or dealing with mathematical skills involving place value or directional or sequential aspects and processes;
- the persistence of difficulties of this kind despite special remedial help.

In general, the policy documents attempt to highlight the strategies within schools that should be developed. They argue that the overwhelming majority of children with learning difficulties should have their needs met within the normal school environment and that such children have a right to receive a broad and balanced curriculum. In planning to meet the needs of such children one LEA, representative of others, suggested schools should ensure that:

- there is a procedure within school aimed at identifying children with special educational needs;
- there is routine systematic assessment of children identified as likely to have special educational needs;
- there is systematic recording of the assessment of needs and of decisions taken as to how the needs should be met;
- parents are actively involved;
- appropriate channels of communication exist to enable each teacher involved with the child to be aware of the child's needs and how it is proposed to meet those needs;
- appropriate channels of communication exist between teachers and support services including inspectors, educational psychologists, specialist teachers from special schools, classes and peripatetic services, education welfare officers, and staff of Health Service and Social Services;

- information is published in response to the Education Act 1980, regarding arrangements made by the school to meet children's special educational needs;
- channels of communication with governors are such as to enable governors to discharge their responsibility under the Act.

Governors are reminded of their responsibilities under the Act which states they should:

- use their best endeavours ... to secure that if any registered pupil has special educational needs the special educational provision that is required for him is made;
- secure that, where the responsible person has been informed by the LEA that a registered pupil has special educational needs, those needs are made known to all who are likely to teach him; and
- secure that the teachers in the school are aware of the importance of identifying, and providing for, those registered pupils who have special educational needs.

The documents suggest that schools need, therefore, to consider and review aspects of their in-service requirements: curriculum; teaching strategies; allocation of specialist responsibilities; early identification; observation and assessment strategies; record keeping; communication and use of other support services.

Factors related to provision by the LEA rather than by the schools are also highlighted. In general, the suggestion is made that the LEA will act in such a way as to further its policy that wherever possible children will receive their entitlement to a broad and balanced curriculum within their normal mainstream setting. A differentiated curriculum response rather than a traditional remedial response is suggested.

In order to support this, the policy documents suggest that LEAs will provide advisory support services including some extra direct teaching support if necessary: educational psychology support; in-service training geared towards awareness raising, whole-school approaches and making all teachers specialists; formal assessment procedures under the Education Act 1981; guidelines; and in some instances, forms of 'screening' to aid early identification. In general, the recommendations for increasing provision for SpLD within LEAs attempted a 'best fit' model of matching the continuum of provision to the continuum of severity of needs. There did appear to be an emphasis upon increasing the support services provision.

Education Act 1981: 'statementing procedure'

Q.4: 'Are statements under Section 5 of the Education Act 1981 prepared for pupils with specific learning difficulties?'

Yes: 71 (89.9 per cent)   No: 8 (10.1 per cent)

The vast majority of LEAs do provide 'statements', it appears. Many comments, however, were added, such as 'not usually', 'in some cases', 'not normally', 'if appropriate', 'sometimes'. These would suggest that there is considerable variance between LEAs and within an LEA as to when a 'statement' is provided. When parents disagree with an LEA's decision to make a statement or not to, or the description of provision, they may contend the decision.

$Q.5$: 'With reference to children with specific learning difficulties, during 1988 has the LEA been involved in:'

(a) Court cases
Yes: 4 (5.1 per cent), No response: 3 (3.8 per cent), No: 72 (91.1 per cent)

(b) Local appeals
Yes: 29 (36.7 per cent), No response: 3 (3.8 per cent), No: 47 (59.5 per cent)

Only a small number of cases appear to need to be resolved in court. This figure may reflect the resolution of differences at local appeal stage. Local appeals had occurred in 29 authorities. Such appeals are only available when an authority intends to provide a statement and the parents wish to appeal against the type of provision being offered or made. Where the authority decides not to provide a statement no statutory right to a local appeal exists. In such a situation parents have the right to appeal to the Secretary of State and three respondents mentioned that this had occurred. From the survey we cannot be sure of the overall number of such appeals.

As part of the current inquiry, the DES was asked for the number of appeals received under Section 5(6) of the Education Act 1981. In a letter dated 15 September 1989, we were informed that 'The Secretary of State has received a total of 144 appeals under Section 5(6) of the 1981 Act. Twenty-four appeals were received in the period January to December, 1988'. In a subsequent letter dated 16 November 1990, it was stated that in 1989 alone 'The Secretary of State received a total of 99 appeals under the Education Act 1981. Of this total 50 were under Section 5(6) and 49 under Section 8(6) of the 1981 Act'.

The DES does not have separate figures for the number of appeals on behalf of children with specific learning difficulties. It would be interesting to know whether the apparent trend to an increasing use of litigation and appeal procedures indicated in the above figures is continuing. It would be of particular interest to know whether pupils with specific learning difficulties are increasingly involved in such actions. Voluntary associations have suggested that this is the case. Is it a trend that is likely to continue?

Identification

Respondents were asked, 'What steps are taken by the LEA to identify pupils with SpLD?' The question led to a variety of responses, which were clearly overlapping and not mutually exclusive. Rather, they seemed to reflect the different perceptions of what might be considered to be 'identification', or indeed SpLD and whether any special or particular steps were taken to identify SpLD as opposed to any other form of special educational needs. The responses are outlined in Table 13.2.

It is important to note that the replies reflect authority strategies, not individual or particular responses. The first four categories may well describe similar strategies. It was clear that the vast majority of LEAs employ a system of 'staged

Table 13.2: Approaches to identification

	Number	Percentage of responding LEAs (N=7)
Normal methods of referral	20	25.3
Staged assessment, for all, as outlined in the Warnock Report	18	22.7
Within-school steps leading to referral to educational psychologist and/or support teachers	22	27.8
No special or specific steps undertaken	14	17
Total:	74	92.8
Screening or survey	18	22.8
In-service training	4	5.1
Private assessments	2	2.5
Referral by parents	11	13.9
Referral by GP	1	1.3

NB: Categories are not mutually exclusive.

assessments' as described in the Warnock Report and DES Circular 1/83 outlining procedures and practices in the identification and assessment of children with special educational needs under the 1981 Act. Many of these did not feel a need for specific strategies of identification of SpLD beyond those appropriate for any other form of special educational need. The initial stages of identification were seen to involve teachers and parents without necessarily involving external specialists. It was noted that teachers may well benefit from guidance and training geared to enable identification of SpLD; only four LEAs referred to their in-service provision in this area. It was, perhaps, felt that the informal, day-to-day guidance and support from support teachers and educational psychologists was of more relevance to the issue of identification.

'Screening' was mentioned in about 23 per cent of the responses. No indication was given of whether the screening procedures were sensitive to SpLD, were accurate in identifying or were linked to resource allocation. The fact that only 23 per cent of the responding LEAs used such procedures may be related to the importance of the above factors (Lindsay, 1984). Screening that proved insensitive and inaccurate would be of little use in enabling difficulties to be overcome or to be avoided more easily. Early identification of SpLD is beset with problems (see Chapters 1, 2 and 6).

Provision

The questionnaire next asked 'What range of provision does the LEA make for children with specific learning difficulties?' The most common responses are summarized in Table 13.3. Once again it should be noted that the categories mentioned were not mutually exclusive and each reply might include several categories.

Table 13.3: LEA provision

Provision	Number	Percentage of responding LEAs (N=79)
No specific provision	6	7.6
Dyslexia unit	5	6.3
Special units and/or classes	27	35.5
Direct daily/sessional teaching within schools	18	22.8
Residential/independent/'out of county'	22	27.8
Support via the educational psychology service (EPS)	18	22.8
Advice and support via a central 'support service'	40	50.6
(within support service some referred to specialist teachers for SpLD)	11	13.9
Joint support from EPs and 'support service'	9	11.4
'Statemented provision'	8	10.1
Full range of provision	8	10.1

NB: Categories are not mutually exclusive.

Other provision mentioned included:

- Advice to class teachers;
- A primary school for children with SpLD;
- Reading centre/reading development unit/progress centre/learning resource centres;
- A school for children with moderate learning difficulties;
- Units for children with emotional or behavioural difficulties;
- A school for children with physical disabilities;
- Units for the hearing or visually impaired;
- A 'facility' for secondary aged children;
- Special school/unit provision where the problem is associated with other difficulties;
- Additional home tuition;
- School-based resources, such as IT;
- LEA-determined extra resources, such as IT;
- Extra daily or sessional teaching support;
- Secondary school's own resources;
- 'Coordinators' within every school;
- Child and parent groups;
- Counselling and support groups run by educational psychologists;
- Language units and special schools available to all;
- Support from the special educational needs adviser;
- Additional non-teaching assistants;
- Data-Pac precision teaching programmes.

The variety of responses highlighted a number of important issues. It is clear that the vast majority of children regarded as having SpLD are being provided for within their own mainstream schools and that a policy of 'least disruption' is employed by most LEAs. That is, the most common view appeared to be that children with SpLD have a right to a broad and balanced curriculum alongside the rest of their peers. Additional provision is, in general, only considered if the severity of the difficulties is seen to be beyond the capabilities of the class teacher. The question arises: 'seen by whom?'

A range or continuum of provision, as described earlier, is the usual response by LEAs to match the continuum of the severity of difficulties experienced. Such provision enables the flexible and efficient use of resources. A representative response was:

> The range of provision is from class-teacher based assessment and teaching, to special needs teaching in primary and secondary schools, to additional teaching linked to statements, to specialist provisions in secondary schools, to the use of 'out-county' resources.

Some LEAs might regard such a range of provision as 'available, as appropriate, for all children'. The range of provision is made to cater for the wide variety of learning difficulties found and no particular provision is made specifically for children with SpLD. The survey responses in the categories 'No specific provision', 'Full range of provision' and many of those within 'Support from a central support service' did suggest such an interpretation. It is unclear in such circumstances whether statements are made to protect provision made to particular children.

Statements tend to be made only for the most severe of difficulties but differential responses are made between LEAs and within some large counties. Some LEA responses suggested a clear indication of when Statements are provided. An example of one such response is given in Figure 13.1.

The majority of responses did not suggest such a clearly formulated position but rather emphasized the 'continuum of provision to support integration, quality, range and efficient use of resources'. At what point within the continuum statements are made is questionable. This is also illustrated in Figure 13.1. Firstly, it demonstrates a continuum of provision and, secondly, a hypothetical cut-off point when moving from help provided under Section 2 of the Education Act 1981 to help provided following assessment under Section 5 (Reason, Farrell and Mittler, 1990).

Other issues highlighted by the responses were differential provision across primary and secondary age sectors and the apparent trend towards the establishment of teacher support services or strengthening existing teaching support services. In relation to LEA provision for the different age-groups, the following was a typical description of provision.

At primary level

A peripatetic teaching-cum-advisory service supplemented by tutorial centres for withdrawal.

At secondary level

The policy has been that each school will be resourced adequately to make appropriate arrangements; however, in small schools that do not have the economies of scale, there is a system of special classes.

There appears to be a trend towards providing a centrally coordinated teacher support service for the primary aged children. These support services offer advice, support and some direct teaching of individuals or groups. The support services are provided to meet the wide variety of special educational needs within mainstream schools and are not necessarily geared to SpLD in particular. Some LEAs indicated that within their teacher support service they had teachers with relevant qualifications who were regarded as 'specialists' and their time was dedicated to meeting the needs of children with SpLD. A few responses indicated some concern that *ad hoc* provision was resulting in the additional teaching time or support, appointed either within school or via a support service, being provided by teachers with limited experience in the field of SpLD.

Figure 13.1: Section 2 and Section 5 (Education Act 1981)

Not Statemented (Section 2)	• Mainstream school	
	• Mainstream school	with support from 'in-house' or visiting SEN staff
	• Mainstream school	with access to a special centre
Statemented (Section 5)	• Mainstream school	with allocated teacher, ancillary or equipment plus visiting or in-house specialist
	• Mainstream school	with boarding facilities where SpLD are associated with emotional difficulties
	• Special school	where provision is made for significant emotional difficulties associated with SpLD

Provision of INSET

The question was asked: 'What range of provision does the LEA make for training teachers about specific learning difficulties?' The most frequent responses are shown in Table 13.4.

Other responses made were as follows:

• Course provided at a local college of further education (1 such response);
• Residential courses (1);
• Two-day courses (1);
• Reading centre provides courses upon request (5);
• Individual support by teaching support service (2);

- Use of 'Baker' days (3);
- Secondment (2);
- Courses provided by adviser for SEN (3);
- Advisory pamphlets/information provided by educational psychology service (2).

Table 13.4: Provision of INSET

Provision	Number	Percentage of responding LEAs (N=79)
Little or some specific provision	14	17.7
A range; within the context of programmes for learning difficulties generally	24	30.4
Centrally or school based provided by educational psychology service	24	30.4
Centrally or school based provided by teaching support service or specialist teachers	11	13.9
Joint provision by psychology and teaching support services	7	8.9
Provision of INSET by external group such as Dyslexia Assoc./Inst.	13	16.5
Day-to-day guidance and support from educational psychology service	7	8.9
Accredited courses via universities or polytechnics	12	15.2
RSA diplomas	8	10.1
Sessions provided for head, coordinators, or head of SEN departments	6	7.6

NB: Categories are not mutually exclusive.

From the above information there might appear to be a great diversity of INSET provision within and between LEAs. However, the categories used are not mutually exclusive and may, to a large extent, hide common or prevalent LEA strategies. Thirty per cent of respondents reported that the INSET provision made was not specifically geared to SpLD but for learning difficulties in general. The number of LEAs using such an approach may well be higher as responses within some of the other categories may include a similar strategy. Full-time secondment to courses was rarely mentioned but a significant number made reference to higher level accredited courses provided by universities or polytechnic colleges, or jointly by the LEA and educational institutions. Some of these courses are also likely to be directed to studying learning difficulties in general rather than SpLD in particular. A number of LEAs mentioned the RSA diploma qualification. Only one response referred to using the local college of further education to aid teacher staff development. A relatively large number referred to central and school-based INSET provided by educational psychologists.

Future plans

The final section of the questionnaire requested respondents to: 'Outline any impending changes in your LEA services for children with SpLD.' The most frequent responses are outlined in Table 13.5.

Table 13.5: Future plans

Response	Number	Percentage of responding LEAs (N=79)
No answer	7	8.9
No plans for change	20	25.3
Currently reviewing provision for all SEN	10	12.7
Extension of 'unit' provision	7	8.9
Rationalizing, or additional staffing for teacher support service	8	10.1
Increasing school-based tuition or non-teaching assistance	7	8.9
Stop or reduce placements external to LEA	4	5.1
Developments in INSET	10	12.7
Changes envisaged because of Local Management of Schools	4	5.1

NB: Categories are not mutually exclusive.

Other responses made were as follows:

- More flexible support (3 responses);
- Development of a policy statement (2);
- More consistent assessment procedures (2);
- More coordination/cooperation (2);
- Better records of learning achievement (2);
- Establish specialist educational psychologist post (2);
- Resource schools better (1);
- Increase in provision at local school for SpLD;
- Annual summer course;
- Weekly support group for parents;
- Increase residential provision;
- Search for more preventative approaches;
- Set up standing interest group;
- Improve liaison with British Dyslexia Association;
- Set up 'Local Neighbourhood Management Teams' to coordinate all special needs support;
- Provision of 'guidelines for schools'.

The most frequent response made was that no planned change currently existed in respect of SpLD. However, in many replies this was placed within the context of planning being difficult when virtually *everything is changing*. Such a perspective was evident in comments such as 'planning is a luxury' and 'learning to thrive in chaos'. It was felt to be too early to be sure of the consequences of the Education Reform Act 1988 and inherent issues such as the National Curriculum and Local Management of Schools with their implications for centrally retained funding and LEA organization.

Within the constraints of recent legislation there was, in general, a wish to further the development of an increased range and flexibility of support. This would entail providing a continuum of resources matched to the continuum of need supporting the practice of 'integration', or rather, 'non-segregation'. There was a general trend evident towards 'in-class' support rather than withdrawal. In a few replies some conflict of views was recorded. For example, in one response differences of opinion were noted between the LEA's adviser and its head-teachers and psychologists. The adviser wanted to increase the emphasis on advisory work while the headteachers and psychologists were promoting the retention of some withdrawal sessions. There was some concern that the needs of children with emotional problems associated with SpLD would not be adequately met if withdrawal was not retained. A number of LEAs were hoping to increase provision via extending the teacher support service or increasing 'unit' provision. In both cases there appeared to be a majority wishing to extend provision to the secondary sector. A desire to reduce provision within 'out-of-authority' schools was also evident.

Planned developments in INSET included providing an increase in 'awareness' training for all teachers; adopting RSA qualification diploma courses; local training workshops; the development of a 'home-grown' package with higher education accreditation; and training directed specifically for teacher support team staff.

Discussion

The evidence gathered through this part of the survey supplements that of the previous survey and our existing knowledge of practice. To a large extent the evidence echoes the previous findings but also shows how the policies of LEAs have continued to develop following the implementation of the Education Act 1981.

Terms

It is clear that there is a general acceptance of the terms specific learning difficulties and dyslexia by LEAs. There is, however, a definite preference for using the term SpLD rather than dyslexia. The former term is felt to be more accurately descriptive and more appropriate within an educational context. The term dyslexia is recognized by LEAs and accepted as one which has become popular. In some instances, LEAs have used the terms jointly. In others they appear to have used them synonymously and in yet others dyslexia appears to be seen as but one form of SpLD. Whatever their views on terminology, there was a general agreement that certain children did exist who needed help in only specific academic skills, particularly those associated with literacy. Some documents included an attempt to describe SpLD by means of a symptomology. They tended to provide a hybrid of opinion, a few including outdated views and a minimum of recent research.

Warnock philosophy

While there is some lack of clarity about the use of terminology there appears to be a clear majority favouring the philosophy outlined in the Warnock Report. The vast majority of LEAs believe that SpLD should be seen and responded to as one form of learning difficulty. Just as in the previous report, it was noted that LEAs tended to hold as one of their central tenets that pupils with SpLD should be seen within the general context of learning difficulties. It is argued that the procedures for identification, assessment and provision should be a part of the general resources available to all children with any form of learning difficulty. This response is based upon a belief in the appropriateness of a curriculum entitlement model, including differentiation, rather than a pragmatic response to limited resources. It is argued that all children have a right to a broad, balanced and relevant education and that such a commitment will be possible within the constraints of the National Curriculum.

Policy statements

Similar findings to the earlier survey were also evident concerning the formulation of LEA policies and the development of provision. About 50 per cent of LEAs claim to have a policy in relation to SpLD, about half of these having a written one. It was noted that for many LEAs a policy specifically for SpLD may not have been reported on if there existed a policy for learning difficulties inclusive of SpLD.

Provision

The reports to education committees made it clear that the provision of a graduated range of responses was seen as necessary for learning difficulties in general, including SpLD. The prevailing approach relates this graduated range to the continuum of needs based on the severity of difficulties experienced. This stance complements the school of thought that regards SpLD as part of a continuum of literacy ability, rather than a distinctive disability. The continuum of needs, however, does not relate exclusively to SpLD type difficulties, and may include children experiencing difficulties for a variety of reasons and who possess various levels of compensatory capability.

This 'best fit' model of matching provision to needs may be a result of LEAs having to deal with a crucial dilemma of resourcing. In a situation of limited resources, the LEA needs to reconcile allocation to the intensive needs of a few, with the allocation of resources to the needs of the vast majority of children with SpLD whose numbers are increasing. A continuum of provision may enable an LEA to be more flexible in its use of resources (see Chapters 6 and 7).

Within the reports on provision there was a trend towards seeking to increase the staffing of support services, both teacher and psychological services. There were clear emphases upon strengthening resources to further 'integration', or 'non-segregation', and it was accepted that the vast majority of children with SpLD should be educated within their normal mainstream setting. Within this there appears to be a trend towards 'in-class' support rather than withdrawal. The term 'support' seems to be anything but precise and may include a variety of responses to SpLD.

Only a few documents referred to teaching methods. Paired or shared reading, precision teaching, multi-sensory methods and 'dyslexia unit' methods and materials are variously mentioned in these. The first two techniques were developed independently of dyslexia/SpLD theory. One or two documents showed concern that the appropriateness and benefits of LEA provision were not being fully appreciated.

Statements

The trend for requesting increased resources seems to have followed the implementation of the Education Act 1981 in April 1983. Arguments were put forward that the number of children identified as having SpLD were increasing for a number of reasons, not least of which was the increasing awareness of classroom teachers. Perhaps actual increases in resources and the arguments for this have been strengthened by the provision of statements of special educational needs in those situations where a pupil's needs were not being adequately met. The requirement to provide statements might influence an LEA to ensure that adequate levels of support were generally available. Flexible use of resources would then be possible rather than LEAs having to make specified allocations to particular individuals. It is also evident from the comments received that in many areas resources for the area of special educational needs have increased substantially.

Although 89.9 per cent of replies suggested statements were made in relation to children with SpLD, it was made clear that this happened only in cases where the severity of learning difficulties and needs were greatest. It is not clear what criteria are used to determine whether a statement is provided. The wording of the Act would imply a statement should be provided if 'special education provision' is required, 'special educational provision' being that which is over and above what is 'generally available'. LEAs would perhaps wish to argue that their continuum of provision was 'generally available'. It is a moot point, given the competing priorities on support staff time, whether support is available in any particular case. The interpretation of support being generally available might significantly reduce the necessity of providing statements of special educational needs.

The possible interpretations of the law are many. For example, if individual direct teaching is seen to be required and provided by a support service, is this over and above that which is generally available? Views may differ! Is the support produced over and above that which is generally available within that particular school? Is it over and above that generally available across the LEA? If the latter view is taken then an LEA might actually provide extra resources to enable a specific child to receive support but appoint those resources to their central support service, thereby avoiding the necessity of providing a statement. The child and his or her parents would not then have those extra resources provided under the 'protection' of a statement of special educational needs. It might be asked whether statements are drawn up to protect the child or to protect the allocation of a resource.

It appears that disagreements between LEAs and parents rarely need to be resolved in formal appeals. Successful negotiation appears to be the norm. In relation to continua of provision and needs it is not clear how in any given situation provision is matched to needs if there is any contention between those involved. The 'staged' procedures for assessments following the Education Act 1981 and subsequent circulars are followed by LEAs. In most cases formal assessments under Section 5 of the Education Act 1981, or the provision of the statements under Section 7, are not involved. The earlier stages involve parents, teachers and other professionals in a 'partnership' to ensure that pupils' needs are recognized, assessed and provided for.

If there are disagreements between professionals and parents then a decision to initiate a formal, multidisciplinary assessment under Section 5 of the Act may be taken. Even so, the criteria for resolving issues, related to whether or not a statement is issued, or the level of support that is provided, remain unclear.

The wording of the legislation itself is open to various interpretations. It appears that a number of factors will influence these decisions such as LEAs' policies, the views of parents and of professionals and the levels of support currently provided. It is clear that the majority of LEAs respond to the needs of children with SpLD within the context of their particular range of resources. It is also clear that the range of provision of LEAs differs widely. It is likely, therefore, that responses to SpLD or the provision made will differ. In such circumstances, parents need to be empowered to have informed participation in the procedures. That is, LEAs need to communicate as much as is possible with parents concerning their policies and practices. If not, parents may look at the provision of neighbouring authorities and believe that the 'grass is greener'.

There would also appear to be a difference in most LEAs as to the provision made within the primary as opposed to the secondary sector. Within the primary sector there is a trend towards establishing or increasing existing teacher support services that provide advice and support, including some direct individual or small group teaching. In the secondary sector the schools are, in general, expected to meet the needs of pupils with SpLD from within their own resources. Case law will continue to exert a powerful influence on the development of LEA policies on SpLD (Chasty and Friel, 1991).

Whole-school policies

The Education Act 1980 ensures that schools must inform parents of their arrangements to meet the needs of pupils with special educational needs. LEAs are encouraging schools to adopt 'whole-school' policies that enable a differentiated curriculum response (see Chapter 8). It is suggested that such policies also require schools to ensure they have efficient and effective methods of identification, teaching and assessment strategies, use of support services and inservice provision. The Education Act 1986 required LEAs to provide 'curriculum statements' for their schools to develop. The comments received suggest LEAs offer to act to support a 'whole-school' approach by providing guidelines, inservice training, educational psychology and teaching support services. Both schools and LEAs, therefore, are required to make clear their policies and practices. It may be beneficial for LEAs and schools to consider and review just how successful they are in communicating their policies and practices to parents and the community.

Future plans

The majority of LEAs appeared to have no immediate plans for changes in their provision for children with SpLD. Of those that did, their plans were directed towards increasing and making more comprehensive the general continua of provision including support services and unit provision. Authorities were, it appeared, attempting to ensure some degree of flexible use of resources. A number of LEAs reported intentions to reduce the number of 'out-of-community' placements and transfer the resources so as to promote 'integration'. Developments in in-service education were seen as a priority in a number of LEAs. Both short courses and longer accredited courses were seen to be required. Sadly the current GEST funding arrangements are of little help to LEAs in INSET provision concerned with SpLD.

LEAs ought to consider how they might raise concerns within the community about the provision they make. Officers of an authority may feel they are making substantial provision for children with SpLD within the context of the resources available to all children with learning difficulties. In some cases parents have felt that LEA officers and professionals were conspiring to prevent their child receiving extra help. Perhaps such suspicions might not arise if parents are fully informed of the LEA's policies and concerns to provide a balanced curriculum, as well as the graduated range of provision.

Education Reform Act 1988

Relatively few mentions were made of the possible effects of the Education Reform Act 1988. No concern was expressed about the implications of the National Curriculum and related assessments in relation to children with SpLD and no mentions were made of the possible usage of 'modifications' or 'disapplications'. It is felt that there must be a consideration of process as well as content in terms of the delivery of the National Curriculum in relation to children with SpLD. Such children have an equal right to a broad curriculum and should not be faced with unnecessary barriers. Local Management of Schools was the subject of some concern. It was felt that this might adversely affect the provision made for those pupils who were not the subject of a statement. Further, it was suggested that the support offered to all children would be seriously affected if support services were not maintained as central services under LEA schemes of delegation. Indeed a number of LEAs wished to increase both their psychological and teacher support services but their future may be affected by these issues relating to locus of financial control and pressures on the allocation of limited 'discretionary' budgets.

Summary

- The questionnaire on LEA policy and practice was completed by 79 out of 106 LEAs (including the Isle of Man and the Isles of Scilly), giving a response rate of 74.5 per cent.
- A policy for pupils with SpLD had been formulated by 42 authorities (53.2 per cent) and of these 23 (54.8 per cent) had documents specifying their policy. Some authorities felt that their policies in respect of learning difficulties in general included SpLD and that a specific policy for SpLD would be inappropriate.

- As in the previous inquiry, most authorities felt that the identification, assessment procedures and provision for children with SpLD should be seen within the context of the resources available for learning difficulties in general.
- Most LEAs attempt to provide a continuum of provision to match a continuum based on the severity of needs. The vast majority of children will have their needs met within their normal mainstream class. Depending on the severity of needs, the following may be provided: advice; teaching support within-class; withdrawal for teaching support; provision within a unit, special school, or 'out-of-community' residential placement.
- The documents received suggested that LEAs encourage schools to consider aspects of their in-service requirements: curriculum; teaching strategies; identification, observation and assessment strategies; record keeping; communication and use of support services. In essence, they encourage 'whole-school' approaches.
- The documents suggest that, for their part, LEAs will provide psychological and teaching support services: in-service training geared towards awareness raising and whole-school approaches; formal assessment procedures and 'guidelines'.
- It is clear that the provision made for children with SpLD has been substantially increased since the implementation of the Education Act 1981.
- Although most LEAs do provide statements of special educational needs for children with SpLD, they do so only for the most severe cases. The criteria as to when a statement is provided are not clear. Only in a very few instances does there appear to be a need to resort to Local Appeals or court cases. However, information from the DES may indicate a marked increase in appeals to the Secretary of State.
- A range of in-service training was reported to be provided. This range is within the context of programmes of learning difficulties generally. In-service training provided by educational psychology services is reported by a similar number of LEAs. In a number of cases accredited courses provided by higher education institutions are employed. In the majority of cases, however, LEA internal resources are used.
- Within the current context of change in the education service it is not surprising that the most frequent response in relation to future plans was that there were none imminent. Of those LEAs who did report development plans there are a number intending to rationalize or increase the staffing levels of support services. Others hoped to increase unit provision or to develop their in-service provision.

Recommendations

13.1. LEAs have an explicit policy on pupils with specific learning difficulties to be either particular to these difficulties or set in the context of a policy for learning difficulties in general.

13.2. The inclusion of specific learning difficulties within such a policy be clearly communicated to parents and other interested parties by LEAs.

13.3. LEAs review and monitor all aspects of their service delivery to children with specific learning difficulties.

13.4. Within the current context of reviewing LEA organization and provision, ensure that resources for children with specific learning difficulties are firmly embedded within their range of services.

13.5. LEAs develop and evaluate their continua of resources to ensure that, for each type or degree of difficulty experienced, there is adequate resourcing to meet the requirements for identification, assessment and provision.

13.6. In the context of the 1988 Education Reform Act, LEAs ensure that school governors are in an informed position to fulfil their responsibilities in relation to specific learning difficulties.

13.7. LEAs assist schools in meeting the legal requirement that each school develops a policy on special educational needs in general and specific learning difficulties in particular.

13.8. LEAs ensure that a range of in-service training opportunities exists whereby teachers and educational psychologists are enabled to identify, assess and alleviate special educational needs stemming from specific learning difficulties.

Chapter 14

Educational Psychologists' Views and Practices

Introduction

I am not a member of the dyslexia lobby ... but I think they are right in stressing the blighting effect of SpLD on children and adults. I find these conditions very common in a mild form and they explain a lot of difficulties at school and at home.

SpLD is a way of describing a normal pattern of skill or ability variation between and within individuals. We regard such a variation as a difficulty because it impinges on skills of a high social value.

For most parents dyslexia equals difficulty in reading, writing and/or spelling, and no one can be blamed for it.

The idea of dyslexia and the actual word has been politically useful in getting help for children.

Dyslexia sounds like an incurable disease.

Dyslexia has become a commercial product and journalistic victim. Professionalism has been corrupted by the subject, with little objectivity remaining.

The assumption appears to be that children with learning deficits in specific areas should be identified as having needs which are different from children with learning difficulties in many areas.

These selected comments illustrate the flavour and range of views expressed in the 882 questionnaires returned by educational psychologists in the winter and spring of 1989.

The working group deliberately decided to keep the questionnaire very brief. The format was limited to two sides of A4 paper and consisted of a combination of yes/no and open ended questions. A total of 1780 questionnaires were sent to the overlapping membership of the DECP and the AEP in England, Wales and Northern Ireland.

Although the Education Reform Act 1988 had been passed, few supporting documents or circulars were available at the time. The nature of the National Curriculum and its assessment, and the implications of Local Management of Schools were uncertain to respondents.

Processing the results

Responses to the objective (closed) questions were coded for all 882 question-naires received. In addition, a 20 per cent sample (N=170) was made by taking every fifth form in order of receipt. The comments on these forms were coded under the following four section headings:

Overall view
Identification
Provision
Professional development

Ideally, of course, comments should have been coded for all 882 responses. This proved impossible because members of the working group could not devote that amount of time to the analysis of results.

Prior examination of all questionnaires had identified the kinds of issues raised by respondents, which could be grouped into manageable categories. The comments of the 20 per cent sample were then coded as to whether or not an item had been mentioned. This was felt to be less subject to bias than attempting to collate the comments in note form. In some instances, however, the coding adopted may have hidden disagreements or blurred distinctions.

Results

Representation of the sample

Tables 14.1 and 14.2 show that the majority of respondents were maingrade edu-cational psychologists employed by county councils. The response rate of princi-pal educational psychologists was probably depressed because they also completed a second separately mailed questionnaire concerned with LEA policy (see Chapter 13).

Overall view

Three questions were asked under this heading: firstly, whether respondents found the term 'specific learning difficulties' useful in their professional work; secondly, whether they found the term 'dyslexia' useful in their professional work; and, thirdly, whether they considered the two terms synonymous. Table 14.3 shows that 87.4 per cent of respondents considered the term specific learn-ing difficulties useful. Those objecting to the term did so because they avoided the use of any categorical descriptions.

Nearly all those finding the term dyslexia useful (30.5 per cent) felt the same about specific learning difficulties, and a minority considered the two terms synonymous (22 per cent). Many reported that they did not themselves refer to dyslexia but accepted its use by others, parents in particular. A few reserved dys-lexia for the most severe cases where there appeared to be evidence of neuro-logical impairment. Others, however, rejected the term because it implied a neurological cause. Answers between different grades of LEA psychologist did

Table 14.1: Post of respondents

Status	Number returned	Percentage of return	N in post	Percentage replying
PEP	50	5.7	99	50.5
SEP	178	19.6	321	55.5
EP	522	59.2	1029	50.1
Clin P	12	1.4	*	*
Lecturer/ researcher	31	3.5	*	*
Retired	35	4.0	*	*
Other	44	5.0	*	*
Missing	15	4.7	*	*
Total	882	100		

* These replies are not from defined populations.

Table 14.2: Employer of respondents

Employer	Number returned	Percentage of return	N in post	Percentage replying
County council	435	49.3	770	56.5
Met. B. council	119	19.2	381	31.2
Inner and outer London	90	10.2	230	39.1
Welsh county	31	3.5	76	40.7
N. Ireland	17	1.9	44	38.6
Other public	38	4.3	*	*
Voluntary	7	0.8	*	*
Private practice	28	3.2	*	*
Other/retired/ missing	67	7.6	*	*
Total	882	100		

* These replies are not from defined populations.

not differ. Bearing in mind the small numbers involved, Table 14.4 shows that psychologists in private practice were more likely to find dyslexia useful than were LEA educational psychologists.

Additional comments for the 20 per cent sample (N=170) have been classified in Table 14.5. Reservations about using either term centred on the difficulties of

Table 14.3: Overall view

Question	Yes		No		Not applicable/ no response	
	N	%	N	%	N	%
SpLD useful?	771	87.4	79	9.0	31	3.6
Dyslexia useful?	269	30.5	580	65.8	32	3.7
Terms synonymous?	194	22.0	640	72.6	48	5.5

Table 14.4: Term found useful

	Do you find dyslexia useful?				Do you find SpLD useful?			
	LEA EP		Private		LEA EP		Private	
Yes	223	(31%)	18	(69%)	661	(90%)	26	(100%)
No	508	(69%)	8	(31%)	72	(10%)	0	

Table 14.5: Comments volunteered for questions 1, 2 and 3 ($N = 170$)

Comment	N	%
SpLD wider than dyslexia	42	25
Dyslexia used by parents	30	18
Dyslexia emotive	20	12
Dyslexia not a single condition	20	12
Dyslexia appears neurological	16	9

NB: Some respondents made more than one comment, others none.

having an agreed definition and doubts as to the rightness of singling out one particular form of learning difficulty for possibly preferential treatment within an overall group of children with special educational needs.

An unwillingness to refer to dyslexia was often because the term appeared to explain the difficulties in a medical way, which was unhelpful in an educational context: *'I see dyslexia as a negative label which can be used to imply that school-based intervention will not succeed because the fault lies within the child.'*

There was much awareness of the importance of terminology for parents and children and the dangers of misunderstanding: *'Dyslexia appears to mean a syndrome or medical cause which can have good or bad consequences, e.g. sympathy for the sufferer versus the belief that little can be done to help.'*

The difficulties and distress that some children and their parents were experiencing were also recognized: '*I am very concerned for parents who are misunderstood by staff and labelled over-anxious or criticized for jumping the dyslexia bandwagon. We need to improve our response to parents who are justifiably concerned...*'

Comments suggest that there was often little real difference between psychologists who answered the formal questions differently: '*I have answered "no" since I do not use the term SpLD to categorize children. I do, however, refer to any SpLD the child may have.*'

There was also awareness of the effect of the label 'dyslexia' in the competition for limited educational resources: '*The continuum of special educational needs described in the Warnock Report is being seriously undermined by the "dyslexia campaign". I dislike the term if it is used to denote an elite subgroup of children who have reading problems.*'

Identification

Respondents were asked 'What do you look for in identifying an individual pupil with SpLD?' As the space on the questionnaire did not permit lengthy answers, comments were inevitably very general. Table 14.6 groups the comments under headings defined by those members of the working group who analysed the responses of the 20 per cent sample (170 psychologists). It should be noted that 22 responses could not be categorized, usually because the respondents had stated in the previous question that the term specific learning difficulties was not useful in their professional work.

As discussed earlier, the grouping of comments might have blurred finer distinctions. Furthermore, results could only reflect that which had been mentioned. For example, respondents might have taken standardized tests of literacy for granted and not mentioned them. Consequently, Table 14.6 has probably underrepresented that category. Similarly, psychologists would consider emotional and social factors in all cases they see and not single out that aspect only for specific learning difficulties. The table can therefore only be considered indicative of the range of responses.

The headings in Table 14.6 are not mutually exclusive; comments by one respondent could result in entries under several of the headings. Commonly, educational psychologists considered a wide range of information including reports from parents and teachers, learning history, classroom observation, the effect of intervention as well as information from standardized tests. Reference was also made to parental needs and expectations: '*Some parents have expectations of the form of the assessment. It is better to move with the current and add your own assessments.*'

Of interest is the frequency of the notion of some kind of discrepancy in attainments (mentioned by 80 per cent), which did not necessarily relate to assessments of ability: '*I am looking for performance discrepancies rather than hypothetical abilities*'; '*I look for strengths and skill deficits and try to help*'.

Psychologists differed considerably in the content of their assessments. Some firmly supported normative approaches. '*I feel very strongly that an individual test of intelligence should be used, e.g. WISC-R, BAS. It is not possible to identify all pupils with SpLD on the basis of attainments only.*' '*Discrepancy between verbal IQ and reading and spelling ages; reversals of letters, words, etc.; high*

Table 14.6: Grouped comments for 'What do you look for in identifying an individ-ual pupil with SpLD?' (N = 148 as 22 of 170 sample had no comments or could not be coded)

	N	%
Some kind of discrepancy	119	80
Results of curriculum-based assessment and qualitative error analysis	83	56
Learning history (observations over time)	48	32
Cognitive, e.g. memory, sequencing	46	31
Results of normative tests of attainment	32	22
'Soft signs', e.g. laterality, clumsiness	17	11
Emotional and social, e.g. frustration	16	11

NB: The response groupings are not mutually exclusive.

level of frustration with reading and writing despite good general comprehen-sion.'

Others gave lists of characteristics without specifying the method of assess-ment. 'Short term memory deficits, sequencing problems, coding problems, "soft" signs, word retrieval problems during conversation, unusual transfor-mations/reversals, familial history, evidence of higher learning rates for non-symbolic material.'

Many psychologists (56 per cent in Table 14.6) were committed to cur-riculum-based assessment combined with qualitative error analysis. 'Unusual strategies in reading, writing and spelling.' 'Marked difficulties with print recog-nition and reproduction combined with interest in content and good use of con-textual cues. All this within an educational ethos which encourages both enthusiasm in literacy and provides systematic teaching as necessary.'

Respondents were also asked 'Do you normally assess discrepancies between abilities and attainments?' 687 (78 per cent) reported that they did so in some form and 131 (15 per cent) that they did not. The remainder omitted this ques-tion. Comments from the 20 per cent sample illustrate the range of interpre-tations given by those who answered 'yes':

This information is a by-product of skills analysis, not the reason for making the assessment. I am looking at existing skills and learning style.

Yes, if it will help parents or school, or application for resources. No, if we can design a teaching programme which works. At first involvement I aim at the teaching plan approach.

Normally but not essentially.

Only as part of the assessment – the response to teaching is more infor-mative.

The issue of the validity of 'discrepancy' is open to further research. The curriculum and teaching methods used must also be considered.

This is by no means the main focus of assessment for SpLD … It is not only bright children who can have SpLD.

Yes, but the quality of mistakes in reading and writing is more diagnostic.

Where sufficient information was given in the questionnaires completed by the 20 per cent sample, comments were analysed in terms of commitment to formal tests of ability. Results are given in Table 14.7 and include responses from those who reported that they did not assess discrepancies. Table 14.7 shows the range of opinion and the frequency of the qualified or defensive responses illustrated in the quotes given above.

Table 14.7: The range of opinions about tests of ability (*N* = 132)

	N	*%*
Important/always	41	31
Qualified support	33	25
Reluctant/defensive use	27	20
Not used	31	23

NB: These categories *are* mutually exclusive.

Formal assessment under the 1981 Education Act

Statutory Assessments of Special Educational Needs under the 1981 Education Act require educational, psychological and medical advice as well as administrative involvement. LEA policies and procedures in making such assessments and providing statements of special educational needs vary (cf. Chapter 13).

When there is additional teaching support or equipment within the pupils' own schools, a statement of special educational needs is not mandatory. It may be felt, however, that a statement 'protects' the provision or 'controls' the additional resources. Formal assessment is not necessarily required for part-time or short-term attendance at a reading centre or similar provision as long as the requirements of the National Curriculum are also met. As practices between authorities vary, it is important to exercise caution in interpreting the responses of the individual psychologists who responded to the questionnaire.

Table 14.8 shows that the majority of respondents (68 per cent) were writing formal assessment advice about children with specific learning difficulties. Some educational psychologists who had not contributed to statutory assessments explained that this was because they held specialist posts, such as pre-school work, rather than from any point of principle. Similarly, principal educational psychologists undertook fewer assessments because of the administrative nature

Table 14.8: Advice on formal assessments for SpLD

Advice given	N	%
Yes	600	68
No	205	23.3
No information or not applic.	77	8.7
Total	882	100

Table 14.9: Number of children formally assessed for SpLD in the last year (1988) (where applicable)

No. of assessments	No. of psychs	Percentage of psychs
0*	224	28.2
1– 4	260	32.7
5– 9	126	15.9
10–14	109	13.7
15–19	20	2.5
20–24	21	2.6
25–29	7	0.9
30–49	16	2.0
50+	12	1.5
	795	100.0

* While we identified psychologists who specifically wrote that this question was not applicable to them, it is possible that a number of non-applicables have been included as nil returns.

of their work. It should also be noted that the DECP includes members who are not practising educational psychologists involved in formal assessments.

Table 14.9 shows that the number of formal assessments completed during the previous year ranged from 0 to more than 50! It should be noted, however, that the question may have been taken by some to include all formal assessments and not only those relating to SpLD. In view of the apparent general increase in the number of formal assessments undertaken in local authorities, this aspect certainly needs further investigation.

Provision

Replies suggest that educational psychologists are tailoring interventions to the needs of the individual rather than favouring particular styles/methods of tuition.

Whilst Table 14.10 gives the highest percentages of mention to 'bottom-up' structured approaches (cf. Chapter 3), comments by respondents emphasize a combination of approaches. Interventions are said to take account of learning history, present difficulties and curricular needs. There is awareness of the variety of options available in both remedial programmes and curricular support. *'Plenty of paired/shared reading together with learning to read through writing, i.e. dictation of own stories which are then read and re-read leading to the writing of own stories in conjunction with systematic practice of phonics and sight words only in this context, not as isolated drill.'* 'It is difficult to answer as the interventions are usually custom built and make use of micros...'

Table 14.10: Curriculum provision suggested (*N* =170)

Method	N	%
Data-Pac, precision teaching, graded, structured	67	39
Multisensory, Alpha to Omega. Gillingham. Fernald	43	25
Paired, shared, relaxed reading	40	24
Spelling programme	30	18
Counselling	24	14
Phonics	19	11
Computing, word processing, typing	19	11
Access to the curriculum	19	11
Language experience	10	6
Tape recorder	10	6
Process training, e.g. Frostig	6	4
Other	29	17

NB: Categories are not mutually exclusive.

In addition to the kinds of teaching methods listed in Table 14.10, access to the curriculum is emphasized by those who mention it. This relates particularly, but not only, to secondary schools. *'Using word processors, spelling checkers, tape recorders and support within the class...'* *'Teaching study skills to ensure efficient use of time...'* *'Alternative means of recording.'* *'Encouraging staff to supply written notes and accept oral contributions.'*

Spelling difficulties are addressed through a variety of multisensory and precision teaching approaches often in association with paired, shared or 'relaxed' reading. The importance of motivation is stressed with the mention of reducing anxiety and developing confidence. There was no relationship between the use or non-use of the term 'dyslexia' and the curriculum interventions recommended.

Some psychologists also described the staffing available for the additional help referring, for example, to specialist reading or SpLD support services (cf. Chapter 8 for a discussion of these services). Those who mentioned such services made fewer curricular suggestions than those who were apparently the main or only source of external advice to the school. Table 14.11 provides a summary of the person resources mentioned by the 20 per cent sample of respondents.

Table 14.11: Person resources mentioned ($N = 170$)

Resource	N	%*
Class teacher	18	11
School remedial teacher	12	7
Parent	17	10
Peer	4	2
Reading support service	32	19
SpLD support service	25	15
Unit or part time off site	21	12
Special school	6	4

* Rounded up.

NB: Categories are not mutually exclusive.

The concern for the needs of a wider group of children was expressed by a recently retired educational psychologist: *'One predominant thought during my working years has been that there are thousands of children at all IQ levels who have particular learning difficulties. They all need help. It is inequitable to single out for special help those who are fortunate enough to be allocated a label such as dyslexia.'* These opinions reflect the discussion in Chapter 2.

In-service training

Educational psychologists often contribute to in-service education for teachers (INSET) both on an authority-wide basis and within the particular schools they serve. The questionnaire only asked about their contributions relating to SpLD in 1988. Of the respondents, 305 (34 per cent) had contributed, with the percentage of principal psychologists higher than that of main grade psychologists. Comments made showed that psychologists answering 'no' with regard to the value of the term SpLD had sometimes contributed to courses concerned with more general aspects of reading or learning difficulties.

Parent groups

Some regions have very active parent groups concerned with dyslexia or specific learning difficulties. Respondents were asked about their contact with such groups as distinct from consultation with individual parents about their children or contact with parent groups concerned with special educational needs in general. Some 165 psychologists (19 per cent) reported such involvement in 1988 with a bias towards principal and senior psychologists.

Professional development requests

Educational psychologists were asked about their own professional development needs with regard to specific learning difficulties. Table 14.12 tabulates the results for the 20 per cent sample of respondents.

Table 14.12: Professional development needs mentioned (*N* = 170)

Interventions	N	%
Ways of helping	46	27
Remediation	15	9
Evaluation of interventions	14	8
Use of computers	6	4
Whole-school policy	5	3
Theoretical issues		
Clarification of terms	14	8
Psych. and neurol. research	27	16
Evaluation of assessment methods	15	9
Early identification	9	5
Policy and practice		
Resource allocation	12	7
LMS	3	2
National curriculum	4	2
Cooperation with advisers	6	4
Interdisciplinary cooperation	9	5
Exam allowances	4	2

NB: Categories are not mutually exclusive.

It can be seen that aspects to do with intervention were mentioned most frequently. Some requests were directed towards remedial programmes in the traditional sense, others towards whole-school approaches and access to the curriculum. There was a wish to keep up with current research including a hope that the present publication will help to make the task more manageable.

Policy issues were felt to be important both in relation to the 1981 Education Act and the implications arising from the Education Reform Act 1988. Emphasis was placed on policies which would enable equitable distribution of resources. The importance of inter-disciplinary cooperation in case work, service planning and the sharing of information about theory and intervention were highlighted by a number of respondents.

Discussion

As the present questionnaire differed significantly in content and format from that distributed in 1983, few direct comparisons can be made. Whilst the previous survey focused on the range of possible terminology, the present opted for a simple comparison between specific learning difficulties and dyslexia. In inquiring about methods of identification, the previous survey listed tests of abilities and achievements. The present survey asked respondents to describe what they looked for in the identification process and to mention methods recommended for the purposes of intervention.

Both surveys have in common the recognition of the existence of pupils with unexpected and baffling difficulties in acquiring basic literacy (and sometimes numeracy). Both surveys can be compared with the detailed work undertaken by the Grampian Region psychological services in 1985–86 described in Chapter 6.

Previous chapters have considered at length the theoretical aspects and practical implications of psychological and psychoeducational approaches to specific learning difficulties. These issues will therefore not be reconsidered here. Key themes emerging from the survey will be described in the final section of the book.

Summary

A questionnaire was completed by 882 psychologists belonging to the DECP and/or the AEP. Responses to objective (closed) questions were coded for all and comments analysed for a 20 per cent sample. It would, of course, have been desirable to analyse comments for the whole sample but the time available to the volunteer working group did not permit that. The following are the main results of the survey.

- *Terminology.* 'Specific learning difficulties' was considered useful by almost all the respondents (87 per cent). Whilst 'dyslexia' was regarded as useful by 30 per cent, comments showed that this meant for many an acceptance of other people using 'dyslexia'.
- *The continuum of special educational needs.* Although no particular question addressed this issue, comments favoured a view of specific learning difficulties within the overall context of learning difficulties and special educational needs, linked with the 'Warnock philosophy' of identifying those needs.
- *Identification.* A range of factors was considered including educational history, present attainments, response to intervention, general competence and results of standardized tests.
- *Provision.* The vast majority was made within the pupils' own schools through visiting support services when available. When specialist literacy services were involved, the psychologists were less likely to make detailed teaching suggestions. The approaches recommended included the direct teaching of literacy skills through published cumulative programmes, paired or shared reading, individual programmes for phonics or spelling, approaches based on language experience and counselling. Arrangements for access to the curriculum through teacher support, additional preparation of materials or the use of technology was also part of the provision mentioned.

- *Formal assessment (1981 Education Act).* Sixty-eight per cent of the psychologists had provided advice for children with specific learning difficulties during the year prior to the inquiry; that is, during 1988.
- *Identification and terminology.* Whether or not psychologists 'found the term dyslexia useful' did not make a difference to the attributes considered in identifying specific learning difficulties, the likelihood of writing formal advice or the type of provision recommended.
- *Equal opportunities.* Psychologists were concerned that provision should be made in ways that reflected pupil needs rather than response to pressure.
- *Implications of new legislation.* Concern was expressed about the effects of the Education Reform Act 1988 but in early 1989 sufficient information was not available for more explicit comments. Subsequent correspondence with the DES concerning appeals to the Secretary of State suggests that these are increasing and that this trend is likely to continue.
- *Access to psychologist.* The British Psychological Society maintains a Register of Chartered Psychologists (British Psychological Society, 1990). This register is available in major libraries. A number of those psychologists listed are involved in the identification and alleviation of SpLD. Educational and child psychologists are usually employed by local authorities.

Recommendations

14.1. The term 'specific learning difficulties', rather than 'dyslexia', be used in reports.

14.2. Close collaboration between educational psychologists, teachers, professionals and voluntary bodies be extended in identifying and alleviating specific learning difficulties, building on existing best practice.

14.3. Educational psychologists clarify the theoretical and operational definitions of specific learning difficulties.

14.4. Educational psychologists evaluate the efficacy of the interventions they recommend and disseminate findings.

14.5. Educational psychologists extend their involvement in INSET related to specific learning difficulties.

14.6. Work in this controversial and multidisciplinary area be considered an essential aspect of initial and continuing professional development for educational psychologists.

Chapter 15

Views of Other Organizations and Individuals

Introduction

In order to canvas the opinion of other bodies in addition to LEAs, the working party invited submissions from respondents to the previous DECP survey in 1983, other organizations, the public and organizations abroad. A letter to the national press explained that the purpose of the new inquiry was to provide a disinterested and objective account of current educational policies and practices, and to make recommendations. It asked for comments on five points:

- The concept of specific learning difficulties (dyslexia)
- Identification and assessment
- Prevention
- Teaching methods
- Provision of resources

Table 15.1 lists the respondents who replied at length in 1983 and/or 1990. This chapter is largely based on the 1990 submissions. Where representations were made, edited extracts are presented under the above headings. References have been deleted. Individuals wishing to read the full submissions should contact the particular organizations. Several brief submissions were also received. These are summarized in Table 15.2.

The concept of specific learning difficulties (dyslexia)

Discussion of the concept of specific learning difficulties centred around terminology and definition. Table 15.3 summarizes preferred terms and definitions.

Comments: preferred term

The term 'specific learning difficulties' was acceptable to all except the British Dyslexia Association, the Dyslexia Unit Bangor and the National Association for Remedial Education. BDA and DUB preferred the term 'dyslexia' while NARE preferred to consider special educational needs without any exclusive term. The Department of Education and Science also avoided 'labelling', concentrating instead on 'identifying each child's individual needs and ensuring that those needs are being met'. Interestingly, the BDA incorporates the phrase 'National Organisation for Specific Learning Difficulties' in its heading in the publication *Dys-*

Table 15.1: Views submitted: full submissions

	Respondents	1983	1990
Statutory bodies	Department of Education and Science	✓	✓
Voluntary bodies	British Dyslexia Association	✓	✓
	Dyslexia Institute	✓	✓
University	Dyslexia Unit, Bangor	✓	✓
Professional bodies	Assistant Masters and Mistresses Association		✓
	National Association of Remedial Education		✓
	National Association of Schoolmasters and Union of Women Teachers		✓
	United Kingdom Reading Association	✓	✓
Letters	Adults with specific learning difficulties		3
	Medical personnel		2
	Dyslexia associations		7
	Education otherwise		3
	Parents		22
	Solicitor		1
	Teachers		40
	Dyslexic pupils		1

lexia Contact. All submissions seemed to state in some form that there is an information processing difficulty resulting in below expected levels of attainment in literacy skills in particular.

Identification and assessment

Factors mentioned as relevant to identification and assessment are summarized in Table 15.4.

Comments from organizations

There was much consensus on identification and assessment procedures. The main differences centred on the use and interpretation of standardized tests of ability. The British Dyslexia Association, the Dyslexia Institute and the Dyslexia

Table 15.2: Views submitted: brief submissions

Body	Summary
National Bureau for Students with Disabilities	• No specialist knowledge on specific learning difficulties • Aware of widely differing views of specific learning difficulties • Extra resources required
Professional Association of Teachers of Students with Specific Learning Difficulties	• Sent members' contributions • Details of their contributions • List of centres for RSA Diploma Course • Brochure detailing Diploma Course
Royal Society of Arts	• Provides Diploma Course leading to RSA Diploma for teachers of pupils with specific learning difficulties • The charity 'Defining Dyslexia' funds new courses approved by RSA
Secondary Heads Association	• Policies to assist pupils with specific learning difficulties vary greatly • Each LEA has own strategies and policies

Ten submissions from abroad were received. They have not been included here.

Unit Bangor all looked at patterns of abilities and difficulties. The United Kingdom Reading Association regarded general ability as only one of a wide range of criteria.

There was agreement on as wide-ranging an assessment as possible, taking account of information from teachers and parents and the child's responses to teaching programmes. In accordance with the wider notion of specific learning difficulties as part of a continuum of special educational needs, a concept supported by most, a broad range of assessment was seen to enable each child to be given an individual programme of objectives targeted to his or her specific needs across the curriculum.

Extracts relating to identification and assessment are presented below.

Department of Education and Science

Under the 1981 Education Act, local education authorities have a responsibility to secure the provision of education for children with specific learning difficulties, just as they have to make provision for the needs of all other children with special educational needs in their area. It is the responsibility of each LEA to decide on the kind of provision to be made in individual cases, but the majority of authorities have taken account of the advice offered by the committees referred to above and to offer remedial help in schools. Where this provision is made by support on an in-school or a peripatetic basis, any disruption to

Table 15.3: Preferred terms and definitions

Body	Preferred term	Reasons for preferred term	Definition
DES	SpLD and SEN	'…aim to focus on the child himself, rather than on the disability since progress depends not only on the nature and severity of his difficulty but on his personal resources and attributes…'	'…children of at least average ability who experience such difficulties in one or more of reading, writing, spelling and mathematics and … require special arrangements…'
UKRA	SpLD	SpLD is a term which is useful for educational purposes. …The term dyslexia is at the one time more helpful in its reference quite specifically to 'difficulty with lexis' (i.e. words or language symbols) and less helpful educationally as it is restrictive in the sense of not including related difficulties of dysgraphia and dyscalculia.	… difficulties which relate to reading, writing and spelling … difficulties in learning which affect coordination of gross as well as fine motor movement patterns and of speech as well as language difficulties to the extent that the difficulties derive from learning problems (difficulty or difference).
BDA	Dyslexia	'Specific learning difficulties is only an improvement on "dyslexia" if it is assumed that the use of the word "dyslexia" implies, more than does the phrase "specific learning difficulties", a definite aetiology and a circumscribed form of remedial treatment and that it applies only to children of average and above average intelligence. As none of these implications are true, the case for using the term "specific learning difficulties" falls.' 'We need a word which has meaning outside the education service.' [See note below – Eds]	'A specific difficulty in learning, constitutional in origin, in one or more of reading, spelling and written language, which may be accompanied by difficulty in number work. It is particularly related to mastering and using a written language (alphabetic, numerical and musical notation) although often affecting oral language to some degree.' '… phonological coding difficulties.'
DI	SpLD	But a label should be chosen which: best describes the child; motivates…to improve his learning and literacy skills; guides and inspires the practitioner in the most effective way, and be prepared to change the label.	…organizing or learning deficiencies which restrict the student's competencies in information processing in motor skills and working memory, so causing limitations in some or all of the skills of speech, reading, spelling, writing, essay writing, numeracy and behaviour.

Table 15.3: cont.

Body	Preferred term	Reasons for preferred term	Definition
DUB	Dyslexia	It is certainly on record that 'the government recognise dyslexia' (*Hansard*, 13 July 1987).	...a *distinctive* group who consistently show the same problems and have the same needs.
NARE	SEN	...more effective not to use terms such as 'dyslexia' or any of its variations which have lost the objectivity and usefulness they may once have possessed....[It prefers] pragmatically to consider a number of headings under which the educational needs of a child can be examined and so lead to the positive planning of teaching objectives towards solving the problem.	Learning difficulties cannot be neatly split into general difficulties and specific learning difficulties as separate needs. They must be viewed by the LEA and the schools as part of a continuum of special educational provision where the differences may be expressed in the expectancy of results, the rate of learning and the methods of working.
AMMA	SpLD	As an Association representing teachers, we feel it is preferable to use the term 'specific learning difficulties' which is likely to be acceptable to all our members, rather than 'dyslexia' which tends to arouse strong reactions, and for which there is no generally agreed definition. ...as there is disagreement about the definition of dyslexia, its aetiology and which pupils fall within its parameters...more productive to keep the broader and less controversial term.	...those pupils who experience difficulty in certain areas of learning and who will display an uneven profile of scores if given a full psychological assessment. Within this larger group, there are some pupils whose difficulties with sequencing, short-term memory, and visual and/or auditory discrimination, give rise to problems in mastering the written side of language (reading and writing).
NAS/ UWT	SpLD	...attempts to use 'dyslexia' as a general description rather than the more precise term 'specific learning difficulties' in respect of reading, writing, spelling or mathematics, has made it harder to address the problems which are associated with a clearly defined learning disability.	[BMA, 1980 definition:] ...a learning disability which initially shows itself by difficulty in learning to read, and later by erratic spelling and by difficulty in writing as opposed to words. It tends to lessen as the child grows older, and is capable of considerable improvement especially when appropriate help is offered at the earliest opportunity. It is not due to intellectual inadequacy, nor is it associated with emotional or anatomical defects.

Table 15.4: Identification and assessment factors

Body	LEA responsibility	Early identification	Family history	Self-image	Coordination	Language	Ability	Reading	Spelling	Hand writing	Written work	Perceptual	Memory	Sequencing	Association	Number	Educational history	Laterality
DES	✓	✓		✓	✓	✓	✓	✓	✓	✓	✓	✓	✓	✓	✓		✓	
UKRA					✓	✓	✓	✓	✓		✓	✓	✓	✓	✓	✓	✓	✓
BDA		✓	✓		✓	✓	✓	✓	✓	✓	✓	✓	✓	✓	✓	✓		
DI					✓	✓	✓	✓	✓			✓	✓		✓	✓		
DUB	✓			✓	✓	✓	✓	✓	✓	✓	✓	✓	✓	✓	✓	✓	✓	✓
NARE	✓		✓	✓			✓											
AMMA	✓	✓	✓		✓		✓											
Letters	✓	✓									✓	✓		✓	✓			

the child's normal programme is minimized. Early identification of a child's special educational needs is vital in ensuring that those needs can be effectively met.

United Kingdom Reading Association

We assume that we are referring to difficulties that include the following:

- below expected level in reading, writing or spelling yet otherwise generally able;
- specific difficulties such as:
  attention/sustained attention (discrimination);
  memory, such as word finding, retrieval (association), recall
  (revisualizing, reauditorizing motor memory/other associations,
  analysis and synthesis (phonemic segmentation/blend sequencing,
  pacing/spacing, directional factors integrating and
  transferring/generalizing learning;
- possibly associated anxieties, frustration, energy level fluctuations;
- possibly early language delay or difficulties.

Further to Dr Thackray's statement in the 1983 inquiry and endorsing his point, which was shared with others, that there should be assessment that includes 'seeing how children work and what kinds of responses they make over a period of time to a teaching programme', we would also like to note that there is a substantial loss of knowledge in those areas in which there has been a rejection of the use of standardized tests of general ability and reliance solely on observation and reports. It is not that we would wish to see a dependence on test batteries but that the systematic research, which is facilitated by sensitive profiling using well trialled reliable batteries of relevant subtests, can provide important insights into the nature and extent of the difficulties across the population. It can supplement, but not substitute classroom observation and analysis. We would further recommend that samples of children's work be collected so that norms can be established for skills such as handwriting rate, fluency and legibility as well as a range of vocabulary in different types of writing for different audiences, taking account of successions of drafts and the developmental steps taken both independently and with teacher 'conferencing' (intervention/advice). The inclusion of examples of work showing specific learning difficulties along with the full range of work for samples of the age-range could contribute valuable material not only for research but also for the development of teacher education materials.

It is anticipated that if the New National Curriculum Guidelines for English broadly follow the Cox Report's recommendations and the Guidelines for Mathematics and Science, and the TGAT Report's recommendations are followed with reference to the ten levels of attainment, it is more likely that the on-going recording of progress of children with SpLD, along with their peers, will reveal the importance of cumulative, open records with examples of work. We recommend that every effort be made to link research and teacher education with INSET related to the National Curriculum, so that there is increased awareness not only of what SpLD are like for the child and teacher but of what can be done to adapt teaching to meet the special educational needs of such pupils.

British Dyslexia Association

We believe strongly that early identification and assessment are of crucial importance. We believe that it is important that when a child is first admitted to school there should be good liaison with the health services and that appropriate information (relevant family history and any weakness in the child's developmental profile) should be transferred from the health services to the school. The infants school should screen the children. This will require training for all teachers in infants schools. Points to look for include: dyslexia in the family; birth history; early speech and language difficulty; early hearing problems; specific difficulty with rhyme and alliteration and naming difficulties; uncertain laterality; poor auditory sequential memory as shown by difficulty in remembering days of the week, months of the year or the alphabet.

There should be a screening procedure at the age of six. Marie Clay has described one such procedure. We take the view that reading, writing and spelling problems at the age of six should be a cause for concern, irrespective of the origin of those problems. Screening at the age of six should begin with a checklist completed by the class teacher. Other screening devices that might be considered include *McCleod*, the *Bury Infant Check* and the *Aston Index*. We are establishing a working party to develop a screening procedure.

Assessment. Dyslexic people require a comprehensive assessment to ascertain their:

- levels of comprehension of spoken and written language and expressive vocabulary;
- levels of reading and spelling skills relative to their general ability;
- reading and spelling strategies, as evidenced by an error analysis;
- competence in number work;
- competence in writing an original passage;
- cognitive profile, to be derived from standardized tests such as the *WISC-R* or the *British Ability Scales* – the IQ scores themselves derived from these tests are of secondary importance;
- auditory–vocal skills especially in relation to speech–sound processing;
- visual–motor perceptual abilities, particularly directional scanning and eye–hand coordination;
- verbal and visual memory competence.

At the beginning of the assessment it is essential to take a careful history of the child's educational difficulties. An accurate assessment is best related to the way in which the child functions. Discussion of the results is, therefore, essential in order to plan the teaching help required.

The assessment has a number of purposes. The first is to provide an explanation to the individual and, where appropriate, to the parents of the difficulties. In some cases the identification of the difficulties in itself transforms a child's existence. What has seemed like laziness, obstinacy or stupidity can now be seen as reactions to dyslexia. The second purpose is to offer an explanation to professionals dealing with the child. A third and very important purpose is to offer a guide to the development of teaching strategies.

Psychologists will have to devolve much assessment to teachers. Well-trained teachers could undertake the task very effectively. There should be more collaboration and discussion between teachers and psychologists. In too many cases, teachers are not shown psychologists' reports. The individual teaching programme developed as a result of the assessment should include longer term targets and a time-scale. Full account should be taken of cultural, environmental and personality factors that affect test results. Those using the tests should be aware that standard errors of measurement of subtests of the *WISC-R* or *British Ability Scales* can be relatively large.

Assessments are also required by examination boards to establish what examination allowances should be given to dyslexic candidates. We believe that it is important to establish clear and relevant criteria, which can be applied by officers of examination boards (see Chapter 16).

Dyslexia Institute

The purposes of the assessment process are (i) to identify the student with specific learning difficulties in the ordinary classroom; and having surveyed all the influences upon his learning, (ii) to highlight the abilities and difficulties he brings to the learning process; which determine (iii) his attainment in the basic reading, spelling, writing and numeracy competencies required in the curriculum; so (iv) enabling a provision to be specified that meets the student's special educational needs.

In the assessment procedure followed in the Dyslexia Institutes, the *Wechsler Intelligence Scales*, in their revised forms, are the preferred instruments for determining the student's cognitive competencies. *British Ability Scales* are used extensively for diagnostic purposes, but in its present form, at age 5:0 to 7:11, our experience has shown that 4 out of 10 required subtests on the IQ Estimate (General, Visual and Verbal) and at age 8:0 to 17½, 4 out of 8 subtests are found to be difficult by students with specific learning difficulties. On the *WISC* batteries, usually 3 or 4 out of 10 subtests are affected and one of these, Digit Span, is deleted from the IQ calculation. These differences in test structure and procedure result in lowered *BAS* IQ estimates compared with *WISC* scores. These different patterns in scores are not diagnostically significant, but may alter parent/teacher/local education authority expectations of the student in an undesirable way.

It must be stressed that level of intelligence is not a significant factor. SpLD students are not always clever. Students with high average or low levels of intellectual ability may have specific learning difficulties. The patterns of abilities and difficulties that determines the learner's linguistic competence is much more important.

Dyslexia Unit, Bangor

It is important not to overlook the research evidence that now exists on the subject of dyslexia in the narrow sense. There is little doubt that the difficulties arise at the phonological level. What this means, in effect, is that dyslexic individuals have distinctive difficulty in converting environmental stimuli into speech sounds. This makes sense not only of their lateness in learning to read and their poor spelling, but of their weak memory for visually and auditorily presented digits, their longer response latencies in picture and colour naming, and much else. Despite this considerable body of evidence one still meets people who like to tell the world how little we know about dyslexia; this over-pessimistic view needs to be corrected.

This is not to be an uncritical defender of traditional intelligence tests. They are of use, however, in determining whether a child's difficulties are general or specific, and it may often be important to show the child (not to mention the child's parents and teachers) that there are certain areas where they are extremely talented. Most psychologists are aware that the dyslexic child is likely to have distinctive difficulties on the four ACID items of the *WISC* (that is, Arithmetic, Coding, Information and Digit Span), and it follows that, when *WISC* results are reported, they are not likely to be very helpful unless details are given of all the subtest scores. With respect to statementing, we should like to think that help can often be given without the elaborate procedures necessarily involved. However, the situation may vary from one LEA to another, and in a particular case there may be a good reason why statementing is necessary.

National Association for Remedial Education

The 1981 Act sets out the legal framework for formal assessments of children with safeguards for parents. LEAs have a duty to identify children needing special educational provision.

> Assessment is not merely seen as a diagnostic tool but as a means of under-standing a child's learning difficulties, providing a guide to his education and a basis for monitoring progress. There will be a need to establish a part-nership between the LEA and the parents and there will be a responsibility to achieve an analysis of the child's learning difficulties, the specification of the child's educational needs and the facilities required to make the correct educational provision available.

NARE advocates a carefully organized screening procedure, which will identify not only those children whose areas of weakness are obvious from a simple test assessment, but also the complexities of the problem found within children who have specific learning difficulties.

The school, the support services and the school psychological service should examine all the relevant details of the background to the problem and a collection of baseline data should then be collated.

NARE strongly recommends (a) that all teachers are helped to become competent to take part in the assessment procedures, and (b) that schools are able to continue the move away from the use only of norm-referenced tests and further the employment of criterion-referenced tests where these are closely geared to the curriculum and can lead to the formulation of relevant objectives for each individual child. Each child should be assessed carefully in the usual learning situation and in the most objective way possible so that the teacher may see:

- what is the class/lesson/curriculum subject requirement;
- what the child has to do in a certain task so that an acceptable level of mastery can be achieved;
- what are the specific areas or ways in which the child is not achieving at that level.

There are three relatively informal stages that precede, and often avoid, the formal assessment procedures for school-age children. These informal stages are not new, simply a reiteration of present good practice.

Stage 1. Occurs usually when a class teacher observes a child experiencing difficulty with his or her work or, perhaps, in making satisfactory relationships. Discussions involving the class teacher, the headteacher and the parents ensue. Often an internal solution is quickly devised: a change of teaching method or a change of group might be adequate.

Stage 2. Occurs when a simple change, such as those mentioned above, proves to be ineffective. Usually, a member of the support service is included in the consultations and a further internal solution is attempted. This may comprise, for example, extra tuition in language related skills, or, maybe, support by a peripatetic teacher for hearing impaired children.

Stage 3. Relates to discussions about a child's problems involving an educational psychologist as well as the school staff, the peripatetic specialist and the parents. Even at the third stage, internal strategies may be set up and prove appropriate. The headteacher (or a senior member of staff) should monitor and maintain a record of parental consultations and the steps taken for Stages 1 and 3.

Included in Stage 1 would be the normal follow-up to a screening procedure, and here it is worth rehearsing the reasons for screening as the LEA and school responsibility.

The collection of initial data is designed to establish (a) whether the child has a learning difficulty (in the area of reading, spelling, handwriting or mathematics), and (b) whether these difficulties are of a specific rather than a general nature. As a minimum, therefore, the basic data will include the following:

- criterion-referenced testing for spelling and handwriting;
- a description of phonic skills mastered;
- an estimate of sight vocabulary;
- examples of copied writing;
- examples of free writing;
- examples of dictated writing.

We would also expect to find evidence to indicate that the difficulty is chronic; that is, that all existing remedial resources have been harnessed, but have been shown to have met with little success.

Following this detailed analysis, a profile of needs involving additional educational support should be considered. This will necessitate a consideration of the best way in which this can be achieved, the right sort of in-service training, the type of teaching objectives involved and the frequency of review that will be necessary.

The difficulties arise in the building up of a profile of special educational needs within the field of communication, where there is an overlap of possible causes more likely to illustrate a general area of difficulty rather than a specific one. It should be noted that some of the following characteristics might influence the way in which a child has difficulty in acquiring one or a combination of the skills of reading, spelling, handwriting or mathematics:

- visual, hearing or motor handicaps;
- low intelligence (there is a problem of definition; maybe one should merely mention low receptive language skills);
- emotional problems or maladjustment;
- poor home/environmental circumstances;
- lack of schooling, especially in the early years;
- inappropriate teaching;
- poor self-image with negative attitudes to learning to read;
- parental pressure.

There may be difficulties with emotional problems or maladjustment, in that consideration must be given to whether specific learning difficulties are a product of emotional problems or emotional/behavioural problems are a consequence of having specific learning difficulties, or are both due to something else. Similarly with a lack of schooling in the early years: is this cause or effect? The overriding consideration, however, must be the child's specific difficulty.

There are certain areas of weakness that are more likely to lead to a diagnosis of a *specific* rather than a *general* learning difficulty but whose peculiarities may also be evident with children who have a general need caused by the items listed above.

These specific indicators are as follows:

- a history of delayed speech and language development;
- letter-order confusion;
- poor left–right discrimination;
- poor auditory memory;
- difficulty with sound blending;
- difficulty with sequencing and ordering in speech and language;
- bizarre spelling patterns;
- confusion of b/d, p/q;
- reversals of letters;
- use of mirror writing;
- poor visual memory;
- early clumsiness;
- poor concentration span;
- similar familial history.

The early stages of building up a profile should look in detail at these specific areas in addition to an examination of all normal tests of reading and spelling that are used in schools. This is a continual process, which should be evaluated throughout the early years of a child's schooling and through the recording involved in the first three stages of assessment. If, at the end of this careful analysis of special educational needs within the field of communication skills, it is still found that a deep-seated problem exists for which extra resources may be needed, then it will be necessary to consider formal assessment with a view to making a statement of special educational needs for the child as recommended in the Education Act 1981 and its circulars (8/81 and 1/83). Not all LEAs will be inclined to maintain a statement for the children with specific learning difficulties.

Assistant Masters and Mistresses Association

Early identification is important, so that steps can be taken to provide appropriate help and support, before any difficulties that are present become compounded by feelings of anxiety and a sense of failure. Where the difficulties are mild, early intervention may largely overcome the problem, while in more severe cases, the sooner the pupil receives help, the more effective that help is likely to prove.

Because these pupils' weaknesses are sometimes matched by strengths in other areas of learning, it is easy for their difficulties to be overlooked. They may be thought of as lazy, or lacking in perseverance. If the child becomes anxious, or the parents are concerned, or if the child's teachers are perplexed by the pupil's apparent inability to master certain skills, an assessment by an educational psychologist can be of great value in pinpointing the true nature of the child's difficulties.

Letters

Teachers and parents stressed the need for early screening and identification, based on difficulties with perceptual tasks, sequencing, rhyming, phonic analysis, coordination, oral/written anomaly and family history. Many parents reported difficulties in having their children's problems assessed, sometimes because they did not know where to go and sometimes because 'statementing' was too slow. Some were confused and upset because they said local education authorities would not recognize dyslexia as an entity but called it specific learning difficulties and did not act upon diagnoses from educational psychologists working for dyslexia associations. A few teachers sought the uniform acceptance of the existence of the problem by educational psychologists. Several parents felt that special educational needs were defined according to available resources rather than actual needs. A clinical medical officer noted that identification was often not possible because the educational psychologist's time was used by most schools for 'more urgent' and obvious special educational needs. A solicitor wanted to know at what age identification and a statement of needs is possible. Further education teachers remarked that they had no tutors with expertise at identifying specific learning difficulties.

Prevention

It was generally agreed that those specific learning difficulties that were constitutional in origin, could not be prevented, but that associated educational failure could be alleviated by early intervention and appropriate teaching and support. Views are summarized below.

United Kingdom Reading Association

What we would aim to prevent are the following:

- failure to recognize the difficulties at an early stage of schooling if not at pre-school/through home and health links;

- failure to provide an appropriate range of teaching approaches and re-sources to meet individual needs within the normal classroom, with ad-ditional support in those cases with such needs as cannot be met by the class teacher;
- development of negative attitudes and rejection of literacy-related school work as a result of frustration and anxiety associated with stress;
- teachers having a lack of awareness of access to advice and support regard-ing methods and approaches suitable for assisting children with SpLD;
- home–school liaison difficulties arising from insufficient knowledge or clarity of policy on the part of the individual schools, education authorities or national providers.

We would suggest that the following factors be taken into account in attempting to achieve these aims.

Home support. Establish an early alert system and home support for pre-school/parents. This might include special programmes mediated through health visitors, perhaps along the lines of the Portage Programme but with appropriate content and style of mediation.

Screening. Screening of hearing and sight to include not only testing of acuity under 'optimal' (1:1) situations in quiet surroundings but with realistic classroom working noise and visual distraction. Such 'dynamic assessment' in context would aim to take account also of factors relating to attention and responses in-volving speech and language.

Maintaining appropriate records. These include notes of teaching/learning meth-ods, not only resources/books used by pupils. The records would be particularly important over the first few months of school and at the stages of fostering emergent writing and reading. Observations of children's development of ability to work collaboratively, involving communication through listening and speak-ing as well as thinking and doing, could be monitored along with their progress in constructing, drawing and 'writing'. The emphasis we are placing is on more intensive and shared classroom observation by teacher-teams who are appro-priately trained and used to working in the classroom together.

Avoidance of cumulative difficulties. The avoidance of cumulative difficulties building up as a result of a lack of positive intervention requires close monitoring of individualized teaching, and judicious use of relaxation training for the child, possibly also the parents and the teachers. The key ages of 7 and 11, linked to the new National Curriculum assessment, could be used for checking, by routine screening of handwriting for pace as well as fluency of letter formation, links and legibility. The early identification of a need for special training to use scribes or other methods of coping with handwriting difficulties or written language dif-ficulties could be effected by simple copying tests. Up-to-date norms for British children's writing pace could be established and the maintenance of samples of work arranged through appropriate programmes of research and development in the field. This would provide a practical means of checking, before entry to se-condary school, that all children could keep a suitable pace for the required study skills to be employed or for essential help to be sought.

Access. The exercise in which we are involved in this inquiry could lead directly to more widespread access to the range of sources that could be of assistance in the design and communication of policy and practice in this field. With the increased access and facility of technological aids, it is likely that computer data-banking could provide a means of organizing and disseminating relevant information.

British Dyslexia Association

Dyslexia, which is constitutional in origin, cannot be 'prevented'. Early identification will, however, prevent what Stanovich has described as the 'Matthew effect' (to him that hath shall be given and from him that hath not shall be taken away, even that which he hath). If children are helped at a young age, an accumulation of learning difficulties and, more importantly, emotional and behavioural difficulties can be prevented.

Dyslexia Institute

Individual differences in learning style are evident in the SpLD child's early development. In those important formative years before the child attends school, learning is not subject to the bias of the formal prestige presentation of the material to be learned, in a specific way, by teachers. Children relate to, survey and learn in their own environment, in their own way. There are clearly evident characteristics in unbiased early learning that give indications of the child's later learning preferences, which must be considered if we are to understand how the child learns. Generally, children with SpLD seem to have difficulty in building 'little skills' into 'bigger skills'. Little things they can do very well; bigger, more complex schemas they handle much less effectively.

Three major areas of pre-school experience, which is of considerable relevance to later language learning, should be considered: (1) fine motor skills in the preferred hand; (2) working memory skills; and (3) speech skills.

National Association Remedial Education

Nursery and pre-school early screening should be given a priority place in order to assist the parent to help those children with potential learning problems to overcome these, at the latest, by the time of school entry. The Warnock Report gave this area a priority position and yet, throughout the community, there is no real growth in pre-school provision or in increasing support for parents whose children are already beginning to encounter areas of difficulty that could become a communication problem at a later stage. In the near future the statutory requirement for LEAs to provide nursery education should be restored and this Association would, therefore, strongly recommend as the first line of attack in this field that there should be investment for the future in nursery provision, pre-school screening and parental involvement. This could become one of the best investments for the future and help to avoid the intervention at a later stage from being an uphill struggle to overcome learning apathy and lack of motivation. It has been recommended during the last few years that education should be more accountable' and yet the resources to make preventive education a reality are not even considered. The 1981 Education Act was clear in its definition of areas of responsibility. A great deal of emphasis has been placed on the future role of the parent but this has rarely been translated into areas of real advice. This Association would wish to see more guidelines given on how this largely untapped source of expertise can best be brought into practice.

Sections 4, 5 and 6, together with Schedule 1 of the 1981 Act, set out the legal framework for formal assessments of children with the safeguards for parents, but clearly, these are not enough. LEAs have a duty to identify those children whose special educational needs require special educational provision. Assessment is not seen merely as a diagnostic tool but as a means of understanding a child's learning difficulties, providing a guide to his education and a basis for monitoring progress. There will be a need to establish a partnership between the LEA and the parents and there will be a responsibility to achieve an analysis of the child's learning difficulties, the specification of the child's learning difficulties, the specification of the child's educational needs and the facilities required to make the correct educational provision available.

This responsibility starts at the age of two years and we would advocate a planned programme from the pre-school stage, through into the primary sector of education and into the secondary stage as and where it is found to be necessary.

The majority of local authorities now have some system of screening in existence as a means of identifying major areas of weakness in the pattern of children's learning in the basic subjects. The machinery, therefore, is in existence – the greater danger is that this screening may be used only for collecting statistical evidence and not for planning well organized intervention programmes designed to build up individual work for children with learning difficulties. They may even be successful where the learning difficulty has a simple cause and effect process but they do not at the moment fulfil the needs of pupils with specific learning difficulties. Many of the children who have this need are missed at the early screening stages because they may have managed to achieve reading ages that are above the cut-off levels designed by the tester. In no way is the use of a simple normative reading or spelling test sufficient to diagnose in depth those areas of communication that are likely to increase in difficulty as the child advances through the school.

The Association advocates a carefully organized screening procedure, which will identify not only those children whose areas of weakness are obvious from a simple test assessment, but also the complexities of the problem found within children who have specific learning difficulties.

The school psychological services have a vital role to play and they should be increased to a level where they can fulfil not only the demands of the 1981 Education Act but also the obligations of being part of a team organized to help those children with specific difficulties and carry out the necessary preventive measures whilst working closely with specialist teaching support staff and classroom teachers.

Assistant Masters and Mistresses Association

While there is little to be done to counteract genetic factors (dyslexic tendencies are said to run in families), or perinatal damage, teachers are able to have some influence through early intervention and an awareness of the effects of different teaching styles. Early referral and prompt diagnosis should be followed by ensuring that the pupils receive the appropriate teaching and additional support that they require.

Teachers dealing with such children need to be flexible in their approach, so that they can, as far as possible, find a method that suits the pupil, rather than expecting that all pupils will learn in the same way.

Letters

The letter that was received from a pupil with severe and prolonged literacy problems was by Zachary (reproduced at the front of this book). The points he makes are important and clearly put. We are indebted to him for writing to us.

It was generally agreed that prevention of specific learning difficulties was not possible, but the prevention of subsequent educational difficulties and associated problems could best be achieved by early intervention. Several teachers and parents blamed whole-book/word/look-and-say teaching methods and felt that the problem might have been alleviated with analytic/word-building approaches to teaching reading and spelling.

Other parents described their own efforts to help their child in the face of what they saw as LEA prevarication and obstructiveness. The development of teaching materials by parents, including the writing of computer programs, was described. The relief experienced by parent and child when the nature of the problem was seen as largely 'within-child', was marked. Parental appreciation of effective tutorial assistance was profoundly moving. The acceptance that progress would almost certainly be slow was generally acknowledged. Our correspondents were realistic in their expectations. As with all of us, they and their child needed both hope and help.

Teaching methods

A variety of teaching strategies was mentioned. Table 15.5 summarizes the main ones.

Comments

The range of teaching methods and materials advocated is in accordance with the wider concept of specific learning difficulties as part of a continuum of special educational needs. DES and NARE both stress that class teachers or subject teachers have a major responsibility for meeting their children's special educational needs and must coordinate partnerships between child, teacher(s), parents and support services.

All agree that, wherever possible, the child should be supported in fully accessing the curriculum in a normal school. Extracts from the submissions are presented below.

Table 15.5: Teaching methods

Body	Responsibility of class/subject teacher	Support from specialist teacher	Perceptual training	Memory training	Sequencing training	Motor skills training	Letter formation training	Phonics	Spelling rules	Contextual cues	Word recognition	Language skills	Reading strategies	Writing strategies	Automaticity	Metacognition	Multisensory	Number	Curriculum support	Essay practice	Study skills	Objectives	Enjoyment of reading and writing	Paired/peer reading	Typewriters	Word processors	Tapes	Behavioural skills	Counselling
DES	✓	✓						✓	✓		✓						✓	✓	✓		✓					✓	✓		
BDA			✓	✓	✓				✓			✓	✓	✓	✓	✓	✓	✓	✓		✓							✓	
DI			✓	✓	✓					✓							✓												
DUB						✓		✓									✓			✓									✓
AMMA																	✓					✓							
NARE	✓	✓	✓			✓		✓		✓		✓									✓	✓	✓						
NAS/UWT																													
UKRA		✓	✓	✓			✓	✓		✓					✓		✓		✓			✓	✓	✓		✓	✓		✓
Letters																	✓		✓			✓			✓	✓	✓		

Specific techniques listed by UKRA and in Letters included Marie Clay, Writing Road to Reading, Kathleen Hickey, Hornsby's Alpha to Omega, Grace Fernald, Mnemonics, Edith Norrie Letter Case, Bradley's Plastic Letters, Brand Word Families, Rhyme and Rhythm, Slingerland, Gillingham and Stillman, Montessori, Yule and Joyce Morris (see Chapter 7 for further details of these methods).

Department of Education and Science

Students should be introduced to ways of identifying children with special educational needs, helped to appreciate what the ordinary school can and cannot do for such children and given some knowledge of the specialist help available and how it can be enlisted.

Training for teachers of children with special educational needs in ordinary schools was one of the priority areas of in-service training support under the Department's grant scheme. Under the LEATGS, local educational authorities are able to support courses of their own choosing to meet local needs. These courses attract 50 per cent central government funding. The Royal Society of Arts has validated a one-year part-time diploma for teachers of pupils with specific learning difficulties.

United Kingdom Reading Association

We consider that no single method is likely to meet every aspect of the special educational needs of all pupils who have SpLD. There are methods for teaching reading and writing that are well trialled and have proved to be helpful in some cases. These tend to be described as 'multisensory' but should be carefully considered in terms of their potential for adaptation so that appropriate emphases on particular approaches (such as through mainly auditory avenues) can be provided within a framework aimed to provide for maximal reinforcement through differently sequenced routes where relevant.

What seems to be necessary in all cases is the observation of ways in which the child can demonstrate more effective recall, and how effective is his or her processing of mental images, whether a visualizer or auditorizer or with relatively greater facility with learning by other associations or constellations of clues.

Basic awareness of the sound–symbol relationship in English needs to be developed to a level of automaticity for fluent writing and spelling as well as reading. We would consider it to be an unfortunate and false dichotomy between teaching by 'story approach' and by 'phonics'. What matters is the growth of confidence in the individual child as he or she enjoys reading and writing, and through informed teaching and shared enjoyment of play and work with letters and words, the child acquires familiarity and competence in control over the symbol system. With many children, who have had prolonged difficulties and not responded successfully to more open-ended approaches including ways in which story approach is employed by some teachers, the introduction of more structured approaches with systematic records provided by use of carefully graded materials can bring about desirable changes. This does not suggest, however, that the story sessions should be dropped and a diet of 'phonics' substituted.

It is helpful to have a bank of tape-recorded stories so that no child is denied the pleasure of gaining access to the meaning of the print even if he or she cannot decode it. Audio tape-recording and use of microcomputers are perhaps underused avenues at present, possibly due to lack of teacher planning time and training in the design of individual educational programmes (IEPs, see below). Classroom management skill in using paired and peer reading and conferencing with individuals or small groups is required in order to make time within the routine classwork for working with the individuals who have SpLD. Those approaches to developing writing and reading that employ such methods can facilitate the adaptation of teaching and learning to meet individual needs.

We would wish to emphasize the fact that we are not recommending a single 'scheme' but that teachers be aware of the theoretical rationale for the materials they use and the pacing and sequencing of the increments in complexity of the linguistic challenges and symbolic representations involved. The matter of awareness of textual cohesion and its implication for the child's memory load to be considered in selecting and using particular passages or stories is a further factor in the planning and preparation for teaching and for homework.

We consider that children with SpLD require individualized teaching, preferably for some time every day, and that specially trained teachers should be available to assist with the support for the child, the class or subject teacher and for homework/parental liaison. This does not imply solely one-to-one teaching or that a specialist teacher would be needed every day. The design of a suitable programme for basic literacy does need to be related to the child's whole curriculum and to work in a class situation. The matter of assisting with such design and keeping track of the child's development is perhaps the most important aspect of the specialist's potential contribution.

British Dyslexia Association

The most important requirement is a detailed analysis of the cognitive skills of the child. Teaching must then be matched to the needs of the child. Where a child has specific problems in, for example, short-term memory, fine motor control or left and right confusion, teaching will need to be addressed to developing those skills in younger children and by bypassing the deficits in older children.

With regard to literacy, it is important to analyse the strategies being used by the child. Children who are relying exclusively on word recognition strategies will need to be taught phonic strategies. Because some 80 per cent of English words follow regular spelling rules, rule-based approaches are very helpful for a great many children. Their reading strategies must, however, be monitored to ensure that they do not develop an exclusive reliance on phonic approaches but are able to use a combination of word recognition, phonic approaches and context. There may be some children who are unable to achieve this goal. A child with a good visual memory may, for example, achieve more by relying primarily on word recognition and context than by attempting to develop rule-based strategies.

Similar considerations apply to spelling. Methods that rely on visual memory such as 'look–cover–write–check', or rule-based methods relying on the development of phonic strategies should be used, according to the strength of the child.

Multisensory teaching intuitively seems sensible where children have phonological coding difficulties, often associated with short-term memory problems and other organizational difficulties. The value for reading and spelling progress of learning how to split words into their constituent speech sounds has been demonstrated. It has also been shown that tracing can help. Many workers have found multisensory approaches to be successful. Properly controlled large-scale studies of different teaching approaches are both difficult and costly and we know of no such studies. On the other hand, such evidence as has been collected about traditional remedial approaches would suggest that these are not very effective.

We still encounter a great many cases in which children with literacy problems are, for that reason, not given access to the full curriculum. We regard it as of vital importance that children with specific learning difficulties are given support both in the normal classroom and by having access to a support tutor outside the classroom. We find many cases where children with literacy problems are withdrawn to a remedial class for the whole or a large part of their curriculum and denied access to the full curriculum. Even if unable to read effectively they can study English literature by using talking books. They can make use of tape-recorded notes. Their written work can be much improved if they are equipped with word processors with spelling checkers and taught the necessary keyboard and word processing skills. Above all, there must be an understanding from all who teach them that they may have many talents and skills. Their abilities must not be measured purely on the basis of their difficulties in acquiring literacy.

It is important to teach study skills to children. For those who have problems with organization of information, such teaching is vital. Teachers need to be trained for this work.

We believe that there is a need for detailed investigation into the causes of numeracy problems and the remediation of those problems. Some problems with numeracy can be associated with dyslexia. Mastering the functions of arabic and algebraic symbols is a similar process to mastering the functions of alphabetic symbols. Problems in understanding sequence and order can affect understanding of place value. A proportion of dyslexic children have memory problems that interfere with their learning number bonds and tables. Some mathematics topics, however, require visuo-spatial abilities. At present there is little more that we can say than that the teaching of children with numeracy problems must address their particular difficulties and that it is important, therefore, that those difficulties are analysed.

Dyslexia Institute

The child will have available wide-ranging sources of information, sights, sounds, feelings, tastes and smells from which he may learn. If he is to learn effectively from this environment he must: (1) survey the whole of that environment and attend to all the major senses from it; (2) focus his attention in an analytical way to take in important aspects; (3) sequence the results of his analysis of environment into a required order; (4) move himself, his limbs or his ideas to explore and give different perspectives to that environment; (5) integrate separate aspects of that environment into a more meaningful pattern for him; (6) represent that ongoing experience (a) in feeling or motor terms, (b) visually in pictures or (c) verbally in words. The final vital aspect of his learning package is to (7) recall his experiences and thoughts for later use through verbal, visual or motor channels.

We therefore see the major building blocks in a hierarchical structure of learning as being:

- surveying/attending;
- analysing and focusing attention;
- sequencing;

- moving, the child, his limbs, the environment, or elements of the environment;
- integrating parts to build an individually meaningful whole;
- representing ideas: (a) in motor terms, (b) visually in pictures and (c) verbally in words;
- recalling for later use through (a), (b) and (c) above, or any combination of these channels. This is the vital delivery process of learning.

While all the skills listed above may be acquired by the child from experience, children do not all acquire these skills at the same rate. Individual differences will be apparent both in the overall rate of acquisition and the development and use of these skills. In the past teachers have tended to adopt a *laissez-faire* attitude, leaving the child to acquire learning skills as best he can, from the experiences he has available to him. But the skills listed above are all teachable. Should our approach not be to teach the child the major learning skills that he finds difficult?

The range of teaching provisions to be made for students with specific learning difficulties will be wide and varied. The provision made must be individual and related to the abilities and difficulties in learning experienced by the student. The provision should cover (a) learning skills, (b) (i) language skills, (ii) numeracy skills, (c) study/thinking skills, and (d) behavioural skills, and should (e) link effectively to the school curriculum. For the majority of students this can be arranged and managed in the ordinary school. Others with greater difficulty will need to be withdrawn to a unit for small group teaching. A few will have such serious difficulties that they cannot sustain the broad curriculum of the ordinary school and must be sent to a school that makes special provision where skill development is directly related to curriculum load.

Dyslexia Unit, Bangor

We should not underestimate the extent to which it is possible to *transform a child's existence* (we mean this) by making clear to him and to his parents the nature of the difficulties. What *had* seemed like laziness, cussedness, stupidity, and reluctance to try can now be seen as the child's reactions to the dyslexia – that is, reactions to a constitutionally caused anomaly of development for which he is not to blame. If one presents the picture in this way, all sorts of pressure, guilt feeling and the like are thereby removed, including those which have arisen when well-intentioned teachers have told him, 'You can do it if you try'. To carry out this kind of therapeutic discussion successfully it is, of course, necessary for the psychologist to know the kinds of things that a dyslexic does and does not find difficult. There are plenty of discouraged dyslexics who will respond, 'Can't do it' on almost every occasion; and the important skill is to know when to say, 'Yes, I quite understand', for instance if the task is the verbatim memorization of a long sentence, and when to say cheerfully, 'Have a go'!, for instance if the task is the completion of a matrix. We have found the *Bangor Dyslexia Test* a useful basis for such discussion. For instance, in the case of the left–right item one can ask not only, 'Did you have difficulty when you were younger?' (as per the manual), but 'Were you teased about this?', 'Did you feel a fool?', and the like. What is important – however this is accomplished – is that the child should be encouraged to talk about his difficulties and be helped to come to an accurate understanding both of his strengths and of his weaknesses.

One sometimes finds similar pessimism with regard to teaching methods. Provided the word 'dyslexia' is used in the strict, narrow sense indicated earlier, there is no need for controversy. The structured multisensory teaching, which is now being used by an increasing number of trained teachers, is not only effective in practice, but is supported by research evidence. There is room for controversy only if the word 'dyslexic' is used of a range of children with many different problems; this usage generates claims that dyslexia is not a 'single condition' and that there is 'no agreed teaching method'. Such talk confuses the issue. It seems far better to say simply that children whose difficulties arise from an original weakness at the phonological level have distinctive needs. With regard to meeting these needs much can in fact be done to forestall future problems if no child is allowed to leave junior school without a knowledge of letter–sound correspondence and correct letter production. It is not in dispute that for skilled readers there may be advantages in 'skimming', but this is certainly not true in the case of dyslexic individuals. The older dyslexic individual needs considerable practice in essay writing.

It is important not to overlook the many social problems that can arise from dyslexia, for example missed appointments from an uncertain sense of time (or even from misreading a notice!), failure to relay messages as a result of poor immediate memory or linguistic uncertainty, and inappropriate responses in relation to others through failure to read their body language. A counselling service at the secondary and tertiary stages of education seems to be a 'must'.

National Association for Remedial Education

After careful individual assessment in the usual learning situation, a programme should then be devised to remedy the shortcomings.

The important point is to create an atmosphere in which children with specific learning difficulties are accepted as part of the whole-school responsibility, and that the school staff are not placed in a position of disadvantage where the only people who seem to know how to help these pupils are outside the main school system. At present, the media have persuaded many parents that their children can only receive help from outside agencies and 'experts', and the emphasis by some writers on a 'medical' diagnosis of specific learning difficulties, or 'dyslexia', is not helpful. Neither, we believe, is the mystique that is often associated with the phenomenon of specific learning difficulties because, in the end, the only useful solution to the problem derives from skilled, sensitive and sustained teaching – professional qualities needed by all teachers and which are particularly needed by class teachers working on the problem of specific learning difficulties (and others) in conjunction with special educational needs staff.

The basis for the competent helping of children with specific learning difficulties is not greatly different from that for the careful teaching of literacy (or other) skills to children in general, but each LEA should first have a team of experienced and trained teachers capable (a) of delivering a programme of individual, or small-group, additional tuition preferably in the pupils' own schools, and (b) of advising colleagues. The team's training should be fashioned from the elements listed and discussed below.

This training must cover the needs of children with specific learning difficulties, particularly in reading, spelling and handwriting, in order that these teachers have a thorough knowledge of the learning processes in these areas and of the problems various children with specific learning difficulties encounter. We believe that the equivalent of 40 hours' in-service training contact time for this initial course is a minimum period in which to provide a foundation of knowledge on which must be built further supervised 'on-the-job' training.

The areas to be covered are the understanding of language competence through performance in the linguistic skills of listening, talking (that is, receptive and expressive spoken language skills), reading and writing through multi-sensory approaches. Assessment and monitoring skills should be taught to the teacher-students so that they can make pertinent use of their own analyses of children's errors and miscues, criterion-referenced tests and the children's rate of learning as a means of (a) identification, (b) the prescription of learning objectives and (c) their application.

Assistant Masters and Mistresses Association

A multisensory approach is one way of helping to give these pupils the opportunity to learn in a way that is appropriate to them. If, for instance, there is an auditory weakness, they may be able to compensate by absorbing information that is presented visually. As each pupil's needs will be different, too great an emphasis on any one method should be avoided.

It may also be helpful to bear in mind that these pupils are less likely to pick up information simply by being placed in a learning situation, and that they often respond best to a more structured approach. They may need more specific teaching than other pupils, where the learning steps are carefully worked out in advance and they are given plenty of time to consolidate each new skill before moving on to the next stage.

National Association of Schoolmasters, Union of Women Teachers

The provision for children within this category of need (SpLD) should include individual learning programmes based on specialist advice from advisory teachers within the field of special education as well as educational psychologists, appropriate multisensory teaching and ancillary support, and also arrangements for pupils to be statemented in cases where there is a particularly severe problem.

In-service training leading to a recognized qualification should be available for teachers in special and in ordinary schools, to enable them to respond to the needs of pupils with different sensory impairment, among which are those learning difficulties that collectively are described as 'dyslexic'. The NASUWT believes that the process of identification and assessment is a task that can more readily be carried out in a school where there are teachers who have both the theoretical and practical knowledge of the problems associated with specific learning difficulties, and can adapt their teaching methods in devising learning programmes that are appropriate and match the needs of the pupils concerned.

Letters

Many teachers and parents advocated an individual structured teaching programme using multisensory techniques. Some stressed the need for support in other curriculum areas and felt that computers, word processors, typewriters and tape-recorders could be used. Teachers, parents, dyslexia associations and dyslexic individuals stressed the importance of raising and maintaining self-esteem. A range of teaching strategies and systems being used were included in the replies received.

Several teachers stressed the need to be willing to try various methods, to encourage wide reading and to teach skills of written presentation. Only two teachers and one parent advocated special school placement, and only for a short time. Two parents had been upset at having to do regular teaching to a strict programme and felt that they had failed in it. One teacher admitted that, after many years' experience, she still could not specify any particular methods. Zachary appreciated that he needed specialist help (see his letter at the front of this book).

Provision of resources

Edited extracts from submissions are presented below.

Department of Education and Science

The Warnock Report (GB.DES, 1978) identified a number of areas where further research was considered necessary. Among these was the assessment and education of children with specific learning difficulties in reading, writing and spelling, and the evaluation of different approaches. The Department subsequently funded a programme of four main research projects or proposals. The results of these four projects were the subject of a seminar organized by the Department in May 1984.

United Kingdom Reading Association

The major area of provision we would consider to be in-service education of teachers. We would like to be of assistance in the planning of ways in which teachers could be more fully informed at pre-service level as well as at in-service level. We would stress the importance of introducing any work on SpLD within a framework of language development and an understanding of the concept of special educational needs and not in isolation from an awareness of child development and speech and language difficulties as well as differences that should also be considered in a cultural context and with appreciation of multiethnic and multilingual factors.

The design of school buildings should be considered in planning for areas for relatively distraction-free, small-group work and individualized teaching. Classrooms which have wide, open-plan areas require to be equipped with areas that are adaptable for study-offices, either at the periphery or free-standing like little telephone booths, for individual short work sessions. Additional resources for audio and microtechnological use would ease the teachers' burden once they are confident in design of group and individual education programmes (IEPs).

Take-home audio cassettes and additional books are likely to be valuable further resources. More research is required into case studies of a range of children with SpLD affecting different aspects of learning and in different school contexts.

We have commented already on the need for screening, through testing and research linked projects to monitor the effectiveness of the recommendations that have been offered in earlier sections of this brief paper.

We would be pleased to be consulted in any further work on this aspect of developing literacy and learning.

British Dyslexia Association

We believe strongly that early identification and effective teaching strategies before the age of seven will, in the long term, reduce demands for provision for special educational needs in later years and will not, therefore, add to the net cost of provision. We deprecate very much an approach that suggests that choices have to be made between different categories of children with special edu-cational needs and that providing for dyslexic children implies the deprivation of other categories of children. There is evidence from, for example, Project Read that multisensory methods help a wide range of children with literacy problems. Local education authorities have duties to make provision for children with special educational needs whether or not they maintain statements of educational needs for those children (Education Act 1981, Section 4).

Many professionals who assess children are reluctant to define needs other than in terms of the resources available. This is the phenomenon described by Goacher *et al.* (1988). They say:

> These tensions and differences in interpretations were manifested at the inter-service meetings which were held at the University of London Institute of Education as part of our research strategy. There was one school of thought that maintained that it was naïve, even hypocritical, to expect professionals to write about needs with no regard to the likelihood of pro-vision being made. Administrators who expressed this view were quite can-did about the fact that professionals had been told not to put into advice the need for facilities that could not be made available.

Dyslexia Institute

It is apparent from *Regina* (the Queen) *v. Surrey County Council Education Committee, ex parte H*, July 1984 that 'There is no question of Parliament having placed the local education authority under the obligation to provide a child with the best possible education. There is no duty on the authority to provide such a Utopian system, or to educate him or her to his or her maximum potential'. This must be tempered by the fact that in the case of most children with SpLD the education authority is demonstrably failing to educate the child at a normal level of expectation, never mind maximum potential. The education authority is also under constraints to take due account of the efficient use of resources. Yet the later judgement in *Regina v. Inner London Education Authority, ex parte F*, June 1988 makes it clear that the priorities must be (i) meeting the child's needs, and (ii) the resources.

In making judgements about a provision, consideration must be given to the clear relationship between the teaching provision, in hours per week, the dur-ation of the provision in weeks, the cost of provision, and the progress made by the child in receipt of that provision. Experience in the Dyslexia Institute suggests that inadequate provision in terms of hours per week may appear to be superficially cheap but results in slow progress. When costed and related to the progress recorded by a similar child who receives a much fuller provision, greater child skill gain is seen to be related to greater provision cost. Calculations show that diminishing returns are evident and an educationally and financially efficient programme can be established. However this suggests that up to an identifiable point a fuller provision over a shorter time is a more efficient use of resources.

In the Dyslexia Institute's view, in making such a restricted provision, which takes into account only crude cost unrelated to skill gains, the education authority may be in breach of the statutory requirement to make efficient use of financial resources.

Skilled teachers who can undertake the necessary work either in a school classroom or a 'unit' setting are a very scarce resource. Central government should take appropriate supportive steps to ensure that such key staff are appropriately trained and available in the right proportion to meet individual needs. This training is a costly capital investment in teaching skills and should be funded by the DES as a priority.

It is evident that appropriate teaching for children with special educational needs is expensive when judged by ordinary class teaching standards. The Dyslexia Institute considers that central government should make a grant of between £1000 and £5000 per child to local authorities to defray the extra costs of educating all children with such serious special needs that they require the protection of a statement. What we need is national *understanding* of the 'dyslexic' child's skills in learning as well as his difficulties in literacy, *appreciation* of what can be done by effective teaching, *vision* in creating the necessary structures within the education authorities in this country, and *unity* in seeking maximum practical support (money and resources) from central government through the DES to enable this work to take place. The Dyslexia Institute will gladly cooperate with education authorities and other voluntary bodies at any stage in the process of understanding, appreciation, vision or unity.

Dyslexia Unit, Bangor

More specialist teachers need to be trained, and there should be more 'general awareness' courses for class teachers. We are not convinced that promoting teacher awareness is as expensive an exercise as some have supposed. In contrast, the cost of *not* taking the dyslexia problem seriously seems to be horrendous: the child and parents will in that case have not only the dyslexia itself to contend with but lack of sympathy and understanding. At the very least they are put under considerable strain; there is a serious risk to health, and in some cases a risk that the child will turn 'agin' society and become delinquent. Even when the child sits at the back of the class and gives no trouble, his lack of literacy skills will mean that much of the money spent on his education is being wasted. In purely financial terms therefore – and quite apart from any humanitarian considerations – it is more economical to take the dyslexia problem seriously than to sweep it under the carpet.

National Association for Remedial Education

The first point to be emphasized is that class teachers should be given the support and in-service training necessary to enable them to be considered as 'specialist teachers', particularly at the primary stage of education. There has been a positive danger in the past of reliance for specialist 'remedial' teaching to be on the peripatetic services. This has led to a withdrawal of responsibility for such work by some teachers and the stretching of the resources of the support services to a point where their intervention has been too limited to be effective. There will, however, be cases where the schools cannot meet adequately the educational needs of some of those children, and the LEAs should be extending their support services within the field of learning difficulties, language difficulties and sensory impairment to a level where direct specialist intervention can be available as part of the follow-up in Stage 2 of assessment and following the screening procedure.

Wherever possible the child with a specific learning difficulty should be helped within the classroom with the work allied to the curriculum. There will, however, be occasions when some children may need structured individual teaching away from the main body of the class for a controlled period of time. Every survey of remedial provision in the past has been critical of the lack of liaison between teachers in the classroom and the peripatetic services. This must be overcome by a planned programme between the class teacher and the visiting support teacher in order to provide a structured series of learning objectives designed to suit the individual needs of the children and to allow them to feel a total part of the class structure. Time for this liaison is vital and must be part of the planning.

There can be different ways in which this extra help can be organized but the major factor is the acceptance by the LEA that this is part of their overall responsibility under the 1981 Education Act. The criteria must be firm and satisfy the specific nature of the difficulty, and the teachers concerned must have received adequate training in this field. Where the children's difficulties in reading, spelling or handwriting cannot be explained by interrupted schooling, inadequate intelligence, poor teaching or adverse social and cultural factors, then additional specialist teaching should be provided in the ordinary school. The tutors would work under the guidance of an advisory teacher and/or educational psychologist and in liaison with the class and subject teachers.

It is preferable for this additional specialist help to be given within the familiar surroundings of the child's own school, rather than necessitating regular visits to an outside unit, centre, clinic or special school. This will also facilitate a close working relationship between the specialist teacher and members of staff, which is vital if continuity in the child's individual programme is to be maintained.

Withdrawal from the ordinary school situation tends to place the child in a 'special' category and might encourage teachers to abdicate their responsibilities towards alleviating the child's learning difficulties. Regular attendance at an outside establishment necessitates missing part of the school day, which could include lessons or activities that the child enjoys, in which the child experiences success, or which the child should not miss.

Nevertheless, it is the implementation of the course of action most likely to help a child best that must remain the paramount consideration. Besides, it may be desirable for the child to tackle problems in the context of a fresh environment. Careful discussion between parents, the child, the headteacher, members of staff and the agency concerned is an essential part of planning such a course of action. When a child attends a centre that is part of local authority provision, every effort should be made by the specialist teacher to liaise with the child's school in order to maintain continuity in the helping programme.

In some instances, referral to an independent agency outside the LEA's jurisdiction might have been suggested. It is important that parents are acquainted with the services already available to them from the local education authority before such a course of action is taken. Evidence shows that parents can feel obligated to pay for additional help themselves when adequate help is already available within their local education authority.

There is also a legal dimension that might be brought into the discussion when a private arrangement leads to parents withdrawing their child from a school session for tuition elsewhere. A child should attend full-time, that is for both sessions in each day the school is open where s/he is a registered pupil, for parents to fulfil their obligations under the Education Act 1944 (Section 39).

More important, perhaps, are the stress and fatigue that will almost certainly accompany after-school private lessons when a child with specific learning difficulties has spent an exhausting time in school trying to keep up. It is to be regretted that many parents feel compelled to resort to these measures to help their child, but clearly they should be counselled as to the probable increased pressure on the child when this is arranged. Their well-intentioned move could well prove counter-productive.

Taking all these factors into consideration, additional help is best provided in the child's own school and within the school day, with care to select times for tutoring that will disturb the usual curriculum as little as possible. This strategy is, after all, but a variation of the integrative thrust of the 1981 Act, and emphasizes a resourcing responsibility to which the DES, together with unproviding LEAs, must address themselves.

It is vital that the programme is regularly evaluated. The specific areas of need discovered, the teaching programme to be employed and the method(s) and resource(s) to be used should be fully described. Evaluation, after three terms' tuition, should involve the specific learning difficulties teacher, class teacher/form tutor and the educational psychologist or special needs advisory teacher whoever is responsible for supervising the programme. A decision should then be taken as to whether or not the additional provision needs to be continued. Parental involvement is most important. Attainment and mastery levels need to be considered along with the child's morale and attitude at each step. If these are adequate and it is decided that the additional tuition can be discontinued, at least for the time being, follow-up checks on the maintenance of progress should be made in the school's routine of continuing assessment.

National Association of Schoolmasters, Union of Women Teachers

The provision of adequate resources at both central government and LEA levels is central to the development of coherent and effective policies which, in the light of the Education Act 1981, are required in helping to identify, assess and provide for children with special educational needs, including those who are the subject of the DECP national inquiry.

Letters

The majority of letters received from the parents of dyslexic pupils expressed extreme frustration concerning delays in the recognition by LEAs, some psychologists and sometimes by teachers and headteachers, of their child's learning difficulties. Without exception, parents used the term 'dyslexia' rather than 'specific learning difficulties'. Some professionals are reported in parents' letters as having said that they considered dyslexia to be no more than a psychologically suspect but socially respectable label that appealed to some parents. Inadequate resources for efficient diagnosis/identification of dyslexia was seen as a major failing of the state system. Long, drawn-out 'battles' with local authorities over identification were described in telling detail, some culminating in legal appeals.

Parents were equally critical concerning the provision available in many LEA schools. The absence of teachers who had undertaken advanced courses of training in the identification and alleviation of specific learning difficulties (dyslexia) was also frequently voiced. A small number of parents had deliberately withdrawn their children from the state system and were educating them at home. Parents generally accepted that their child's progress would be slow in most cases, irrespective of where the child was educated. The demand for places at day or residential schools specializing in this field was expressed by some respondents.

It is appreciated that satisfied parents tend not to write in response to requests, such as ours, for their comments. However, a small number wrote in appreciative terms of the endeavours of particular professionals, both within the state system, and independent of it, who were perceived as having helped them and their child come to terms with, and begin to make progress in reducing, the adverse effects of SpLD (dyslexia). Parents need guidance on what is available.

Summary

Introduction

Submissions were invited from various bodies on:

- The concept of specific learning difficulties (dyslexia)
- Identification and assessment
- Prevention
- Teaching methods
- Provision of resources

Tables 15.1 and 15.2 summarize the responses received.

Concept of Specific Learning Difficulties (Dyslexia)

Responses centred around terminology and definition. Table 15.3 summarizes these.

Identification and Assessment

There was much consensus on the use of a range of assessment procedures, with some differences about the relevance of standardized intelligence tests. Profiles of abilities and attainments were considered important. Screening surveys were advocated. Table 15.4 summarizes responses.

Prevention

It was generally agreed that specific learning difficulties, being constitutional in origin, could not be prevented, but that associated educational failure could be alleviated by early intervention and appropriate teaching and support.

Teaching Methods

A range of teaching methods was suggested, reflecting the view of specific learning difficulties as part of a continuum of special educational needs. Table 15.5 summarizes responses received.

Provision of Resources

Factors considered were:

- in-service education of teachers;
- LEA responsibility under the Education Act 1981;
- research and evaluation;
- partnership;
- school-based resources.

Recommendations

Based on the consensus of responses, the following recommendations are made.

Concept of Specific Learning Difficulties (Dyslexia)

15.1. The term 'specific learning difficulties' (SpLD) be used and seen as part of a continuum of special educational needs whilst acknowledging that the term 'dyslexia' has a considerable currency.

Identification and Assessment

15.2. Teachers and parents be informed of the LEA's responsibility, under the Education Act 1981, to make provision for children with special educational needs, including SpLD, and to initiate formal assessment when additional resources are needed.

15.3. Screening procedures should be further developed and their effects evaluated.

Prevention

15.4. Early intervention is needed to minimize the subsequent educational failure and emotional difficulties associated with SpLD, and continuing support be provided as required.

15.5. Courses of initial training for teachers include consideration of the nature, identification and alleviation of SpLD.

Teaching Methods

15.6. Professional awareness and use of a range of teaching techniques be developed and applied in the context of school-based curriculum support for pupils with SpLD.

15.7. Responsibility for teaching of and learning by pupils with SpLD be seen as involving collaboration between the pupils, class and subject teachers, specialist teachers, advisory teachers, parents and educational psychologists.

Provision of Resources

15.8. Teachers' awareness of SpLD be enhanced and fully supported in the classroom by specialists.

15.9. LEAs encourage teachers to undertake INSET courses on the identification and alleviation of SpLD.

15.10. The cost–benefit ratios of the above provision be investigated.

Chapter 16

Examination Board Policies and Practices

Introduction

Educational psychologists have been involved in writing and submitting reports to schools and other institutions about pupils thought to have specific learning difficulties ever since the profession began. Many of these reports found their way to the examining boards prior to a pupil entering or taking a public examination, some with and others without, the psychologist's knowledge. Consequently there were no clear and systematic data on the use of psychologists' reports to seek special consideration for pupils with specific reading and writing difficulties when the first national DECP survey was started in 1981 (Cornwall, Hedderly and Pumfrey, 1984). In some respects the situation in 1989 has become much clearer, but in many other respects, despite the considerable advances in assessment processes and procedures, the issues are more confused.

Some issues remain the same as described in the earlier survey. For example, it is still true that the majority of handicaps are certified by doctors. There is an assumption that the educational and therefore assessment issues are clearly understood for the majority of medical conditions that give rise to a disability or an assessment problem. The introduction of the Education Act 1981 does ensure the involvement of a psychologist with children having disabilities or handicapping conditions and most 'permanently' disabled pupils are recorded as such through the issue of a statement of special educational provision as defined by the Education Act 1981. Pupils who are temporarily impaired at examination time through a broken arm or something similar are not generally the concern of the psychologist.

The examination boards still appropriately reserve the right to determine their assessment procedures and concessions for handicapped students. In the earlier report it was suggested that the examining boards had as 'much trouble attempting to sort out a policy (for dyslexia students) as have other organisations'. No doubt this is still true but it is also evident that the boards have been much more pro-active and positively successful in their attempts to produce policies and procedures than have most other organizations, including the British Psychological Society. Whether this has been achieved despite the changes in the examination and assessment processes that have taken place in the last few years, or because of them, is difficult to determine, but nevertheless such achievements should be emulated. This chapter will address some of the issues facing educationalists with the view to making clear recommendations on a range of actions.

The role of the psychologist

In 1980 educational psychologists took some comfort from the knowledge that the Schools' Council for the Curriculum and Examinations issued a letter to all examination boards. This letter indicated that the British Medical Association (BMA), in consultation with examining boards, had stressed that the BMA 'was particularly anxious that both schools and examination boards should be made aware that the questions of "dyslexia" are the province of the educational psychologist and not that of the general practitioner'. This is ironical since in 1989 at a major international conference on dyslexia it became apparent that the diagnoses and treatment of dyslexia as a medical condition were still very much live issues. New evidence for this standpoint has been produced from autopsy studies (Masland, 1990). Educational psychologists should be questioning again whether 'dyslexia' is solely the province of psychologists. It may become necessary to involve doctors more frequently in the assessment of dyslexic pupils under the assessment arrangements introduced by the Education Reform Act 1988 for pupils with learning difficulties that affect their access to the National Curriculum.

Since 1980 all examination boards have cooperated to refine and agree a policy on arrangements for examining dyslexic candidates. This has come about partly because of the introduction of the General Certificate of Secondary Education (GCSE), which was introduced fully in 1988 to replace the old system of O-level GCEs (General Certification of Education), and the CSEs (Certificate of Secondary Education). The need for the boards to standardize their procedures and to ensure comparability across geographical areas extended to the procedures for examining handicapped candidates. The new procedures include, in almost all cases, the requirement for a report from a qualified psychologist to be submitted through the candidate's school.

Another major change since the publication of the previous report has been the full introduction on April 1983 of the Education Act 1981. This Act required that a pupil with a significantly greater difficulty in learning than the majority of pupils of his or her age should have a multidisciplinary assessment. Part of the assessment process required that a psychological report be provided giving 'advice' to the authority to enable special educational provision to be determined for the pupil. There has been some debate in the literature, mentioned in earlier chapters, as to whether specific learning difficulties require special provision according to the Education Act 1981. Examining boards currently do not require that a child with dyslexia should have been the subject of a multidisciplinary assessment, even though most other disabled students receiving concessions in examinations will have had a full assessment. These students will generally be so severely handicapped that they will be, or will have been, the subject of a statement of special educational provision.

Legal basis of specific learning difficulties (dyslexia)

The 1984 DECP Inquiry described the background to the legal basis of dyslexia up to the introduction of the Education Act 1981 and therefore the information is not repeated here (Cornwall, Hedderly and Pumfrey, 1984). The High Court judgements referred to in that publication are still relevant, although recent events have tended to clarify various situations rather than to change any fundamental understanding of them (Chasty and Friel, 1991).

The Education Act 1981 governs the conduct of assessments and, like every other Act, it is a law which cannot be switched on and off at will. Although many of us at times disobey the road traffic Acts (not the authors of course!), we all appreciate that when we are doing so we may be breaking the law and if found out we expect to suffer some sort of penalty. Failure to comply with the education Acts tends not to carry the same penalty and professionals tend to refer to statutory and non-statutory assessments as though we are able to differentiate clearly between the two situations. Even the DES Circular 22/89 issued in September 1989 refers to the two kinds of assessments although it is clear that the non-statutory version is the routine assessment by teachers of a child's progress in school rather than a multidisciplinary assessment. In law it is the local education authority that conducts the assessment under the Education Act 1981. It is wise for professionals to be cautious when carrying out their duties because, as employees of a local authority, they are almost inevitably undertaking an assessment as defined by the Education Act 1981 if the pupil comes within the definition outlined in Section 1 of the Act. Now that the Education Reform Act 1988 is in force the need to ensure that parents have been informed of the full purpose and procedure for an assessment becomes more important, particularly for dyslexic pupils who might have their curriculum modified or disapplied as an outcome of the assessment (GB.DES, 1989g).

Because the 1981 Act has been in force for several years there is some guidance in the form of case law. An early, interesting judgement was made by Mr Justice Taylor in 1985 in the case of *Regina v. Hampshire County Council ex parte J*. Mr Justice Taylor ruled that 'dyslexia' was clearly a disability and therefore the Education Act 1981 requirements applied. J had a learning difficulty which called for an assessment. When he had been assessed it was a requirement that the authority should ask themselves three questions. First of all does J have special educational needs? Secondly, if he does what provision does he require; and thirdly, is the authority able to make provision within their normal or special resources? Because J had a disability, the full multidisciplinary assessment was required. From such an assessment presumably the need for concessions in examinations would have been evident if they applied to his handicap. Any other provision that he needed would also be identified and recorded in a statement. The provision that he needed would also be identified and recorded in a statement. The provision would then subsequently be made and reviewed at least on an annual basis.

A further relevant judgement arose a year later from the *Hereford and Worcester County Council and Another ex parte Lashford* (1986). This judgement made it clear that under the Education Act 1981 there were two groups of children with special needs. The first small group consisted of children with special needs that called for the authority to determine the special provision and to make a statement. For the second group it was unnecessary for the authority to determine the special provision and therefore no statement was required. It was the second group who were the responsibility of the governors of an ordinary school who are charged in the 1981 Act to use 'their best endeavours' to meet the pupil's needs in the ordinary school. In both cases reported above, 'dyslexic' pupils were involved and a full multidisciplinary assessment was required by the Act before the authority could make a decision.

Although it is not relevant to the issue of examination boards, another judgement might well be considered here because of its general relevance. In the case of *Regina v. Secretary of State for Education and Science ex parte Davis*, held before Lord Justice Watkins and Mr Justice Auld in November 1988, it was ruled that: 'an authority had *no* duty to make special educational provision for a child for whom it was responsible before completing the procedure in Section 7 of the Act and making a final statement of the child's special educational need.' This is an important decision because parents have the duty to see that their child is educated according to his or her age, ability and aptitude and with regard to any special educational needs that he or she has. Many parents of dyslexic children 'jump the gun' and make independent provision. The ruling from this judgement ensures that the parents are responsible financially as well as in every other way for such a decision and placement if it is made before the outcome of the assessment. This of course is not an excuse for authorities to delay an assessment and the regulations attached to the Education Act 1981 and the Education Reform Act 1988 will ensure that there is a maximum time from the initiation of the assessment to the completion. At the moment it is suggested in DES Circular 22/89 that this period should be no more than six months. Most parents and many professionals would regard even this length of time as excessive in the short time between the ages of 5 and 16 that a child is in school.

Another High Court judgement, which might bring some consolation to those working in a local educational authority setting, came in July 1984 in the case of *Regina v. Surrey County Council ex parte H*. Here the judge said that: 'There was no question of Parliament having placed the local education authority under the obligation to provide a child with the best possible education. There is no duty on the authority to provide a Utopian system, or to educate him or her to his or her *maximum* potential.' The duty to educate the child rests with the parents. It is the local authority's duty to provide facilities and resources appropriate for the children in its area. This is done to enable parents to carry out their duty.

Many dyslexic children will not even be achieving at a level expected of the average for the peer group and they are often regarded as being educated at a level well below their 'true potential'. The assessment process under the 1981 Act is at least designed to improve this. In a more recent judgement in June 1988 in the case of *Regina v. the Inner London Education Authority ex parte F*, it is made clear that the priorities for an assessment are first to identify and meet the child's needs and secondly to consider the resources.

In summary then it transpires that dyslexia is now a legally recognized disability. The local education authority is required to assess all pupils with disabilities that might affect their educational needs in order to discover whether the authority is called upon to make special provision. Mr Justice Taylor's judgement reasoned that even if the authority made extensive provision for blind children, for example, an assessment was still necessary when the pupil had a known disability. The local education authority is also required to assess a child with *specific* learning difficulties which cause the pupil to have significantly greater difficulties than the majority of pupils of his or her age. The authority must also assess a pupil if there is a *prima facie* case that the pupil may have educational needs that require the authority, rather than the school, to determine any *special* provision. This situation could, of course, occur when there is no learning difficulty but some other psychological problem that requires 'special' provision. There is evidence from the DES that the number of appeals to the Secretary of State under sections 5 and 8 of the Education Act 1981 is increasing markedly (see Chapters 2 and 13 for details).

The Education Act 1981 requires that children with special educational needs are educated alongside others who do not have special needs. Resources can therefore only be used efficiently if they achieve this goal. Exceptions to this include the situation where the special education for the child with difficulties is incompatible with the efficient education of others, or where there is a parental request for separation from the majority. The fact that an authority has already resourced a special school should not come before the requirement to make integrated provision. The National Curriculum requirements apply to almost all pupils, regardless of their handicap. The assessment procedures will apply to children throughout their progress within the National Curriculum. Therefore the methods of assessment and concession for children with disabilities including dyslexia will become increasingly important issues in the next few years. These need to be addressed before an individual commences a GCSE course, and much earlier if possible.

Survey of examination boards

Background

In preparation for the introduction of the General Certificate for Secondary Education (GCSE) in 1987, as a replacement for the GCE and CSE examinations, the 22 examination boards were reorganized into six groups. These groups are based on geographical regions as follows:

LEAG	London East Anglian Group
MEG	Midlands Examining Group
NEA	Northern Examining Association
SEG	Southern Examining Group
NISEC	Northern Ireland Schools Examination Council
WJEC	Welsh Joint Education Committee

The secretary or assistant secretary for each and every one of the boards within each group was approached by letter with a request for information on their examining board's policy and practice for all handicapped or disabled candidates. In addition they were all asked about their arrangements for pupils with specific learning difficulties and for any statistical information that they had. All boards replied to the letter, although several wrote quite short replies. This usually occurred when they only referred to the common agreement in their region or to the statement made by the Joint Council for the GCSE and accepted by all examining groups. Relevant sections of this statement are reproduced in Appendix II. With the introduction of the National Curriculum, the guidance is particularly useful.

The boards were requested to give statistical information on the number of requests for concessions for candidates with specific learning difficulties. Many of the replies mentioned the difficulty of obtaining accurate information. The boards gave a number of reasons for this. One reason was that because the arrangements for handicapped candidates were usually delegated to the school or examination centre, exact details may not have been kept centrally. Some boards said that anyway this information was not kept for individual handicaps. Some mentioned the fact that because certificates were not endorsed it was not felt necessary to record the data. Nevertheless, some replies included statistical information.

The London East Anglian Board recorded that in 1988 they received 20,301 appeals for special concessions for GCSE candidates while for the GCE (advanced level and alternative ordinary level) they received 10,381 requests. The categories of handicap were not differentiated.

The Welsh Board recorded that in 1988 there were 1495 requests for special consideration at the GCSE stage. Of these 93 were for dyslexic candidates. Dyslexic candidates therefore represented 6.2 per cent of all handicapped pupils taking examinations in the Welsh Board's area.

In the last DECP survey we reported that the percentage of 'dyslexic' candidates at the O-level stage varied between 0.25 and 1.25 per cent and that at the CSE stage, from 0.25 to 1.5 per cent (Cornwall, Hedderly and Pumfrey, 1984). Now that the examination procedure has changed significantly with the introduction of the GCSE, it appears that it is slightly more difficult to obtain a 'true' estimate of incidence. Two of the examination boards indicated that they were intending to employ people to analyse their data for this kind of information when time permitted. They rightly pointed out that most of their efforts in the last two years had been geared to the successful introduction of the curriculum and assessment format of the GCSE, leaving little time for data analysis. Several of the boards' responses indicated that there was some evidence of an increase in the number of appeals for concessions for dyslexic candidates in recent years and at the GCSE level it was thought that the incidence of identified dyslexic candidates (including those identified as having a specific learning difficulty) was now from 0.25 per cent to as much as 2 per cent of the total number of candidates.

Perhaps the most comprehensive data were supplied by the Joint Matriculation Board (JMB). This is useful and interesting because this board also provided information for the previous report and therefore some comparisons may be made. The statistics and their background also reflect some of the historical changes in the examination of pupils at the end of their statutory secondary education.

Prior to 1985 the JMB made special awards to handicapped candidates at grade E only at A-level and at Grade C at O-level. From 1985 and for subsequent examinations the board's awarding committee agreed that special awards should be made where warranted at all grades. This change resulted in other procedural changes, one of which was that the board stopped the practice of differentiating for statistical purposes between special awards made to dyslexic candidates and those made to other handicapped candidates. In 1987 the board also stopped differentiating between appeals received on behalf of dyslexic candidates and other candidates. As explored later in this chapter, this procedure may have implications for professionals when considering the severity of a pupil's handicap.

There is an added problem that mitigates against the easy collection of statistical information by the JMB. This also occurred in a somewhat similar way in some other regions. The JMB and four northern CSE boards combined to constitute the Northern Examining Association (NEA), which is responsible for GCSE examinations in the northern area of England, although entries are still accepted from outside the area. Local examination centres submit appeals to the NEA board in their own area and the JMB also takes appeal entries from outside. The appeals are then dealt with for each examination subject by the NEA board responsible for the administration of that particular subject. This is often a different board from the local one to which the appeal was submitted. The JMB therefore is unable to supply for the GCSE years any data regarding the number of appeals received and the outcome for candidates with specific learning difficulties. Thus for these reasons the statistical information is less comprehensive for 1985 and subsequent years.

Tables 16.1 and 16.2 provide information for the years 1978 to 1988 for A-level (Table 16.1) and for O-level or since 1988 GCSE (Table 16.2).

It is difficult to analyse the data precisely but for A-level students there seems to be a gradual increase in the number of appeals received by the board. This may reflect the increase in the number of candidates. The proportion of dyslexic candidates in relation to the total number of candidates or to the total number of handicapped candidates seems to be rising. In 1978 only 1.85 per cent of handicapped candidates were classed as 'dyslexic', but by 1986 this percentage was 5.73 per cent. It also appears from anecdotal data that in 1988 the raw numbers of 'dyslexic' candidates are two to three times the number apparent in 1978.

The analysis of the O-level data also reveals a similar pattern. In 1978 only 4.3 per cent of handicapped candidates were dyslexic but by 1986, 8.4 per cent of the handicapped candidates were dyslexic. Again, the raw numbers seem to show a slow but gradual increasing trend. The change from the CSE to GCSE system may 'explain' some of the apparent increase.

Perhaps one can be more confident about the other trend emerging from these data: that in both the A-level stage and GCSE stage the number of successful appeals or grade improvements made for handicapped candidates has increased significantly. In the late 1970s only 10 per cent of candidates' appeals were successful to the extent that they received an award, but by the late 1980s the success rate increased to around 20 per cent. This trend was apparent before the change in the board's procedures and the same pattern has been observed in other regions according to anecdotal evidence from other boards. It is not clear, however, whether the dyslexic candidate benefits by this trend or not. One assistant secretary did suggest that the procedure where scripts are re-marked with a view to disregarding spelling errors was producing a change in grade more often in recent years than was the case ten years ago. Because the number of candidates involved is quite small, any interpretation must be made with caution but it does seem that dyslexic students are being identified more frequently today than they were in the late 1970s. The JMB statistics suggest that at A-level the percentage of the total of dyslexic candidates who were awarded a grade E on appeal increased from 2.22 per cent in 1978 to 16.13 per cent in 1982 and 14.28 per cent in 1983. In the following year (1984) no dyslexic candidates achieved an improved grade. At the O-level stage the percentage of 'dyslexic' candidates gaining improved grades remained throughout at between 3.5 and 4.5 per cent. This contrasts with the other handicapped students where between 16 and 18 per cent obtained a grade improvement in most years.

Policy of boards

As mentioned above the boards had accepted a general statement (see Appendix II). The principles that a board adopted were reported in the previous DECP working party report and essentially remain the same. These are that:

- all candidates should be given every opportunity to perform to the best of their ability;
- a handicapped candidate must not be placed at an advantage over other candidates of similar age, ability and aptitude in the subject;
- the users of a certificate (such as employers or higher education) should not be misled.

Table 16.1: JMB statistics on concessions for A-level (1978–88)

Year	'Dyslexic' candidates				Other candidates			
	Appeals received		Awards made		Appeals received		Awards made	
	Candidates	Subjects	Candidates	Subjects	Candidates	Subjects	Candidates	Subjects
1978	45	113	1	2	2426	—	191	200
1979	30	62	3	3	1754	—	176	188
1980	62	138	3	3	1847	—	177	187
1981	25	47	3	3	1527	—	171	180
1982	31	54	5	5	1918	—	213	220
1983	37	63	5	7	1925	—	244	248
1984	108	225	0	0	2290	—	248	260
1985	128	274	—	—	2865	4685	441	513
1986	133	226	—	—	2322	3508	474	555
1987	—	—	—	—	2774	4187	481	554
1988	96	192	—	—	2760	4141	543	627

—, Information not available.

Table 16.2: JMB statistics on concessions for O-Level (1978–87)

Year	'Dyslexic' candidates				Other candidates			
	Appeals received		Awards made		Appeals received		Awards made	
	Candidates	Subjects	Candidates	Subjects	Candidates	Subjects	Candidates	Subjects
1978	103	301	4	4	2359	—	375	403
1979	142	575	5	5	2557	—	357	401
1980	215	615	7	8	2697	—	388	422
1981	167	481	8	9	2928	—	351	377
1982	237	780	10	10	3296	—	492	520
1983	232	604	7	8	3524	—	580	620
1984	228	521	8	17	3467	—	568	601
1985	263	574	—	—	3852	6657	778	908
1986	243	459	—	—	2869	4742	606	773
1987	—	—	—	—	3014	4486	569	636

—, Information not available.

In a useful article that described some of the GCSE working party processes, it was reported that the examination boards were concerned to be able to compensate for whatever limitations were imposed upon a candidate by their disability (Cullen, 1988). This had to be achieved without giving the candidate an unfair advantage. The examination boards also stress in their joint notes of guidance that the examination groups wish to be as free as possible to tailor provisions to individual needs. The boards are willing to be flexible if approached with a sound case.

It should be appreciated that this is in order to give candidates a 'fair' advantage. In the first paragraph of general guidance to centres (2.1) there is a clear suggestion that the syllabuses of all the examining groups should be investigated because some schemes are more readily adapted than others. One headmaster of a special residential school has reported to the author of this chapter that this policy pays dividends, particularly for dyslexic candidates. He claimed that the amount of written work required from different boards for the course work and in the examination in the same subject varied by more that 100 per cent in some cases. This same headmaster also entered his dyslexic students for the GCSE English examination through the Welsh Board. Is this poetic licence, poetic justice or just good sense in view of his pupils' special needs? There seems to be little doubt that the syllabus from one area could suit pupils better than the syllabus from the local regional board and it is accepted as reasonable to consider the child's needs as well as the centre's needs when examination entries are being made. As this chapter was being written there were press reports of a study that isolated some differences between examination boards and regions, in the marking of scripts and in the ease with which pupils passed (*Huddersfield Examiner*, 25 October 1989, p. 1).

Perhaps the most important advice to centres is not to draw on previous experience or hearsay evidence. The boards want hard data. This should include the exact nature of the handicap and how the disability interferes with the assessment of the pupil's skills and knowledge. For dyslexic candidates exact data on reading levels and speed, writing levels and speed and incidence of spelling errors in a script, perhaps expressed as a percentage error rate, would seem to be appropriate. It is important to be aware that the scripts produced by dyslexic candidates can be readily compared with those produced by candidates who apparently have no specific difficulty. It would not be regarded as unusual in the GCSE scripts, for example, for there to be a spelling error rate of 5 per cent (that is, five words in every hundred contained a minor or major spelling error). Many so-called 'dyslexic' candidates produce a lower error rate and yet manage to obtain concessions. If the board also notice that the legibility and number of words written is quite within normal limits, the credibility gap starts to widen. The nature of the difficulty might limit the candidate's opportunity to demonstrate his or her skills to the best advantage but is this not an experience many others have had at examination times for quite different reasons?

Concessions available

All six regions issue a document on the procedure for requests for special provision and special consideration in the GCSE examinations. The statement accepted by all boards through the Joint Council for GCSE was included with the document or with the literature sent by the boards.

One important point for psychologists and teachers to notice and observe is that applications for candidates with a disability should be notified to the board as early as possible. All boards refuse to accept applications for concessions after the results have been published, although there is usually a provision for a check if the published result is bizarre in some way and a marking error is suspected. With many subjects the GCSE is based on course work and therefore the handicapped pupil should be made known to the board at the commencement of the course, which should have been chosen specifically as mentioned above. Examination boards also like to know the difficulties that a candidate has even if there is no concession available for that difficulty. As we will discuss further in this chapter, there is little credibility in the discovery of 'dyslexia' at A-level or degree level if no one noticed a significant handicap at an early stage. This is not to say that late detection does not happen. Many boards take the view that a grade A, B or C in the GCSE English examination is an indication of a certain level of fluency in English that would imply to an employer or to a higher education institution that the candidate has mastered that subject to a level which would allow him or her to use written English in pursuit of their chosen career or studies. Where A-level candidates have obtained good GCSE grades in English it is not thought possible for developmental dyslexia to appear this late. When considering older students, the student's performance in previous written examinations should be looked at carefully. Anecdotal evidence from examination boards still includes the stories of the pupils with grade A passes in English language and literature who are the subject of a request for concessions in science subjects, for example, because they cannot write or spell. In Table 16.1 it is evident that in only a few cases of appeal at A-level are grades subsequently improved. In 1984 none of the 108 candidates received a higher grade than that which was awarded normally. At least one interpretation of these results is that the pupil was able to demonstrate his or her ability in the examination satisfactorily.

The main concessions for dyslexic candidates were the same in each region. These fell into the following areas:

- Extra examination time for reading.
- Extra examination time for writing answers.
- Compensation for spelling errors. These are not generally penalized in examinations other than in language assessment. Most boards adopt a system of referring scripts of handicapped candidates to the senior examiners at their meeting for the award of grades. The senior examiners are asked to ensure that the candidates are not penalized for poor spelling, minor inaccuracies or for any other reason directly attributable to their handicap.
- Compensation for handwriting difficulties. The usual method of presenting work may be allowed if this is, for example, through the use of a typewriter, tape recorder, amanuensis or a word processor. There is still some variation between regions and boards with this and therefore a check must be made with the appropriate board. Some boards allow a 'translation' of an illegible written script provided it accompanies the original.
- Compensation for concentration/arousal difficulties. This usually applies to pupils with muscular atrophy or dystrophy who need regular, supervised breaks in the course of an examination.
- Oral examination.

All boards allow extra time for examinations. This is usually up to a maximum of 25 per cent of the total examination time. Extra time is not allowed in examinations where speed is a factor, for example in GCSE typewriting. It may not be appropriate to seek time concessions for pupils with specific reading and writing difficulties in subjects like cookery or art and design and they probably would not be allowed unless there was another reason for an extension. Concessions were not allowed to the same extent for English language and literature, for obvious reasons. Several boards, for example, specifically ruled out the possibility of a candidate having a paper read to him or her in GCSE English language and the modern and classic languages. At A-level the JMB, for example, does not approve a request for sighted students to have any paper read to them.

Course work is completed at school and sometimes at home as well and may be done more or less in the subject's own time scale. One of the major advantages of the GCSE for dyslexic pupils is that they are able to persevere with course work at their own level and to some extent the work produced reflects motivation as well as ability. Word processors and re-written or typed written final copies from a draft will be accepted in most subjects involving course work if this is the student's normal mode for presentation. This work is subject to a 'moderation' process that also takes account of the examination where applicable. Boards are aware of the criticism that some subjects are susceptible to parental involvement and each board obviously scrutinizes the candidate's work to ensure that it is that of the candidate. Guidelines for the use of word processors are included in Appendix II.

Most boards expect the school to submit an application on behalf of candidates with a specific learning difficulty within the 18-month period preceding the examination concerned. There is some ambiguity for the GCSE because the board's advice also asks schools to be aware of special needs prior to the commencement of the GCSE course, which is almost two years before the examination. The application for concessions must be accompanied by an educational psychologist's report.

Currently all examination boards do everything possible to avoid endorsing certificates to indicate that concessions have been made.

Concerns of psychologists

Although the examination boards have an agreed policy, the interpretation of this policy does vary. This concerns psychologists, teachers, and parents. The different interpretations make difficulties for schools when selecting the appropriate syllabus and board for pupils. One teacher, Roger Lewis, of the Harrow base for specific learning difficulties, argued for much more consistency across the GCSE Boards (Lewis, 1991). He suggested that the Joint Council for the GCSE should adopt one set of regulations that is fair and clearly set out and written in understandable English with a summary flow chart, guidelines and standardized application forms for concessions. He compared four examination boards (LEAG, SEG, MEG and NEA) and indicated that there were inconsistencies, particularly where an amanuensis or a reader was required. He reported, for example, that only the Southern Examining Board (SEG) stated that they required evidence that the concession that was being sought reflected the candidate's normal method of recording. In practice, for some of the more unusual requests for concessions, all boards would normally expect evidence that the mode of recording for the examination did reflect the candidate's normal situation. Some of the inconsistencies were probably more to do with the interpretation of each local board's requirements than an actual difference in the assessment process for each candidate. What is clearly required from the teacher's point of view is some clarity on each board's policy and the dissemination of the board's requirements. The boards no doubt will wish to place the responsibility for selecting the appropriate examination and concession on the teacher, but this can only be done if their policies are clear. Examples were provided by practising psychologists of differences in interpretation by different boards. Usually this related to the ease with which extra time was agreed to by some boards (usually it seems in the Midlands and the South), and the difficulty in obtaining the same concessions from other boards (usually in the north). Some boards were not prepared to allow 25 per cent extra time on top of a concession allowing questions to be read to the candidate.

The Joint Council was reported to have obtained advice from a professional psychologist that defined dyslexia or specific learning difficulty in terms of: 'a pupil with a *WISC-R* Intelligence Quotient of 110 or above and a reading age of 7 or below'. The controversy that this comment generated among the educational psychology profession was quite intense. There is, however a serious point here because examining boards are dealing with measurement and need hard, reliable criteria in order to apply concessions fairly. Whereas all members of the working party were most disconcerted to hear that such advice had allegedly emanated from a member of the profession, it was also thought that the profession needed to offer a viewpoint based on objective criteria. In the absence of criteria it is not appropriate to criticize. It has already been suggested that the profession should emulate the good practice of the boards and produce a common policy.

The need to move with the times was considered appropriate by several teachers and psychologists and in particular it was suggested that the use of the Dictaphone and word processor should be encouraged. Pupils should not only be taught at school to use these technological aids, but they also should be allowed to use them routinely in examinations. The emphasis on the 'pen and ink' method of recording seems unnecessarily limiting and particularly so for those with a specific difficulty. Fortunately, other outputs are increasingly accepted.

Another related concern was the lack of a clear definition of dyslexia or of specific learning difficulty. It was thought that this led to differential rates of identification. Again there is some evidence that dyslexia is centred on the southern commuter areas, along the motorway network and in the mainly 'white' spa towns of Bath and Harrogate, for example, and in the affluent areas around Birmingham. Many psychologists working in local authorities felt that it was too easy for people who could pay for a psychologist's report to be able to seek concessions in examinations when a local authority psychologist would not identify the problem as serious. The view that there really is no such thing as dyslexia and that any concession made in an assessment is giving an unfair advantage to the middle classes and financially well off is still widely held (Whittaker, 1982).

On the same theme, some psychologists pointed out that many pupils with specific learning difficulties obtain most of their marks in a graded examination paper at the beginning of a test. This also applies to the general population, but it is thought to apply particularly to children with sequential processing and attention deficit problems. Therefore recommending more time for an examination may not help the pupil (Ullman, Sleator and Sprague, 1984). Some argue that it at least relieves anxiety, but objective evidence for this is hard to find.

Concerns of examining boards

The examining boards, as has already been indicated, have collectively produced a policy and guidelines and are no doubt continuing to work towards a nation-wide approach. The establishment of an advisory body consisting of representatives of the profession teaching handicapped pupils was mentioned by several boards as a means whereby concerns arising from the assessment of handicapped students could be resolved. Concern was expressed by a number of boards over the variety of the reports received from educational psychologists in support of applications for concessions for handicapped pupils. It was felt by the boards that a more consistent method of presenting data on handicapped pupils by the reporting psychologist would be helpful and the highlighting of relevant objective data are essential. This point was also made by some psychologists and appears in a document produced by the West Midlands Principal Psychologists group. Examples of useful reporting styles were given as the style produced by the Dyslexia Institute, which recorded all test data at the beginning of the report with a summary of pupils' areas of difficulty plus a summary of positive skills. Also the report in the publication from ILEA on examination provision for pupils with SpLD was recommended as being helpful (Bostock, 1987).

One obvious concern of the boards was the discrepancy between the script produced by a dyslexic candidate and the expected problem. Many candidates managed to produce perfectly reasonable course work and examination papers with only a normal average rate of spelling errors and a normal number of total words written in the time available, as has already been mentioned. Some boards thought that this was due to normal maturation and understood that the specific problems could reduce. However, at this stage it was thought that there could be a credibility gap and that psychologists should be aware of the problem. This particularly applies to A-level students who have already achieved good O-level success and seek concessions for the first time. It is generally recognized that there is quite a difference between O-level and A-level and some students find it hard to adjust to the different intellectual demands required. The suggestion that they have a 'dyslexic' handicap is not always believed. One examinations officer wrote: 'I cannot escape the impression that a fair number of the requests we receive are made on behalf of marginal cases who were spotted more by chance than because of a serious disability while there may well be other candidates more seriously afflicted on whose behalf we receive no plea.'

Another board commented on the difference in referral rates between the state and private sector, the latter producing more than twice as many as the board would have expected, particularly in view of the statutory provision for severe difficulties.

A further comment referred to the range of the reading and spelling ages in reports. 'We receive applications for an increase of 25 per cent of extra time for a pupil with a reading and spelling age of thirteen plus at the same time as we receive applications for the same amount of extra time for pupils with spelling and reading ages around seven years.'

This was seen by the board as grossly unfair even when motor/writing problems were involved. The same board also indicated an awareness of parental pressures on teachers when parents are understandably fighting for the best provisions for their children. The board said that 'The best judge of the amount of extra time required should be the psychologist writing the report, but there seem to be very few who consider the relative needs of those whose dyslexia is far more severe than that of the subject of the report'. Normative considerations are important. At present, the essential data are not available.

The examining boards have experienced difficulty in dealing with the reports of educational psychologists. These vary between a single paragraph couched in vague terms to reports extending to several pages of detailed observations and data. In the former case it is difficult for the board to decide whether or not there is a problem requiring action. In the latter case there is often far more information than is needed for the purposes of deciding eligibility for concessions. The board may still have a problem determining how best to assess the pupil even when they can clearly appreciate that there is a problem. The solution most often put forward is for psychologists to have a common format for reporting. They should consider the guidelines produced by the Joint Council and the nature of the skill being assessed in the GCSE examination and course.

The issue of the qualifications of the psychologist has also caused concern. At the time of writing this chapter (1991) the Joint Council's Standing Agreement No. 4 indicates that the school should obtain a report from a psychologist recognized as competent by the British Psychological Society. The Association of Educational Psychologists believes that the report should be from a competent educational psychologist and that the pupil should have been observed in school over a period of time. In 1990 the BPS set up for the first time a Register of Chartered Psychologists and this is intended to provide greater safeguards for members of the public. The Register of Chartered Psychologists is now widely available in public libraries and therefore the BPS believes that examination boards should be more explicit in their advice to schools. It suggested that the wording of Section 24 of the Joint Council's statement should read:

> Where a candidate attends a LEA or grant maintained school or is funded at a non maintained provision by the LEA because of special educational need the report should normally be provided by the LEA Educational Psychologist. Where a candidate is educated privately the psychologist, who should not be a member of staff at the educational establishment concerned, should normally be a Chartered Educational Psychologist and or a Full or Affiliate member of The Association of Educational Psychologists. The Examining Group reserve the right to accept reports from other Chartered Psychologists in which case the Examining Group concerned should be consulted as to the acceptability of the report...

Clearly this requires that psychologists work towards consistent criteria. The need for agreement over definitions, measurement and even competence becomes very important. The changes in funding of schools and the availability of LEA psychologists for this work will also become an issue in some areas but at the very least teachers and examining boards will be able to check the Register of Chartered Psychologists. This is likely to be the first step towards improved consistency and the boards could produce their own local list from the register of 'approved' psychologists. This might not find favour in all quarters, particularly among those psychologists who believe that there should have been evidence of a learning difficulty that was sufficiently greater than that of the majority of pupils of the same age for an assessment under section 5 of the Education Act 1981 to be required. In these cases it could be argued that the assessment of concessions should almost always be done by an educational psychologist who has known the pupil over a considerable period.

Early in 1991, the issue of penalizing poor spellers was raised by the Secretary of State for Education. GCSE examination boards reacted strongly (SEAC, 1991).

Summary

This chapter has considered the assessment of dyslexic pupils by examining boards and has also given an overview of the legal basis for dyslexia and the role of educational psychologists. The examining boards have made considerable progress in determining methods of examination generally and in developing a common policy for considering requests for concessions. The discussion has indicated the need for their recommendations to be made better known to practising educational psychologists, although some recommendations may have implications for other agencies.

The data collected in the current survey are not conclusive or reliable but they suggest that referrals for concessions for dyslexic candidates are on the increase. It appears that more candidates are being identified at A-level even though the same candidates have achieved success in English at O-level. A further trend suggests that 'dyslexic' candidates either already obtain satisfactory results or that the application of concessions is less likely to result in an improved grade than is the case for other handicapped pupils. Nearly all other handicapped pupils receiving concessions will have been the subject of a full multidisciplinary assessment. Psychologists' reports 'referring' candidates for concessions are addressing a wide variation in ability and it is suggested that there is a need for the profession to take action to improve this situation.

There is now a legal requirement to assess pupils with specific learning difficulties if these are greater than the majority of pupils in the age range. 'Dyslexia' is also established as a disability coming within the meaning and jurisdiction of Section 1 of the Education Act 1981 and therefore if this is suspected, Section 5 of the same Act applies and a multidisciplinary assessment must be carried out to determine whether the authority should be called upon to make extra educational provision for the pupil. This assessment should be completed in less than six months. There will not necessarily be a statement of special provision at the end of it but, if examination concessions are required, then these should have been identified and recorded in the advice. Pupils with difficulties falling within the normal range, and which are not serious or which are not qualitatively different from the difficulties experienced by anxious introverts or poorly prepared candidates or poorly motivated candidates, for example, should not be the subject of educational psychologists' recommendations to examining boards.

A BPsS/DECP working party could attempt to make further recommendations to help to resolve some of these issues. Certainly one aspect of professional behaviour which should be considered relates to the Education Act 1981. Many 'dyslexic' children and children with specific learning difficulties are being dealt with by psychologists working with teachers in what is known as an 'informal' way. Many parents and schools are happy with this approach and indeed if the school is willing to use its 'best endeavours' (to quote the Act) to resolve the learning difficulty then there would seem to be no reason for the multidisciplinary assessment under Section 5 of the Act. It is also argued that educational psychologists are a scarce resource, and therefore if they are needed to help schools resolve an individual's learning problems then this in itself suggests that there is a *prima facie* case for an assessment. In legal circles 'best endeavours' is usually interpreted as just that. Governors (and therefore the teachers they employ) are called upon to do their best, as they would for all pupils, but they are not expected to do more than their best for isolated individual pupils. The education authority is expected to intervene with 'special provision' at this point. The Education Act 1981 changed the law to ensure that parents received written professional advice so that they can make better informed decisions about their child's educational needs. Many psychologists need to remember that it is the parent(s)' duty to ensure that their child is educated according to the child's age, ability and aptitude and it is frequently the parents of handicapped children who wish to obtain a fair and just appraisal of their child. Parents and the children themselves are the prime consumers of a local education authority psychological service and there must be no conspiracy among professionals to deny basic legal rights to children with disabilities or to take over parental responsibilities. The parents of a child with special educational needs have a right to the basic assessment advice and recommendations that professionals can provide.

Following this argument through suggests that several changes in current practice could be made that would help to clarify procedures for examination boards and for parents. The first is that no pupil should receive a recommendation for examination board concessions unless he or she has had a multidisciplinary assessment under Section 5 (or 7) of the Education Act 1981. From this it follows that no recommendation for concessions would be made unless the pupil had a disability or significantly greater difficulty in learning than the majority of children of his or her age. Many psychologists will argue with this approach but most of the arguments will centre around the need for more resources and the problems with the 'pupils who were not identified early'. The resource question will never be resolved if professionals conspire to shore up the system and ignore individuals' legal rights to information. Perhaps another radical approach would be to ask the examination boards to endorse the certificates of candidates who were not the subject of an Education Act 1981 assessment but nevertheless receive concessions. Most of the handicapped population then would still receive certificates that were not endorsed, but this would allow people with less obvious difficulties to receive concessions. It can be deduced from the statistical data that most of the group concerned could be advised that concessions would not usually help them and therefore the individual could then determine whether or not to go for an endorsed certificate. This approach might serve employers' and higher education establishments' needs better than the present system in which certificates are not endorsed.

There is little doubt that the candidates at issue are the students who have difficulty with the 'academic' recording of information. It would be possible if there were sufficient psychologists available to assess all dyslexic pupils in relation to each of the subjects of the National Curriculum over a period of time. This would be a more appropriate method for determining the exact nature of the problem and whether the problem differed for each subject area. The emphasis on the assessment teaching model adopted appropriately by many psychologists would then be maintained as an appropriate problem-solving strategy and this may even help students to the extent that they need no concessions. Certainly the need would be clarified in a way that 'one off' assessments cannot be (Reynolds and Hobbs, 1988). There is indeed a danger for some candidates that the extra time they are allowed may actually reduce their chances in an examination because of other psychological factors, such as lower anxiety, fatigue and poor answering strategy (such as spending too long on the favourite question). The ongoing assessment over a period of time can address more appropriately the problems students have in formal and other assessment situations.

A further approach might be to offer all candidates, regardless of any measured difficulty, the opportunity for some of the concessions such as extra time, although clearly more research would be needed to enable us to know whether this made any difference to grades made. Presumably, if extra time concessions were available to all candidates on request, some endorsement of certificates would be required to show that the candidate requested and was granted extra time.

It was argued by some psychologists in their evidence that educational psychologists will wish to take action on occasions in order to make a pupil or his or her parent feel less anxious about the examinations at GCSE. Even though parents and pupils are told that examination boards ignore spelling errors in subjects other than English, it has been suggested that pupils are relieved and more able to tackle the examination when they know that the board understands their difficulty. In conversation with some of the boards it seems that some chief examiners are content to accept this situation and even consider that some reports are already written in a form of 'code' that asks the board to consider the pupil's difficulties although it is in fact highly unlikely that anything other than a 'normal' GCSE result will follow. This strategy is also considered in the model report in the publication by Bostock (1987). The examining board is only called upon to 'understand' the problem. The examining boards emphasized that all handicapped pupils did receive equal and fair treatment from their system. However it is difficult to ensure that the psychological profession would be able to be fair to all the thousands of examination candidates who feel the need to be understood unless an approach such as that outlined above was developed.

Another change in professional practice suggested by the consideration of this issue is that psychologists' reports should confine themselves at this stage to relevant 'hard' data, such as reading speed levels and writing speed levels, with clear statements on the pupil's usual mode of recording knowledge and skills. Data could be presented in a clear manner that makes it possible for another psychologist to replicate the observations and determine their reliability and validity. Therefore actual measures or test scores should be quoted. The data should take into account that the examining board will also be collecting a considerable amount of material on the pupil. Care should be taken to ensure that the subject matter assessed by the examining board is considered by the psychologist to avoid situations where examining boards are at a loss to understand how the handicap affected the pupil's GCSE or A-level examination. The criterion for disability in connection with an assessment should be determined somehow by the profession. Is it one standard deviation from the norm, say, in terms of writing speed or should it be the score obtained by someone in the bottom 20 per cent on the particular measure? Some of these questions cannot be resolved here but some firm recommendations follow.

Recommendations

16.1. As part of the LEA's statutory responsibilities, teachers and educational psychologists continue to assess and review progress throughout the whole curriculum of children with specific learning difficulties.

16.2. Educational psychologists identify, develop and recommend to schools and examination boards appropriate methods for the assessment of pupils with specific learning difficulties.

16.3. Professionals develop operational definitions of terms such as dyslexia and specific learning difficulties so that communication with examining boards, parents, schools and other organizations is improved.

16.4. Criteria for concessions be presented in a manner that makes it possible to replicate the observations and determine their validities and reliabilities.

16.5. Professionals consider concessions only for pupils who have been or *who would have been* the subject of a multidisciplinary assessment under the Education Act 1981 based on data collated over a period of time before the concessions are required.

16.6. Examination boards, educational psychologists and subject specialists develop agreed schemata for reports based on the published principles of the examination boards.

16.7. A working party of chartered educational psychologists, under the aegis of the British Psychological Society, be set up to consider and make further recommendations with regard to the professional practice issues relating to assessments within the National Curriculum and by external examination boards (for handicapped pupils).

Key Themes and Recommendations

The relationship between theory and practice is analogous to that between Siamese twins. This book aims to inform practitioners and interested lay readers about both. It focuses on the challenges presented, and responses made, in many different areas of research and practice to the conceptualization, identification and alleviation of specific learning difficulties. Its purpose is to stimulate discussion and action in all these areas.

Professionals will draw on a range of experience and specialisms in applied psychology, education, medicine and administration. Lay readers will include members of many voluntary organizations and individuals who are concerned with the issues addressed.

We appreciate that a book such as this has to balance breadth and depth of coverage, bearing in mind its intended readership. The decision to include an extensive bibliography was taken so that readers can follow up in detail any points discussed.

The first section of the book outlined issues to be addressed in subsequent sections. Looking back, we note those themes that have appeared most frequently throughout the chapters.

Financial considerations

It has been difficult to separate that which belongs to psychology, education or medicine from that which relates to politics, finance and administration. Chapter 1 has introduced this dilemma through a discussion of definitions and incidence in relation to funding. In Chapter 2 the issue of 'potential' versus 'performance' has illustrated how values and priorities determine which children receive what share from the limited public purse. Chapter 4 has developed the theme through a consideration of social and emotional factors, particularly in relation to equality of opportunities. The costing of support services has received attention in Chapter 8 through detailed examples. Finally, survey responses have included comments illustrating the administrative frustrations of those whose fundamental concern is for the best interests of the individual (Chapters 13 and 14).

Legal implications

The effects of legislation can be similarly traced through the chapters of the book. It has been claimed that imprecise definitions of special educational needs, and the subset of specific learning difficulties, have resulted in exhortations for operational definitions or '*prima facie* cases' to determine where cut-off lines might be drawn. This has been well illustrated in Chapter 16 concerned with examination board policies and practices. As has been argued in Chapters 1 and 4, research into learning difficulties might be trivialized through either mindless empiricism, the over-inclusiveness of legally determined categories as has happened in the USA or, alternatively, the lack of categories evident in Britain. Several chapters have referred to the increase in the number of appeals to the

Secretary of State during 1989 and the precedents set by litigation, possibly indicating an increasing trend towards courts deciding issues which remain controversial to practitioners (Chapter 1, 13 and 16).

Nature versus nurture

Some have regarded specific learning difficulties as caused by relatively minor cognitive problems exacerbated through lack of appropriate opportunities to learn. Others have assumed, in contrast, that the difficulties mirror cognitive impairments that can only be alleviated or circumvented but not overcome or 'cured'. These viewpoints reflect different conceptions of the relative roles played by 'nature' and 'nurture' at particular stages of development.

In discussing the manuscript and the recommendations arising from the various chapters, members of the DECP working group found that they themselves held differing assumptions about the nature and severity of the difficulties under consideration. Those emphasizing the educational context, as in Chapter 3, were thinking of children who had not easily acquired the skills of print recognition and reproduction and needed more carefully planned opportunities for so doing. Conversely, those focusing on constitutional factors, for example in Chapter 9, had in mind a smaller proportion of pupils likely to struggle with a lifelong disability. The recognition of our own differing concept became important in deriving a consensus in terms of the recommendations made.

In practice, specific learning difficulties can be regarded along a continuum, ranging from mild to severe. Those at the 'mild' end would eventually become labelled 'severe' if they lacked adequate opportunities to make progress. In other words, marked and persistent problems with basic literacy, and other associated competencies, would best be identified in relation to the quality and quantity of intervention received and response to it.

Educational history

An emphasis on a pupil's educational history as a focus for identification has run through many of the chapters. The theory and research in the psychological and psychoeducational sections has been illustrated in the practices described by LEAs and educational psychologists and in the requirements of examination boards. That emphasis differs from the exclusion criterion defined by the phrase 'despite conventional instruction' introduced by the World Federation of Neurology in 1968 (Chapter 1). Recognition is given to the importance of investigating what 'conventional instruction' entails.

The notion of discrepancy

When examining constitutional factors, consideration has been given to qualitatively distinct but varied patterns of individual functioning. The heterogeneity of the population of pupils with specific learning difficulties has been recognized. The evenness or unevenness of achievement has been a central aspect in the identification of specific learning difficulties (Chapters 6 and 14).

For psychologists, the notion of various discrepancies between attainments has been frequently, but not necessarily, related to cognitive test results. Alternative conceptions have focused on particular aspects of learning, for example on the discrepancies between well developed use of context and poorly developed recognition of print in the acquisition of literacy.

'Top-down' or 'bottom-up'

Inevitably reference to particular methods of intervention has remained general. Whilst Chapters 2 and 3 have discussed the continued tensions between 'top-down' and 'bottom-up' approaches, Chapter 7 has considered teaching methods in more detail. Throughout there has been frequent mention of the interdependent nature of assessment and intervention.

A cognitive rationale for the cumulative and repetitive practice of aspects relating to phonology has been provided in Chapter 5 and has largely been endorsed by educational psychologists in Chapter 14. Nevertheless, Chapters 3 and 4 have stressed the broader context of language learning and the crucial part played by emotional factors. Finally, the psychomedical section has pointed to future possibilities, rather than currently proven educational interventions.

Recommendations

Most chapters have concluded with a set of recommendations agreed by members of the working group. These were intended to present a consensus of opinion derived after discussion of the chapter in question. It was felt that the recommendations would only make sense to others if they had also first read the chapters. A full list has therefore not been reproduced out of context.

We have nevertheless selected a few 'key' recommendations from each chapter in order to illustrate the general flavour of opinion within the working group. These recommendations might be regarded as reflecting current trends of good practice and provide a fitting end for the book.

1.3. All professionals encourage cooperation between statutory and voluntary organizations concerned with any pupil currently identified as experiencing specific learning difficulties.

1.6. In cooperation with schools, psychological services build up epidemiological data on the nature, extent and responses to interventions of children experiencing specific learning difficulties.

2.2. All of the many interested parties contribute towards a wider public appreciation of the complexities and costs involved.

3.2. Practitioners ensure that their knowledge base remains sufficiently broad to avoid over-ready focus on limited aspects of literacy acquisition.

3.5. Specific learning difficulties must not become defined in terms of sociocultural background.

4.1. Specific learning difficulties be examined in the context of personal experiences and interpersonal relationships, recognizing the emotional impact of a prolonged struggle with literacy.

4.2. Educationalists be mindful of the pitfalls that allow labels limited to within-child variables to detract attention from instructional conditions, organizational aspects and general policies.

5.1. Teachers and other adults engaged in pre-school work place an increasing emphasis upon oral activities, emphasizing rhyme, rhythm and repetition in playful speech with all children.

5.3. Further techniques be developed to assist with cognitive and linguistic weaknesses of children with specific learning difficulties, involving educational psychologists, teachers and speech therapists.

6.1. Given the present state of knowledge, dogmatic assertions concerning either the conceptual basis or the incidence of specific learning difficulties be treated with caution.

6.2. It be recognized that cut-off points with regard to additional provision remain to a large extent administrative and financial decisions dependent on political will.

6.3. Identification procedures and operational definitions include consideration of the child's previous learning history and present development.

7.1. The symbiotic relationship between assessment and teaching be appreciated by all professionals involved with pupils identified as having SpLD.

7.6. The communalities between all pupils learning to read and the distinctive characteristics of those with SpLD be explicated and their instructional implications both considered and investigated.

8.3. Suggestions for differentiation made in the National Curriculum guidelines be evaluated and developed.

8.7. Pupils' views about the nature and quality of the support they receive or consider desirable, be sought.

9.2. Practitioners ensure that their assessments of children with specific learning difficulties be undertaken with an awareness of possible neuropsychological factors and be based on a comprehensive view of literacy skills.

10.3. Awareness of research on the role of visual factors in the diagnosis and treatment of specific learning difficulties and advice to clients on the significance or otherwise of such findings be developed.

11.1. Those evaluating the efficacy of psychopharmacological treatment of specific learning difficulties have a thorough technical appreciation of research design and methodology.

13.1. LEAs have an explicit policy on pupils with specific learning difficulties to be either particular to these difficulties or set in the context of a policy for learning difficulties in general.

14.4. Educational psychologists evaluate the efficacy of the interventions they recommend and disseminate findings.

14.6. Work in this controversial and multidisciplinary area be considered an essential aspect of initial and continuing professional development for educational psychologists.

15.1. The term specific learning difficulties be used and seen as part of a continuum of special educational needs whilst acknowledging that the term dyslexia has a considerable currency.

16.6. Examination boards, educational psychologists and subject specialists develop agreed schemata for reports based on the published principles of the examination boards.

Appendix I

Submission Received from the Department of Education and Science (May 1989)

A National Enquiry 1989: Specific Learning Difficulties
Dyslexia – Challenges, Responses and Recommendations

Thank you for your letter of 30 January, requesting the Department's views on specific learning difficulties or dyslexia. Please accept my apologies for the long delay in replying.

You sought a statement of five particular areas and I shall respond to these in turn.

1. The concept of specific learning difficulties (dyslexia)

Over the years there has been considerable disagreement about the existence of dyslexia as a special condition or syndrome. DES takes the view that under the Education Act 1981, the precise name used to describe a child's learning difficulties is not important. That Act deliberately tries to avoid the concept of labelling children and concentrates instead on identifying each child's individual needs and ensuring that those needs are met. In doing so the procedures aim to focus on the child himself, rather than on the disability since progress depends not only on the nature and severity of the difficulty, but on his personal resources and attributes, as well as the help and support he receives both at home and at school.

The issue of dyslexia has been considered by a number of eminent committees who have advised successive Secretaries of State. In the light of their reports, the Department takes the line that there are some children of at least average ability who experience such difficulties in one or more of reading, writing, spelling and mathematics and that those children require special arrangements, normally in the form of good remedial teaching in ordinary schools. None of the reports has recommended the adoption of the term 'dyslexia'. The existence of specific learning difficulties is nevertheless recognised by this Department as a specific problem.

2 and 3. Identification and assessment/prevention

Under the 1981 Education Act, local education authorities have a responsibility to secure the provision of education for children with specific learning difficulties, just as they have to make provision for the needs of all other children with special educational needs in their area. It is the responsibility of each LEA to decide on the kind of provision to be made in individual cases, but the majority of Authorities have taken account of the advice offered by the committees referred to above and to offer remedial help in schools. Where this provision is made by support on an in-school or a peripatetic basis, any disruption to the child's normal programme is minimised. Early identification of a child's special educational needs is vital in ensuring that those needs can be effectively met.

4 and 5. Teaching methods and provision of resources

The Secretary of State's criteria for initial teacher training courses require that students should be prepared through their subject method work and educational studies to teach the full range for pupils whom they are likely to encounter in an ordinary school, across the diversity of disability, behaviour, social background and ethnic and cultural origin. Students should be introduced to ways of identifying children with special educational needs, helped to appreciate what the ordinary school can and cannot do for such children and given some knowledge of the specialist help available and how it can be enlisted.

Training for teachers of children with special educational needs in ordinary schools was one of the priority areas of in-service training support under the Department's grant scheme. Under the LEATGS, local education authorities are able to support courses of their own choosing to meet local needs. These courses attract 50% central Government funding. The Royal Society of Arts has validated a one-year part-time Diploma for teachers of pupils with specific learning difficulties.

The Warnock Report (May 1978) identified a number of areas where further research was considered necessary. Among these was the assessment and education of children with specific learning difficulties in reading, writing and spelling, and the evaluation of different approaches. The Department subsequently funded a programme of four main research projects or proposals: brief details are given in the attached Appendix. The results of these four projects were the subject of a seminar organised by the Department in May 1984.*

I hope this text is suitable for your purposes.

Your sincerely

MRS G. W. DISHART
Schools 2 Branch

---

* Appendix not included. The full report has been published (GB.DES, 1984b).

Appendix II

Extract from 'GCSE: Arrangements for Candidates with a Disability' (Statement made by the Joint Council for GCSE in 1987)

Notes for the guidance of those responsible for examination candidates and entries

Introduction

1.1 The Boards responsible for the GCE O level and CSE examinations, which are being replaced by GCSE examinations, have always been willing to make arrangements to enable candidates placed at a disadvantage by circumstances outside their control to provide evidence on which a grade appropriate to their attainment in the subject can be awarded. It was recognised, however, that differing approaches to the same problems were confusing to centres, candidates, parents and associations working on behalf of candidates with disabilities. For some years, the GCE Boards collectively and the CSE Boards collectively took steps designed to eliminate anomalies while retaining flexibility. The introduction of GCSE has been a catalyst for renewed attempts at appropriate standardisation of provision in the interests of the candidates

1.2. Examining Groups represented on the Joint Council for GCSE have agreed a framework within which all Examining Groups are making provision for each candidate according to need. The Northern Examining Association has provided more detailed guidelines for the use of centres.

The purpose of sections 1–4 of this document is to set in context the agreed framework (known to Examining Groups as Standing Agreement No. 4). It is recognised that both Standing Agreement No. 4 and these notes of guidance may seem very brief to those who work with students with disabilities and who know the complexity and variety of handicaps and the many aspects which have to be considered when making appropriate examination provision.

There are at least as many different solutions as there are different candidates and Examining Groups wish to be as free as possible to tailor provision to individual needs. The encyclopaedic volume of solutions, if it were ever deemed desirable, would best be built on GCSE case-law rather than on GCE and CSE case-law. The disadvantage of briefer notes is that they may not completely eliminate variations of interpretation but it is expected that this will be more than

offset by the establishment of an Advisory Committee composed of representatives of the Examining Groups and representatives of those with experience
of teaching handicapped students.

General guidance to centres about procedures for obtaining special arrangements with any examining group

A centre which is entering a candidate with any form of handicap which could
make it more difficult for a candidate to be awarded a grade appropriate to the attainment in the subject should follow the advice below.*

2.1. Remember to investigate all the syllabuses of all the Examining Groups.
Some schemes of examination are more readily adapted than others.
2.2. Write early to the Examining Group(s) (see section 4.5) but ensure that there
is awareness by all concerned that the condition of a candidate may change (better or worse) between the initial enquiry and the actual examination.
2.3. Do not draw conclusions based on previous experience nor on hearsay. (See
section 3.5.)
2.4. Give the Examining Group a clear statement of
(a)   the exact syllabus and the papers or sections (where there are options)
         for which the candidate is to be entered,
(b)   the year of the examination and whether the request refers to the
         Summer or to the Winter series,
(c)   the nature of the disability or disabilities,
(d)   a succinct statement of which aspects of the assessment are affected
         by the disability and how they are affected,
(e)   the means by which the candidate normally studies and communi-
         cates and, therefore, what provisions seem appropriate to the needs
         of the candidate,
(f)   what medical or psychological reports are available or could be pro-
         vided if they were required. (Remember also to alert in good time
         any people who may be asked to provide reports.)
2.5. Inform the Examining Group immediately if the provisions made by the
Group in response to the initial request of the centre appear inadequate, so that
further investigation/consultation is initiated.
2.6. Report to the Examining Group immediately after the examinations have
been taken if the arrangements were not satisfactory in practice and suggest why
this may have been so. If there is no report, it will be assumed that the arrangements were satisfactory.
2.7. Remember that the Examining Groups are seeking to ensure that the certificates awarded to all candidates retain public credibility by means of special provisions which support, rather than inhibit, handicapped candidates, and that this
can only be achieved by mutual recognition, on the part of the Examining Group
and centres, of constraints and by a mutually sympathetic and imaginative
approach to solutions to problems.

* Note: Centres which have regularly entered a number of severely handicapped candidates for the
examinations of particular Boards or Groups will have established a method of working which is satisfactory to all concerned, and the above guidance should not be interpreted as a need to change
mutually acceptable practices.

2.8. Remember that the Examining Group should be contacted in writing for each series in each year that a candidate is entered for one or more subjects, but reference can be made to earlier correspondence to avoid lengthy repetition of information.

3. Principles on which Examining Groups will base special arrangements

3.1. The purpose of the special arrangements is to compensate for the limitations imposed by handicaps but not otherwise to advantage the student.

3.2. The examination must be a fair test of the handicapped candidate's attainment in terms of the particular syllabus.

3.3. To the greatest extent possible, Examining Groups will make arrangements which will enable the handicapped candidate to demonstrate that an assessment objective has been met. Examining Groups and centres will do everything possible to avoid the necessity of endorsing the certificate while this remains part of the National Criteria. Where exemptions from the National Criteria are permitted (e.g. that relating to Spoken English) centres may, nevertheless, discuss with Examining Groups ways of enabling candidates who wish to do so to meet the National Criteria.

3.4. The Examining Groups will try to avoid unnecessary documentation (such as a medical certificate for a candidate who the Head of a centre confirms was in hospital and unfit to take the examination) but they must be able to meet their responsibility for ensuring that their willingness to make special arrangements is not abused.

3.5. It is the responsibility of the centre to inform the Examining Group in good time of the possible need for special arrangements. For some cases, contact with the Examining Group may be best made before a final decision is made to take the course; for others, contact during the first year of the course is desirable; for many, contact is most helpful at the beginning of the term before that in which the examination is to be taken. Common sense, and a willingness of centres to enquire of the Examining Group about particular students, will better help the handicapped candidate than specific 'rules' (which would never cover every eventuality). The emphasis on assessment during the course for GCSE, however, means that contact should generally be made earlier than was necessary for GCE O level or CSE.

4.5. For candidates with learning dysfunction

(Including specific learning difficulties/dyslexia, neurological dysfunction/minimal brain damage.)

(a) General

Attention is particularly drawn to the notes 2.1 (in relation to choice of syllabus) and 2.4(d) and (e). It is important to indicate which aspects of the GCSE assessment are likely to be affected by the individual candidate's specific learning difficulty, e.g. reading (accuracy, speed), spelling, written presentation (legibility, speed, fluency). The means by which the candidate normally studies (e.g. use of tapes to take in information or to present answers, use of typewriter, etc.) should be clearly described.

(b) Presentation and interpretation of examination materials

If reading the questions is likely to be a significant and major problem, a full description of the candidate's reading level (as measured by a named test with the date of administration given) should be provided, including, if relevant, information regarding speed of reading. The Examining Group should be informed whether there is a deficiency in reading ability such that misinterpretation of a question is likely.

(c) Time allowances

If speed of reading or writing is a specific difficulty, try to establish the candidate's average speed and send your conclusions to the Examining Group to support the recommendation. It may be helpful to test writing speed under timed pressure as well as in a non-pressurised situation.

In considering the value of extra time allowances, it should be borne in mind that some candidates, if having concentration and attention difficulties, would not necessarily gain.

(d) Presentation of answers

i   *Spelling* – Factors which should be noted in preparing brief notes for Examination Groups to consider are spelling age (naming the test and giving the date of administration), the extent to which spelling errors lead to completely unrecognisable words, and the effect of pressure on spelling. Spelling errors, provided the words are recognisable, are not generally penalised in examinations other than language papers.

ii   *Legibility* – The usual method of presenting work used by the candidates should be indicated, e.g. typewriter, tape, amanuensis. It is not anticipated that these would be the normal mode of presentation for any but candidates with extremely severe problems in co-ordination and medical evidence regarding co-ordination problems would generally be expected in these few cases.

iii   Where candidates have a problem with written work, including speed and fluency, it is particularly important that candidates are taught at school to show appropriate brief essay plans, perhaps showing key words, and use note form competently. This may involve little penalty except in subjects where ability to produce prose is an essential part of the assessment, e.g. some parts of English, Welsh, modern foreign language and classical language papers.

(e) Oral examinations

Where these are part of the assessment, pupils with specific learning difficulties are unlikely to be disadvantaged and their performance in this part of the assessment can be usefully compared with written tasks. For candidates who are not able to communicate by means of vocalised speech, investigate the use of other forms of communication. (See 4.2(c).)

(f) Practical examinations

Some pupils with neurological dysfunction have particular problems of organisation and clumsiness. In the latter case, factors affecting the safety of the candidate and other candidates need to be borne in mind.

Conditions for the use of word processors in the written components of GCSE examinations

1.   The provision for the use of a word processor* is restricted to candidates with a handicap which prevents them from writing in the normal way. This should be taken to include those with specific learning difficulties. Applications should be supported by medical/psychological evidence where appropriate.

2.   The use of a word processor should be seen as an alternative to handwriting and should afford the user no advantage over other candidates except the facility to type, check and amend material before producing hard copy.

3.   Candidates should not have access to material stored in memory other than an appropriate word processing program. The retrieval of data or information during an examination should be regarded as an infringement. Similarly, candidates should not have access to special facilities which would give them an unfair advantage over others (e.g. there should be no access to spell checks in any examination where the use of dictionaries is prohibited or access to calculation facilities where the use of an electronic calculator is prohibited).

4.   The examinations of candidates using word processors should be conducted separately from those of the other candidates, but subject to the same regulations.

5.   Additional time should be allocated on the same basis as agreed for handicapped candidates generally. Printing out should be accommodated within the time allowed for each candidate.

6.   Special consideration should not be given to candidates because of problems arising from errors made by them in operating the machine or from machine faults. It is the responsibility of centres/candidates to ensure that the user is proficient and that the machine is functioning correctly at the time of the examination (this is similar to the Group's regulation on the use of calculators).

7.   Manufacturer's operating manuals must not be made available to candidates during the examinations.

8.   Word processors must be used by candidates only and not by an amanuensis on their behalf.

9.   It is the responsibility of centres to ensure that all the above conditions are met.

---

* For the purposes of this document a word processor is a free-standing, dedicated word processor or a micro-computer with a word processing facility.

References

ABRAMS, F. (1991). 'The vitamin case's deficiency', *Times Educational Supplement*, 3897, 8 March, p. 6.

ABRAMSON, L.Y., SELIGMAN, M.E.P. and TEASDALE, J.D. (1978). 'Learned helplessness in humans: a critique and reformulation', *Journal of Abnormal Psychology*, 87, 47–74.

ACKERMAN, D. and HOWES, C. (1986). 'Sociometric status and after-school activity of children with learning disabilities', *Journal of Learning Disabilities*, 2, 416–19.

ADAMS, R. (1969). 'Dyslexia: a discussion of its definition', *Journal of Learning Disabilities*, 2, 616–68.

ADELMAN, H.S. (1989). 'Beyond the learning mystique: an interactional perspective on learning disabilities', *Journal of Learning Disabilities*, 22, 5, 301–4.

ADULT LITERACY AND BASIC SKILLS UNIT (1988). *After the Act: Developing Basic Skills Work in the 1990s*. London: Adult Literacy and Basic Skills Unit.

AINSCOW, M. (Ed.) (1989). *Special Education in Change*. London: Fulton in association with the Cambridge Institute of Education.

AINSCOW, M. and MUNCEY, J. (1984a). 'Learning difficulties in the primary school: an in-service training initiative', *Remedial Education*, 18, 3, 116–24.

AINSCOW, M. and MUNCEY, J. (1984b). *Special Needs Action Programme (SNAP)*. Swansea: Drake Educational Associates.

AINSCOW, M. and TWEDDLE, D. (1979). *Preventing Classroom Failure: An Objectives Approach*. Chichester: Wiley and Sons.

AKERMAN, T., GUNELT, D., KENWARD, P., LEADBETTER, P., MASON, L., MATTHEWS, C. and WINTERINGHAM, D. (1983). *DATAPAC: an Interim Report*. Department of Educational Psychology, University of Birmingham.

AMERICAN PSYCHOLOGICAL ASSOCIATION (1985). *Standards for Educational and Psychological Tests*. Washington, DC: APA.

ANDREWS, N. and SHARE, J.E.H. (1986). 'The efficacy of teaching dyslexics', *Child Care, Health and Development*, 12, 1, 53–62.

ARKELL, H. (n.d.). *On Being Dyslexic*. A publication available from the Helen Arkell Dyslexia Centre.

ARKELL, H. (1970). 'The Edith Norris Letter Case'. In: FRANKLIN, A.W. and NAIDOO, S. (Eds) *The Assessment and Teaching of Dyslexic Children*. London: ICAA.

ARNOLD, H. (1984). *Making Sense of It*. Sevenoaks: Hodder and Stoughton Educational.

ASSESSMENT OF PERFORMANCE UNIT (1988). *Language Performance in Schools*. London: ICAA.

ASSOCIATION FOR CHILDREN WITH LEARNING DISABILITIES (1986). 'ACLD description: specific learning disabilities', *ACLD Newsbriefs*, 160.

ATKINSON, E.J., GAINS, C.W. and EDWARDS, R. (1991). *The A–Z List of Reading Books* (6th edn). Stafford: National Association for Remedial Education.

AUBREY, C., EAVES, J., HICKS, C. and NEWTON, M. (1982). *Aston Portfolio Assessment Checklist*. Cambridge: Learning Development Aids.

AUGUR, J. (1986). 'The concept of dyslexia, specific policies, strategies and techniques for its remediation and their more general application in the ordinary classroom', *Early Child Development and Care*, 23, 4, 215–61.

AUGUR, J. and BRIGGS, S. (Eds) (1991). *The Hickey Multi-sensory Language Course*. London: Whurr.

AXLINE, V.M. (1964). *Dibbs: In Search of Self*. London: Gollancz.

BABCOCK, D.S. and HAN, B.K. (1982). 'Ultrasonography of the head'. In: McLAURIN, J. (Ed.) *Paediatric Neurosurgery*. Orlando, FL: Grune and Stratton.

BADDELEY, A.D. (1979). 'Working memory and reading'. In: KOHLERS, P., WROLSTAD, M. and BOUNA, H. (Eds) *Processing of Visible Language*. New York: Plenum.

BADDELEY, A.D., ELLIS, N.C., MILES, T.R. and LEWIS, V.J. (1982). Developmental and acquired dyslexia: a comparison', *Cognition*, 11, 185–99.

BADDELEY, A.D., THOMPSON, N. and BUCHANAN, M. (1975). 'Word length and the structure of short-term memory', *Journal of Verbal Learning and Verbal Behaviour*, 14, 75–89.

BAKER, L. (1985). 'Working memory and comprehension: a replication', *Bulletin of the Psychonomic Society*, 23, 28–30.

BAKER, L. and BROWN, A.L. (1984). 'Metacognitive skills and reading'. In: PEARSON, P.D. (Ed.) *Handbook of Reading Research*. New York: Longman.

BAKKER, D.J. (1972). *Temporal Order in Disturbed Reading*. Rotterdam: University Press.

BAKKER, D.J. (1984a). 'Hemispheric differences and reading strategies: two dyslexias?', *Bulletin of Orton Society*, 29, 84–100.

BAKKER, D.J. (1984b). 'The brain as dependent variable', *Journal of Clinical Neuropsychology*, 6, 1, 1–16.

BAKKER, D.J. (1990a). 'Neuropsychological treatments of dyslexia'. In: HALES, G., with HALES, M., MILES, T. and SUMMERFIELD, A. (Eds) *Meeting Points in Dyslexia: Proceedings of the First International Conference of the British Dyslexia Association*. Reading: British Dyslexia Association.

BAKKER, D.J. (1990b). *Neuropsychological Treatments of Dyslexia*. Oxford: Oxford University Press.

BAKKER, D.J., BOUMA, A. and GARDIEN, C.J. (1990). 'Hemisphere-specific treatment of dyslexia subtypes: a field experiment', *Journal of Learning Disabilities*, 23, 7, 433–8.

BAKKER, D.J. and SATZ, P. (Eds) (1970). *Specific Reading Disability*. Rotterdam: Rotterdam University Press.

BALD, J. (1990). 'Lenses pass the eye test'. *Times Educational Supplement*, 5 November, p. 10.

BALDWIN, G. (1968). *Patterns of Sound*. London: Chartwell Press.

BANDURA, A. (1977). *Social Learning Theory*. Englewood Cliffs, NJ: Prentice-Hall.

BANNATYNE, A. (1967). 'The colour phonics system'. In: MONEY, J. (Ed.) *The Disabled Reader*. Baltimore, MD: Johns Hopkins University Press.

BANNATYNE, A. (1974). 'Diagnosis: a note on the recategorisation of the WISC scaled scores', *Journal of Learning Disabilities*, 7, 272–3.

BANNISTER, D. and FRANSELLA, F. (1971). *Inquiring Man: The Theory of Personal Constructs*. Harmondsworth: Penguin.

BARKING and DAGENHAM LEA SCHOOL PSYCHOLOGICAL SERVICE (in association with University College, London) (1982). *Barking Reading Project Test Battery*. Barking: Barking and Dagenham LEA.

BARRS, M., ELLIS, S., HESTER, H. and THOMAS, A. (1988). *The Primary Language Record*. London: ILEA.

BARTLETT, F.C. (1932). *Remembering: A Study in Experimental and Social Psychology*. Cambridge: Cambridge University Press.

BASTIAN, H.C. (1898). *A Treatise on Aphasia and other Speech Defects*. London: H. K. Lewis.

BATEMAN, B. (1965). 'An educational view of a diagnostic approach to learning disorders'. In: HELLMUTH, J. (Ed.) *Learning Disorders*, Vol. 1. Seattle WA: Special Child Publications.

BEAIL, N. (Ed.) (1985). *Repertory Grid Technique and Personal Constructs*. London: Croom Helm.

BEGLEITER, H. (1985). 'Cognitive EPs: technique and application'. In: CRACCO, R.P., BRENNER, P. and WESTMORLAND, C. (Eds) *State of the Science in EEG – 1985*. Atlanta, GA: EEG Society.

BEGLEY, J., BROWN, M. and CAMERON, R. (1989). 'Special needs: spelling', *Support for Learning*, 4, 1, 12–18.

BELLAN, R. (1986). 'The integrated method of reading therapy', *Journal of Learning Disabilities*, 19, 5, 271–3.

BENDER, L. (1957). 'Specific reading disability as a maturational lag', *Bulletin of the Orton Society*, 7, 9–18.

BENNETT, N., DESFORGES, C., COCKBURN, A. and WILKINSON, B. (1984). *The Quality of Pupil Learning Experiences*. London: Lawrence Erlbaum Associates.

BENTON, D. and ROBERTS, G. (1988). 'Effects of vitamin supplementation on intelligence of a sample of school children', *Lancet*, 23 January, 140–3.

BERLIN, R. (1887). *Eine Besondere Art der Wortblindheit (Dyslexie)*. Wiesbaden: Verlag von J. F. Bergmann.

BERTELSON, P. (1986). 'The onset of literacy: liminal remarks', *Cognition*, 24, 1–30.

BERTELSON, P., MORAIS, J., ALEGRIA, J. and CONTENT, A. (1985). 'Phonetic analysis capacity', *Nature*, 313, 73–4.

BIBBY, G. (1990). 'An evaluation of in-class support in a secondary school', *Support for Learning*, 5, 1, 37–42.

BIRCH, H. and BELMONT, L. (1964). 'Auditory–visual integration in normal and retarded readers', *American Journal of Orthopsychiatry*, 34, 852–61.

BIRD, C., CHESSUM, R., FURLONG, F. and JOHNSON, D. (Eds) (1981). *Disaffected Pupils*. Massachusetts: Brunell University Press.

BISHOP, D.V.M. (1989a). Reading attainment in 8-year-olds with a history of language delay: a longitudinal study. Paper presented at the Rodin remediation Academy International Conference, University College of North Wales, September.

BISHOP, D.V.M. (1989b). 'Unfixed reference, monocular occlusion and developmental dyslexia – a critique', *British Journal of Opthalmology*, 73, 81–5.

BISHOP, D.V.M., JANCEY, C. and STEEL, A. McP. (1979). 'Orthoptic status and reading disability', *Cortex*, 15, 659–66.

BISHOP, D.V.M. and ROBSON, J. (1989). 'Accurate non-word spelling despite congenital inability to speak: phoneme–grapheme conversion does not require subvocal articulation', *British Journal of Psychology*, 80, 1–15.

BLANCHARD, J.S., MASON, G.E. and DANIEL, D. (1987). *Computer Applications in Reading* (3rd edn). Newark, DE: International Reading Association.

BLAU, H. and LOVELESS, E.J. (1982). 'Specific hemispheric routing – TAKV to teach spelling to dyslexics: VAK and VAKT challenged', *Journal of Learning Disabilities*, 15, 8, 461–6.

BODER, E. (1973). 'Developmental dyslexia: a diagnostic approach based on three atypical reading patterns', *Developmental Medicine and Child Neurology*, 15, 663–87.

BODER, E. and JARRICO, S. (1982). *Boder Test of Reading–Spelling Patterns*. New York: Grune and Stratton.

BOOTH, T., POTTS, A. and SWAN, W. (1987). *Preventing Difficulties in Learning*. Oxford/Milton Keynes: Blackwell/Open University Press.

BOS, W. (1988). Een onderzoek naar de effektiviteit van een neuropsychologische behandeling bij twee dyslectische jongens. MA Thesis, Free University, Amsterdam.

BOSTOCK, A. (1987). *Examination Provision for Candidates with Specific Learning Difficulties (GCSE Edition)*. London: ILEA.

BRADLEY, L. (1981). 'The organisation of motor patterns for spelling: an effective remedial strategy for backward readers', *Developmental Medicine and Child Neurology*, 23, 83–91.

BRADLEY, L. (1984). *Assessing Reading Difficulties: A Diagnostic and Remedial Approach*. London: Macmillan.

BRADLEY, L. (1985). *Poor Spellers, Poor Readers: Understanding the Problem*. Centre for the Teaching of Reading, University of Reading.

BRADLEY, L. (1989). 'Predicting learning disabilities'. In: DUMANT, J.J. and NAKKEN, H. (Eds) *Learning Disabilities. Vol. 2. Cognitive, Social and Remedial Aspects*. London: Academic Press.

BRADLEY, L. (1990). 'Rhyming connections in learning to read and spell'. In: PUMFREY, P.D. and ELLIOTT, C.D. (Eds) *Children's Reading, Spelling and Writing Difficulties: Challenges and Responses*. Lewes: Falmer Press.

BRADLEY, L. and BRYANT, P.E. (1983). 'Categorising sounds and learning to read: a causal connection', *Nature*, 301, 419–21.

BRADLEY, L. and BRYANT, P.E. (1985). *Rhyme and Reason in Reading and Spelling*. Ann Arbor, MI: University of Michigan Press.

BRADLEY, L., MACLEAN, M.E., CROSSLAND, J. and BRYANT, P.E. (submitted). 'Rhyme and knowledge of letters are powerful predictors of children's reading'.

BRADSHAW, J.R. (1990). 'A service to ourselves or our clients?', *Support for Learning*, 5, 4, 205–10.

BRAND, V. (1984). *Spelling Made Easy*. Baldock: Egon Publications.

BRANSTON, P. (1988). 'Reading: it's all in the mind'. In: REID, K. (Ed.) *Troubled Children*. Oxford: Blackwell.

BRANSTON, P. and PROVIS, M. (1986). *Children and Parents Enjoying Reading*. London: Hodder and Stoughton.

BRANWHITE, A.B. (1983). 'Boosting reading skills by direct instruction', *British Journal of Educational Psychology*, 53, 3, 291–8.

BRENNAN, W.K. (1979). *Curriculum Needs of Slow Learners*. Schools Council Working Paper, 63. London: Evans/Methuen.

BRENNAN, W.K. (1987). *Changing Special Education Now*. Milton Keynes: Open University Press.

BRETT, M. (Ed.) (1990). *Education Year Book 1990*. London: Longman.

BRITISH MEDICAL ASSOCIATION (1980). 'Dyslexia is not a medical problem', *British Medical Association News Review*, January 1970.

BRITISH PSYCHOLOGICAL SOCIETY (1989). *Psychological Testing. Guidance for the User*. Leicester: British Psychological Society.

BRITISH PSYCHOLOGICAL SOCIETY (1990). *Register of Chartered Psychologists*. Leicester: British Psychological Society.

BROMLEY LEA (in association with Thames Polytechnic) (1989). *Bromley Screening Pack*. Bromley: Bromley LEA.

BROWN, B., HAEGERSTROM-PORTNOY, G., ADAMS, A.J., YINGLING, D.G., GALLIN, D., HERRON, J. and MARCUS, M. (1983b). 'Predictive eye movements do not discriminate between dyslexic and control children', *Neuropsychologia*, 21, 2, 121–8.

BROWN, B., HAEGERSTROM-PORTNOY, G., YINGLING, C.D., HERRON, J., GALIN, D. and MARCUS, M. (1983a). 'Dyslexic children have normal vestibular responses to rotation', *Archives of Neurology*, 40, 370–3.

BROWN, E.N. (1981). 'Coding strategies and reading comprehension'. In: FRIEND-MAN, D.A.A. and O'CONNOR, N. (Eds) *Intelligence and Learning*. New York: Plenum Press.

BROWN, E.N. (1990). 'Children with spelling and writing difficulties: an alternative approach'. In: PUMFREY, P.D. and ELLIOTT, C.D. (Eds) *Children's Reading, Spelling and Writing Difficulties: Challenges and Responses*. Lewes: Falmer Press.

BRUCK, M. (1988). 'The word recognition and spelling of dyslexic children', *Reading Research Quarterly*, 23, 5, 1–69.

BRUN, A. (1975). 'The subpial granular layer of the foetal cerebral cortex in man', *Acta Pathologica et Microbiologica Scandinavia*, Suppl. 179, 40.

BRUNER, J.S. (1986). *Actual Minds, Possible Worlds*. London: Harvard University Press.

BRUNER, J. and HASTE, H. (Eds) (1990). *Making Sense*. London: Routledge.

BRYANT, P.E. (1985). 'The question of prevention'. In: SNOWLING, M. (Ed.) *Children's Written Language Difficulties*. Windsor: NFER-NELSON.

BRYANT, P.E. (1990). 'Phonological development and reading'. In: PUMFREY, P.D. and ELLIOTT, C.D. (Eds) *Children's Difficulties in Reading, Spelling and Writing*. London: Falmer Press.

BRYANT, P.E. and BRADLEY, L. (1980). 'Why children sometimes write words which they do not read'. In: FRITH, U. (Ed.) *Cognitive Processes in Spelling*. London: Academic Press.

BRYANT, P.E. and BRADLEY, L. (1985). *Children's Reading Problems*. Oxford: Blackwell Scientific Publications.

BRYANT, P.E. and GOSWAMI, U. (1990). 'Comparison between backward and normal readers: a risky business', *The British Psychological Society Education Section Review*, 14, 2, 3–10.

BRYANT, P.E. and IMPEY, L. (1986). 'The similarities between normal readers and developmental and acquired dyslexics', *Cognition*, 24, 121–37.

BRYANT, P.E., MACLEAN, M.E., BRADLEY, L. and CROSSLAND, J. (1990). 'Rhyme and alliteration, phoneme detection and learning to read' (in press).

BURNS, R.B. (1986). *The Self-concept in Theory, Measurement, Development and Behaviour*. London: Longman.

BURT, C. (1921). *Word Reading Test*. Revised by VERNON, P.E. (1938–67) as *Burt (Rearranged Word Reading Test)*. Re-normed by SHEARER, E. and APPS, R. (1975). London: Hodder and Stoughton.

BUSHELL, R. and CRIPPS, C. (1988). *Specific Learning Difficulties*. Stafford: National Association for Remedial Education.

BUTKOWSKY, I.S. and WILLOWS, D.M. (1980). 'Cognitive–motivational characteristics of children varying in reading ability; evidence of learned helplessness in poor readers', *Journal of Educational Psychology*, 72, 3, 408–22.

BUTT, N. (1986). 'Implementing the whole school approach at secondary level', *Support for Learning*, 1, 4, 10–15.

CAMBRELL, L., WILSON, R. and GANTT, W. (1981). 'Classroom observations of task attending behaviours in good and poor readers', *Journal of Educational Research*, 17, 400–21.

CAMPION, J. (1982). 'Dyslexia, past, present and future trends', *Association of Educational Psychologists' Journal*, 5, 9, 54–7.

CANT, R. and SPACKMAN, P. (1985). 'Self-esteem, counselling and educational achievement', *Educational Research*, 27, 1, 68–70.

CARBO, M., DUNN, R. and DUNN, K. (1986). *Teaching Students to Read through their Individual Learning Styles*. Englewood Cliffs, NJ: Prentice-Hall.

CARNINE, D. and SILBERT, J. (1979). *Direct Instruction Reading*. Orlando, FL: Charles Merrill.

CATALDO, S. and ELLIS, N. (1988). 'Interactions in the development of spelling, reading and phonological skills', *Journal of Research in Reading*, 1, 2, 86–109.

CATALDO, S. and ELLIS, N. (1990). 'Learning to spell, learning to read'. In: PUMFREY, P.D. and ELLIOTT, C.D. (Eds) *Children's Difficulties in Reading, Spelling and Writing*. London: Falmer Press.

CHAPMAN, E.K. and STONE, J.M. (1988). *The Visually Handicapped Child in Your Classroom*. London: Cassell.

CHASE, C.H., SCHMITT, R.L., RUSSELL, G. and TALLAL, P. (1984). 'A new chemotherapeutic investigation: piracetam effects on dyslexia', *Annals of Dyslexia*, 34, 29–48.

CHASTY, H. and FRIEL, J. (1991). *Children with Special Needs: Assessment, Law and Practice – Caught in the Act*. London: Kingsley.

CHOMSKY, C. (1979). 'Approaching reading through invented spelling', In: RESNICK, O.L. and WEAVER, P. (Eds) *Theory and Practice in Early Reading*, Vol. 2. Hillsdale, NJ: Lawrence Erlbaum.

CICCI, R. (1987). 'Dyslexia: especially for parents', *Annals of Dyslexia*, 37, 203–11.

CLARK, C.R. and DAVIES, C.O. (1979). *Peabody Rebus Reading Program*. Circle Pines, MN: American Guidance Services.

CLARK, M.M. (1970). *Reading Difficulties in Schools*. Harmondsworth: Penguin.

CLARK, M.M. (1976). *Young Fluent Readers*. London: Heinemann.

CLARK, M.M. (1979). *Reading Difficulties in Schools* (2nd edn). London: Heinemann.

CLAY, M. (1979a, NZ; 1981, UK). *The Early Detection of Reading Difficulties: A Diagnostic Survey with Recovery Procedures*. Auckland: Heinemann Educational.

CLAY, M. (1979b). *Reading: The Patterning of Complex Behaviour*. London: Heinemann.

CLAYTON, P. (1987). 'Scotopic sensitivity', *Optician*, 25 September, p. 22.

CLUNIES-ROSS, L. and WIMHURST, S. (1983). *The Right Balance: Provision for Slow Learners in Secondary Schools*. Windsor: NFER-NELSON.

COLES, G.S. (1987). *The Learning Mystique: A Critical Look at Learning Disabilities*. New York: Pantheon Books.

COLES, G.S. (1989). 'Excerpts from the learning mystique: a critical look at learning disabilities', *Journal of Learning Disabilities*, 22, 5, 267–77.

COLLINS, J.E. (1961). 'The effects of remedial education', *Educational Monographs*, 4.

COLTHEART, M. (1981). 'Disorders of reading and their implications for models of normal reading', *Visible Language*, 15, 245–66.

COLTHEART, M. (1982). 'Surface dyslexia and its implications for models of normal reading'. In: BROADBENT, D.E. and WEISKRANTZ, L. (Eds) *The Neuropsychology of Cognitive Function*. London: The Royal Society.

COLTHEART, M. (1984). 'The right hemisphere and disorders of reading'. In: YOUNG, A.W. (Ed.) *Functions of the Right Hemisphere*. London: Academic Press.

COLTHEART, M. (Ed.) (1987a). *The Psychology of Reading*. Hove: Erlbaum.

COLTHEART, M. (1987b). 'Varieties of developmental dyslexia: a comment on Bryant and Impey', *Cognition*, 27, 97–101.

COLTHEART, M., MASTERSON, J., BYNG, S., PRIOR, M. and RIDDOCH, M.J. (1983). 'Surface dyslexia', *Quarterly Journal of Experimental Psychology*, 35A, 469–95.

COLTHEART, M., PATTERSON, K. and MARSHALL, J.C. (Eds) (1980). *Deep Dyslexia*. Boston, MA: Routledge and Kegan Paul.

CONGDON, P. (1990). 'Better vision', *Times Educational Supplement*, 19 January, p. 18.

CONNORS, C.K., BOUIN, A.G., WINGLEE, M., LOUGE, L., O'DONNELL, D. and SMITH, A. (1984). 'Piracetum and event-related potentials in dyslexic children', *Psychopharmacology Bulletin*, 20, 667–73.

CONWAY, N.F. and GOW, L. (1988). 'Mainstreaming special class students with mild handicaps through group instruction', *Remedial and Special Education*, 9, 5, 34–40.

COOTER, R.B. Jr (1988). 'Effects of Ritalin on reading', *Academic Therapy*, 23, 461–8.

CORNWALL, K.F., HEDDERLY, R. and PUMFREY, P.D. (1984). 'Specific learning difficulties: the specific reading difficulties versus dyslexia controversy resolved?', *Occasional Papers of the Division of Educational and Child Psychology of the British Psychological Society*, 7, 3 (complete edition).

CORNWALL, K.F. and SPICER, J. (1982). 'DECP enquiry: the role of the educational psychologist in the discovery and assessment of children requiring special education', *Occasional Papers of the Division of Educational and Child Psychological Society*, 3, 1, 3–10.

COTTERELL, G. (1985). *Teaching the Non-reading Dyslexic Child*. Wisbech, Cambs: Learning Development Aids.

COX, A.R. (1983). 'Programming for teachers of dyslexics', *Annals of Dyslexia*, 33, 221–33.

COX, A.R. (1985a). 'Alphabetic phonics: an organisation and expansion of Orton–Gillingham', *Annals of Dyslexia*, 35, 187–98.

COX, A.R. (1985b). *Structures and Techniques: Remedial Language Training*. Bath: Better Books.

CRITCHLEY, M. (1970). *The Dyslexic Child*. London: Heinemann.

CRITCHLEY, M. (1981). 'Dyslexia: an overview'. In: PAVLIDIS, G. Th. and MILES, T.R. (Eds) *Dyslexia Research and its Applications to Education*. Chichester: Wiley.

CRUICKSHANK, W.M. (1968). 'The problem of delayed recognition and its correction'. In: KEENEY, A.H. and KEENEY, V.T. (Eds) *Dyslexia: Diagnosis and Treatment of Reading Disorders*. St Louis, MO: Mosby.

CULLEN, H. (1988). 'Special provision for pupils with learning difficulties in GCSE examinations', *Support for Learning*, 3, 3, 182–3.

CUNNINGHAM, C.C. and DAVIS, H. (1985). *Working with Parents: Framework for Collaboration*. Milton Keynes: Open University Press.

DANEMAN, M. and CARPENTER, P.A. (1980). 'Individual differences in working memory and reading', *Journal of Verbal Learning and Verbal Behaviour*, 19, 450–66.

DARKE, S. (1988). 'Anxiety and working memory capacity', *Cognition and Emotion*, 2, 145–54.

DAVIDSON, J. (1990). 'The use of speech in computer-assisted learning programmes for beginning readers', *Support for Learning*, 5, 4, 216–9.

DAVIDSON, P.M. (1988). 'Word processing and children with specific learning difficulties', *Support for Learning*, 3, 4, 210–4.

DAVIE, R., BUTLER, N. and GOLDSTEIN, H. (1972). *From Birth to Seven*. London: Longman.

DAVIES, J.D. and DAVIES, P. (1988). 'Developing credibility as a support and advisory teacher', *Support for Learning*, 3, 1, 12–15.

DAVIS, C. and STUBBS, R. (1988). *Shared Reading in Practice*. Milton Keynes: Open University Press.

DAYAN, G. and AUGUR, J. (1990). 'Facts about dyslexia', *Newscheck*, 7, 5, 10–11.

DE FRIES, J.C. (1991). 'Genetics and dyslexia: an overview'. In: SNOWLING, M. and THOMSON, M. (Eds) *Dyslexia: Integrating Theory and Practice*. London: Whurr.

DECKER, S.N. and DeFRIES, J.C. (1981). 'Cognitive ability profiles in families of reading-disabled children', *Developmental Medicine and Child Neurology*, 23, 217–27.

DELACATO, C. (1959). *The Diagnosis and Treatment of Speech and Reading Problems* (6th edn). Springfield, IL: Charles C. Thomas.

DENCKLA, M.B. (1977). 'Learning for language and language for learning'. In: BLAW, M.E., RAPIN, I. and KINSBOURNE, M. (Eds) *Child Neurology*. New York: Spectrum.

DENCKLA, M.B. and RUDEL, R. (1976). 'Rapid "automatized" naming RAN: dyslexia differentiated from other learning disabilities', *Neuropsychologia*, 14, 471–9.

DESSENT, T. (1987). *Making the Ordinary School Special*. Brighton: Falmer Press.

DIENER, C.I. and DWECK, C.S. (1978). 'An analysis of learned helplessness: continuous changes in performance, strategy and achievement cognitions following failure', *Journal of Personality and Social Psychology*, 36, 451–62.

DIIANNI, M., WILSHER, C.R., BLANK, M.S., CONNORS, C.K., CHASE, C.H., FUNKENSTEIN, H.H., HELFGOTT, E., HOLMES, J.M., LOUGEE, L., MALETTA, G.J., MILEWSKI, J., PIROZZOLO, F.J., RUDDEL, R.G. and TALLAL, R. (1985). 'The effects of piracetam in children with dyslexia', *Journal of Clinical Psychopharmacology*, 5, 272–8.

DINSMORE, J.A. and ISAACSON, D.K. (1986). 'Tactics for teaching dyslexic students', *Academic Therapy*, 21, 3, 293–300.

DOBBINS, D.A. (1986). 'An empirical classification of children with reading difficulties', *Educational and Child Psychology*, 3, 2, 70–80.

DOBBINS, D.A. (1988). 'Yule's "hump" revisited', *British Journal of Educational Psychology*, 58, 338–44.

DOBBINS, A. (1990a). *Specific Reading Difficulties: Prevalence and Characteristics* (in preparation).

DOBBINS, A. (1990b). 'An exclusionary approach to the identification of pupils with unexplained underachievement in reading', In: HALES, G. with HALES, M., MILES, T. and SUMMERFIELD, A. (Eds) *Meeting Points in Dyslexia: Proceedings of the First International Conference of the British Dyslexia Association*. Reading: British Dyslexia Association.

DOBBINS, D.A. and TAFFA, E. (1990). 'The "stability" of identification of underachieving readers over different measures of intelligence and reading.' Personal communication.

DODRILL, G.B. and TROUPIN, A.S. (1977). 'Psychotropic effects of carbamazepine in epilepsy: a double blind comparison with phenytoin', *Neurology*, 27, 1023–8.

DONALDSON, M. (1988). *Sense and Sensibility: Some Thoughts on the Teaching of Literacy.* Reading: Reading and Language Information Centre, University of Reading.

DOWNING, J., AYERS, D. and SCHAEFER, B. (1983). *Linguistic Awareness in Reading Readiness.* Windsor: NFER-NELSON.

DRAKE, W.E. (1968). 'Clinical and pathological findings in a child with a developmental learning disability', *Journal of Learning Disabilities*, 1, 486–502.

DREBY, C. (1979). '"Vision" problems and reading disability: a dilemma for the reading specialist', *The Reading Teacher*, 32, 7, 787–95.

DREVER, J. (1964). *A Dictionary of Psychology.* Harmondsworth: Penguin.

DREW, A.L. (1956). 'A neurological appraisal of familial congenital word blindness', *Brain*, 79, 44.

DRIVER, R. (1983). *The Pupil as Scientist?* Milton Keynes: Open University Press.

DUANE, D.D. (1991). 'Neurobiological issues in dyslexia'. In: SNOWLING, M. and THOMSON, M. (Eds) *Dyslexia: Integrating Theory and Practice.* London: Whurr.

DUDLEY-MARLING, C.C. (1981). 'WISC and WISC-R profiles of learning disabled children: a review', *Learning Disabilities Quarterly*, 4, 307–19.

DUFFY, F.H., DENCKLA, M.B., BARTELS, P.H., SANDINI, G. and KIESSLING, L.S. (1980). 'Dyslexia: automated diagnosis by computerised classification of brain electrical activity', *Annals of Neurology*, 7, 421–8.

DUNLOP, P. (1972). 'Dyslexia: the orthoptic approach', *Australian Orthoptic Journal*, 12, 16–20.

DVORAK, K. and FEIT, J. (1977). 'Migration of neuroblasts through partial necrosis of the cerebral cortex in newborn rats. Contribution to the problems of morphological development and development period of cerebral mycrogyria', *Acta Neuropathologica*, 38, 203–12.

DYER, C. (1988). 'Which support?: an examination of the term', *Support for Learning*, 3, 1, 6–11.

EDWARDS, D. and MERCER, N. (1987). *Common Knowledge: The Development of Understanding in the Classroom.* London: Methuen.

EDWARDS, J.H. (1990). Emotional reactions to dyslexia: case studies. Unpublished M.Ed. Thesis, University of Wales.

EHRI, L. (1979). 'Linguistic insight: threshold of reading acquisition'. In: WALKER, T. and McKINNON, G. (Eds) *Reading Research: Advances in Theory and Practice.* New York: Academic Press.

EHRI, L. (1985). 'Sources of difficulty in learning to spell and read'. In: WOLRAICH, M.L. and ROUTH, D. (Eds) *Advances in Developmental and Behavioural Paediatrics.* Greenwich, CT: JAI Press Inc.

ELLIOTT, C.D. (1983). *British Ability Scales, Handbook and Technical Manual.* Windsor: NFER-NELSON.

ELLIOTT, C.D. (1989). 'Cognitive profiles of learning disabled children', *British Journal of Developmental Psychology*, 7, 171–9.

ELLIOTT, C.D. (1990a). 'The definition and identification of specific learning difficulties.' In: PUMFREY, P.D. and ELLIOTT, C.D. (Eds) *Children's Reading, Writing and Spelling Difficulties: Challenges and Responses.* Basingstoke: Falmer.

ELLIOTT, C.D. (1990b). *Differential Ability Scales.* San Antonio, TX: The Psychological Corporation.

ELLIOTT, C.D. and TYLER, S. (1987). 'Learning disabilities and intelligence test results: a principal components analysis of the British Ability Scales', *British Journal of Psychology*, 78, 325–33.

ELLIS, A.W. (1979). 'Developmental and acquired dyslexia: some observations on Jorm', *Cognition*, 7, 413–20.

ELLIS, A.W. (1984). *Reading, Writing and Dyslexia: A Cognitive Analysis.* Hillsdale, NJ: Lawrence Erlbaum.

ELLIS, N. (1981). 'Visual and name coding in dyslexic children', *Psychological Research*, 43, 201–18.

ELLIS, N. (1988). 'The development of literacy and short-term memory'. In: GRUNEBERG, M.M., MORRIS, P.E. and SYKES, R.N. (Eds) *Practical Aspects of Memory II*. Chichester: John Wiley.

ELLIS, N. (1990). 'Reading, phonological skills and short-term memory: interactive tributaries of development', *Journal of Research in Reading*, 13, 2, 107–22.

ELLIS, N. and LARGE, B. (1987). 'The development of reading: as you seek so shall you find', *British Journal of Psychology*, 78, 1–28.

ELLIS, N. and LARGE, B. (1988). 'The early stages of reading: longitudinal study', *Applied Cognitive Psychology*, 2, 47–76.

ELLIS, N. and MILES, T. (1981). 'A lexical encoding deficiency: experimental evidence'. In: PAVLIDIS, G.Th. (Ed.) *Dyslexia Research and its Applications to Education*. New York: John Wiley.

ENGELMANN, J., OSBORN, E. and ENGELMANN, J. (1969). *Distar: An Instructional System*. Chicago; IL: SRA.

EPPS, S., YSSELDYKE, J.E. and ALGOZZINE, B. (1983). 'Impact of different definitions of learning disabilities on the number of students identified', *Journal of Psychoeducational Assessment*, 1, 341–52.

EULER, C. von, LUNDBERG, I. and LENNERSTRAND, G. (Eds) (1989). *Brain and Reading: Structural and Functional Anomalies in Development Dyslexia with Special Reference to Hemispheric Interactions, Memory Function, Linguistic Processes and Visual Analysis in Reading*. Proceedings of the Seventh International Rodin Remediation Conference. London: Macmillan.

EVANS, M.M. (1982). *Dyslexia: An Annotated Bibliography*. London: Greenwood Press.

EYSENCK, M.W. (1979). 'Anxiety, learning and memory: a reconceptualisation', *Journal of Research in Personality*, 13, 363–85.

EYSENCK, M.W. (1982). *Attention and Arousal (Cognition and Performance)*. Berlin: Springer Verlag.

FARRELL, P., DUNNING, T. and FOLEY, J. (1989). 'Methods used by educational psychologists to assess children with learning difficulties', *School of Psychology International*, 10, 47–55.

FAWCETT, A. (1989). 'Automacity: a new framework for dyslexic research'. Paper presented at the First International Conference of the British Dyslexia Association.

FEINGOLD, B.F. (1975). 'Hyperkinesis and learning disabilities linked to artificial food flavours and colors', *American Journal of Nursing*, 75, 797–803.

FERNALD, G. (1943). *Remedial Techniques in the Basic School Subjects*. New York: McGraw-Hill.

FERREIRO, E. and TEBEROVSKY, A. (1983). *Literacy before Schooling*. London: Heinemann.

FINN, J.D. (1982). 'Patterns in special education placement as revealed by the Office for Civil Rights survey'. In: HELLER, K.A., HOLTZMAN, W.H. and MESSICK, S. (Eds) *Placing Children in Special Education: A Strategy for Equity*. Washington, DC: National Academy Press.

FISH, J. (1989). *What is Special Education?* Milton Keynes: Open University Press.

FLETCHER, J.M., ESPY, K.A., FRANCIS, D.J., DAVIDSON, K.C., ROURKE, B.P. and SHAYWITZ, S.E. (1989). 'Comparisons of cut off and regression based definitions of reading disabilities', *Journal of Learning Disabilities*, 22, 6, 334–8.

FLYNN, J.M. and DEERING, W.M. (1989). 'Subtypes of dyslexia: investigation of Boder's system using quantitative neurophysiology', *Developmental Medicine and Child Neurology*, 31, 2, 215–23.

FONSECA, A.M. (1990). Automaticity and the free writing vocabulary of top infants. Unpublished M.Ed. dissertation, University of Manchester School of Education.

FORNESS, S.R. and KAVALE, K.A. (1983). 'Remediation of reading disabilities. Part 2. Classification and approaches', *Learning Disabilities*, 2, 12, 153–64.

FORNESS, S.R. and KAVALE, K.A. (1988). 'Psychopharmacologic treatment: a note on classroom effects', *Journal of Learning Disabilities*, 21, 3, 144–7.

FORRESTER, A. (1985). *Embedded Pictures*. Available from Tameside Educational Psychology Service, UK.

FRANCIS, H. (1982). *Learning to Read: Literate Behaviour and Orthographic Knowledge*. London: Allen and Unwin.

FREDMAN, G. (1989). 'Critical review of the classification of reading disorders', *Association of Child Psychology and Psychiatry Newsletter*, 11, 4, 5–10.

FREDMAN, G. and STEVENSON, J. (1988). 'Reading processes in specific reading retarded and reading backward thirteen year olds', *British Journal of Developmental Psychology*, 6, 1, 97–106.

FREEBODY, P. and TIRRE, W.C. (1985). 'Achievement outcomes of two reading programmes: an instance of aptitude–treatment interaction', *British Journal of Educational Psychology*, 55, 1, 53–60.

FRICK, R.W. (1988). 'Issues of representation and limited capacity in the auditory short-term store', *British Journal of Psychology*, 79, 213–41.

FRITH, U. (1980). 'Unexpected spelling problems'. In: FRITH, U. (Ed.) *Cognitive Processes in Spelling*. London: Academic Press.

FRITH, U. (1981). 'Experimental approaches to developmental dyslexia: an introduction', *Psychological Research*, 43, 97–109.

FRITH, U. (1985). 'Beneath the surface of surface dyslexia'. In: PATTERSON, K., MARSHALL, J.R. and COLTHEART, M. (Eds) *Surface Dyslexia*. Hillsdale, NJ: Lawrence Erlbaum.

FRITH, U. and SNOWLING, M. (1983). 'Reading for meaning and reading for sound in autistic and dyslexic children', *British Journal of Developmental Psychology*, 1, 329–42.

FROSTIG, M. and HORNE, D. (1964). *The Frosting Programme for the Development of Visual Perception*. Chicago, IL: Folett.

FROSTIG, M., LEFEVER, D.W. and WHITTLESEA, J.R.B. (1964). *The Marianne Frosting Developmental Test of Visual Perception*. Palo Alto, CA: Consulting Psychologists Press.

FROSTIG, M., LEFEVER, W. and WHITTLESEA, J.R.B. (1966). *Developmental Tests of Visual Perception* (3rd edn). Palo Alto, CA: Consulting Psychologists Press.

FROSTIG, M. and MASLOW, P. (1970). *Movement Education: Theory and Practice*. Chicago, IL: Follett.

FUNNEL, E. (1983). 'Phonological processes in reading: new evidence from acquired dyslexia', *British Journal of Psychology*, 2, 159–80.

GADDES, W.H. (1985). *Learning Disabilities and Brain Function: A Neuropsychological Approach* (2nd edn). New York: Springer-Verlag.

GADOW, K.D. (1983). 'Pharmacotherapy for learning disabilities', *Learning Disabilities: An Interdisciplinary Journal*, 2, 10, 127–40.

GAINES, K. (1989). 'The use of reading diaries as a short term intervention strategy', *Reading*, 23, 3, 141–5.

GALABURDA, A.M. (1979). 'Cytoarchitectonic abnormalities in development dyslexia: a case study', *Annals of Neurology*, 6, 94–100.

GALABURDA, A.M. and EIDELBERG, P. (1982). 'Symmetry and asymmetry in the human posterior thalamus. II. Thalamic lesions in a case of developmental dyslexia', *Archives of Neurology*, 39, 333–6.

GALABURDA, A.M., SHERMAN, G.F., ROSEN, G.D., ABOITZ, F. and GESCHWIND, N. (1985). 'Developmental dyslexia: four consecutive patients with cortical abnormalities', *Annals of Neurology*, 18, 222–33.

GALABURDA, A.M., SIGNORET, J.C. and RONTHAL, M. (1985). 'Left posterior angiomatous anomaly and developmental dyslexia: report of five cases', *Neurology*, 35, suppl., 198.

GANSCHOW, L. (1984). 'Analysis of written language of a language learning disabled (dyslexic) college student and instructional implications', *Annals of Dyslexia*, 34, 271–84.

GARNER, R. (1988). *Metacognition and Reading Comprehension*. Norwood, NJ: Ablex.

GARNER, R. and REIS, R. (1981). 'Monitoring and resolving comprehension obstacles: an investigation of spontaneous text lookbacks among upper-grade good and poor comprehenders', *Reading Research Quarterly*, 12, 569–82.

GATHERCOLE, S.E. and BADDELEY, A.D. (1989). 'Evaluation of the role of phonological STM in the development of vocabulary in children: a longitudinal study', *Journal of Memory and Language*, 28, 200–13.

GATHERCOLE, S.E. and BADDELEY, A.D. (1990). Phonological memory deficits in language disordered children: is there a causal connection? *Journal of Memory and Language*, 29, 3, 336–60.

GENTILE, L.M. and McMILLAN, M.M. (1987). *Stress and Reading Difficulties: Research, Assessment and Intervention*. Newark, DE: International Reading Association.

GENTILE, L.M. and McMILLAN, M.M. (1988). 'Re-examining the role of emotional maladjustment'. In: GLAZER, S.M., SEARFOSS, L.W. and GENTILE, L.M. (Eds) *Re-examining Reading Diagnosis: New Trends and Procedures*. Newark, DE: International Reading Association.

GESCHWIND, N. (1980). 'Brain "miswired" in dyslexics?', *Medical News*, 6 March.

GESCHWIND, N. (1983). 'Biological associations of left handedness', *Annals of Dyslexia*, 33, 29–39.

GESCHWIND, N. and BEHAN, P.O. (1982). 'Left handedness: association with immune disease, migraine, and developmental learning disorders', *Proceedings of the National Academy of Sciences*, 79, 5097–100.

GESSERT, B. (1976). 'Specific reading difficulties in Great Britain'. In: TARNAPOL, L. and TARNAPOL, M. (Eds) *Reading Disabilities: An International Perspective*. Baltimore, MD: University Park Press.

GIBSON, E.J. (1985). 'Trends in perceptual development: implications for the reading process'. In: SINGER, H. and RUDDELL, R.B. (Eds) *Theoretical Models and Processes of Reading* (3rd edn). Newark DE: International Reading Association.

GIBSON, E.J. and LEVIN, H. (1975). *The Psychology of Reading*. Cambridge, MA: MIT Press.

GILLINGHAM, A. and STILLMAN, B.U. (1956). *Remedial Training for Children with Specific Disability in Reading, Spelling and Penmanship* (5th edn, 1969). Cambridge, MA: Educators Publishing Service.

GILMORE, V.J. and GILMORE, C.E. (1968). *Gilmore Reading Test*. New York: Harcourt Brace Jovanovich.

GIPPS, C., GROSS, H. and GOLDSTEIN, H. (1987). *Warnock's Eighteen Per Cent: Children with Special Needs in the Primary School*. London: Falmer Press.

GITTLEMAN, R. (1983). 'Treatment for reading disorders'. In: RUTTER, M. (Ed.) *Developmental Neuropsychiatry*. New York: Guilford.

GITTLEMAN, R. and FEINGOLD, I. (1983). 'Children with reading disorders. I. Efficacy of reading remediation', *Journal of Child Psychology and Psychiatry*, 24, 2, 167–91.

GITTLEMAN, R., KLEIN, D. and FEINGOLD, I. (1983). 'Effects of methylphenidate in combination with reading remediation', *Child Psychology and Psychiatry*, 24, 2, 193–212.

GJESSING, H.J. and KARLSEN, B. (1989). *A Longitudinal Study of Dyslexia*. New York: Springer Verlag.

GLANZER, M., FISCHER, B. and DORFMAN, D. (1984). 'Short-term storage in reading', *Journal of Verbal Language and Verbal Behaviour*, 23, 467–86.

GLYNN, T. and McNAUGHTON, S. (1985). 'The Mangere home and school remedial reading procedure: continuing research on their effectiveness', *New Zealand Journal of Psychology*, 14, 66–77.

GOACHER, B., EVANS, J., WELTON, J. and WEDELL, K. (1988). *Policy and Provision for Special Educational Needs: Implementing the 1981 Education Act.* London: Cassell.

GOODMAN, A.G., RALL, T.W., NIES, A.S. and TAYLOR, P. (Eds) (1985). *The Pharmacological Basis of Therapeutics,* 8th edn. New York: Pergamon.

GOODMAN, K. (1967). 'Reading: a psycholinguistic guessing game', *Journal of the Reading Specialist,* 6, 126–35.

GOODMAN, Y. (1983). 'Beginning reading development: strategies and principles'. In: PARKER, R. and DAVIES, F. (Eds) *Developing Literacy: Young Children's Use of Language.* New York: International Reading.

GOSWAMI, U. (1986). 'Children's use of analogy in learning to read: a developmental study', *Journal of Experimental Child Psychology,* 42, 72–83.

GOSWAMI, U. (1988). 'Children's use of analogy in learning to spell', *British Journal of Developmental Psychology,* 6, 21–33.

GOSWAMI, U. and BRYANT, P. (1990). *Phonological Skills and Learning to Read.* Hove, Sussex: Erlbaum.

GOULANDRIS, N. (1985). 'Extending the written language skills of children with specific learning difficulties – supplementary teaching techniques'. In: SNOWLING, M. (Ed.) *Children's Written Language Difficulties: Assessment and Management.* Windsor: NFER-NELSON.

GRAMPIAN REGION PSYCHOLOGICAL SERVICE (1988). *Reeling and Writhing: Children with Specific Learning Difficulties.* Aberdeen: Grampian Education Authority.

GRANT, E.C.G., HOWARD, J.M., DAVIES, S., CHASTY, H., HORNSBY, D. and GALBRAITH, J. (1988). 'Zinc deficiency in children with dyslexia: concentrations of zinc and other minerals in sweat and hair', *British Medical Journal,* 296, 607–9.

GRAY, W.S. (1963). *Gray Oral Reading Test.* Austin, TX: Pro-Ed.

GREAT BRITAIN. DEPARTMENT OF EDUCATION AND SCIENCE (1967). *Children and their Primary Schools* (The Plowden Report), 3 vols. London: HMSO.

GREAT BRITAIN. DEPARTMENT OF EDUCATION AND SCIENCE (1968). *Psychologists in Education Services.* London: HMSO.

GREAT BRITAIN. DEPARTMENT OF EDUCATION AND SCIENCE (1972). *Children with Specific Reading Difficulties.* Report of the Advisory Committee on Handicapped Children (Chairperson: Professor J. Tizard). London: HMSO.

GREAT BRITAIN. DEPARTMENT OF EDUCATION AND SCIENCE (1975a). *The Discovery of Children Requiring Special Education and the Assessment of their Needs* (Circular 2/75). London: HMSO.

GREAT BRITAIN. DEPARTMENT OF EDUCATION AND SCIENCE (1975b). *A Language for Life.* Report of the Committee of Inquiry. (Chairperson: Sir Alan Bullock, FBA). London: HMSO.

GREAT BRITAIN. DEPARTMENT OF EDUCATION AND SCIENCE (1978). *Special Educational Needs.* Report of the Committee of Inquiry into the Education of Handicapped Children and Young People (Chairperson: H. M. Warnock). London: HMSO.

GREAT BRITAIN. DEPARTMENT OF EDUCATION AND SCIENCE (1981a). *Education Act 1981* (Circular 8/81). London: DES.

GREAT BRITAIN. DEPARTMENT OF EDUCATION AND SCIENCE (1981b). *Slow Learning and Less Successful Children in Secondary Schools.* London: HMSO.

GREAT BRITAIN. DEPARTMENT OF EDUCATION AND SCIENCE (1981c). *West Indian Children in our Schools.* Interim Report of the Committee of Enquiry into the Education of Children from Ethnic Minority Groups (Chairperson: G. Rampton). London: HMSO.

GREAT BRITAIN. DEPARTMENT OF EDUCATION AND SCIENCE (1983). *Assessments and Statements of Special Educational Needs (Circular 1/83).* London: HMSO.

GREAT BRITAIN. DEPARTMENT OF EDUCATION AND SCIENCE (1984a). *Slow Learning and Less Successful Pupils in Secondary Schools.* London: DES.

GREAT BRITAIN. DEPARTMENT OF EDUCATION AND SCIENCE (1984b). Report of a seminar, held by the Department on 22 May, to disseminate the findings of four research projects on specific learning difficulties. London: DES.

GREAT BRITAIN. DEPARTMENT OF EDUCATION AND SCIENCE (1988a). *Information Technology from 5 to 16* (Curriculum Matters Series). London: HMSO.

GREAT BRITAIN. DEPARTMENT OF EDUCATION AND SCIENCE (1988b). *Report of the Committee of Inquiry into the Teaching of English Language* (Chairman: Professor J. Kingman). London: HMSO.

GREAT BRITAIN. DEPARTMENT OF EDUCATION AND SCIENCE (1988c). *Local Management of Schools* (Circular 7/88). London: DES.

GREAT BRITAIN. DEPARTMENT OF EDUCATION AND SCIENCE (1988d). *Assessments and Statements of Special Educational Needs: Procedures within the Education, Health and Social Services.* (Draft revision of Circular 1/83). London: HMSO.

GREAT BRITAIN. DEPARTMENT OF EDUCATION AND SCIENCE (1988e). *Education Reform Act 1988.* London: HMSO.

GREAT BRITAIN. DEPARTMENT OF EDUCATION AND SCIENCE (1989a). *English in the National Curriculum.* London: HMSO.

GREAT BRITAIN. DEPARTMENT OF EDUCATION AND SCIENCE (1989b). *A Survey of Pupils with Special Educational Needs in Ordinary Schools.* London: DES.

GREAT BRITAIN. DEPARTMENT OF EDUCATION AND SCIENCE (1989c). *School Curriculum and Assessment* (Circular 5/89). London: DES.

GREAT BRITAIN. DEPARTMENT OF EDUCATION AND SCIENCE (1989d). *National Curriculum: From Policy to Practice.* London: DES.

GREAT BRITAIN. DEPARTMENT OF EDUCATION AND SCIENCE (1989e). *Ethnic Monitoring of Teachers* (Circular 8/89). London: DES.

GREAT BRITAIN. DEPARTMENT OF EDUCATION AND SCIENCE (1989f). *Assessments and Statements of Special Educational Needs: Procedures within the Education, Health and Social Services (Circular 22/89; Revision of Circular 1/83).* London: DES.

GREAT BRITAIN. DEPARTMENT OF EDUCATION AND SCIENCE (1989g). *Education Reform Act 1988: Temporary Exceptions from the National Curriculum* (Circular 15/89). London: DES.

GREAT BRITAIN. DEPARTMENT OF EDUCATION AND SCIENCE (1989h). *A Survey of Support Services for Special Needs.* London: DES.

GREAT BRITAIN. DEPARTMENT OF EDUCATION AND SCIENCE (1989i). *The School Teacher Appraisal Pilot Study. National Steering Group's Report.* London: HMSO.

GREAT BRITAIN. DEPARTMENT OF EDUCATION AND SCIENCE (1990a). *The Education (National Curriculum) (Assessment Arrangements for English, Mathematics and Science) Order 1990* (Circular 9/90). London: HMSO.

GREAT BRITAIN. DEPARTMENT OF EDUCATION AND SCIENCE (1990b). *Staffing for Pupils with Special Educational Needs* (Draft Circular /90). London: DES.

GREAT BRITAIN. DEPARTMENT OF EDUCATION AND SCIENCE AND THE WELSH OFFICE (1987a). *National Curriculum Task Group on Assessment and Testing: A Report* (The Black Report). London: DES/WO.

GREAT BRITAIN. DEPARTMENT OF EDUCATION AND SCIENCE AND THE WELSH OFFICE (1987b). *National Curriculum Task Group on Assessment and Testing: A Digest for Schools.* London: HMSO.

GREAT BRITAIN. DEPARTMENT OF EDUCATION AND SCIENCE AND THE WELSH OFFICE (1988). *English for Ages 5 to 11.* Proposals of the Secretaries of State (Chairman: Professor B. Cox). London: DES.

GREAT BRITAIN. DEPARTMENT OF EDUCATION AND SCIENCE (1991a). *The Teaching and Learning of Reading in Primary Schools: A Report by HMI.* London: DES.

GREAT BRITAIN. DEPARTMENT OF EDUCATION AND SCIENCE (1991b). *An Enquiry into LEA Evidence on Standards of Reading of Seven Year Old Children: A Report by NFER.* London: DES.

GREENING, M. and SPENCELEY, J. (1987). 'Shared reading: support for inexperienced readers', *Educational Psychology in Practice*, 3, 1, 31–7.

GREGG, P.J. (1988). 'Dyslexia and tinted lenses: a small research project', *Optician*, 29 January, pp. 17–20.

GREGORY, R.P. (1988). *Action Research in the Secondary School: The Psychologist as Change Agent*. London: Routledge.

GREGORY, R.P., HACKNEY, C. and GREGORY, N.M. (1981). 'Corrective reading programme: the use of educational technology in a secondary school', *School Psychology International*, 2, 2, 21–5 (reprinted in Gregory, 1988).

GREGORY, R.P., HACKNEY, C. and GREGORY, N.M. (1982). 'Corrective reading programme: an evaluation', *British Journal of Educational Psychology*, 52, 33–50 (reprinted in Gregory, 1988).

GROSSER, G.S. and SPAFFORD, C.S. (1989). 'Perceptual evidence for an anomalous distribution of rods and cones in the retinas of dyslexus: a new hypothesis', *Perceptual and Motor Skills*, 68, 3, (1), 683–98.

HACKETT, G. (1989). 'DES waters down right to special help', *Times Educational Supplement*, No. 3822, 29.

HADLEY, H.R. (1988). 'Improving reading scores through a self-esteem intervention program', *Elementary School Guidance and Counselling*, 23, 248–52.

HAGBERG, B. (1978). 'Defects of immediate memory related to the cerebral blood flow distribution', *Brain and Language*, 5, 366–7.

HALES, G., HALES, M., MILES, T. and SUMMERFIELD, A. (Eds) (1990). *Meeting Points in Dyslexia: Proceedings of the First International Conference of the British Dyslexia Association*. Reading: British Dyslexia Association.

HALL, N. (1987). *The Emergence of Literacy*. London: Hodder and Stoughton with UKRA.

HALLGREN, B. (1950). 'Specific dyslexia', *Acta Psychiatrica et Neurologica*, 65, 1–287.

HAMMILL, D.D. (1990). 'On defining learning disabilities: an emerging consensus', *Journal of Learning Disabilities*, 23, 2, 74–84.

HAMMILL, D.D. and McNUTT, G. (1981). *The Correlates of Reading: The Consensus of Thirty Years of Correlational Research*. Austin, TX: Pro-Ed Monograph.

HAMPSHIRE, S. (1981). *Susan's Story*. London: Sidgwick and Jackson.

HANNON, P. and JACKSON, A. (1987). 'Educational home visiting and the teaching of reading', *Educational Research*, 29, 182–91.

HARDING, L.M. (1984). 'Reading errors and reading style in children with specific reading disability', *Journal of Research in Reading*, 7, 103–12.

HARRIS, T.L. and HODGES, R.E. (Eds) (1981). *A Dictionary of Reading and Related Terms*. Newark, DE: International Reading Association.

HART, D.M. and HELLYER, P. (Eds) (1989). *National Association of Head Teachers Guide to the Education Reform Act 1988*. Haywards Heath: NAHT.

HARVEY, B. (1983). 'Life with dyslexia', *Parents' Handbook*, 2. Staines: Dyslexia Foundation.

HAWKES, R.C., HOLLAND, G.N., MOORE, W.S. and WORTHINGTON, B.S. (1980). 'Nuclear magnetic resonance (NMR) tomography of the brain: a preliminary clinical assessment with demonstration of pathology', *Journal of Computed Tomography*, 4, 577–86.

HEALY, J.M. (1982). 'The enigma of hyperlexia', *Reading Research Quarterly*, 17, 219–39.

HEATON, P. and WINTERTON, P. (1986). *Dealing with Dyslexia*. Bath: Better Books.

HEDDERLY, R. (1978). 'Orange juice therapy', *Association of Educational Psychologists' Journal*, 5, 9, 24–8.

HEDDERLY, R. (1979). 'Applied psychology or unethical conduct?', *Bulletin of the British Psychological Society*, 32, 135–6.

HEDDERLY, R. (1981). Characteristics of a clinical sample of dyslexic children. Unpublished study. Huddersfield.

HELVESTON, E.M. (1987). 'Management of dyslexia and related learning disabilities', *Journal of Learning Disabilities*, 20, 415–18.

HENDERSON, S.E. (1987). 'The assessment of "clumsy" children: old and new approaches', *Journal of Child Psychology and Psychiatry*, 28, 511–29.

HERBERT, D. and JONES, G.D. (1984). *A Classroom Index of Phonic Resources* (3rd edn). Stafford: NARE Publications.

HERMAN, K. (1959). *Reading Disability*. Stockholm: Munksgaard.

HERSON, M. (1986). *Pharmacology and Behavioural Treatment: An Integrated Approach*. New York: Wiley.

HESSLER, G.L. (1987). 'Educational issues surrounding severe discrepancy', *Learning Disabilities Research*, 3, 1, 43–9.

HEWISON, J. and TIZARD, J. (1980). 'Parental involvement and reading attainment', *British Journal of Educational Psychology*, 50, 3, 209–15.

HICKEY, M. (1977). *Dyslexia. A Language Training Course for Teachers and Learners*. Bath: Better Books.

HICKS, C. (1980). 'The ITPA visual sequential memory task: an alternative interpretation and its implications for good and poor readers', *British Journal of Educational Psychology*, 50, 1, 16–25.

HICKS, C. (1986). 'Remediating specific reading disabilities: a review of approaches', *Journal of Research in Reading*, 9, 1, 39–55.

HICKS, C. and SPURGEON, P. (1982). 'Two factor analytic studies of dyslexic subtypes', *British Journal of Educational Psychology*, 52, 3, 289–300.

HINSHELWOOD, J. (1900). 'Congenital word-blindness', *Lancet*, 21, 1506–8.

HINSHELWOOD, J. (1902). 'Congenital word-blindness, with reports of two cases', *Opthalmic Review*, 21, 91–9.

HINSHELWOOD, J. (1904). 'A case of congenital word-blindness', *British Medical Journal*, 2, 1303–7.

HINSHELWOOD, J. (1907). 'Few cases of congenital word-blindness occurring in the same family', *British Medical Journal*, 2, 1229.

HINSHELWOOD, J. (1909). 'Four cases of congenital word-blindness occurring in the same family', *British Medical Journal*, 2, 1229–32.

HINSON, M. and KELLY, T.A. (1986). 'Specific learning difficulties: one LEA's approach in practice', *Support for Learning*, 1, 2, 19–28.

HIRSH-PASEK, K. (1986). 'Beyond the great debate: finger spelling as an alternative route to word identification for deaf or dyslexic readers', *Reading Teacher*, 40, 3, 340–3.

HO, H.-Z., GILGER, J.W. and DECKER, S.N. (1988). 'A twin study of Bannatyne's "genetic dyslexic" subtype', *Journal of Child Psychology and Psychiatry*, 29, 63–73.

HOLDAWAY, D. (1980). *Independence in Reading* (2nd edn). Sydney: Ashton Scholastic.

HOLLIGAN, C. and JOHNSTON, R.S. (1988). 'The use of phonological information by good and poor readers in memory and reading tasks', *Memory and Cognition*, 16, 522–32.

HORNSBY, B. and FARRER, M. (1990). 'Some effects of a dyslexia centred teaching programme'. In: PUMFREY, P.D. and ELLIOTT, C.D. (Eds) *Children's Difficulties in Reading, Spelling and Writing*. London: Falmer Press.

HORNSBY, B. and MILES, T.R. (1980). 'The effects of a dyslexia-centred teaching programme', *British Journal of Educational Psychology*, 50, 3, 236–42.

HORNSBY, B. and SHEAR, F. (1975). *Alpha to Omega: the A–Z of Teaching Reading, Writing and Spelling*. London: Heinemann.

HOUSE OF COMMONS EDUCATION, SCIENCE AND ARTS COMMITTEE (1987). *Special Educational Needs; Implementation of the Education Act 1981*. London: HMSO.

HOWELL, E. and STANLEY, G. (1988). 'Colour and learning disability', *Clinical and Experimental Optometrics*, 71, 2, 66–71.

HUDSON, E. and CLUNIES-ROSS, G. (1984). 'Evaluation of interventions: a study of the integration of children with intellectual handicaps into regular schools', *Australia and New Zealand Journal of Developmental Disabilities*, 10, 165–77.

HULME, C. (1981a). 'The effects of manual tracing on memory in normal and retarded readers: some implications for multi-sensory teaching', *Psychological Research*, 43, 179–91.

HULME, C. (1981b). *Reading Retardation and Multi-sensory Teaching*. London: Routledge and Kegan Paul.

HULME, C. (1988). Working memory and learning to read (in preparation).

HULME, C. (1989). 'A longitudinal case study of phonological dyslexia'. Paper presented at the First International Conference of the British Dyslexia Association, Bath.

HULME, C., BICKERSTAFF, A., MORAN, A. and McKINLAY, I. (1982). 'Visual, kinaesthetic and cross-modal judgements of length by clumsy and normal children', *Developmental Medicine and Child Neurology*, 24, 461–71.

HULME, C. and BRADLEY, L. (1984). 'An experimental study of multi-sensory teaching with normal and retarded readers'. In: MALATESHA, R.M. and WHITAKE, H.A. (Eds) *Dyslexia: A Global Issue*. The Hague: Nijhoff.

HULME, C., THOMSON, N., MUIR, C. and LAWRENCE, A. (1984). 'Speech rate and the development of short-term memory span', *Journal of Experimental Child Psychology*, 38, 241–53.

HUMPHRIES, L.L. (1981). 'Medication and reading disability', *Journal of Research and Development in Education*, 14, 4, 54–7.

HUSTON, A.M. (1987). *Common Sense about Dyslexia*. Lanham, MD: Madison Books.

HUSTON, A.M. (1990). 'The effects of poor visual memory on reading and writing'. Paper read at the UKRA Annual Conference, University of Nottingham, 23–26 July.

HUSTON, A.M. (1991). *Understanding Dyslexia*. New York: Madison Books.

HYND, G.W. and COHEN, M. (1983). *Dyslexia: Neuropsychological Theory, Research and Clinical Differentiation*. New York: Grune and Stratton.

HYND, G.W., CONNOR, R.T. and NIEVES, N. (1987). 'Learning disabilities subtypes: perspectives and methodological issues in clinical assessment'. In: TRAMONTANA, M.G. and HOOPER, S.G. (Eds) *Assessment Issues in Child Neuro-psychology*. New York: Plenum Press.

HYND, G.W. and HYND, C.R. (1984). 'Dyslexia: neuroanatomical/neurodiagnostic perspectives', *Reading Research Quarterly*, 19, 482–98.

HYND, G.W. and OBRZUT, J.E. (1977). 'The effect of grade level and sex on the magnitude of the dichotic ear advantage', *Neurophychologicia*, 15, 689–92.

HYND, G.W., QUACKENBUSH, R. and OBRZUT, J.E. (1980). 'Training school psychologists in neuropsychological assessment: current practices and trends', *Journal of School Psychology*, 18, 148–53.

HYND, G.W. and WILLIS, W.G. (1988). *Pediatric Neuropsychology*. Orlando, FL: Grune and Stratton.

HYNDS, J. (1987). 'Diagnosing dyslexia', *ACE Reports – Journal of Clwyd Association for Compensatory Education*. Queensferry: Deeside Special Education Centre.

INNER LONDON EDUCATION AUTHORITY (1981). *Development of Reading and Related Skills with Pupils of Secondary Age (DORRS)* (ILEA Working Party. Chairperson: M. C. Roe). London: ILEA Learning Materials Service.

INNER LONDON EDUCATION AUTHORITY (1982). *Classroom Observation Procedure*. London: ILEA.

INTERAGENCY COMMITTEE ON LEARNING DISABILITIES (1987). *Learning Disabilities: A Report to the US Congress*. Bethseda, MD: National Institute of Health.

IRLEN, H. (1983). 'Successful treatment of learning disabilities'. Paper presented to the 91st Annual Convention of the American Psychological Association at Anaheim, California, August.

JACKSON, S. (1989). School focussed study. Dissertation submitted for the Diploma in Advanced Study in Specific Learning Difficulties (Literacy). University of Manchester.

JANSEN, M. (1985). 'Language and concepts: play and work? – Seriousness or fun? Basic or creativity?' In: CLARKE, M. (Ed.) *New Directions in the Study of Reading*.

JASTAK, S. and WILKINSON, G.S. (1984). *Wide Range Achievement Test (Revised)*. Wilmington, DE: Jastak Associates.

JEFFREE, D. and SKEFFINGTON, M. (1985). *Let Me Read*. London: Souvenir Press.

JOHNSON, D.J. (1978). 'Remedial approaches to dyslexia'. In: BENTON, A.J. and PEARL, D. (Eds) *Dyslexia: An Appraisal of Current Knowledge*. New York: Oxford University Press.

JOHNSTON, R.S. (1982). 'Phonological coding in dyslexic readers', *British Journal of Psychology*, 73, 455–60.

JOHNSTON, R.S. (1983). 'Developmental deep dyslexia', *Cortex*, 19, 133–9.

JOHNSTON, R.S., RUGG, M.D. and SCOTT, T. (1987). 'Phonological similarity effects, memory span and developmental reading disorders: the nature of the relationship', *The British Journal of Psychology*, 78, 205–13.

JORM, A.F. (1979). 'The cognitive and neurological basis of developmental dyslexia: a theoretical framework and review', *Cognition*, 7, 19–32.

JORM, A.F. (1983). 'Specific reading retardation and working memory: a review', *British Journal of Psychology*, 74, 311–42.

JORM, A.F., SHARE, D.L., MACLEAN, R. and MATTHEWS, R. (1984). 'Phonological confusability in short-term memory for sentences as a predictor of reading ability', *British Journal of Psychology*, 75, 393–400.

JORM, A.F., SHARE, D.L., MACLEAN, R. and MATTHEWS, R. (1986). 'Cognitive factors at school entry predictive of specific reading retardation and general reading backwardness', *Journal of Child Psychology and Psychiatry*, 27, 45–54.

KAPPERS, E.J. (1988). 'Neuropsychologische behandeling van initiele dyslexie'. In: VAN DER LEIJ, A. and HAMMERS, J. (Eds) *Dyslexie, 1988*. Lisse, The Netherlands: Swets and Zeitlinger.

KAPPERS, E.J. (1990). 'Neuropsychological treatment of dyslexic children', *Euro News Dyslexia*, 3, 9–15.

KASS, C. and MYKLEBUST, H. (1969). 'Learning disability: an educational definition', *Journal of Learning Disabilities*, 2, 377–9.

KATZ, R.B. (1986). 'Phonological deficiencies in children with reading disability: evidence from an object naming test', *Cognition*, 22, 225–57.

KAVALE, K. (1987). 'Theoretical issues surrounding severe discrepancy', *Learning Disabilities Research*, 3, 1, 12–20.

KAVALE, K. and FORNESS, S. (1985). *The Science of Learning Disabilities*. Windsor: NFER-NELSON.

KAVANAUGH, D. (Ed.) (1978). *Listen to Us!* New York: Workman Publishing.

KAY, J. and MARCEL, A. (1981). 'One process, not two, in reading aloud: analogies do the work of nonlexical rules', *Quarterly Journal of Experimental Psychology*, 33A, 397–413.

KEENEY, T.J., CANIZZO, S.R. and FLAVELL, J.H. (1967). 'Spontaneous and induced verbal rehearsal in a recall task', *Child Development*, 38, 953–66.

KELLY, G.A. (1955). *The Psychology of Personal Constructs*. New York: W. W. Norton.

KEMP, G. (1986). 'Reading across the curriculum: matching reading skills to reading materials', *Support for Learning*, 1, 1, 7–12.

KEPHART, N.C. (1960). *The Slow Learner in the Classroom*. Columbus, OH: Merrill.

KIRK, S.A. (1962). *Educating Exceptional Children*. Boston, MA: Houghton Mifflin.

KIRK, S.A. and CHALFANT, J.C. (1984). *Academic and Developmental Learning Disabilities*. London: Love Publishing.

KIRK, S.A. and KIRK, W.D. (1971). *Psycholinguistic Learning Disabilities: Diagnosis and Remediation*. Urbana, IL: University of Illinois Press.

KIRK, S.A., McCARTHY, J.J. and KIRK, W.D. (1968). *The Illinois Test of Psycholinguistic Abilities*. Urbana, IL: University of Illinois Press.

KIRKMAN, S. (1990). 'A chance to go into the top set', *Times Educational Supplement*, 8 June.

KLEIMAN, G.M. (1975). 'Speech recoding in reading', *Journal of Verbal Learning and Verbal Behaviour*, 14, 323–33.

KNUSSON, C. and CUNNINGHAM, C.C. (1988). 'Stress, disability and handicap'. In: FISHER, S. and REASON, J. (Eds) *Handbook of Life Stress, Cognition and Health*. Chichester: Wiley.

LAM, Y.Y. and HENDERSON, S.E. (1987). 'Some applications of the Henderson revision of the test of motor impairment', *British Journal of Educational Psychology*, 57, 389–401.

LAMM, O. (1989). Failure in achieving automatic performance of psychomotor skills. Paper presented at the First International Conference of the British Dyslexia Association, Bath.

LANE, C. (1990). 'ARROW: alleviating children's reading and spelling difficulties'. In: PUMFREY, P.D. and ELLIOTT, C.D. (Eds) *Children's Difficulties in Reading, Spelling and Writing*. London: Falmer Press.

LARSON, S. and PARLENVI, P. (1984). 'Patterns of inverted reading and sub groups in dyslexia', *Annals of Dyslexia*, 34, 195–203.

LASHLEY, K.S. (1938). 'Factors limiting recovering after cerebral nervous system lesions', *Journal of Nervous and Mental Diseases*, 88, 733–55.

LAVERS, P., PICKUP, M. and THOMPSON, M. (1986). 'Factors to consider in implementing an in-class support system within secondary schools', *Support for Learning*, 41, 1, 7–12.

LAWRENCE, D. (1973). *Improved Reading Through Counselling*. London: Ward Lock.

LAWRENCE, D. (1985). 'Improving self-esteem and reading', *Educational Research*, 27, 3, 194–200.

LAWRENCE, D. (1987). *Enhancing Self-esteem in the Classroom*. London: Paul Chapman.

LAWRENCE, D.H. (1915). *The Rainbow*. London: Heinemann.

LAWSON, J.S. and INGLIS, J. (1984). 'The psychometic assessment of children with learning disabilities: an index derived from a principal components analysis of the WISC-R', *Journal of Learning Disabilities*, 17, 517–22.

LAWSON, J.S. and INGLIS, J. (1985). 'Learning disabilities and intelligence test results: a model based on a principal components analysis of the WISC-R', *British Journal of Psychology*, 76, 35–48.

LAZARUS, R.S., DELONGIS, A., FOLKMAN, S. and GRUEN, R. (1985). 'Stress and adaptational outcomes: the problem of confounded measures', *American Psychologist*, 40, 770–9.

LAZARUS, R.S. and SMITH, C.A. (1988). 'Knowledge and appraisal in the cognition–emotional relationship', *Cognition and Emotion*, 2, 281–300.

LEFCOURT, H.M. (1981). *Research with the Locus of Control Construct*. Vol. 1. *Assessment Methods*. New York: Academic Press.

LEIJ, A. van der (1989). Can dyslexic children become automatic readers? Paper presented at the First International Conference of the British Dyslexia Association, Bath.

LEONG, C.K. (1987). *Children with Specific Reading Disabilities*. Berwyn: Swets North America.

LERER, R.J. *et al.* (1979). 'Handwriting deficits in children with minimal brain dysfunction: effects of methylphenidate (Ritalin) and placebo', *Journal of Learning Disabilities*, 12, 7, 450–55.

LEVINSON, H.N. (1980). *A Solution to the Riddle Dyslexia*. New York: Springer Verlag.

LEVINSON, H.N. (1989). 'Abnormal optokinetic and perceptual span parameters in cerebellar-vestibular dysfunction and learning disabilities or dyslexia', *Perceptual and Motor Skills*, 68, 1, 35–54.

LEVY, D.L. (1982). A case study of two dyslexic identical twins with specific language disability. Paper read at the University of Manchester International Conference on Dyslexia, Holly Royde College, Manchester.

LEVY, P. and GOLDSTEIN, H. (Eds) (1984). *Tests in Education*. London: Academic Press.

LEWIS, L. (1976). *Attack-a-Track*. Bath: Better Books.

LEWIS, R. (1991). Special arrangements at GCSE for students having specific learning difficulties (personal communication).

LEWKOWICZ, N.K. (1980). 'Phonemic awareness training: what to teach and how to teach it', *Journal of Educational Psychology*, 72, 686–700.

LIBERMAN, I.Y., SHANKWEILER, O., ORLANDO, C., HARRIS, K.S. and BERTI, F.B. (1971). 'Letter confusions and reversals of sequence in the beginning reader: implications for Orton's theory of developmental dyslexia', *Cortex*, 7, 127–42.

LINDSAY, G. (Ed.) (1984). *Screening for Children with Special Needs*. London: Croom Helm.

LINDSAY, G., EVANS, A. and JONES, B. (1985). 'Paired reading versus relaxed reading', *British Journal of Educational Psychology*, 55, 3, 304–9.

LLOYD-SMITH, M. and SINCLAIR-TAYLOR, A. (1988). 'Inservice training for "designated teachers"', *Support for Learning*, 3, 3, 166–72.

LORD, R. and HULME, C. (1988). 'Visual perception and drawing ability in clumsy and normal children', *British Journal of Developmental Psychology*, 6, 1–9.

LOSSE, A., HENDERSON, S.E., ELLIMAN, D., HALL, O., KNIGHT, E. and JONGMANS, M. (1991). 'Clumsiness in children – do they grow out of it? A ten year follow-up study', *Developmental Medicine and Child Neurology*, 33, 55–68.

LUNDBERG, I., OLAFSSON, A. and WALL, S. (1980). 'Reading and spelling skills in kindergarten', *Scandinavian Journal of Psychology*, 21, 159–73.

LYON, G.R. (1983). 'Subgroups of learning disabled readers: clinical and empirical identification', In: MYKLEBUST, H. (Ed.) *Progress in Learning Disabilities*, Vol. V. New York: Grune and Stratton.

LYSLEY, A. (1989). 'Getting into the mainstream: Robert', *Times*.

MACLEAN, M., BRYANT, P.E. and BRADLEY, L. (1987). 'Rhymes, nursery rhymes and reading in early childhood', *Merill-Palmer Quarterly*, 33, 255–82.

MANCHESTER CITY COUNCIL EDUCATION DEPARTMENT (1989). *English National Curriculum Key Stage 1 Resource Pack*. EDS North, Manchester M10 8WP.

MANN, V.A. (1984). 'Longitudinal prediction and prevention of early reading difficulty', *Annals of Dyslexia*, 34, 117–36.

MANN, V.A. (1986). 'Phonological awareness: the role of reading experience', *Cognition*, 24, 65–92.

MARCEL, T. (1980). 'Phonological awareness and phonological representation: investigation of a specific spelling problem'. In: FRITH, U. (Ed.) *Cognitive Processes in Spelling*. London: Academic Press.

MARIA, K. (1987). 'A new look at comprehension instruction for disabled readers', *Annals of Dyslexia*, 37, 264–78.

MARKIDES, A. (1983). *The Speech of Hearing-impaired Children*. Manchester: Manchester University Press.

MARSH, G., FRIEDMAN, M., WELCH, V. and DESBERG, P. (1981). 'A cognitive–developmental theory of reading acquisition'. In: MACKINNON, E. and WALLER, T.G. (Eds) *Reading Research: Advances in Theory and Practice*, 3. London: Academic Press.

MARSHALL, J.C. (1987). 'The cultural and biological context of written languages: their acquisition, deployment and breakdown'. In: BEECH, J. and COLLEY, A. (Eds) *Cognitive Approaches to Reading*. Chichester: Wiley.

MARSHALL, J.C. and NEWCOMBE, F. (1973). 'Patterns of paralexia: a psycholinguistic approach', *Journal of Psycholinguistic Research*, 2, 175–99.

MARSHALL, J.C. and NEWCOMBE, F. (1980). 'The conceptual status of deep dyslexia: an historical perspective'. In: COLTHEART, M., PATTERSON, K. and MARSHALL, J.C. (Eds) *Deep Dyslexia*. London: Routledge and Kegan Paul.

MARTIN, A. (1989). *The Strugglers*. Milton Keynes: Open University Press.

MARTIN, T. (1986). 'Leslie: a reading failure talks about failing', *Reading*, 20, 1, 43–52.

MASLAND, R.L. (1981). 'Neurological aspects of dyslexia'. In: PAVLIDIS, G.T. and MILES, T.R. (Eds) *Dyslexia Research and its Applications to Education*. Chichester: Wiley.

MASLAND, R.L. (1989). Neurological aspects of dyslexia. The John Glen memorial lecture. Paper presented to the BDA International Conference, Bath, 29 March 1989.

MASLAND, R.L. (1990). 'Neurological aspects of dyslexia'. In: HALES, G., HALES, M., MILES, T. and SUMMERFIELD, A. (Eds) *Meeting Points in Dyslexia. Proceedings of the First International Conference of the British Dyslexia Association*. Reading: British Dyslexia Association.

MASON, R.R. (1989). 'Unfinished action research: alleviating spelling correctively involving educationally novel technologies in school time (U AR A SCIENTIST)', *Educational Psychology in Practice*, 5, 2, 110–11.

MASTROPIERI, M.A. (1987). 'Statistical and psychometric issues surrounding severe discrepancy: a discussion', *Learning Disabilities Research*, 3, 1, 50–6.

MAY, F.B. (1986). *Reading as Communications: An Interactive Approach* (2nd edn). Columbus, OH: Merrill.

MAYEUX, R. and KANDEL, E.R. (1985). 'Natural language, disorders of language and other localisable disorders of cognitive functioning'. In: KANDEL, E.R. and SCHWARTZ, J.H. (Eds) *Principles of Neural Science* (2nd edn). New York: Elsevier.

McBRIDE, M.C. and KEMPER, T.L. (1982). 'Pathogenesis of four-layers microgyric cortex in man', *Acta Neuropathologica*, 57, 93–8.

McCLURE, P. and HYND, G. (1983). 'Is hyperlexia a severe reading disorder or a symptom of psychiatric disturbance?', *Clinical Neuropsychology*, 5, 145–9.

McKAY, M.F., NEALE, M.D. and THOMPSON, G.B. (1985). 'The predictive validity of Bannatyne's WISC categories for later reading achievement', *British Journal of Educational Psychology*, 55, 280–8.

McNAUGHTON, S., GLYNN, T. and ROBINSON, V. (1987). *Pause, Prompt, and Praise*. Birmingham: Positive Products.

MEDCALF, J. (1989). 'Comparison of peer tutored remedial reading using pause, prompt and praise procedure with individual tape assisted reading programme', *Educational Psychology*, 9, 3, 253–66.

MEEK, M. (1982). *Learning to Read*. London: Bodley Head.

MELCK, E. (1986). *Finding out about Specific Learning Difficulties/Dyslexia*. A publication available from 2 Manor House, Church Lawford, Warwickshire CV23 9EG.

MELLARD, D.F. (1987). 'Educational issues surrounding severe discrepancy: a discussion', *Learning Disabilities Research*, 3, 1, 29–31.

MILES, E. (1982). *The Bangor Teaching Programme*. Bangor: Dyslexia Unit.

MILES, E. (1989). *The Bangor Dyslexia Teaching System*. London: Whurr.

MILES, T.R. (1961). 'Two cases of developmental aphasia', *Journal of Child Psychology and Psychiatry*, 2, 48–70.

MILES, T.R. (1983a). *Bangor Dyslexia Test*. Cambridge: Learning Development Aids.

MILES, T.R. (1983b). *Dyslexia: The Pattern of Difficulties*. London: Collins Educational.

MILES, T.R. (1988). 'Counselling in dyslexia', *Counselling Psychology Quarterly*, 1, 97–107.

MILES, T.R. and ELLIS, N.C. (1981). 'A lexical encoding deficiency. II. Clinical observations'. In: PAVLIDIS, G.T. and MILES, T.R. (Eds) *Dyslexia Research and its Applications to Education*. Chichester: Wiley.

MILES, T.R. and MILES, E. (1990). *Dyslexia: A Hundred Years On*. Milton Keynes: Open University Press.

MILICH, L.C. and SHELDON, E. (1986). *I'm Edukationable. A Parents' Guide to Schools for Specific Learning Difficulties*. Ruislip: Defining Dyslexia.

MILLAR, L. (1986). 'Factors involved in supporting visually impaired children in mainstream schools', *Support for Learning*, 1, 4, 16–21.

MILLER, A. (1987). 'Is there still a place for paired reading?', *Educational Psychology in Practice*, 3, 1, 38–43.

MILLER, I.W. and NORMAN, W.H. (1979). 'Learned helplessness in humans: a review and attribution theory model', *Psychological Bulletin*, 86, 93–118.

MILLIDOT, M. (1986). *Dictionary of Optometrics*. London: Butterworths.

MILLS, K. (1988). 'Approaching an extended role for meeting special educational needs in high schools', *Support for Learning*, 3, 1, 20–6.

MITCHELL, J.V. (Ed.) (1985). *The Ninth Mental Measurement Yearbook*. Lincoln, NE: Nebraska, Buros Institute of Mental Measurements.

MITCHELL, J.V. (Ed.) (1987). *Buros' Mental Measurement Yearbook*. Lincoln, NE: University of Nebraska Press.

MOMMERS, M.J.C. (1987). 'An investigation into the relationship between word recognition, reading comprehension and spelling skills in the first two years of primary school', *Journal of Research in Reading*, 10, 122–43.

MONTGOMERY, D. (1981). 'Do dyslexics have difficulty accessing articulatory information?', *Psychological Research*, 43, 235–43.

MOON, C. and WELLS, G. (1979). 'The influence of home on learning to read', *Journal of Research in Reading*, 2, 53–62.

MOORE, P.J. (1988). 'Reciprocal teaching and reading comprehension: a review', *Journal of Research in Reading*, 11, 1, 3–14.

MORAIS, J., BERTELSON, P., CARY, L. and ALEGRIA, J. (1986). 'Literacy training and speech segmentation', *Cognition*, 24, 45–64.

MORAIS, J., CARY, L., ALEGRIA, J. and BERTELSON, P. (1979). 'Does awareness of speech as a sequence of phones arise spontaneously?', *Cognition*, 7, 323–31.

MORGAN, R.T.T. (1976). 'Paired-reading tuition: a preliminary report on a technique for cases of reading deficit', *Child Care, Health and Development*, 2, 13–28.

MORGAN, S.R. (1986). 'Locus control in children labelled learning disabled, behaviourally disordered, and learning disabled/behaviourally disordered', *Learning Disabilities Research*, 2, 10–13.

MORTIMORE, P., SAMMONS, P., STOLL, L., LEWIS, D. and ECOB, R. (1988). *School Matters*. London: Open Books.

MORTON, J. (1980). 'The logogen model and orthographic structure'. In: FRITH, U. (Ed.) *Cognitive Processes in Spelling*. London: Academic Press.

MOSELEY, D.V. (1988). 'Dominance, reading and spelling', *Bulletin d'Audiophonologie, Annales Scientifiques de l'Université Franche-Comte*, 443–64.

MOSELEY, D.V. (1990a). 'Suggestions for helping children with spelling problems'. In: PUMFREY, P.D. and ELLIOTT, C.D. (Eds) *Children's Difficulties in Reading, Spelling and Writing*. London: Falmer Press.

MOSELEY, D.V. (1990b). 'Research into visual function, reading and spelling', *Dyslexia Review*.

MOSELEY, D.V. and NICHOL, C. (1986). *Aurally Coded English Spelling Dictionary*. Wisbech, Cambs: Learning Development Aids.

MOSES, D., HEGARTY, S. and JOWETT, S. (1987). 'Meeting special educational needs support for the ordinary school', *Educational Research*, 29, 2, 108–15.

MOULTON, J.R. (1985). 'The writing process: a powerful approach for the language disabled student', *Annals of Dyslexia*, 35, 161–73.

NAIDOO, S. (1972). *Specific Dyslexia*. London: Pitman.

NAIDOO, S. (1981). 'Teaching methods and their rationale'. In: PAVLIDIS, G.Th. (Ed.) *Dyslexia Research and its Applications to Education*. New York: Wiley.

NAIDOO, S. (1988). *Assessment and Teaching of Dyslexic Children*. London: Invalid Children's Aid Nationwide (ICAN).

NAISMITH, D.J., NELSON, M., BURLEY, V.J. and GETENBYM, S.J. (1988). 'Can children's intelligence be increased by vitamin and mineral supplements?', *Lancet*, 6 August, p. 335.

NATIONAL ADVISORY COMMITTEE ON HANDICAPPED CHILDREN (1968). *Special Education for Handicapped Children (First Annual Report)*. Washington, DC: United States Office of Health, Education and Welfare.

NATIONAL ASSOCIATION FOR REMEDIAL EDUCATION (1985). *Guidelines 6: Teaching Roles for Special Educational Needs*. Stafford: NARE Publications.

NATIONAL CURRICULUM COUNCIL (1988). *Implementing the National Curriculum – Participation by Pupils with Special Educational Needs* (Circular No. 5). York: NCC.

NATIONAL CURRICULUM COUNCIL (1989a). *English Key Stages 1: Non-statutory Guidance*. York: NCC.

NATIONAL CURRICULUM COUNCIL (1989b). *A Curriculum for All*. York: NCC.

NATIONAL FOUNDATION FOR EDUCATIONAL RESEARCH (1970). *Reading Test BD*. Windsor: NFER-NELSON.

NATIONAL FOUNDATION FOR EDUCATIONAL RESEARCH (1989). *Touchstones*. Windsor: NFER-NELSON.

NATIONAL JOINT COMMITTEE ON LEARNING DISABILITIES (1988). *Letter to the Member Organisations of the NJCLD*.

NAYLOR, J.G. and PUMFREY, P.D. (1983). 'The alleviation of psycholinguistic deficits and some effects on the reading attainments of poor readers: a sequel', *Journal of Research in Reading*, 6, 2, 129–53.

NEALE, M.D. (1966). *The Neale Analysis of Reading Ability*. London: Macmillan.

NEALE, M.D. (1989). *The Neale Analysis of Reading Ability* (revised British edition). Windsor: NFER-NELSON.

NEARY, C. and WILKINS, A. (1989). 'Effects of phosphor persistence and the control of eye movements', *Perception*, 18, 257–64.

NEISSER, U. (1967). *Cognitive Psychology*. New York: Prentice-Hall.

NEWBY, M.J.N. (1969). 'Dyslexia and I', *Remedial Education*, 4, 3, 134–5.

NEWCOMER, P.L. and HAMMILL, D.D. (1976). *Psycholinguistics in the Schools*. Columbus, OH: Merrill.

NEWMAN, S.P., KERLE, H., WADSWORTH, J.F., ARCHER, R., HOCKLEY, R. and ROGERS, P. (1985). 'Ocular dominance, reading and spelling: a re-assessment of a measure associated with specific reading difficulties', *Journal of Research in Reading*, 8, 2, 127–8.

NEWMAN, S., WRIGHT, S. and FIELDS, H. (1989). 'Identification of a group of children with dyslexia by means of IQ-achievement discrepancies', *Irish Journal of Psychology*, 10, 4, 647–56.

NEWSON, J. and NEWSON, E. (1977). *Perspectives on School at Seven Years Old*. London: Allen and Unwin.

NEWTON, M.J. and THOMSON, M.E. (1982). *Aston Index (Revised)*. Wisbech, Cambs: Learning Development Aids.

NEWTON, M.J., THOMSON, M.E. and RICHARDS, I.R. (1978). *Readings in Dyslexia: A Study Text to Accompany the Aston Index*. London: LDA/Heinemann.

NEWTON, M.J., THOMPSON, M.E. and RICHARDS, I.L. (1979). *Readings in Dyslexia*. Wisbech, Cambs: Learning Development Aids.

NICHOLSON, C.L. and ALCORN, C.L. (1980). *Educational Applications of the WISC-R: A Handbook of Interpretive Strategies and Remedial Recommendations*. Los Angeles, CA: Western Psychological Services.

NORRIE, E. (1960). *The Edith Norrie Letter Case*. London: Helen Arkell Word Blind Centre.

NORTHWEST SEMERC. (1990). *Northwest SEMERC Software Survey*. Oldham: Northwest SEMERC.

OAKHILL, J. (1982). 'Constructive processes in skilled and less skilled comprehender's memory for sentences', *British Journal of Psychology*, 73, 13–20.

OAKHILL, J. (1984). 'Why children have difficulty reasoning with three-term series problems', *British Journal of Developmental Psychology*, 2, 223–30.

OBRZUT, J.E. and HYND, G.W. (Eds) (1986). *Child Neuropsychology*, Vol. 1, *Theory and Research*; Vol. 2, *Clinical Practice*. London: Academic Press.

O'CONNOR, P.D. and SOFO, F. (1988). 'Dyslexia and tinted lenses. A response to Gordon Stanley', *Australian Journal of Remedial Education*, 20, 1, 10–12.

OKE, A., KELLER, I. and ADAMS, R.N. (1978). 'Lateralization of norepinephrine in the human thalamus', *Science*, 200, 1411–13.

OLDENDORF, F.W.H. and ZABIELSKI, W. (1984). *Basic Principles of Nuclear Magnetic Resonance*. Garden Grove, CA: Medcom, Inc.

OLSEN, R.K., KLIEGL, R. and DAVIDSON, B.J. (1983). 'Dyslexia and normal readers' eye movements', *Journal of Experimental Psychology: Human Perception and Performance*, 9, 5, 816–25.

ORTON, J.L. (1967). 'The Orton–Gillingham approach'. In: MOONEY, J. (Ed.) *The Disabled Reader*. Baltimore, MD: Johns Hopkins University Press.

ORTON, S.T. (1925). 'Word blindness in school children', *Archives of Neurological Psychiatry*, 14, 5, 197–9.

ORTON, S.T. (1926). 'Reading disability', *Genetic Psychology Monographs*, 14, 335–453.

ORTON, S.T. (1937). *Reading, Writing and Speech Problems in Children*. New York: Norton.

PAIN, J.F. (1990). Indicators of specific learning difficulties in infant and junior schools: practical assessment and problems of estimating incidence (personal communication: PDP).

PATTERSON, K.E. (1982). 'The relation between reading and phonological coding: further neurological observations'. In: ELLIS, A.W. (Ed.) *Normality and Pathology in Cognitive Functions*. London: Academic Press.

PATTERSON, K.E., MARSHALL, J.C. and COLTHEART, M. (Eds) (1985). *Surface Dyslexia: Cognitive and Neuropsychological Studies in Phonological Reading*. London: Erlbaum.

PAVLIDIS, G.Th. (1979). 'How can dyslexia be objectively diagnosed?', *Reading*, 13, 3, 3–15.

PAVLIDIS, G.Th. (1981a). 'Do eye movements hold the key to dyslexia?', *Neuropsychologia*, 19, 57–64.

PAVLIDIS, G.Th. (1981b). 'Sequencing, eye movements and the early objective diagnosis of dyslexia'. In: PAVLIDIS, G.Th. and MILES, T.R. (Eds) *Dyslexia Research and its Application to Education*. Chichester: Wiley.

PAVLIDIS, G.Th. (1983). 'Erratic sequential eye-movements in dyslexics: comments and reply to Stanley *et al*.', *British Journal of Psychology*, 74, 189–93.

PAVLIDIS, G.Th. (Ed.) (1990a). *Perspectives on Dyslexia*, Vol. 1, *Neurology, Neuropsychology and Genetics*. Chichester: Wiley.

PAVLIDIS, G.Th. (Ed.) (1990b). *Perspectives on Dyslexia*, Vol. 2, *Cognition, Language and Treatment*. Chichester: Wiley.

PAVLIDIS, G.Th. and MILES, T.R. (1981). *Dyslexia Research and its Applications to Education*. Chichester: Wiley.

PAYNE, T.G. (1989). Secondary school children and their teachers' perceptions of the support available for learning difficulties. Thesis submitted for the degree of master of science in the Faculty of Arts, University of Manchester.

PAYNE, T. (1991). 'It's cold in the other room', *Support for Learning*, 6, 2, 61–5.

PEARSON, L. and LINDSAY, G. (1986). *Special Needs in the Primary School: Identification and Intervention*. Windsor: NFER-NELSON.

PERFETTI, C.A. and LESGOLD, A.M. (1977). 'Discourse comprehension and sources of individual differences'. In: JUST, M. and CARPENTER, P. (Eds) *Cognitive Processes in Comprehension*. Hillsdale, NJ: Erlbaum.

PHELPS, J. and STEMPEL, L. (1987). 'Handwriting: evolution and evaluation', *Annals of Dyslexia*, 37, 228–39.

PHEMISTER, P. (1973). 'Dyslexia from the inside', *Times Educational Supplement*, 4 March, p. 9.

PHILLIPS, E.M. (1989). 'Use and abuse of the Repertory Grid: a PCP approach', *The Psychologist*, 2, 194–8.

PINKERTON, F., WATSON, D.R. and McCELLAND, R.J. (1989). 'A neurophysiological study of children with reading, writing and spelling difficulties', *Developmental Medicine and Child Neurology*, 31, 569–71.

PINNELL, G.S., LYONS, C.A. and DEFORD, D.E. (1988). 'Reading Recovery'. In: SOPRIS WEST INC. *Educational Programmes that Work* (14th edn). Colorado: Sopris West Inc. in cooperation with the National Dissemination Study Group.

PIROZZOLO, F.J. (1979). *The Neuropsychology of Developmental Reading Disorders*. New York: Praeger.

POLLOCK, J. (1978). *Signposts to Spelling*. London: Helen Arkell Dyslexia Centre.

POOLE, H. (1989). Helping children with specific learning difficulties: the evaluation of a pilot project. MSc Thesis, Educational Psychology Special Study, Education Department, University of Sheffield.

PORTER, J. and ROURKE, B.P. (1985). 'Socio-emotional functioning of learning disabled children: a subtypal analysis of personality patterns'. In: ROURKE, B.P. (Ed.) *Neuropsychology of Learning Disabilities: Essentials of Subtype Analysis*. New York: Guilford Press.

POTTER, F. (1982). 'Listening and reading: the recall of 7–9 year olds', *British Journal of Educational Psychology*, 52, 16–24.

POTTON, A. (1983). *Screening*. London: Macmillan.

PRINGLE-MORGAN, W. (1896). 'A case of congenital word blindness', *British Medical Journal*, 2, 1378.

PUMFREY, P.D. (1977). *Measuring Reading Abilities: Concepts, Sources and Applications*. London: Hodder and Stoughton.

PUMFREY, P.D. (1979). 'Improved reading through counselling – Royal Road or cul-de-sac?'. In: THACKRAY, D. (Ed.) *Growth in Reading*. London: Ward Lock.

PUMFREY, P.D. (Ed.) (1980). *O. C. Sampson – Child Guidance: its Provenance, History and Future*. Leicester: Division of Educational and Child Psychology of the British Psychological Society.

PUMFREY, P.D. (1985). *Reading: Tests and Assessment Techniques* (2nd edn). London: Hodder and Stoughton in association with the UKRA.

PUMFREY, P.D. (1990a). 'Literacy and the National Curriculum: the challenge of the 1990s'. In: PUMFREY, P.D. and ELLIOTT, C.D. (Eds) *Children's Reading, Spelling and Writing Difficulties*. Lewes: Falmer Press.

PUMFREY, P.D. (1990b). 'Testing and teaching pupils with reading difficulties'. In: PUMFREY, P.D. and ELLIOTT, C.D. (Eds) *Children's Reading, Spelling and Writing Difficulties*, pp. 187–208. Lewes: Falmer Press.

PUMFREY, P.D. (1990c). 'Integrating: the testing and teaching of reading', *Support for Learning*, 5, 3, 146–52.

PUMFREY, P.D. (1991). *Improving Reading in the Junior School: Challenges and Responses*. London: Cassell.

PUMFREY, P.D. and ELLIOTT, C.D. (Eds) (1990). *Children's Reading, Spelling and Writing Difficulties*. Lewes: Falmer Press.

PUMFREY, P.D. and MITTLER, P. (1989). 'Peeling off the label', *Times Educational Supplement*, 3824, 29–30.

QUIN, V. and MACAUSLAN, A. (1986). *Dyslexia: What Parents Ought to Know*. Harmondsworth: Penguin.

RACK, J. (1985). 'Orthographic and phonetic encoding in normal and dyslexic readers', *British Journal of Psychology*, 76, 325–40.

RACK, J. and SNOWLING, M. (1985). 'Verbal deficits in dyslexia: a review'. In: SNOWLING, M. (Ed.) *Children's Written Language Difficulties: Assessment and Management*. Windsor: NFER-NELSON.

RAPIN, I. (1982). 'Developmental language disorders and brain dysfunction as precursors of reading disability'. In: WISE, G.B., BLAW, M.E. and PROCOPIS, P.G. (Eds) *Topics in Child Neurology*, Vol. 2. New York: Spectrum.

RAVEN, J.C. (1958). *Standard Progressive Matrices*. London: H.K. Lewis.

RAVENETTE, T.A. (1979). 'Specific reading difficulties: appearance and reality', *Association of Educational Psychologist Journal*, 4, 10, 1–12.

RAYBOULD, E., ROBERTS, B. and WEDELL, K. (1980). *Educational Review Occasional Publications*, No. 7. Birmingham: University of Birmingham Press.

RAYBOULD, E. and SOLITY, J. (1985). 'Teaching with precision'. In: SMITH, C. (Ed.) *New Directions in Remedial Education*. Lewes: Falmer Press and the National Association for Remedial Education.

RAYNER, K. (1983). *Eye Movements in Reading: Perceptual and Linguistic Aspects*. New York: Academic Press.

RAYNER, K. (1985). 'Do faulty eye movements cause dyslexia?', *Developmental Neuropsychology*, 1, 1, 3–15.

REASON, J. (1990a). *Human Error*. New York: Cambridge University Press.

REASON, R. (1984). Review of the Boder Test of Reading–Spelling Patterns. In: LEVY, P. and GOLDSTEIN, H. (Ed.) *Tests in Education*. London: Academic Press.

REASON, R. (1990b). 'Reconciling different approaches to intervention'. In: PUMFREY, P.D. and ELLIOTT, C.D. (Eds) *Children's Reading, Spelling and Writing Difficulties*. Lewes: Falmer Press.

REASON, R. and BOOTE, R. (1986). *Learning Difficulties in Reading and Writing: A Teacher's Manual*. Windsor: NFER-NELSON.

REASON, R., BROWN, B., COLE, M. and GREGORY, M. (1988). 'Does the "specific" in specific learning difficulties make a difference to the way we teach?', *Support for Learning*, 3, 4, 230–6.

REASON, R., FARRELL, P. and MITTLER, P. (1990). 'Changes in assessment'. In: ENTWISTLE, N. (Ed.) *Handbook of Educational Ideas and Practices*. London: Routledge.

REEVES, B. (1988). 'Reading through rose tinted spectacles', *Optician*, 29 January, pp. 21–6.

REID, J.F. (1983). 'Into print: reading language growth'. In: DONALDSON, M., GRIEVE, R. and PRATT, C. (Eds) *Early Childhood Development and Education*. Oxford: Blackwell.

REITSMA, P. (1984). 'Sound priming in beginning readers', *Child Development*, 55, 406–23.

RENOUX, G., BIZIERE, K., RENOUX, M., GUILLAUMIN, J.M. and DEGENNE, D. (1983). 'A balanced brain asymmetry modulates T cell mediated events', *Journal of Neuroimmunology*, 5, 227–38.

RENTEL, V.M., CORSON, S.A. and DUNN, B.R. (Eds) (1985). *Psychophysiological Aspects of Reading and Learning Monographs in Psychobiology: An Integrated Approach*. New York: Gordon and Breach, and Harwood.

REYNOLDS, R. and HOBBS, C. (1988). 'Is it too late, the exam's next month? Concessions for special needs students in GCSE', *Educational Psychology in Practice*, 4, 1, 42–5.

RICH, P. (1990). 'Mineral rights and wrongs', *Guardian*, 2 January, p. 26.

RICHARDS, I. (1989). Longitudinal studies of adolescent dyslexics. Paper presented at the First International Conference of the British Dyslexia Association, Bath.

RICHARDSON, A. (1988). 'The effects of a specific red filter on dyslexia', *British Psychological Society Abstracts*, 56.

RICHARDSON, S. (1989). The dyslexia movement in the USA. Paper presented at the First International Conference of British Dyslexia Association, Bath.

RICHENS, A. (1989). 'The effects of anti-epileptic drugs on learning and behaviour', *Educational and Child Psychology*, 6, 2, 44–9.

RICHMAN, L.C. and KITCHELL, M.M. (1981). 'Hyperlexia as a variant of developmental language disorder', *Brain and Language*, 12, 203–12.

ROBERTSON, A.H., HENDERSON, A., ROBERTSON, A., FISHER, J. and GIBSON, M. (1983). *QUEST Screening, Diagnosis and Remediation Kit*. Leeds: Arnold-Wheaton.

ROBINSON, G.L. and MILES, L. (1987). 'The use of coloured overlays to improve visual processing – a preliminary survey', *The Exceptional Child*, 34, 65–70.

RODGERS, B. (1983). 'The identification and prevalence of specific reading retardation', *British Journal of Educational Psychology*, 53, 369–73.

ROOT, B. (1986). *In Defence of Reading Schemes*. Reading: Reading and Language Information Centre, University of Reading.

ROSNER, J. and ROSNER, J. (1987). 'The Irlen treatment: a review of the literature', *Optician*, 25 September, pp. 26–33.

ROTHBAUM, F., WOLFEN, J. and VISINTAINER, M. (1979). 'Coping behaviour and locus of control in children', *Journal of Personality*, 47, 118–35.

ROURKE, B.P. (1988). 'Socioemotional disturbances of learning disabled children', *Journal of Consulting and Clinical Psychology*, 56, 6, 801–10.

RUDEL, R.G. and HELFGOTT, E. (1984). 'Effect of piracetam on verbal memory of dyslexic boys', *Journal of the American Academy of Child Psychiatry*, 23, 695–9.

RUGEL, R.P. (1974). 'WISC subtest scores of disabled readers: a review with respect to Bannatyne's recategorisation', *Journal of Learning Disabilities*, 7, 48–55.

RUMELHART, D.E. (1980). 'Schemata: the building blocks of cognition'. In: SPIRO, R.J., BRUCE, B.C. and BREWER, W.D. (Eds) *Theoretical Issues in Reading Comprehension*. Hillsdale, NJ: Erlbaum.

RUMELHART, D.E. (1985). 'Towards an interactive model of reading'. In: SINGER, H. and RUDDELL, R.B. (Eds) *Theoretical Models and Processes of Reading* (3rd edn). Newark, DE: International Reading Association.

RUMSEY, J.M., DORWART, R., VERMESS, M., DENCKLA, M.B., KRUESI, M.J.P. and RAPOPORT, J.L. (1986). 'Magnetic resonance imaging of brain anatomy in severe developmental dyslexia', *Archives of Neurology*, 43, 1045–6.

RUTHERFORD, W.J. (1909). 'The aetiology of congenital word-blindness: with an example', *British Journal of Children's Diseases*, 6, 484–8.

RUTTER, M., MAUGHAM, B., MORTIMORE, P. and OUSTON, J. (1979). *Fifteen Thousand Hours: Secondary Schools and their Effects on Children*. London: Open Books.

RUTTER, M., TIZARD, J. and WHITMORE, K. (1970). *Health, Education and Behaviour*. London: Longman.

RUTTER, M. and YULE, W. (1973). 'Specific reading retardation'. In: MANN, L. and SABATINO, D. (Eds) *The First Review of Special Education*. Bullonwood Farms: JSE Press.

RUTTER, M. and YULE, W. (1975). 'The concept of specific reading retardation', *Journal of Child Psychology and Psychiatry*, 16, 181–97.

RYE, J. (1982). *Cloze Procedures and the Teaching of Reading*. London: Heinemann Educational.

SABORNIE, E.J. (1989). 'Social mainstreaming of handicapped students. Facing an unpleasant reality', *Remedial and Special Education*, 6, 2, 13–16.

SAFFRAN, V.M., BOGYO, L.C., SCHARTZ, M.F. and MARTIN, O.S. (1980). 'Does deep dyslexia reflect right hemisphere reading?'. In: COLTHEART, M., PATTERSON, K. and MARSHALL, J.C. (Eds) *Deep Dyslexia*. Boston, MA: Routledge and Kegan Paul.

SALAME, P. and BADDELEY, A.D. (1982). 'Disruption of short-term memory by unattended speech: implications for the structure of working memory', *Journal of Verbal Learning and Verbal Behaviour*, 21, 150–64.

SAMPSON, O.C. (1975). 'Fifty years of dyslexia: a review of the literature 1925–1975. I. Theory', *Research in Education*, 14, 15–32.

SAMPSON, O.C. (1976). 'Fifty years of dyslexia: a review of the literature 1924–1975. II. Practice', *Research in Education*, 5, 39–54.

SAMPSON, O.C. (1980). *Child Guidance: Its History, Provenance and Future*. Leicester: British Psychological Society Division of Educational and Child Psychology.

SAWYER, C. and FLANN, C. (1983). 'Microcomputers and children with specific learning difficulties', *Association of Educational Psychologists Journal*, 6, 2, 62–4.

SCARR, S., CAPARULO, B.K., FERDMAN, B.M.N., TOWER, R.B. and CAPLAN, J. (1983). 'Developmental status and school achievements of minority and non-minority children from birth to 18 years in a British Midlands town', *British Journal of Developmental Psychology*, 1, 31–48.

SCHEERER-NEUMAN, G. (1981). 'The utilisation of intra-word structure in poor readers: experimental evidence and a training programme', *Psychological Research*, 43, 155–78.

SCHOENTHALER, S. (1991). *Improve your Child's IQ and Behaviour.* London: BBC Publications.

SCHONELL, F.J. and SCHONELL, F.E. (1942–55). *Schonell Graded Word Reading Test.* Edinburgh: Oliver and Boyd.

SCHONELL, F.J. and WALL, W.D. (1949). 'Remedial education centre', *Educational Review*, 2, 3–30.

SCHOOL EXAMINATIONS AND ASSESSMENT COUNCIL (SEAC) (1991). *Press Digest.* London: SEAC.

SCHOOL FEES INSURANCE AGENCY (1989). *The Parents' Guide to Independent Schools.* Maidenhead: SPIA Educational Trust.

SCHULZE, K.D. and BRAAK, H. (1976). *Hirnwarzen Zeitschrift fur Mikroskopisch–Anatomische Forschung*, 92, 609–23.

SCHWARTZ, M.F., SAFFRAN, E.M. and MARIN, O. (1980). 'Fractionating the reading process in dementia: evidence for word specific print-to-sound associations'. In: COLTHEART, M., PATTERSON, K.E. and MARSHALL, J.C. (Eds) *Deep Dyslexia.* Boston, MA: Routledge and Kegan Paul.

SCIENCE RESEARCH ASSOCIATES (1985). *Direct Instruction.* New York: SRA.

SEARLS, E.F. (1985). *How to use WISC-R Scores in Reading/Learning Disability Diagnosis.* Newark, DE: International Reading Association.

SECRETARY OF STATE FOR EDUCATION (1987). *Special Educational Needs: Implementation of the Education Act 1981. Observations by the Government on the Third Report of the Committee in Session 1986–87.* 15 December. London: HMSO.

SELECT COMMITTEE ON EDUCATION, SCIENCE AND THE ARTS (1987). *Special Educational Needs: Implementation of the Education Act 1981.* London: House of Commons.

SELYE, H. (1976). *The Stress of Life* (revised edn). New York: McGraw-Hill.

SERON, X. and DELOCHE, G. (Eds) (1989). *Cognitive Approaches in Neuropsychological Rehabilitation.* Hillsdale, NJ: Lawrence Erlbaum.

SEYMOUR, P.H.K. (1986). *Cognitive Analysis of Dyslexia.* London: Routledge and Kegan Paul.

SEYMOUR, P.H.K. (1987). 'Individual cognitive analysis of competent and impaired reading', *British Journal of Psychology*, 78, 483–506.

SEYMOUR, P.H.K. and McGREGOR, C.J. (1984). 'Developmental dyslexia: experimental analysis of phonological, morphemic, and visual impairments', *Cognitive Neuropsychology*, 1, 43–82.

SHALLICE, T. (1981). 'Phonological agraphia and the lexical route of writing', *Brain*, 104, 413–29.

SHALLICE, T. and WARRINGTON, E.K. (1980). 'Single and multiple component central dyslexia syndromes'. In: COLTHEART, M., PATTERSON, K. and MARSHALL, J.C. (Eds) *Deep Dyslexia.* London: Routledge and Kegan Paul.

SHALLICE, T., WARRINGTON, E.K. and McCARTHY, R. (1983). 'Reading without semantics', *Quarterly Journal of Experimental Psychology*, 35A, 111–38.

SHANKWEILER, D. and CRAIN, S. (1986). 'Language mechanism and reading disorder: a modular approach', *Cognition*, 24, 139–68.

SHARE, D.L., McGEE, R., McKENZIE, D., WILLIAMS, S. and SILVA, P.A. (1987). 'Further evidence relating to the distinction between specific reading retardation and general reading backwardness', *British Journal of Developmental Psychology*, 5, 1, 35–45.

SHARE, D.L. and SILVA, P.A. (1986). 'The stability and classification of specific reading retardation: a longitudinal study from 7–11', *British Journal of Educational Psychology*, 56, 32–9.

SHARPLEY, C.F. and ROWLAND, S.E. (1986). 'Palliative vs direct action stress-reduction procedures as treatments for reading disability', *British Journal of Educational Psychology*, 56, 1, 40–50.

SHAVELSON, R.J. and BOLUS, R. (1982). 'Self-concept: the interplay of theory and methods', *Journal of Educational Psychology*, 74, 1, 3–17.

SHAVELSON, R.J., HUBNER, J.J. and STANTON, J.C. (1976). 'Self-concept: validation of construct interpretations', *Review of Educational Research*, 46, 407–41.

SHEA, D.R. (1987). 'Medical considerations in learning disorders – a review', *The Mental Retardation Learning Disability Bulletin*, 15, 2, 57–66.

SHEPARD, L. (1980). 'An evaluation of the regression discrepancy method for identifying children with learning disabilities', *Journal of Special Education*, 14, 79–91.

SHEPHERD, I., EVANS, A., CHERRY, C. and HIGGINS, A. (1990). 'Academic engagement: effects of feedback to teachers of "on-task" pupil behaviour', *Educational Psychology in Practice*, 5, 227–34.

SIEGEL, L.S. (1984). 'A longitudinal study of a hyperlexic child: hyperlexia as a language disorder', *Neuropsychologia*, 22, 5, 577–85.

SIEGEL, L.S. (1989). 'IQ is irrelevant to the definition of learning disabilities', *Journal of Learning Disabilities*, 22, 469–78.

SIEGEL, E. and GOLD, R. (1982). *Educating the Learning Disabled*. New York: Macmillan.

SIGMON, S.B. (1989). 'Reactions to excerpts from the learning mystique: a rationale appeal for change', *Journal of Learning Disabilities*, 22, 5, 298–300.

SILVA, P.A., McGEE, R. and WILLIAMS, S. (1985). 'Some characteristics of nine-year-old boys with general reading backwardness or specific reading retardation', *Journal of Child Psychology and Psychiatry*, 26, 407–21.

SIMM, T. (1986). 'The long term results of remedial teaching of reading', *Educational Psychology in Practice*, 1, 4, 142–7.

SIMMONS, K. (1988). 'Writing with a word-processor – what difference does it make?', *Support for Learning*, 3, 4, 207–9.

SINGER, H. and RUDDELL, R.B. (Eds) (1985). *Theoretical Models and Processes of Reading* (3rd edn). Newark, DE: International Reading Association.

SINGLETON, C.H. (1975). 'The myth of specific developmental dyslexia. Part I. History, incidence and diagnosis of the syndrome', *Remedial Education*, 10, 109–13.

SINGLETON, C.H. (1976). 'The myth of specific developmental dyslexia. Part II. Aetiology', *Remedial Education*, 11, 13–17.

SINGLETON, C.H. (1987). 'Dyslexia and cognitive models of reading', *Support for Learning*, 2, 2, 47–56.

SINGLETON, C.H. (1988). 'The early diagnosis of developmental dyslexia', *Support for Learning*, 3, 2, 108–21.

SINGLETON, C.H. (Ed.) (1991). *Computers and Literacy Skills*. British Dyslexia Association Computer Resource Centre, Department of Psychology, University of Hull.

SMITH, F. (1973). *Psycholinguistics and Reading*. New York: Holt, Rinehart and Winston.

SMITH, F. (1978). *Understanding Reading*. London: Holt, Rinehart and Winston.

SMITH, F. (1985). *Reading*. Cambridge: Cambridge University Press.

SMITH, F. (1988). *Understanding Reading. A Psycholinguistic Analysis of Reading and Learning to Read* (4th edn). Hillsdale, NJ: Erlbaum.

SNOWLING, M.J. (1980). 'The development of phoneme–grapheme correspondence in normal and dyslexic readers', *Journal of Experimental Child Psychology*, 29, 219–38.

SNOWLING, M.J. (1981). 'Phoneme deficits in developmental dyslexia', *Psychological Research*, 43, 219–34.

SNOWLING, M.J. (Ed.) (1985). *Children's Written Language Difficulties: Assessment and Management*. Windsor: NFER-NELSON.

SNOWLING, M.J. (1987). *Dyslexia: A Cognitive Developmental Perspective.* Oxford: Blackwell.

SNOWLING, M.J. (1990). 'Dyslexia in childhood: a cognitive–developmental perspective'. In: PUMFREY, P.D. and ELLIOTT, C.D. (Eds) *Children's Difficulties in Reading, Spelling and Writing.* Basingstoke: Falmer Press.

SNOWLING, M.J., GOULANDRIS, N., BOWLBY, M. and HOWELL, P. (1986). 'Segmentation and speech perception in relation to reading skills: a developmental analysis', *Journal of Experimental Child Psychology,* 41, 489–507.

SNOWLING, M.J., HULME, C. and GOULANDRIS, N. (1990). 'Phonological coding deficits in dyslexia'. In: HALES, G. with HALES, M., MILES, T. and SUMMERFIELD, A. (Eds) *Meeting Points in Dyslexia: Proceedings of the First International Conference of the British Dyslexia Association.* Reading: British Dyslexia Association.

SNOWLING, M.J. and STACKHOUSE, J. (1983). 'Spelling performance of children with developmental verbal dyspraxia', *Developmental Medicine and Child Neurology,* 25, 430–7.

SNOWLING, M.J. and THOMSON, D. (Eds) (1991). *Dyslexia: Integrating Theory and Practice.* London: Whurr.

SOLITY, J. and BULL, S. (1987). *Special Needs: Bridging the Curriculum Gap.* Milton Keynes: Open University Press.

SOMERVILLE, D.E. and LEACH, D.J. (1988). 'Direct or indirect instruction? An evaluation of three types of intervention programme for assisting students with specific reading difficulties', *Educational Research,* 30, 1, 46–53.

SPACHE, G.D. (1976). *Investigating the Issues of Reading Disabilities.* Boston, MA: Allyn and Bacon.

SPEECE, D.L., McKINNEY, J.D. and APPELBAUM, M.I. (1985). 'Classification and validation of behavioural subtypes of learning-disabled children', *Journal of Educational Psychology,* 77, 67–77.

SPRING, C. and CAPPS, C. (1974). 'Encoding speed, rehearsal and probed recall of dyslexic boys', *Journal of Educational Psychology,* 66, 780–6.

ST JAMES-ROBERTS, I.A. (1981). 'A reinterpretation of hemispheroctomy findings without functional plasticity of the brain. I. Intellectual function', *Brain and Language,* 13, 31–53.

STANLEY, G. (1975). 'Two-part stimulus integration and specific reading disability', *Perceptual and Motor Skills,* 41, 873–4.

STANLEY, G., SMITH, G.A. and HOWELL, E.A. (1983a). 'Eye movements and sequential tracking in dyslexic and control children', *British Journal of Psychology,* 74, 181–7.

STANLEY, G., SMITH, G.A. and HOWELL, E.A. (1983b). 'Eye movements in dyslexic children: comments on Pavlidis' reply', *British Journal of Psychology,* 74, 195–7.

STANOVICH, K.E. (1980). 'Toward an interactive–compensatory model of individual differences in the development of reading fluency', *Reading Research Quarterly,* 16, 32–71.

STANOVICH, K.E. (1986). 'Matthew effects in reading: some consequences of individual differences in the acquisition of literacy', *Reading Research Quarterly,* 21, 4, 360–407.

STANOVICH, K.E. (1988). 'Explaining the difference between the dyslexic and the garden-variety poor readers: the phonological core model', *Journal of Learning Disability,* 21, 10, 590–604.

STANOVICH, K.E. (1991). 'Discrepancy definitions of reading disability: Has intelligence led us astray?' *Reading Research Quarterly,* XXVI, 1, 7–29.

STANOVICH, K.E., CUNNINGHAM, A.E. and FREEMAN, D.J. (1984). 'Intelligence, cognitive skills and early reading progress', *Reading Research Quarterly,* 19, 278–303.

START, K.B. and WELLS, B.K. (1972). *The Trend of Reading Standards.* Slough: NFER.

STATUTORY INSTRUMENT (1990). *Education (Special Educational Needs) (Amendment) Regulations 1990, No. 1524.* London: HMSO.

STAUFFER, R.G., ABRAMS, J.C. and PIKULSKI, J.J. (1978). *Diagnosis: Correction and Prevention of Reading Difficulties*. New York: Harper and Row.

STEIN, J.F. (1991). 'Vision and language'. In: SNOWLING, M. and THOMSON, M. (eds). *Dyslexia: Integrating Theory and Practice*. London: Whurr.

STEIN, J.F. and FOWLER, S. (1982). 'Ocular motor dyslexia', *Dyslexia Review*, 5, 25–8.

STEIN, J.F. and FOWLER, S. (1985). 'Effect of monocular occlusion on visuomotor perception and reading in dyslexic children', *Lancet*, 13 July.

STEIN, J.F. and RIDDELL, P.M. (1988). 'Disordered vergence control in dyslexic children', *British Journal of Ophthalmology*, 72, 162–6.

STERNE, M. (1990). 'Word blindness', *Times Educational Supplement*, 12 January, p. 20.

STUART, A. (1990). 'The DES Family Reading Group Project – report on work in progress'. Paper presented at the 1990 Annual Conference of the United Kingdom Reading Association, University of Nottingham, July.

STUART–HAMILTON, I. (1986). 'The role of phonemic awareness in the reading style of beginning readers', *British Journal of Educational Psychology*, 56, 271–86.

SUMNER, R. (1987). *The Role of Testing in Schools*. Windsor: NFER-NELSON.

SWANSON, H.L. (1984). 'Semantic and visual memory codes in learning disabled readers', *Journal of Experimental Child Psychology*, 37, 124–40.

SWEETLAND, R.C. and KEYSER, D.J. (1984). *Tests: A Comprehensive Reference for Assessments in Psychology, Education and Business*. Kansas City: Test Corporation of America.

SWEETLAND, R.C. and KEYSER, D.J. (1985). *Tests: A Comprehensive Reference for Assessments in Psychology, Education and Business. Supplement*. Kansas City: Test Corporation of America.

TANSLEY, P. and PANCKHURST, J. (1981). *Children with Specific Learning Difficulties: A Critical Review*. Windsor: NFER-NELSON.

TAYLOR, D.C., FALCONER, M.A., BRUTON, C.J. and CORSELLIS, J.A.W. (1971). 'Focal dysplasia of the cerebral cortex in epilepsy', *Journal of Neurology, Neurosurgery and Psychiatry*, 34, 369–87.

TAYLOR, H.G., SATZ, P. and FRIEL, S. (1979). 'Developmental dyslexia: significance and clinical utility', *Reading Research Quarterly*, 15, 1, 84–101.

TEMPLE, C.M. (1985). 'Reading with partial phonology: developmental phonological dyslexia', *Journal of Psycholinguistic Research*, 14, 523–41.

TEMPLE, C.M. (1986). Acquired and developmental dyslexia: a biological and cognitive perspective. Paper presented to the British Psychological Society, 18–19 September, City University, London.

TEMPLE, C.M. and MARSHALL, J.C. (1983). 'A case study of developmental phonological dyslexia', *British Journal of Psychology*, 74, 517–33.

THOMAS, G. (1986). 'Integrating personnel in order to integrate children', *Support for Learning*, 1, 1, 20–6.

THOMAS, G. (1990). 'Evaluating support', *Support for Learning*, 5, 1, 30–6.

THOMSON, M.E. (1982). 'The assessment of children with specific reading difficulties (dyslexia) using the British Ability Scales', *British Journal of Psychology*, 73, 461–78.

THOMSON, M.E. (1984). *Developmental Dyslexia*. London: Edward Arnold.

THOMSON, M.E. (1988a). *Developmental Dyslexia: Its Nature Assessment and Remediation* (2nd edn). London: Cole and Whurr.

THOMSON, M.E. (1988b). 'Preliminary findings concerning the effects of specialised teaching on dyslexic children', *Applied Cognitive Psychology*, 2, 19–31.

THOMSON, M.E. (1989). *Developmental Dyslexia*, (3rd edn). London: Whurr.

THOMSON, M.E. (1990). 'Evaluating teaching programmes for children with specific learning difficulties'. In: PUMFREY, P.D. and ELLIOTT, C.D. (Eds) *Children's Difficulties in Reading, Spelling and Writing*. London: Falmer Press.

THOMSON, M.E. and WATKINS, W. (1990). *Dyslexia: A Teaching Handbook*. London: Whurr.

Times Educational Supplement (1982). 'Public school admissions give dyslexics big boost', *Times Educational Supplement*, 16 July.

TOPPING, K. (1988). *Peer Tutoring Handbook: Promoting Co-operative Learning*. London: Croom Helm.

TOPPING, K. (1991). Outcome Evaluation of the Kirkless Paired Reading Project. PhD thesis, Division of Education, University of Sheffield.

TOPPING, K. and WOLFENDALE, S. (Eds) (1985). *Parental Involvement in Children's Reading*. London: Croom Helm.

TORRANCE, N. and OLSEN, D. (1985). 'Oral–written differences in the production and recall of narratives'. In: OLSON, D., TORRANCE, and HILLYARD, A. (Eds) *Literacy, Language and Learning: The Nature and Consequences of Reading and Writing*. Cambridge: Cambridge University Press.

TORREY, J.W. (1979). 'Reading that comes naturally: the early reader'. In: WALLER, T. and McKINNON, G. (Eds) *Reading Research: Advances in Theory and Practice*. New York: Academic Press.

TRIEMAN, R. (1985). 'Onsets and times as units of spoken syllables: evidence from children', *Journal of Experimental Child Psychology*, 39, 161–81.

TUCKER, J.A. (1980). 'Ethnic proportions in classes for the learning disabled issues in non-biased assessment', *Journal of Special Education*, 14, 93–105.

TURNER, M. (1990). *Sponsored Reading Failure*. Warlingham: IPSET Education Unit.

TYLER, S. (1990). 'Subtypes of specific learning difficulties: a review'. In: PUMFREY, P.D. and ELLIOTT, C.D. (Eds) *Children's Difficulties in Reading, Spelling and Writing*. London: Falmer Press.

TYLER, S. and ELLIOTT, C.D. (1988). 'Cognitive profiles of poor readers and dyslexic children on the British Ability Scales', *British Journal of Psychology*, 79, 493–508.

TYLER, S. and ELLIOTT, C.D. (in preparation). Discriminant analysis of British Ability Scales profiles in classifying children with specific learning difficulties into subgroups.

ULLMAN, R.K., SLEATOR, E.K. and SPRAGUE, R.L. (1984). 'A new rating scale for diagnosis and monitoring of ADD children', *Psychopharmacology Bulletin*, 20, 160–4.

UNITED STATES OFFICE OF EDUCATION (1975). Public Law 94-142. *Education for All Handicapped Children Act*. US Congress.

UNITED STATES OFFICE OF EDUCATION (1976). *Education of Handicapped Children. Federal Register*, 41:52405. Washington, DC: US Government Printing Office.

UNITED STATES OFFICE OF EDUCATION (1977). *Definition and Criteria for Defining Students as Learning Disabled. Federal Register*, 42:250. Washington, DC: US Government Printing Office.

UNITED STATES OFFICE OF EDUCATION (1988). *Power On: New Tools for Teaching and Learning*. Washington, DC: US Government Printing Office.

VAN DER WISSEL, A. (1987). 'IQ Profiles of learning disabled and mildly mentally retarded children: a psychometric selection effect', *British Journal of Developmental Psychology*, 5, 45–51.

VAN DER WISSEL, A. and ZEGERS, F.E. (1985). 'Reading retardation revisited', *British Journal of Developmental Psychology*, 3, 3–9.

VEITH, G. and SCHWINDT, W. (1976). 'Pathologisch–anatomischer Beitray zum Problem', *Fortschritte de Neurologie, Psychiatrie und Ihrer Grenzgebiete*, 44, 1–21.

VELLUNTINO, F.R. (1979). *Dyslexia Theory and Research*. Cambridge, MA: MIT Press.

VELLUNTINO, F.R. (1987). 'Dyslexia', *Scientific American*, 256, 3, 34–41.

VERMA, G. and PUMFREY, P.D. (Eds) (1988). *Educational Attainments: Issues and Outcomes in Multicultural Education*. Basingstoke: Falmer Press.

VERNON, P.E. (1979). *Intelligence: Heredity and Environment*. San Francisco, CA: W. H. Freeman.

VESS, S.M. (1990). 'Medications commonly used with schoolchildren'. In: THOMAS, A. and GRIMES, J. (Eds) Best Practices in School Psychology II. Washington, DC: The National Association of School Psychologists.

VICKERY, K.S. and REYNOLDS, V.A. (1987). 'Multi-sensory teaching approach for reading, spelling and handwriting. Orton Gillingham based curriculum in a public school setting', *Annals of Dyslexia*, 37, 189–200.

VINCENT, D. (1984). *Reading Tests in the Classroom: An Introduction*. Windsor: NFER-NELSON.

VINCENT, D. with POWNEY, J., GREEN, L. and FRANCIS, J. (1983). *A Review of Reading Tests*. Windsor: NFER-NELSON.

VISSER, J. (1986). 'Support: a description of the work of the SEN professional', *Support for Learning*, 1, 4, 5–9.

VYGOTSKY, L.S. (1962). *Thought and Language*. Cambridge, MA: MIT Press.

VYGOTSKY, L.S. (1978). *Mind in Society: The Development of Higher Psychological Processes*. London: Harvard University Press.

WAGNER, R. and TORGESEN, J. (1987). 'The nature of phonological processing and its causal role in the acquisition of reading skills', *Psychological Bulletin*, 101, 192–212.

WALLACE, C. (1986). *Learning to Read in a Multicultural Society*. Oxford: Pergamon Press.

WATERLAND, L. (1986). *Read with Me: An Apprenticeship Approach to Reading*. Stroud, Gloucestershire: Thimble Press.

WEBSTER, A. and McCONNELL, C. (1987). *Children with Speech and Language Difficulties*. London: Cassell Educational.

WEBSTER, A. and WOOD, D. (1989). *Children with Hearing Difficulties*. London: Cassell.

WEBSTER, J. (1971). *The Rescue Handbook*. Aylesbury: Ginn.

WECHSLER, D. (1974). *Wechsler Intelligence Scale for Children (Revised)*. New York: Psychological Corporation.

WEDELL, K. (1970). 'Diagnosing learning difficulties: a sequential strategy', *Journal of Learning Disabilities*, 3, 6, 23–39.

WEDELL, K. and LAMBOURNE, R. (1980). 'Psychological services for children in England and Wales', *Occasional Papers of the Division of Educational Psychology of the British Psychological Society*, 4, 1 and 2 (complete edition).

WEINBERGER, J. (Ed.) (1989). 'Noninvasive imaging of cerebrovascular disease', *Frontiers of Clinical Neuroscience*, 5 (complete edition).

WEINER, B. (1979). 'A theory of motivation for some classroom experiences', *Journal of Educational Psychology*, 71, 3–25.

WEINER, B. (1985). 'An attributional theory of achievement, motivation and emotion', *Psychological Review*, 92, 548–73.

WELLS, G. (Ed.) (1985a). *Language, Learning and Education*. Windsor: NFER-NELSON.

WELLS, G. (1985b). 'Pre-school literacy: related activities and success in school'. In: OLSON, D., TORRANCE, N. and HILLYARD, A. (Eds) *Literacy, Language and Learning: The Nature and Consequences of Reading and Writing*. Cambridge: Cambridge University Press.

WENDON, L. (1973). *The Pictogram System*. Barton, Cambs: Pictogram Supplies.

WEPMAN, J. (1975). *Auditory Discrimination Test*. Palm Springs, CA: Language Research Association.

WEPMAN, J., CRUICKSHANK, W., DEUTSCH, C., MORENCY, A. and STROTHER, C. (1975). 'Learning disabilities'. In: HOBBS, N. (Ed.) *Issues in the Classification of Children*. San Francisco, CA: Jossey-Bass.

WHEELER, T.J. (1979). *Dyslexia: A Computer Review of Literature from 1966–1979*. Sheffield: Department of Communication Studies, Sheffield Polytechnic.

WHELDALL, K., MERRET, F. and COLMAR, S. (1987). 'Pause, prompt, and praise for parents and peers: effective tutoring of low progress readers', *Support for Learning*, 2, 1, 5–12.

WHITTAKER, M.E. (1981). 'Letter', *Times Educational Supplement*, 13 November.

WHITTAKER, M.E. (1982). 'Dyslexia and the flat earth', *Bulletin of the British Psychological Society*, 35, 97–8.

WHITTAKER, M.E. (1989a). 'The concept of dyslexia', Note to the DECP National Inquiry.

WHITTAKER, M.E. (1989b). 'Letter', *The Psychologist*, 12, 7, 282.

WHITTINGTON, J.E. and RICHARDS, P.N. (1987). 'The stability of children's laterality prevalences and their relationship to measures of performance', *British Journal of Educational Psychology*, 57, 45–55.

WILKINS, A. (1989). 'Photosensitive epilepsy and visual discomfort'. In: KENNARD, C. and SWASH, M. (Eds) *Hierarchies in Neurology: A Reappraisal of a Jacksonian Concept*. London: Springer Verlag.

WILKINS, A. (1990). Visual discomfort and reading. MRC, APU, Cambridge. (To be published in forthcoming book by J. F. Stein.)

WILLES, M. (1983). *Children into Pupils: A Study of Language in Early Schooling*. London: Routledge and Kegan Paul.

WILLIAMS, P.W. (1988). *A Glossary of Special Education*. Milton Keynes: Open University Press.

WILLSON, V.L. (1987). 'Statistical and psychometric issues surrounding severe discrepancy', *Learning Disabilities Research*, 3, 1, 24–8.

WILSHER, C.R. (1980). 'Piracetam treatment of specific written language difficulties (dyslexia) – a discussion', *Dyslexia Review*, 3, 1, 8–9.

WILSHER, C.R. (1986). 'The nootropic concept and dyslexia', *Annals of Dyslexia*, 36, 118–37.

WILSHER, C.R. (1990). 'Treatments for dyslexia: proven or unproven?' In: HALES, G., HALES, M., MILES, T. and SUMMERFIELD, A. (Eds) *Meeting Points in Dyslexia: Proceedings of the First International Conference of the British Dyslexia Association*. Reading: British Dyslexia Association.

WILSHER, C.R., ATKINS, G. and MANFIELD, P. (1979). 'Piracetam as an aid to learning in dyslexia', *Psychopharmacology*, 65, 107–9.

WILSHER, C.R., BENNETT, D., CHASE, C.H., CONNORS, C.K., DIANNI, M., FEAGANS, L., HANVICK, L.J., HELPGOTT, E., KOPLEWICZ, H., OVERBY, P., READER, M.J., RUDEL, R.G. and TALLAL, P. (1987). 'Piracetam and dyslexia: effects on reading tests', *Journal of Clinical Psychopharmacology*, 7, 4, 230–7.

WILSHER, C.R. and TAYLOR, J.A. (1987). 'Remedies for dyslexia: proven or unproven?', *Early Child Development and Care*, 27, 3, 437–49.

WILSON, B.D. and WILSON, J.J. (1980). 'Language disordered children: a neuropsychologic view'. In: FEINGOLD, B. and BANK, C. (Eds) *Developmental Disabilities of Early Childhood*. Springfield, IL: Charles C. Thomas.

WILSON, V.L. (1987). 'Statistical and psychometric issues surrounding severe discrepancy', *Learning Disabilities Research*, 3, 1, 138–42.

WILTSHIRE COUNTY COUNCIL EDUCATION DEPARTMENT (1988). *Early Identification of Special Needs*. Trowbridge: Wiltshire County Council.

WINTER, S. (1987). 'Irlen lenses: an appraisal', *Australian Educational Developmental Psychologist*, 4, 2, 1–5.

WITELSON, S. (1977). 'Developmental dyslexia: two right hemispheres and none left', *Science*, 195, 309–11.

WOLFENDALE, S. (1987). *Primary Schools and Special Needs: Policy, Planning and Provision*. London: Cassell (2nd edn, 1991).

WOOD, J.R.A. and BURNS, R.B. (1983). 'Self-concept and reading ability in ESN (M) pupils', *Research in Education*, 29, 41–55.

WOOSTER, A.D. and CARSON, A. (1982). 'Improving reading and self-concept through communication and social skills training', *British Journal of Guidance and Counselling*, 10, 1, 83–7.

WORLD FEDERATION OF NEUROLOGY (1968). *Report of Research Group on Dyslexia and World Illiteracy*. Dallas, TX: WFN.

WYLIE, R.C. (1979). *The Self Concept*, Vol. 2, *Theory and Research on Selected Topics*. Lincoln, NE: University of Nebraska Press.

YOPP, H.K. (1988). 'The validity and reliability of phonemic awareness tests', *Reading Research Quarterly*, 23, 159–77.

YOUNG, P. and TYRE, C. (1983). *Dyslexia or Illiteracy? Realizing the Right to Read*. Milton Keynes: Open University Press.

YUILL, N. and OAKHILL, J. (1988). 'Understanding of anaphoric relations in skilled and less skilled comprehenders', *British Journal of Psychology*, 79, 173–86.

YUILL, N., OAKHILL, J. and PARKIN, A. (1989). 'Working memory comprehension ability and the resolution of text anomaly', *British Journal of Psychology*, 80, 351–61.

YULE, V. (1988). 'The design of print for children: sales appeal and user appeal', *Reading*, 22, 2, 96–105.

YULE, W. (1973). 'Differential prognosis of reading, backwardness and specific reading retardation', *British Journal of Educational Psychology*, 43, 244–8.

YULE, W. (1988). 'Dyslexia: not one condition but many', *British Medical Journal*, 297, 501–2.

YULE, W., RUTTER, M., BERGER, M. and THOMPSON, J. (1974). 'Over- and under-achievement in reading: distribution in the general population', *British Journal of Educational Psychology*, 44, 1–12.

ZANGWILL, O.L. and BLACKMORE, C. (1972). 'Dyslexics' reversal of eye movements during reading', *Neuropsychologia*, 10, 371–3.

ZATZ, S. and CHASSIN, L. (1983). 'Cognitions of test anxious children', *Journal of Consulting and Clinical Psychology*, 51, 526–34.

ZATZ, S. and CHASSIN, L. (1985). 'Cognitions of test anxious children under naturalistic test-taking conditions', *Journal of Consulting and Clinical Psychology*, 53, 393–401.

Author Index

Subject Index

writing schemes 118
writing skills 7, 14, 17

xenon 149

X-rays 149

Yorkshire 166

Zachary 10, 64, 239, 247